MEDICAL LIBRARY

DUNCAN MacMILLAN HOUSE

Schizophrenia as a Brain Disease

edited by
Fritz A. Henn and Henry A. Nasrallah

New York   Oxford
OXFORD UNIVERSITY PRESS
1982

Copyright © 1982 by Oxford University Press, Inc.

Library of Congress Cataloging in Publication Data

Main entry under title:
Schizophrenia as a brain disease.

  Based on a symposium held at the University of
Iowa in Oct. 1980.
  Includes bibliographies and index.
  1. Schizophrenia—Congresses. 2. Neuropsychiatry
—Congresses. I. Henn, Fritz A. II. Nasrallah,
Henry A. [DNLM: 1. Schizophrenia—Physiopathology
—Congresses. WM 203 S3377 1980]
RC514.S3346   616.89'8207   81-14231
ISBN 0-19-503088-5   AACR2

Printing (last digit): 9 8 7 6 5 4 3 2 1

Printed in the United States of America

Preface

Ideas about the origins of abnormal behavior have undergone enormous changes in the last two decades. Psychiatric theories moved from speculations about the environment to a period in which genetic factors dominated discussions of etiology. Schizophrenia, the most serious of all psychiatric afflictions, is among the clearest examples of this shift. From theories about the schizophrenogenic mother to twin studies, research has increasingly attempted to find causative factors in biological dysfunction. The explosion of knowledge in the neurosciences has fueled this research enterprise. Although the etiology of the disorder is still a mystery, the biological manifestations are being progressively better defined. Schizophrenia has become established as a medical illness with multiple biological correlates and accepted drug treatments.

Many books have been written about schizophrenia but few, if any, have focused on the biomedical concept of schizophrenia as a brain disease. This book presents the evidence for that concept drawn from research in various disciplines.

The book begins with a delineation of schizophrenia from other psychiatric illnesses by Tsuang, who goes on to examine the subgroups within the broad classification of schizophrenia in an effort to find clinical groupings sufficiently homogeneous for biological research. He defines criteria to select patients with long-term poor prognosis and points out that their clinical features suggest organic impairment. Pfohl and Winokur use clinical description and follow-up to construct a research hypothesis. They draw a picture of nonparanoid schizophrenia as an illness with an acute virulent phase followed by a residual defect state, a clinical course that can be an indication of infectious etiology.

These two chapters provide a clinical backdrop for the discussion of more direct evidence of organic involvement in schizophrenia. The first such evidence came from genetic studies. This is reviewed by Ray Crowe, who makes clear the weight of research that supports a genetic contribution to schizophrenia. Although the mode of transmission is not yet known, the question of how broad a schizophrenic spectrum is covered via genetic transmission is discussed by Crowe in some detail. More information on this question may come from prospective studies. The work reviewed by Erlenmeyer-Kimling and her colleagues on populations of children at high risk for developing schizophrenia helps identify both the forms of the disorder and the characteristics that predict its development. The correlation of neuromotor dysfunction, attentional deficits, and the development of clinical illness in children at genetic risk is an encouraging preliminary finding.

Having demonstrated that there is a genetic factor, the discussion shifts to what it may influence. Clearly, the central nervous system is the logical place to look. The next section of the book deals with attempts to localize CNS lesions in schizophrenia. With careful documentation of thought disorder, in analogy to the study of aphasias, Andreasen approaches localization through clinical studies. Such studies require anatomical correlations and several approaches to this question are presented. Stevens reviews the histological studies on schizophrenic brains and presents her own work in this area; forms of gliosis, in her opinion, suggest an infectious or autoimmune process. The use of radiological studies to probe for CNS lesions has been markedly advanced by computerized tomography (CAT). Weinberger and Wyatt review this literature and present a comprehensive study of their own. Their results point to a group of poor prognosis patients with positive CAT scan findings. The division of the schizophrenic population into two clinically distinct groups hinted at in the earlier chapters gains biological support from these CAT studies.

The biochemical and psychopharmacological studies reviewed by Henn and T. Crow and associates also point in the direction of two subgroups of schizophrenic patients. Crow defines these groups in both clinical and biochemical terms and provides a hypothesis that should act as a stimulus for further research. His type I patients are thought to have alterations in dopamine receptors, positive symptoms, and no intellectual impairment. The type II patients have intellectual dysfunction, abnormal CAT scans, negative symptoms, and a chronic course. The latter form of illness, Crow speculates, would be compatible with an infectious etiology. The work on cerebral blood flow and position emission tomography (PET) presented by Ingvar and Buchsbaum highlights the use of non-invasive techniques to explore biological function in patient populations. These measures demonstrate neurophysiological alterations that now must be correlated with biochemical, anatomical, and clinical observations.

The final segment of the book explores two emerging approaches to research, one methodological, the other conceptual. The first deals with the use of computer methods in defining the detailed anatomy of the CNS. The examination of dendritic patterns in normal and disease populations could contribute much to our understanding of brain structure and pathology. The other approach deals with cerebral asymmetry and the schizophrenic brain. The studies reviewed suggest possible left cerebral dysfunction in the schizophrenic brain, and numerous approaches to the study of this model are presented by Nasrallah.

By the end of the book a picture emerges not only of what we know about schizophrenia as a brain disease, but perhaps more importantly, of specific areas where further research is necessary. It is our hope that the book will serve as a summary of current information and as a signpost for future research paths.

This book grew out of a symposium sponsored by the Andrew Woods Fund at the University of Iowa. The Woods family, in supporting this effort, have continued the tradition begun by the late Andrew Woods, M.D., Professor and Chairman of Psychiatry at Iowa, who maintained that psychiatric illnesses would eventually have to be understood in physiological terms.

July 1982   F. A. H.
Iowa City, Iowa   H. N.

ACKNOWLEDGMENTS

We wish to thank the following for support of the Symposium Schizophrenia as a Brain Disease:
The Andrew Woods Fund
Meade Johnson
McNeil
Sandoz

List of Contributors

Nancy C. Andreasen, Ph.D., M.D. University of Iowa, Iowa City, Iowa

Monte S. Buchsbaum, M.D. Biological Psychiatry Branch, National Institutes of Mental Health, Bethesda, Maryland

Barbra Cornblatt, Ph.D. New York State Psychiatric Institute, Columbia University, New York, New York

A. J. Cross, Ph.D. Clinical Research Center, Northwick Park Hospital, Middlesex, England

Timothy J. Crow, M.B., Ph.D. Clinical Research Center, Northwick Park Hospital, Middlesex, England

Raymond R. Crowe, M.D. University of Iowa, Iowa City, Iowa

Sarala Devi, M.D. Clinical Neurology, Columbia University Medical School, New York, New York

L. Erlenmyer-Kimling, Ph.D. New York State Psychiatric Institute, Columbia University, New York, New York

David Friedman, Ph.D. New York State Psychiatric Institute, Columbia University, New York, New York

Fritz A. Henn, Ph.D., M.D. State University of New York at Stony Brook, Stony Brook, New York

David H. Ingvar, M.D. University of Lund, Lund, Sweden

Eve C. Johnstone, M.D. Clinical Research Center, Northwick Park Hospital, Middlesex, England

Seymour Kety, M.D. Mailman Research Center, Harvard Medical School, Boston, Massachusetts

Yvonne Marcuse, Ph.D. New York State Psychiatric Institute, Columbia University, New York, New York

Steven Matthysse, Ph.D. McLean Hospital, Harvard Medical School, Boston, Massachusetts

Henry A. Nasrallah, M.D. University of Iowa, Iowa City, Iowa

Frank Owen, Ph.D. Clinical Research Center, Northwick Park Hospital, Middlesex, England

Bruce Pfohl, M.D. University of Iowa, Iowa City, Iowa

Jacques Rutschmann, D. Sci. New York State Psychiatric Institute, Columbia University, New York, New York

Samuel Simmens, M.A. New York State Psychiatric Institute, Columbia University, New York, New York

Janice R. Stevens, M.D. University of Oregon, Health Sciences Center, School of Medicine, Portland, Oregon

Ming T. Tsuang, M.D., Ph.D. Brown University, Providence, Rhode Island

Daniel R. Weinberger, M.D. Laboratory of Clinical Psychopharmacology, National Institute of Mental Health, Division of Special Mental Health Research, Saint Elizabeth's Hospital, Washington, D.C.

Roger Williams, McLean Hospital, Harvard Medical School, Boston, Massachusetts

George Winokur, M.D. University of Iowa, Iowa City, Iowa

Richard Jed Wyatt, M.D. Laboratory of Clinical Psychopharmacology, National Institute of Mental Health, Division of Special Mental Health Research, Saint Elizabeth's Hospital, Washington, D.C.

Contents

Schizophrenia
as a Brain Disease

1 | Introduction

FRITZ A. HENN and

SEYMOUR KETY

This book summarizes evidence supporting the concept of schizophrenia as a disorder of the brain, with abnormalities in brain structure, arising in part from genetic factors and leading to biochemical and physiological differences in the central nervous system of affected individuals. The contributors offer a wide range of experimental approaches to the study of schizophrenia. That is an important point, for the discussion rests not on theory, but rather on experimental facts. Thus, the character of the arguments is decidedly empirical. The book begins with clinical observations, then moves to anatomical and biochemical studies. The emerging physiological investigations are presented and the book ends with a return to brain structure and some new ways of studying and thinking about the relationship of structure and functions in the central nervous system.

In Chapter 2, Tsuang outlines the historical evidence that delineated the syndrome of schizophrenia from other illnesses. This illustrates the areas of conflict in classification as well as possible subdivisions within the broad category of schizophrenia. It also emphasizes the need for research groups to examine biological variables.

There are two ways to address the latter problem. Either a rigorous clinical division can be made by using restrictive diagnostic criteria, family history, and followup information to classify patients for biological testing or biological measurements can be used to define groups for clinical evaluation and followup. Tsuang's work exemplifies the first approach. In an outcome study of 200 schizophrenic patients who were evaluated 30 to 40 years after their index admission, he showed that one variable was associated with poor outcome in all areas. This was the presence of a memory deficit at the initial admission. This deficit was not found among paranoid schizophrenics, but was stable in nonparanoids over the period of followup. Thus, a clinical group with poor prognosis can be identified by using Feighner diagnostic criteria for nonparanoid schizophrenia with the additional requirement of a memory deficit early in the course of the illness. It would be of great interest to know the family history, history of perinatal injury, and results of CT scans in such patients.

In the next chapter, Pfohl and Winokur review the longitudinal history of a group of carefully diagnosed nonparanoid schizophrenic patients followed over four decades. In these patients they find two classes of symptoms: those that fade away after being seen initially and those that remain relatively constant throughout the course of the disease. The first group includes hallucinations, delusions, violent behavior, and inappropriate affect. The second group includes work impairment and negative symptoms, such as flat affect, poverty of speech, social isolation, negativism, and anhedonia. An interesting point brought out by their study involves a central misconception about schizophrenia that goes back to Kraepelin's description of dementia praecox as an illness in which cognitive abilities gradually diminish. Pfohl and Winokur show in their sample, and mention a variety of other evidence, that diminished cognitive functions exist early in the course of the illness and do not appear to progress. They also point out that the gradual diminution of positive symptoms may actually indicate some improvement in social functioning after the first decade of the illness rather than a relentless downhill course. Hebephrenic schizophrenia is characterized as a dementing illness in which the active stage is limited to the first years after onset with a residual defect state characterized by negative symptoms.

Compelling evidence that biological factors are central in the development of major subgroups of schizophrenia derives from the evaluation of genetic factors. In Chapter 4, Ray Crowe reviews the recent genetic evidence and discusses three questions. First, is there sufficient evidence for genetic contributions to schizophrenia? Second, what diagnostic groups are related to the schizophrenic genotype, or how broad is the schizophrenic spectrum? Third, what is the mode of transmission? The first question, Crowe concludes, has been decisively answered in the affirmative by the numerous family, twin, and adoption studies he reviews. The question of which disorders are inherited with the schizophrenic genotype is complex and Crowe concludes that milder forms of the syndrome exist as borderline schizophrenia, whereas the DSM III diagnosis of acute schizophrenia is not part of the schizophrenic illness on genetic grounds. The concept of a schizophrenic spectrum in general receives support from his review of the genetic studies. In addition, a real role for positive associative mating was demonstrated. In other words, ill probands find ill spouses, though not necessarily ones with the same illness.

There is as yet no definitive answer to the third question—the mode of genetic transmission—since monogenic, recessive and dominant, and polygenic models are all compatible with the data, a situation to be expected if schizophrenia is a syndrome of heterogeneous etiology. In his conclusion, Crowe makes the important point that although "the question of 'nature vs. nurture' in schizophrenia has finally been laid to rest with the realization that schizophrenia is indeed a genetic disease . . . the genetic determinism is not a complete explanation for its etiology and non-genetic factors must be sought as well."

The question of the mode of transmission remains elusive. None of the current theories has enough supporting evidence for acceptance yet. Crowe feels that a biological marker of the illness would be necessary to get a clear picture of the mode of transmission. As if in answer to this plea, subsequent chapters present a variety of possible biological markers.

A line of research inspired by genetic findings has been the study of individuals at high risk for developing schizophrenia in an effort to define a reliable phenotype. In Chapter 5, Erlenmeyer-Kimling and her colleagues review these studies, including their own. Such research is based on the premise that prospective studies of individuals identified by family history to be at high risk for schizophrenia may lead to the identification of behavior patterns or biological alterations that predict the development of schizophrenia. Thus, these studies are aimed at defining groups of indicators of vulnerability to schizophrenia.

In Erlenmeyer-Kimling's review of longitudinal studies, one gets a sense of the substantial number of deficits in normal function that have been observed, but also of the uncertainty surrounding many of these findings. One of the recurrent problems is the finding in some studies that although children at risk for schizophrenia show more dysfunction than do their normal controls, they do not always differ from children at risk for affective disorder. Since the diagnosis of schizophrenia may include patients who might more properly be classified as having an affective disorder, differences in diagnostic criteria between investigators may partly explain this. In the results of the high-risk study that Erlenmeyer-Kimling and her associates have been conducting in New York over the past decade, there is a clear indication that a segment of the high-risk subjects in each of two independent samples have neuromotor and attentional deviations as well as unusual patterns of cortical event-related potentials at early ages. Although the probands in the oldest sample have thus far passed through only about 13% of their total lifetime risk for schizophrenia, and the ultimate determination of clinical outcome cannot be made until they are much older, the interim assessment of current clinical status points to possible relationships between early deviance in the neuropsychological functions examined as indicators of brain dysfunction and psychopathology in late adolescence. The 15 high-risk subjects who were subsequently hospitalized or treated for mental disorder had significantly more indications of motor impairment, depressed IQ scores, and deficient performance in one or more attentional tasks than had the remainder of the high-risk group.

Preliminary results of a path analysis of the neuromotor and attentional data and subsequent clinical status some eight years after initial evaluation indicate a significant correlation between high-risk status and neuromotor functioning, attentional deficits, and current clinical status. Neuromuscular functionings seem to have a large effect on attentional functioning, which in turn, affects clinical status. Even though the data are preliminary and the development of clinical dysfunction is far from having run its course, 30% of the variance in clinical status appears to be accounted for by high-risk status, neuromotor dysfunction, and attentional deficits.

With both clinical and genetic studies suggesting an organic component to schizophrenia, the question of where the defect is located begins to take on some urgency. Several chapters of this book deal with approaches toward localizing central nervous system lesions in schizophrenia. In the first of these, Andreasen discusses her analysis of the speech disturbances that often occur in schizophrenia. In contrast to traditional pessimism about reliability in the rating of thought and language, it was possible to achieve excellent reliability through careful definition of terms and an emphasis on behavioral observation. In comparisons between manic patients and schizophrenics, she has found that derailment and incoherence occur in a high proportion of schizophrenics but not in manics. Longitudinal followup of these two groups indicates that some of the speech disturbances persist in schizophrenics, whereas they are intermittent in manics, returning to normal after the episode. As in aphasia research, such descriptions may provide clues to the cerebral systems involved, particularly if the study of language disorders is correlated with anatomical and radiological studies.

Chapter 7 by Stevens represents the retracing of an old approach to the morbid process in schizophrenia. Her work is indicative of the possibilities that lie in the application of classical neuropathology to schizophrenia, aided substantially by new knowledge of the limbic systems and its ramifications throughout the brain. She approaches schizophrenia as a neurological problem of cerebral localization. In the case of schizophrenia, however, the symptoms are less clearly defined than those seen with neurological lesions and may involve more complex neural systems. Their traces in pathological morphology are not as readily discerned. Recent studies correlating localized stimulation and destruction of animal brains, with careful observations of subsequent behavior, have given us new insights into the relations between morphology and function. In addition, the convergence of neuroleptic drug actions on dopamine transmission guide the neuropathologist in looking for changes.

Stevens also reports on her own recent study of histological sections from 31 schizophrenic patients who died at St. Elizabeth's Hospital in Washington, D.C. between 1955 and 1963. Among the more impressive findings were neuronal fallout, axonal or myelin degeneration in the globus pallidus, and gliosis in the amygdala, hippocampus, or other nuclei of the limbic system. Among the many changes noted in the brains of schizophrenics, which although nonspecific were unusual for individuals in the younger age groups, were gliosis, numerous corpora amylacea, and ependymal granulations. Gliosis, the most ubiquitous abnormality found in the brains of schizophrenics, was maximal at the sites of major pathways and junctions of the limbic system. Stevens has been impressed, as others are becoming, with the possibility that some forms of schizophrenia may result from an infectious or autoimmune process and she states that her pathological findings are consistent with a healed inflammatory process.

Chapter 8 by Weinberger and Wyatt attacks the question of anatomical changes in schizophrenic brains via direct measurement of brains *in vivo*. In the most comprehensive followup to date of the report by Johnstone and Crow (1972) on CAT scans in schizophrenic patients, Weinberger and Wyatt have confirmed and enlarged upon the finding that a subgroup of schizophrenic patients have enlarged ventricles. Studying a younger group of schizophrenics, they have ruled out the possibility that the changes were attributable to old age. Using as controls a group of siblings of the schizophrenics without mental disorder, they have shown that the morphological changes are abnormal and are associated with schizophrenia. They report significant progress in defining the clinical characteristics of schizophrenic patients with and without ventricular enlargement. To the intellectual deficits previously reported by Johnstone and Crow in the group with enlarged ventricles, they have added additional neuropsychological deficits, nonfocal neurological signs, disordered smooth pursuit eye movements, less frequent EEG abnormalities, poor premorbid adjustment, and poor response to neuroleptics. The group without dilated ventricles showed more positive psychotic signs and other features compatible with increased dopaminergic activity. In addition to a better response to neuroleptic therapy, these patients had serum prolactin concentrations that correlated inversely with their psychopathology, as well as a higher spontaneous rate of eye blinking. Since blink rate is diminished and serum prolactin increased following neuroleptic therapy, these appear to be indicators of dopaminergic activity in the brain. Thus, progress is being made in defining two subgroups of schizophrenia on the basis of objective biological measures. It would be useful to obtain further information that might contribute to an etiological differentiation between the two groups.

In Chapter 9, Henn reviews the role that dopamine plays in schizophrenia. He shows that it is unlikely that alterations in dopamine function underlie the negative symptoms of chronic schizophrenia. The lack of clinical response to neuroleptics of chronic amotivational schizophrenics and the lack of specificity in neuroleptic action suggest that dopamine plays a role in psychosis regardless of the specific diagnosis. Dopaminergic pathways play an important modulatory role in the central nervous system, and neuroleptic drugs, which certainly act on these pathways, dampen a variety of central nervous system functions or malfunctions. One way such modulation could take place would involve an intercellular feedback loop between neurons and glia. If astroglia were involved in regulating metabolic rates in the central nervous system, as suggested, this would enable us to correlate the regional changes in glucose metabolism and blood flow demonstrated by Buchsbaum and Ingvar with changes in dopamine activity.

Henn's hypothesis that methionine loading increases the coupling of adenylate cyclase with dopamine receptors in striatal and limbic regions through phospholipid methylation, thus increasing dopaminergic activity, could account for the exacerbation of psychotic symptoms with such loading. In general, the role of phospholipids in the central nervous system is receiving more attention.

In Chapter 10, T. J. Crow and his co-authors define two syndromes in schizophrenia and provide suggestions about different etiologies for the two groups. Type I patients have positive symptoms of psychosis, no intellectual impairment, and possibly an increase in dopamine receptors. Type II patients have negative symptoms, asocial behavior, a chronic course, and enlarged ventricles on CAT scan. Crow is careful to state, as Pfohl and Winokur demonstrated, that Type II patients often go through an initial Type I phase, and that many paranoid schizophrenics never develop Type II symptoms. It is crucial to Crow's scheme to correlate Type I features with postmortem measures showing an increase in dopamine activity. Mackay (1980) has argued that the postmortem material available is likely to come from chronic Type II patients. However, Crow (1980) has shown a good correlation between positive symptoms and an increase in dopamine receptors in a small group of patients whose symptoms had been rated before their death. A persistent problem in these studies is that the patients with positive symptoms are likely to have received neuroleptics to treat these symptoms, so that artifacts due to drug therapy cannot be ruled out.

The symptoms of a disorder depend largely upon the system or systems affected, whereas the course tends to reflect the etiology and nature of the pathological process. If that process is fairly abrupt in onset, relatively short-lived, and reversible, the course of illness will have the same characteristics. If it persists and produces effects repetitively, the course may be intermittent with periods of remission and exacerbation. If the disease process persists and progresses, the course of illness will have the same chronicity and progression. It is reasonable to assume that a system in the brain may be affected by different etiological agents that produce the same symptoms, but over a different course—acute, intermittent, or chronic and progressive—depending upon the nature of the agent and its interactions in the brain. When we are able to characterize a mental disorder in terms of either the system involved or its etiology, we will be able to define the disorder more precisely and describe its course in more appropriate language. Until then it is useful to build upon the body of knowledge about symptoms and course we have in an attempt to define more homogeneous syndromes that constitute subgroups of schizophrenia or manic-depressive illness. That is what Crow and others are doing, and the effort has shed new light on the old distinction between paranoid and nonparanoid schizophrenia.

The course of Type II or nonparanoid schizophrenia suggests an analogy to that of an infectious disease. It may begin acutely, progress through a variety of flare-ups, and end with scarring or deformities. Those who took their medical or psychiatric training in the 1930's or early 1940's remember many patients like those described by Pfohl and Winokur; in fact, they would be representative of what was then called chronic schizophrenia or process schizophrenia. It has often been claimed that such patients are extremely rare today. If that is a valid conclusion and not the result of an arbitary redefinition of schizophrenia, it is possible that modern treatment methods, such as the use of antipsychotic drugs and less prolonged institutionalization, may have helped "cure" such patients. Another possibility, however, is that this very severe form of schizophrenia represents a postencephalitic condition resulting from a virus or other infectious agent that is no longer common. The patients described in Chapter 10 had their onset of illness 15 or 20 years after the great influenza epidemic that left many postencephalitic cases of Parkinson's disorder. That type of Parkinson's disorder was also fairly common in the 1930's and 1940's and has been gradually disappearing, since there have been few new cases to take the place of those who died. Observant psychiatrists of past generations noted an association between influenza and schizophrenia. Menninger (1926) described a form of schizophrenia in the 1920's found commonly in patients who had recovered from the epidemic flu. It is possible that the patients like these who are now becoming rare were the victims of a similar infectious process that attacked a different portion of the central nervous system than that involved in postencephalitic Parkinsonism? A clinical course such as that documented by Pfohl and Winokur is consistent with a viral etiology. As Crow has stated, a genetic predisposition toward a particular viral infection would be a plausible etiology for the course of Type II schizophrenia.

Perhaps the newest and potentially most revealing techniques for delineating functional differences in schizophrenic brains compared to normals are discussed in Chapter 11 by Buchsbaum and Ingvar. These authors describe three physiological approaches to the brain in schizophrenia that have documented a striking reduction in blood flow and glucose utilization in the frontal regions and their correlation with cortical electrical activity. When the nitrous oxide technique was first developed in 1948, it was applied to the measurement of overall cerebral blood and oxygen consumption in schizophrenics. No difference from the normal state was observed, and the inference was made that alterations in these functions either did not occur in schizophrenia or were confined to particular regions of the brain producing changes that were not appreciable in total values. In 1974, applying a method for measurement of regional cerebral blood flow Ingvar found a rather consistent reduction of blood flow in the frontal regions in chronic schizophrenic patients. Since there is a close correlation between local blood flow, metabolism, and functional activity in the brain, this suggested a diminution in the latter two functions. Sokoloff, in 1977, described a method for the measurement of regional glucose metabolism in the brain that, coupled with the technique of positron emission tomography, was applicable to the human brain. Buchsbaum and his associates are finding reduced levels of glucose metabolism in the frontal as compared to the occipital brain regions of schizophrenics, confirming a recent report by Farkas and his associates. Although the EEG is more a measure of the synchrony of cortical functional activity than of its intensity, it is not unreasonable to expect alterations in the wave patterns to be associated with reductions in neuronal function. Buchsbaum reports a number of such changes in frequency and amplitude that are correlated with the changes in glucose metabolism revealed by the PET scan in schizophrenic patients. The possibility of studying regional blood flow and metabolism throughout the human brain has understandably aroused great interest and these preliminary results will undoubtedly be extended by the original investigators and by others. Correlations between these measures, the morphological changes revealed by the CAT scan, and clinical features in subgroups of schizophrenic patients would be illuminating. These studies will also undoubtedly lead to a renewed interest in the physiology and neurochemistry of the frontal lobes. The control of frontal activity by limbic structures may well represent the pathways that are involved in psychosis, where neuroleptics act.

In Chapter 12, Matthysse and Williams emphasize the availability of new techniques that permit quantitative analysis of neuropathological data. The microscopic brain lesions that are known to occur in various neurological and some psychiatric disorders are those that can be demonstrated by classical staining techniques. With biochemical techniques it has been possible to demonstrate such abnormalities as altered dopamine receptors when morphological or histological techniques have not revealed them. Similarly, the CAT scan and measurement of regional blood flow and metabolism have eluciated changes in schizophrenia where none were found or agreed upon previously. In an effort to find the histological abnormalities underlying such changes, Matthysse and Williams have combined classical staining techniques with modern computerized methods for describing and quantifying micro-morphology. They have likened the growth of dendrites in the brain to that of branches on a tree, for which changes in milieu may produce such alterations in growth that quantitative description of large populations of units may be able to demonstrate. The use of computerized techniques may alter the saying that schizophrenia is the graveyard of neuropathology. That has been true only for classical neuropathology. It is possible that a new neuropathology, utilizing the powerful new methods of visualization, demonstration, and quantification may find some flowers among the tombstones.

The last chapter deals with the question of laterality and hemispheric dysfunction, an area in which there have been a number of provocative, but not always consistent findings. After reviewing the evidence for cerebral asymmetry from neurological lesions, intracarotid barbiturate infusion, unilateral application of ECT, commissurotomized patients, and neurochemical and postmortem studies, Nasrallah presents the case for dysfunction of the left cerebral hemisphere in schizophrenia. Studies of handedness in schizophrenic populations and in monozygotic and dizygotic twins concordant and discordant for schizophrenia; observations on skin conductance and lateral eye movements; dichotic listening studies and results of CAT scans, EEG and cortical-evoked potentials also suggest left hemispheric dysfunction in patients with schizophrenia. Nasrallah then turns to the question of interhemispheric communication, reporting his own findings and those of others that a thickening of the corpus callosum occurs in chronic process schizophrenia. On the basis of this and other evidence of failure of coordination between the two hemispheres, he presents an imaginative hypothesis that schizophrenic symptoms may be due to weakened inhibitory mechanisms that mediate left hemispheric dominance for consciousness, resulting in the disinhibition of right hemispheric consciousness. Thus, schizophrenic patients would have two communicating but poorly integrated spheres of consciousness, which could produce a wide variety of psychotic symptoms, delusions, sensory overload, attentional deficits, diffused ego boundaries, withdrawal, and indecisiveness.

The overall impression these chapters give of the direction of progress is that the greatest advances in thinking about schizophrenia will come from the correlation of a variety of laboratory techniques with careful clinical observations. Multiple lines of evidence, including pharmacological, genetic, neurochemical, electrophysiological, radiological, and clinical, clearly point to biological alterations in the schizophrenic brain. We still cannot say where they originate and how they develop, but this volume clearly indicates the potentialities of several new approaches to add to the pharmacological clues investigators have accumulated over the past two decades. Future studies may help localize the pathological process in schizophrenia, and approach the question of etiology more directly.

REFERENCES

Crow, T. J. (1980). Positive and negative symptoms and the role of dopamine—reply. *Brit. J. Psychol.* 137, 383–386.
Mackay, A. V. P. (1980). Positive and negative symptoms and the role of dopamine. *Brit. J. Psychol.* 137, 379–383.
Menninger, K. A. (1926). Influenza and the schizophrenia: An analysis of post influenzal "dementia praecox" as of 1918 and 5 years later. *Amer. J. Psychol.* 5:469–529.

2 | Schizophrenic Syndromes: The Search for Subgroups in Schizophrenia with Brain Dysfunction

MING T. TSUANG

INTRODUCTION

The term schizophrenia was introduced by Bleuler (1908) to describe a splitting or an incongruity of mental functions. Bleuler continued the work of Kraepelin (1896), who defined dementia praecox as a mental illness characterized by early onset and chronic deterioration. Kraepelin stressed the difference between the irreversible nature of dementia praecox and the episodic course of manic-depressive illness. However, even Kraepelin found that nearly 13% of his patients diagnosed as schizophrenic recovered. Although not rejecting the nuclear concept of deteriorating schizophrenia, present researchers have come to view the overall category of schizophrenia as a heterogeneous collection of several disorders. This situation is not simplified by the confusion of theoretical models derived from biological, sociological, and psychological studies on mental functions. The disarray has given rise to the bewildering question whether the term "schizophrenia" is still appropriate.

In view of this situation, a growing consensus has emerged around the need for a nosology based on descriptive findings using epidemiological approaches such as genetic studies using family, twin, adoption, and genetic indicators, psychopharmacological observations of treatment outcome; and computerized axial tomographic studies of the brain. This chapter proposes to identify the subgroups within schizophrenia, based

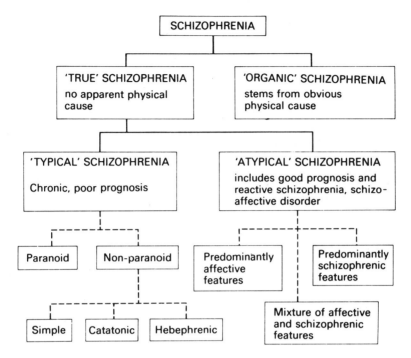

FIGURE 2-1. A Schematic Representation of the Subgroups of Schizophrenia Currently Accepted by Most Psychiatrists. Solid lines, subgroups for which there is established evidence; broken lines, subgroups for which the evidence is unverified or incomplete

on data using current research approaches. The purpose is to identify specific subgroups of disorders that might lead to the eventual validation of diagnosis and reformulation of treatment programs. Figure 2-1 is a schematic representation of subgroups of schizophrenia. The following is a description of each subgroup.

ORGANIC (SYMPTOMATIC) AND IDIOPATHIC (TRUE) SCHIZOPHRENIA

The demarcation between idiopathic and organic schizophrenias rests on the presence or absence of physical precipitating factors. With the new information on the role of biological pathology in schizophrenia that this volume presents, "organic" may not be an appropriate label for schizophrenic symptoms secondary to other physical illnesses; thus we will use the term symptomatic schizophrenia for these illnesses. In symptomatic forms, the expression of schizophrenic symptoms is clearly secondary to an organic precipitant. Causes include such conditions as dementing processes, brain damage, drug or alcohol abuse, epilepsy, or infectious disease. Organic disorders are a heterogeneous group that cannot be characterized by a standard set of symptoms. Nonetheless it is clear that a variety of brain insults can produce clinical conditions resembling schizophrenia.

Schulz (1932) classified cases of schizophrenia according to the presence or absence of organic precipitating factors. He found that the siblings of the idiopathic groups of schizophrenics had twice the incidence of schizophrenia (7.5%) as those of the symptomatic group (3.7%), a highly significant difference ($p < 0.002$). This finding suggests that idiopathic schizophrenia has a heavier genetic loading for schizophrenia than has symptomatic schizophrenia.

Davison and Bagley (1969) reported several clinical features that differentiated the two subgroups at a significant level. The symptomatic subgroup had a higher frequency of catatonic symptoms. Idiopathic schizophrenia had more pronounced thought disorders, flatness of affect, emotional passivity, hallucinations, and delusions. Premorbid schizoid personality and a family history of schizophrenia were almost four times as frequent in idiopathic schizophrenia as in symptomatic.

Even though the symptomatic schizophrenic disorders have been set off from idiopathic syndromes on the basis of organic dysfunction, this does not mean that true schizophrenia is independent of brain function. With improved understanding of the specific factors underlying schizophrenia, future research may disclose more schizophrenias that have an organic base.

TYPICAL AND ATYPICAL CASES
WITHIN IDIOPATHIC SCHIZOPHRENIA

The general category of idiopathic schizophrenia includes two disease processes designated typical and atypical in most of the literature. Atypical schizophrenia deviates significantly from the chronic, deteriorating course of schizophrenia. This category includes schizophrenic disorders that occur as reactions to major environmental stresses (reactive schizophrenias), those in which features promise eventual recovery (schizophreniform psychoses), and mixed forms (schizoaffective disorders). Typical schizophrenia or process schizophrenia is marked by apathy, social withdrawal, and thought disorder manifested by incomprehensible speech. Great interest attends the question of the functional integrity of atypical schizophrenia, as evidenced by the recent trend to relegate this psychosis to affective disorder. The term "schizoaffective disorder" is now a controversial category. In this chapter it will be used interchangeably with atypical schizophrenia. Strong genetic, epidemiological, and clinical arguments, however, exist for maintaining the division of schizophrenia into distinct typical and atypical entities.

With respect to clinical features, the differences between typical and atypical schizophrenia were upheld by Mitsuda (1972). He found that the atypical cases were less severe than the typical in terms of course and clinical symptoms; typical patients had a gradual onset with symptoms of emotional blunting, a high degree of personality deterioration, rigid countenance and posture, disturbed rapport, and a chronic-progressive course. Atypical cases were more episodic, with symptoms of delusional perception, disturbed orientation and apprehension, incoherence, confusion or change of consciousness, insight into illness during the recovery stage, and memory impairment as to pathological experience.

Another study sought to determine whether atypical schizophrenia could be classified with typical schizophrenia or with affective disorder by examining clinical features and other illness-related factors. Tsuang, Dempsey, and Rauscher (1976) chose a group of 85 atypical schizophrenics who were excluded from typical schizophrenia for the following reasons: (1) at admission, a chart diagnosis of schizophrenia was made; (2) according to the Research Criteria of Feighner et al. (1972) for schizophrenia, there were insufficient symptoms or transient symptoms or the possibility of another diagnosis; and (3) there was either a previous, remitting episode of psychiatric illness or the presence of affective symptoms at the time of index admission. This group was compared with 200 schizophrenia cases, 100 cases of mania, and 225 cases of depressive disorders who met Feighner Criteria and who were admitted during the same period (1934 to 1944) to the University of Iowa's Psychiatric Hospital. The striking feature of this study was the virtual dissimilarity between atypical and typical schizophrenia based on non-symptom variables from admission charts. Except for age at admission and family history of schizophrenia, the atypical group differed from the typical in the higher number of females, the presence of precipitating events, a higher rate of recovery, and a larger percentage of family members with affective disorders. Over against both typical schizophrenia and affective disorder patients, the distinguishing characteristic of the atypical schizophrenia group was a higher percentage of environmental precipitating events, especially postpartem-related factors. With the exception of precipitating events and younger age at admission, the atypical group resembled most the manic group for outcome, percentage of females, and family history of illness.

This same group of atypical patients was followed up 30 to 40 years after their index admission. Based on the data collected from followup interviews, outcome status of these patients were rated using marital, residential, occupational, and psychiatric conditions. For all outcome categories combined, the atypical schizophrenic group was better than the typical schizophrenic and worse than the mania. These results show that atypical schizophrenia is different from schizophrenia and affective disorders on the basis of long-term outcome (Tsuang and Dempsey, 1979).

Furthermore, using the sib pair method, Tsuang (1979) found genetic evidence for two variants of schizoaffective disorders. No evidence of genetic independence of schizoaffective disorders was found. The study suggests that there are two variants of schizoaffective disorders or atypical schizophrenia, one associated with schizophrenia and the other with affective disorder. The group with an age of onset before 30 was associated with the typical schizophrenic group; the group with an age of onset after 40 was associated with the affective disorder group. The group in between had no distinctive characteristics. Hence, atypical schizophrenia or schizoaffective disorders appear to be a heterogeneous category with variants associated with typical schizophrenia and affective disorder.

THE POSSIBILITY OF SUBTYPES
WITHIN TYPICAL SCHIZOPHRENIA

The subtyping of schizophrenic symptoms dates back to Kraepelin. He first introduced the term dementia paranoides in 1896 to describe a chronic disorder beginning with non-bizarre, systematic delusions connected with the real world, and occasionally accompanied by hallucinations, that led to a confused state and aberrations of affect. Further observation forced Kraepelin to admit that some of the patients he diagnosed as paranoid did not reach the defect state. This led to the introduction of a tripartite division of paranoid disorder in the eighth edition of his work: paranoid dementia praecox, paraphrenia, and paranoia, with differences based on the longitudinal deterioration of the patient. Bleuler did not emphasize the course of the illness as much as Kraepelin did; instead, he emphasized the cross-sectional clinical picture of patient symptoms. Hence, Bleuler's definition of paranoid schizophrenia was much broader, since it reflected mainly the dominance of persecutory delusions. The provisional character in the diagnosis of paranoid schizophrenia continues into the modern era of nosological approaches. The criteria for paranoid schizophrenia in the ICD-9 resemble Kraepelin's paranoid dementia praecox in that the longitudinal picture beginning with the dominance of stable delusions and leading to thought disorder and affective flattening is stressed. In the DSM-III, a diagnosis of paranoid schizophrenia requires only a prominence of persecutory or grandiose delusions without the specification, in the operational criteria, of whether mental deterioration occurs; this follows the approach of Bleuler.

The confusion in subtyping schizophrenia does not indicate a lack of agreement about the ideal distinction between paranoid and nonparanoid subtypes; the problem is the lack of specific clinical criteria for the establishment of a reliable diagnosis. The paranoid subtype, broadly defined, is marked by a prominence of delusions or hallucinations that are due neither to physical causes nor affective disorders. The criteria for nonparanoid schizophrenia (hebephrenic, catatonic, and undifferentiated) also include delusions and hallucinations, but in more bizarre and incoherent forms, accompanied by catatonic stupor or excitement or hebephrenic features leading to mental deterioration. The controversy in the diagnosis of paranoid–nonparanoid subtypes has focused on thought disorder and affective deterioration; there is disagreement about the diagnostic assignment of patients, who, in addition to their delusions, display confused thoughts or inappropriate affect (Kendler and Tsuang, 1981). To bring some order to this confusion, we shall examine the results of recent studies, present some criteria for diagnosing subtypes, and discuss the results of some preliminary research using these criteria.

Refining Methods of Subtype Research

The move to distinguish paranoid and nonparanoid subtypes has received some impetus from the different responses schizophrenics show to neuroleptic drugs. Of interest is the observation that neuroleptic drugs produce a therapeutic change mostly in patients with positive symptoms (delusions and hallucinations). The negative symptoms (flattening of affect, poverty of speech, and loss of drive) are seen in chronic patients who are less responsive to neuroleptics (Crow, 1980). In addition, the chronic patients showed signs of increased ventricular size according to CAT scans (Johnstone et al. 1978). Subsequently, three studies have independently confirmed increased ventricular size in chronic schizophrenia patients (Weinberger et al., 1979; Donnelly et al., 1980; Golden et al., 1980). These biological findings indicate that there are two syndromes within typical schizophrenia. Patients with the first, which is probably linked to a change in dopamine transmission, have a better chance of recovery. The second syndrome follows an irreversible course and may be associated with intellectual impairment or structural changes in the brain.

Tsuang et al. (1981), in a followup study 30 to 40 years after index admission, found that 10% of nonparanoid schizophrenics and 40.7% of paranoid schizophrenics had a changed subtype diagnoses at followup, according to ICD-8 criteria. Overall, the study group remained highly stable in regard to the diagnosis of schizophrenia, but within that category the tendency was for paranoid schizophrenics to become nonparanoid over a 30- to 40-year period. Furthermore, in a family study of the first-degree relatives of these same probands, Tsuang, Winokur, and Crowe (1980) found no sign that paranoid and nonparanoid subtypes bred true.

Variability of outcome and the lack of a heritable predisposition to either paranoid or nonparanoid subtypes among first-degree relatives indicate that currently held clinical criteria are not adequate for the study of heterogeneity in schizophrenia. It may be that the total preoccupation with paranoid delusions typical to paranoid schizophrenia is a feature that vanishes over time, to be replaced by the random and non-systematized delusions or hallucinations and thought disorder of nonparanoid schizophrenia. The unlikelihood of a changed subtype diagnosis in nonparanoid schizophrenia strengthens this possibility.

RESEARCH CRITERIA

To guarantee more objective subtyping, Tsuang and Winokur (1974) developed specific criteria for the differentiation of hebephrenic and paranoid schizophrenia to augment the research criteria of Feighner. Their criteria are based on the analysis of clinical differences of 260 process schizophrenics diagnosed as nonparanoid (mostly hebephrenic) and paranoid. Generally, the features that distinguish paranoid schizophrenia from nonparanoid schizophrenia are the absence of affective disruption, a pattern of organized thought, and onset after age 25, in paranoid cases.

The future may bring a better understanding of the clinical signs that can be used to distinguish the paranoid from the nonparanoid subgroup. It may also reveal the degree of stability and exchange between these groups. To make progress in this direction, research will have to focus on two aspects: the biological markers that indicate a pattern of syndromes and the relationship between outcome and diagnosis at admission. A preliminary study of this type is presented here as a model for future studies.

OUTCOME STUDY OF GOOD
AND POOR PROGNOSIS SCHIZOPHRENIA

Using specific criteria (Feighner et al., 1972), a long-term outcome study was conducted to determine what clinical features at admission predicted a poor outcome among schizophrenia subgroups. The final outcome of 200 schizophrenics was rated good or poor under three categories: marital status, occupational status, and the presence of psychiatric symptoms at followup 30 to 40 years after index admission (Tsuang and Dempsey, 1979). Finally, all outcome categories were subjected to further analysis to determine, on a global, cross-sectional level, which clinical features at admission were stable over the entire period of followup and which features were associated with poor outcome. Preliminary results (Tsuang, in press) suggest that the one variable that identified poor outcome in all three categories was the presence of memory deficit at index admission. Memory deficit was defined as signs of disorientation and symptoms of recent or remote memory impairment. The research criteria used in the selection of schizophrenia probands for this study excluded acute schizophrenia. Therefore, the acute confusional state was absent; in general, these memory deficits were present without clouding of consciousness.

Since memory deficit was linked with poor outcome, further analysis was carried out to determine which patients had memory deficit. Of the 22 patients who originally presented signs of memory deficit, 20 received a chart diagnosis of nonparanoid schizophrenia. At followup, the majority remained nonparanoid: eight were hebephrenic, 10 catatonic, and two undifferentiated. The omission of the "no information category" left one patient with a diagnosis of paranoid schizophrenia. These findings suggest that schizophrenics with memory deficit are still nonparanoid even 30 to 40 years after admission.

Information on the persistence of memory deficit was also obtained at followup to substantiate the chronic nature of this variable. At the time of followup, 30 to 40 years later, many patients (43%) with memory deficit at admission still complained of impaired memory. In contrast, only 22% of the patients in the group without memory deficit at admission complained of impaired memory. There was no difference in mean age at followup for both groups: the average age in both groups was 53 years. In addition, interviewers rated the respondents for signs of disorientation regarding person, place, or time. An excessive number (62%) of the memory-deficit group showed that they were disoriented, whereas substantially fewer patients (23%) without memory deficit at admission presented signs of disorientation, indicating that memory deficit was a highly stable variable over a 30- to 40-year period.

To evaluate whether schizophrenics with memory deficit at admission eventually led to high mortality, as in the case of well-established diagnostic entities of common organic brain syndrome, we compared rates of mortality at followup in patients with and without memory deficit at admission. Both the rates and the number of survival years between the two groups were similar. This suggests memory deficit at admission in schizophrenics has a prognosis that differs from that seen in common organic brain syndrome. The process might be more subtle and involve a long-term course leading to an end state that does not affect length of survival.

CONCLUSION

If schizophrenia is a heterogeneous group of disorders, consisting of several subgroups, it is futile to search for a single cause of all schizophrenia. The future study of schizophrenia as a brain disease should focus on a discrete group of schizophrenias sharing the same characteristics. Although this method may be criticized in that a representative sample of all schizophrenia is not studied, at least it is assured what kind of schizophrenia is being investigated. Certain conditions should be met in the search for homogeneous subgroups: (1) the selection of a study population should be restricted and well-defined; (2) family studies should be conducted blindly with regard to proband diagnosis; (3) a nonpsychiatric control group should be included; (4) subtyping should use objective biological indicators and clinical features; and (5) a long-term followup study should be included in studies of subtype differences.

Conversely, one could conduct biological studies on all schizophrenias to detect subgroups with different biological indicators. Next, the clinical features and family incidence of schizophrenia in each subgroup could be studied to determine the heritability of this trait. Starting from either the clinical and the familial aspects, or using biological approaches, new hypotheses should be tested on homogeneous subgroups. Studies such as these would elucidate the etiologies of schizophrenia and lead to appropriate treatment of the various forms of the illness.

ACKNOWLEDGMENTS

This study was supported in part by funds from the National Institute of Mental Health, United States Public Service Grants MH24189 and MH31673. Assisting in the analysis and preparation of this manuscript were Jerome A. Fleming, M.Sc., and Bruce McCallum, M.C.S.

REFERENCES

American Psychiatric Association (1980). *Diagnostic and statistical manual of mental disorders*, 3rd ed. American Psychiatric Association, Washington, D.C.

Bleuler, E. (1908). Die Prognose der Dementia praecox (Schizophreniegruppe). *Allg. Z. Psychiat.* 65, 436.

Crow, T. J. (1980). Molecular pathology of schizophrenia: More than one disease process? *Brit. Med. J.* 280, 66–68.

Davison, K., and C. R. Bagley (1969). Schizophrenia-like psychoses associated with organic disorders of the central nervous system: A review of the literature. In *Current problems in neuropsychiatry: Schizophrenia, epilepsy, the temporal lobe* (R. N. Herrington, ed.), Ashford, Kent.

Donnelly, E. F., D. R. Weinberger, I. N. Waldman, and R. J. Wyatt (1980). Cognitive impairment associated with morphological brain abnormalities on computed tomography in chronic schizophrenia patients. *J. Nerv. Ment. Dis.* 168, 305–308.

Feighner, J. P., E. Robins, S. Guze, R. Woodruff, G. Winokur, and R. Munoz (1972). Diagnostic criteria for use in psychiatric research. *Arch. Gen. Psychiat.* 25, 457.

Golden, C. J., J. A. Moses, Jr., R. Zelazowski, B. Graber, L. M. Zatz, T. B. Horvath, and P. A. Berger (1980). Cerebral ventricular size and neuropsychological impairment in young chronic schizophrenics. *Arch. Gen. Psychiat.* 37, 619–623.

Johnstone, E. C., T. J. Crow, C. D. Frith, M. Stevens, L. Kreel, and J. Husband (1978). The dementia of dementia praecox. *Acta Psychiat. Scand.* 57, 305–324.

Kendler, K. S., and M. T. Tsuang (1981). The nosology of paranoid schizophrenia and other paranoid psychoses. *Schizophr. Bull.* 714, 594–610.

Kraepelin, E. (1896). *Ein Lehrbuch fur Studirende and Aerzte.* Ambrosius Barth, Leipzig, East Germany.

Kraepelin, E. (1971). *Dementia praecox and paraphrenia,* 8th ed. (R. M. Barclay, trans.) Krieger Publishing, Huntington, New York.

Kraepelin, E. (1976). *Manic-depressive insanity and paranoia,* 8th ed. (R. M. Barclay, trans.) Arno Press, New York.

Mitsuda, H. (1972). Heterogeneity of schizophrenia. In *Genetic factors in "schizophrenia"* (A. R. Kaplan, ed.), pp. 276–293. Charles C. Thomas, Springfield, Ill.

Schulz, B. (1932). Zur Erbpathologie der Schizophrenie. *Ges. Neurol. Psychiat.* 143, 175.

Tsuang, M. T. (1979). Schizoaffective Disorder. *Arch. Gen. Psychiat.* 36, 633–634.

Tsuang, M. T., and G. Winokur (1974). Criteria for subtyping schizophrenia: Clinical differentiation of hebephrenic and paranoid schizophrenia. *Arch. Gen. Psychiat.* 31, 43.

Tsuang, M. T., and G. M. Dempsey (1979). Long-term outcome of major psychoses. *Arch. Gen. Psychiat.* 36, 1302–1304.

Tsuang, M. T., G. M. Dempsey, and F. Rauscher (1976). A study of "atypical schizophrenia." *Arch. Gen. Psychiat.* 33, 1157–1160.

Tsuang, M. T., G. Winokur, and R. R. Crowe (1980). Morbidity risks of schizophrenia and affective disorders among first degree relatives of patients with schizophrenia, mania, depression and surgical conditions. *Brit. J. Psychiat.* 37, 497–504.

Tsuang, M. T., R. F. Woolson, G. Winokur, and R. R. Crowe (1981). Stability of psychiatric diagnoses. *Arch. Gen. Psychiat.* 38, 535–539.

Tsuang, M. T. (1982). Memory deficit and long term outcome in Schizophrenia: A preliminary study. *Psychiat. Res.* (in press).

Weinberger, D. R., E. F. Torrey, A. N. Neophytides, and R. J. Wyatt (1979). Lateral cerebral ventricular enlargement in chronic schizophrenia. *Arch. Gen. Psychiat.* 36, 735–739.

World Health Organization (1978). Mental disorders: Glossary and guide to their classification in accordance with the ninth revision of the international classification of diseases. WHO, Geneva.

3 | Schizophrenia: Course and Outcome

BRUCE PFOHL and

GEORGE WINOKUR

Knowledge about course and outcome in schizophrenia can be put to many different uses. These include counseling patients and relatives, evaluating the effects of various interventions, planning community health care needs, delineating processes and mechanisms underlying the progression of the disease, and deciding when to obtain biological samples and measurements in order to detect the biological correlates of psychopathology.

Much of the variation in course and outcome reported in the literature can be reconciled by considering the methodology of the various studies. Due consideration must be given to the definition of schizophrenia used and whether only first admission cases were used, in order to avoid overrepresentation of severe cases with multiple admissions. Studies limited to chronically hospitalized patients will miss cases that require only temporary hospitalization. It is likely that schizophrenia is actually a group of diseases, and this is reflected in a variety of diagnostic schemes and biological measures that have been proposed to categorize schizophrenic patients (Wyatt et al., 1981). Although preliminary findings suggest that such subtypes may eventually explain some of the variation in outcome, they will not be considered in detail here.

The following review of the literature is divided into those studies that deal with outcome and those that deal with course. Outcome refers to the cross-sectional distribution of symptoms and disabilities at some specified point after the onset of the disease. Course refers to the longitudinal pattern and changes in symptoms over time.

OUTCOME OF SCHIZOPHRENIA

Kraepelin sought to define schizophrenia illness in a way that would delineate those patients with a severe deteriorating mental illness beginning early in life. He did not provide a set of clear operational criteria for diagnosis, but he described a group of patients among whom only about 4% experienced complete and permanent recovery. Another 13% were said to have mild symptoms with a fair social adjustment. Hoenig (1967) has noted that no one has been able to demonstrate such a poor outcome in any large patient sample defined since that time.

Bleuler preferred to diagnose schizophrenia by the use of certain mental status findings, without reference to longitudinal course, and concluded that schizophrenia has a wide variety of outcomes. Some patients underwent severe deterioration, but a number went on to complete recovery. This broad definition of schizophrenia, with such divergent outcomes, created a need for some additional prognostic factors to determine which patients would do well and which patients would do poorly. This need was met by Langfeldt (1937), in Norway, and later by Vaillant (1964) and Stephens, Astrup, and Mangrum (1966), in the United States.

Vaillant (1964) presents a 10-year followup of 72 consecutive admissions for schizophrenia as diagnosed by the cross-sectional criteria proposed by Bleuler. After 10 years, 41% of his patients were doing relatively well in that they were working more than 50% of the time and had a fair social adjustment; but 28% required chronic hospitalization. If patients with good prognostic signs, such as acute onset, mental confusion, symptoms of less than 6 months duration, and affective symtoms, were removed, the remaining patients had a poor outcome with only 18% described as doing relatively well by the above definition. Stephens, Astrup, and Mangrum (1966) confirmed the validity of these factors.

The utility of the proposed prognostic factors apparently depends on what criteria are used to define the sample initially. If schizophrenia is defined according to more recently proposed research diagnostic criteria or by DSM-III criteria, most of the good prognosis cases are excluded and little is gained by applying the traditional prognostic indicators (Strauss and Carpenter, 1974; Hawk, Carpenter, and Strauss 1975). It is helpful to keep this in mind in reviewing outcome studies of the past decade.

Bland, Parker, and Orn (1978) reported on a 10-year followup of 88 patients. Since diagnosis was by DSM-II criteria, a number of "good prognosis schizophrenics" were probably included. This is also one of the few studies to include only first admission schizophrenics; therefore, more severe cases with multiple admissions are not likely to be over-represented. These factors probably explain the relatively good outcome, with 58% of patients described as being without psychiatric symptoms, although only 35% had normal social relationships and 50% had normal economic productivity. However, 25% were described as severe and chronic with no economic productivity.

Huber, Gross, and Schuttler (1975) report on 502 schizophrenics admitted to a hospital in West Germany with a followup after a mean of 22 years after onset of illness. Twenty-two percent had a complete and apparently lasting remission. Eighty-seven percent were living at home, and 13% were permanently hospitalized, although this might be more indicative of social policy than of outcome. The disease was generally stable or slightly improved by the end of the first decade.

Ciompi (1980) describes a followup study of 289 patients admitted to a hospital in Switzerland between 1900 and 1962. Mean followup was 36.9 years, and mean age at followup was 74 years. A previous discharge diagnosis based on "strict Bleulerian criteria" was used to select the sample. Thus patients who had had symptoms for less than six months were included. Ciompi found 27% of the patients had no psychiatric symptoms at the time of followup, and 27% had severe psychiatric symptoms. Thirty-nine percent of patients lived with their families or on their own, and 44% were in mental institutions. Despite a mean age of 74 years, 50% were still working, at least part of the time.

The study by Tsuang, Woolson, and Fleming (1979), the "Iowa 500," stands out for its careful attention to strict epidemiological methodology. A sample of 200 consecutive admissions for schizophrenia were retrospectively diagnosed by explicit criteria based on a chart review of history and symptoms at time of admission. Six months of continuous symptoms were required for diagnosis. One hundred cases of mania and 225 cases of depression were selected by other criteria. Finally, 160 age- and sex-matched surgical controls without psychiatric problems were also selected from admission records from 1934 to 1944. Outcome criteria and levels within outcome categories were operationally defined and rated blindly with respect to diagnosis by direct interview of patients or relatives. Records of subsequent hospitalizations were also used. Followup extended past 30 years.

Each outcome parameter was measured on a three-point scale. With respect to psychiatric symptoms, 20% of schizophrenics were completely asymptomatic at followup and 55% had severe symptoms. Thirty-five percent of the patients were living with their family or independently, and 15% were in mental institutions. Thirty-five percent were economically productive, and 55% were completely incapacitated. The surgical control group was distinctly different, with over 85% of controls in the better outcome group on each parameter and under 4% in the worst outcome group. The manic and depressive patients were generally indistinguishable as regards outcome and did only moderately worse than the surgical controls. The schizophrenia group experienced excess mortality that could not be fully accounted for either by suicides or by accidental death (Tsuang and Woolson, 1978).

In summary, the literature on outcome for schizophrenia does lead to fairly consistent findings if differences in methodology are taken into account. The diagnoses of schizophrenia that required six months of symptoms and use other criteria that involve longitudinal course result in the greatest homogeneity of outcome. Studies thus designed consistently report that about 20% of schizophrenics are completely asymptomatic one or two decades later. Even so, we must conclude that schizophrenia is most often a severely disabling illness, with about 60% of patients remaining completely nonproductive, economically. About 60% of patients will eventually require some type of chronic institutional care. It appears that the disease is fairly stable after the first decade, generally not becoming any worse and perhaps becoming slightly better.

The above outcome data should apply to patients diagnosed as schizophrenic by DSM-III criteria. Most large, long-term studies only partially overlap the phenothiazine era. but preliminary indications are that the phenothiazines may effect short-term but not long-term prognosis of the disease (Pritchard, 1967; Scarpitti et al., 1964). If criteria for schizophrenia are limited only to cross-sectional measures, such as those proposed by Bleuler, the number of asymptomatic patients after a decade increases to about 40%.

COURSE OF SCHIZOPHRENIA

Course refers to the order and timing of various signs and symptoms and how these change over time. Knowledge about course can indicate possible etiological factors and suggest further diagnostic subtypes and when it would be appropriate to obtain various psychological and bio-chemical data in order to further our understanding of the disease.

Two recent developments may lead to an improved understanding of the various changes that occur during the course of schizophrenia. The first is the previously discussed development of more precise diagnostic criteria. The second is the refinement of psychological testing to more clearly delineate components of mental function. Recent advances in this area are reviewed by Chapman (1979). Unfortunately, most of the studies about to be reviewed were undertaken without the benefit of precise diagnosis or the newer measurement techniques.

Many studies of longitudinal course are made on chronically hospitalized schizophrenics. Although the outcome of such groups might not be representative of that of all schizophrenics, studying these worst cases may still provide valuable information about the nature of the disease. The conventional wisdom since Kraepelin has been that schizophrenia is generally characterized by a development of severe psychotic symptoms over a period of months, followed by a slow progressive dementia over the next few decades. Although the outcome is generally poor, it is interesting that the studies of the past two decades suggest a somewhat different pattern of progression.

Most studies place the onset of schizophrenia before age 35, in the vast majority of patients. The Iowa 500 found a median age of onset of 25 for the hebephrenic subtype and 31 for the paranoid subtypes (Tsuang and Winokur, 1974). Most clinicians have seen schizophrenia develop in persons with normal premorbid social adjustment and above average intelligence, but there is no question that chronic schizophrenics, taken as a group, differ premorbidly from the rest of the population.

Albee, Lane, and Reuter (1964) have published a number of studies in which school records of children who later became schizophrenic are compared with various control groups, with careful investigation of such possible confounders as social class. They conclude that schizophrenics as a group definitely have lower premorbid IQs then controls. Other studies (Schwartzman and Douglas, 1962; Offord, Cross, and Hershey 1971; Robins, 1966) verify the occurrence of low IQ and academic difficulties, premorbidly, and suggest that premorbid IQ is directly correlated with age of onset. Siblings of schizophrenics appear to have an IQ that is intermediate between the premorbid IQ of the schizophrenics and the IQ of the controls. In studies that separate acute from chronic schizophrenics, low premorbid IQ was more pronounced in the chronic group but it is possible that this is because the diagnosis of acute schizophrenia is more likely to include affective disorders by contemporary criteria.

Offord, Cross, and Hershey (1971) verify that paranoid schizophrenics have a higher premorbid IQ than hebephrenics. They make the interesting suggestion that the genetic contribution to IQ is independent from that to schizophrenia and that high IQ leads both to later onset of symptoms and to a predisposition toward paranoid versus hebephrenic symptomatology.

Measurement of premorbid personality is necessarily more subjective than measurement of intellect. Slater and Roth (1969) state that 30 to 50% of schizophrenics have no prior mental abnormality. Those that were abnormal had personalities characterized by paranoid traits, eccentricities, lack of feeling, and lack of sympathy. Zigler, Glick, and Marsh (1979) measured premorbid social competence by applying a rating scale to chart review information of a consecutive series of 92 schizophrenics, 98 "psychoneurotic" patients, and 89 affective disorder patients. Only first admission patients were included. The schizophrenic group had by far the lowest premorbid social competence score. Since the onset of schizophrenic symptoms is often insidious, it is difficult in many of these studies to be sure that the premorbid period used truly antedates the beginning of the schizophrenic symptoms.

In a study now in progress by the present authors, the premorbid history of 52 hebephrenic schizophrenics from the Iowa 500 was reviewed. All patients met the Feighner criteria for schizophrenia (Feighner et al., 1972). The criteria for hebephrenia carefully defined elsewhere (Tsuang and Winokur, 1974) include bizarre behavior, inappropriate or flat affect, catatonic motor symptoms, and early onset. Catatonic schizophrenics were included in the hebephrenic group because of similarities explained in the above reference. Three-page interviews of relatives were generally available in the chart, and great care was taken to avoid recording behavior from the 2 years preceding first hospitalization. About 45% of patients appeared to have some type of personality disorder premorbidly. In about one-half of these cases, the disorder appeared to loosely meet DSM-III criteria for schizoid personality.

In the same series of 52 hebephrenics, the onset of symptoms was generally insidious, occurring about 1 year before first hospitalization. Work impairment, inappropriate affect, and avolition were the symptoms most frequently reported by friends and relatives in the early stages.

Strauss, Carpenter, and Bartko (1974) have suggested that the symptoms of schizophrenia be considered as falling into three main catagories: positive symptoms, such as delusions, hallucinations and motor phenomena; negative symptoms, such a blunted affect, apathy, poverty of thought, and certain types of formal thought disorder; and finally, disorders in relating, such as having few friends and limited social interaction and tending not to marry.

The positive symptoms are usually present early in the course of the disease and are often the reason why the patient is first brought to medical attention. Despite their prominence in various proposed diagnostic criteria, they clearly are not unique to schizophrenia and in themselves are not useful in predicting outcome (Strauss, Carpenter, and Bartko, 1974; Knight et al., 1979). Bridge, Cannon, and Wyatt (1978) summarize several studies that show that halluciations and delusions are much less frequent after the first decade in chronically hospitalized schizophrenics.

In our study of 52 hebephrenics, 85% had persecutory delusions of some type during the first 3 years after onset. After 10 years, 50% still had such delusions, and after 20 years, 40% had. We observed a similar pattern for hallucinations. Figure 3-1 is a graph of the percent of the 52 hebephrenics who had auditory hallucinations each year after the onset of the illness.

Motor symptoms are also conceptually positive symptoms. For reasons that are unclear, catatonia and steretypies appear to be much less frequent than previously reported; however, they may be present early in the course of the disease. Unfortunately, neuroleptics can also cause disorders of muscle tone as well as various involuntary movements. Owens and Johnstone (1980) report a sample of 524 patients who met Feighner criteria for schizophrenia. Most of the patients had been chronically hospitalized; the mean age was 60. They found that 72% had some type of neurological abnormality involving extrapyramidal signs or spontaneous involuntary movement disorders. Surprisingly, they report that such abnormalities were equally frequent in a subgroup of 52 patients who had never had neuroleptics administered to them.

Of the negative symptoms, flat affect has been repeatedly demonstrated to be correlated with chronicity (see reviews by Strauss, Carpenter, and Bartho, 1974, and Knight et al., 1979). Its usefulness is somewhat lessened by the fact that it is frequently not present early in the illness, and if it is not severe, reliable measurements are difficult to obtain. In our sample of 52 hebephrenics, 50% had flat affect at the time

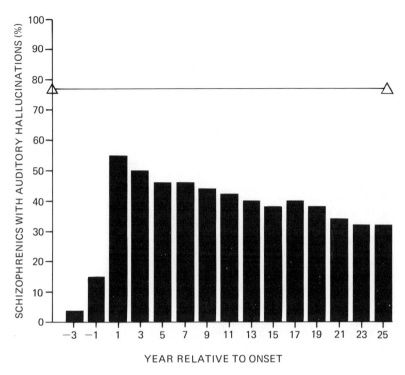

FIGURE 3-1. The Number of 52 Hebephrenic Schizophrenics with Auditory Hallucinations at 2-Year Intervals after First Hospitalization. Horizontal line, percent of schizophrenics who have ever had auditory hallucinations

of first hospitalization, and 80% had it by the 10th year of hospitalization. Inappropriate affect, by contrast, tended to be noticed by the family even prior to hospitalization by which time 73% of patients were affected. This number gradually dropped to 62% over the next 20 years.

Table 3-1 shows the distribution of selected symptoms in our study group of 52 hebephrenics. The first column is simply the percent of patients who had that symptom at any time during the course of the illness. The second column is the mean number of years from the time of hospitalization until that symptom appeared. This number can be negative if onset of that symptom frequently occurred before first hospitalization.

The third column is the percent of patients in whom that symptom

TABLE 3-1.

PERCENTAGE OF 52 HEBEPHRENIC SCHIZOPHRENICS DEVELOPING
SYMPTOM, PERCENTAGE LOSING SYMPTOM, AND MEAN NUMBER OF
YEARS FROM TIME OF FIRST HOSPITALIZATION TO SYMPTOM ONSET AND
SYMPTOM RESOLUTION, RESPECTIVELY

	Onset		Resolution	
Symptom	%	Mean yr	%	Mean yr
Avolition	94	0.2	4	21
Decreased social interaction	94	1.6	18	12
Work impairment	100	−1.1	6	13
Mannerisms	61	6.0	48	9
Inappropriate affect	87	−0.3	42	15
Flat affect	94	5.0	6	23
Persecutory delusions	85	0.2	61	10
Auditory hallucinations	77	0.9	62	12

disappeared. Only patients who once had this symptom are used in the denominator of this calculation. The fourth column is the mean number of years from the time of first hospitalization until that symptom disappeared.

Until recently there was no reliable scale for rating the full range of thought disorder that has been traditionally described in schizophrenics. Andreasen (1979) has developed and tested such a scale—the Scale for the Assessment of Thought, Language and Communication (TLC)—which has been demonstrated to be reliable. In a series of 45 schizophrenics meeting Spitzer's Research Diagnostic Criteria, 30% of the patients had poverty of speech, 40% had poverty of content of speech, 56% had derailment, 16% had incoherence, and 44% had loss of goal. Blocking was present in only 4%, despite the fact that blocking is reported in much higher percentages by clinicians who use the term more loosely.

The currently available longitudinal studies of thought and language disorder in schizophrenia generally deal with various measures of associational defects and with verbal and non-verbal intelligence, which has a direct bearing on the whole issue of dementia in schizophrenia. Kraepelin reported that most schizophrenics become more and more demented over a period of years. It may be that Kraepelin was observing the effects of poor institutional conditions in combination with the generally shorter life-span present during the 1800s. In any case, there is now abundant evidence that even in chronically institutionalized schizophrenics almost all the intellectual deterioration occurs during the first few years after onset. After this there is a mild decline in certain mental faculties, but this is no more rapid than in the general population.

Schwartzman and Douglas (1962) report a study of 50 schizophrenic Canadian male war veterans for whom premorbid IQ testing was available. The schizophrenics had a lower IQ than a matched veteran control group, premorbidly. Although the schizophrenics had a very significant drop in scores after onset, the control group had somewhat improved scores at the time of repeat testing.

Foulds et al. (1962) report a carefully controlled study of 270 schizophrenics and 280 age- and sex-matched neurotics. Raven's Progressive Matrices were used as a measure of nonverbal intelligence, the Mill Hill Vocabulary test as a measure of verbal ability. On Progressive Matrices, the schizophrenics scored considerably below the neurotics, with the paranoid subtype scoring somewhat higher than catatonic and hebephrenic subtypes. On retesting 2 years later, both schizophrenics and neurotics showed a slight decline, but in both cases the decline did not exceed the norms for the general population on this test. The effects of duration of hospitalization were statistically assessed after partialling out the effects of age, and there was no indication that hospitalization per se contributed to lower performance.

On the Mill Hill Vocabulary test, schizophrenic performance was also significantly poorer than was neurotic performance, although the difference was less pronounced than the difference for Progressive Matrices. Repeat testing 2 years later showed no significant change from previous scores for either group. Two other studies have also shown no decrement in verbal performance of schizophrenics over time (Ginett and Moran, 1964; Moran, Gorham, and Holtzman, 1960). Wynne (1963) did report a correlation between poor verbal performance and length of hospitalization; however, length of hospitalization may have been confounded by severity of illness.

Flekkoy (1975) reports the results of formal word association testing of 72 schizophrenics, with repeat testing 16 years later. There was a trend for associations to normalize over time, with the schizophrenics who were early in their course at first testing showing the most gain. They conclude that there is little evidence for chronic deterioration in schizophrenia.

Bridge, Cannon, and Wyatt (1978) reviewed 10 longitudinal followup studies, seven of which included more than 100 schizophrenics. The evidence is strong that even among chronically hospitalized schizophrenics progressive deterioration of intellect after the early stages of the disease did not occur. Not only were delusions and hallucinations less frequent, but patients who had shown little interest in anything for years began to take interest in some social contact. It is difficult to know if some of these encouraging findings are related to the introduction of phenothiazines during the 1950s.

There is one misconception about the course of schizophrenia that appears to be challenged by recent research findings. Slater and Roth (1969, p. 306) define dementia as "impairment of intelligence, in contrast to impairment of personality." They go on to state that "schizophrenia does not lead to dementia." Evidence from computerized axial tomography of the brain (CAT scans) suggest that the decline in IQ in schizophrenics is more than the result of psychotic symptoms interfering with concentration.

Johnstone et al. (1978) reported the results of intelligence testing of 18 chronic schizophrenics, a group of age-matched patients chronically hospitalized because of physical impairment, and age-matched normal controls. The chronic schizophrenics had the lowest IQ and significantly larger ventricles on CAT scanning than either of the other two groups. There was a direct correlation between the amount of ventricular enlargement measured on the scans and the amount of intellectual impairment.

Asano (1967) reported from a series of pneumoencephalographic studies that schizophrenics under 40 years of age were just as likely to show enlarged ventricles as were schizophrenics over 40 years of age. This suggests that whatever ventricular enlargement occurs, occurs relatively early in the course of the illness. These findings are now supported by two independent studies that report CAT scans and psychological testing on a series of schizophrenics diagnosed by research diagnostic criteria (Weinberger et al., 1979; Golden et al., 1980). Both studies were limited primarily to schizophrenics under 50 years old. Not only did the schizophrenics have significantly enlarged ventricles compared to controls, but there was a direct correlation between the amount of atrophy and the amount of intellectual deterioration. In neither study were length of illness and amount of ventricular enlargement correlated.

Although it is true that atrophy of brain tissue does not necessarily imply decreased intellectual function, consistent findings and a correlation with decreased intellectual function on formal testing strongly implicate schizophrenia as a truly dementing illness. Further study will be required to determine if schizophrenia without cerebral atrophy represent a milder form of the same disease process or a completely different type of schizophrenia.

The concept of schizophrenia as a dementing illness with an active stage limited to the first few years after onset is important to the scientist attempting to discover biological changes to explain the disease process. Biological samples should probably be taken from schizophrenics during the first few years of their disease. The ideal sampling time might very well be in the months soon after the patient has met the DSM-III criteria of 6 months duration of symptoms.

At the very least, researchers should be alert to the possibility that duration of illness may explain some of the variance in the data.

REFERENCES

Albee, G. W., E. A. Lane, and J. M. Reuter (1964). Childhood intelligence of future schizophrenics and neighborhood peers. *J Psychol.* 58, 141–144.

Andreasen, N. C. (1979) Thought, language and communication disorders. *Arch. Gen. Psychiat.* 36, 1325–1330.

Asano, N. (1967). Pneumoencephalographic study of schizophrenia. In *Clinical Genetics in Psychiatry: Problems in Nosological Classification* (H. Mitsuda, ed.) Tokyo, Igaku Shoin Ltd., pp. 209–219.

Bland, R. C., J. H. Parker, and H. Orn (1978). Prognosis in schizophrenia. *Arch. Gen. Psychiat.* 35, 72–77.

Bridge, T. P., H. E. Cannon, and R. J. Wyatt (1978). Burned-out schizophrenia: Evidence for age effects on schizophrenic symptomatology. *J. Gerontol.* 33, 835–839.

Chapman, L. J. (1979). Recent advances in the study of schizophrenic cognition. *Schizophrenia Bul.* 5, 568–580.

Ciompi, L. (1980). The natural history of schizophrenia in the long term. *Brit. J. Psychiat.* 136, 413–420.

Feighner, J. P., E. Robins, S. Guze, R. A. Woodruff, G. Winokur, and R. Munoz (1972). Diagnostic criteria for use in psychiatric research. *Arch. Gen. Psychiat.* 26, 57–62.

Flekkoy, K. (1975). Changes of associative performance in hospitalized schizophrenics: A 16-year followup. *Acta Psychiat. Scand.* 52, 330–335.

Foulds, G. A., P. Dixon, M. McClelland, and W. J. McClelland (1962). The nature of intellectual deficit in schizophrenia. *Brit. J. Soc. Clin. Psychol.* I, 141–149.

Ginett, L. E., and L. J. Moran (1964). Stability of vocabulary performance by schizophrenics. *J. Consult. Psychol.* 28, 178–179.

Golden, C. J., J. A. Moses, M. A. Zelazowski, B. Graber, L. M. Zatz, T. B. Horvath, and P. A. Berger (1980). Cerebral ventricular size and neuropsychological impairment in young chronic schizophrenics. *Arch. Gen. Psychiat.* 37, 619–623.

Hawk, A. B., W. T. Carpenter, and J. S. Strauss (1975). Diagnostic criteria and 5 year outcome in schizophrenia. *Arch. Gen. Psychiat.* 32, 343–347.

Hoenig, J. (1967). The prognosis of schizophrenia. *Brit. J. Psychiat.* Special Publication #1 by A. Coppen, and B. Walk, eds.) 115–131.

Huber G., G. Gross, and R. Schuttler (1975). Psychiatric course of illness and prognosis. *Acta Psychiat. Scand.* 52, 49–57.

Johnstone, E. C., T. J. Crow, C. D. Frith, M. Stevens, L. Kreel, and J. Husband (1978). The dementia of dementia praecox. *Acta Psychiat. Scand.* 57, 305–324.

Knight, R. A., J. D. Roff, J. Barrnett, and J. L. Moss (1979). Concurrent and predictive validity of thought disorder and affectivity: A 22-year follow-up of acute schizophrenics. *J. Abnorm. Psychol.* 88, 1–12.

Langfeldt, G. *Schizophreniform States.* Copenhagen: E. Munksgaard, 1939.

Moran, L. J., D. R. Gorham, and W. H. Holtzman (1960). Vocabulary knowledge and usage of schizophrenia subjects. *J. Abnorm. Soc. Psychol.* 2, 246–254.

Offord, D. R., L. A. Cross, and P. A. Hershey (1971). Adult schizophrenia with scholastic failure or low I.Q. in children. *Arch. Gen. Psychiat.* 24, 431–436.

Owens, D. G. C., and E. C. Johnstone (1980). The disabilities of chronic schizophrenia. *Brit. J. Psychiat.* 136, 384–395.

Pritchard, M. (1967). Prognosis of schizophrenia before and after pharmacotherapy. *Brit. J. Psychiat.* 113, 1345–1359.

Robins, L. N. (1966). *Deviant Children Grown Up*, Williams & Wilkins, Baltimore.

Scarpitti, F. R., M. Lefton, S. Dnitz, and B. Pasamanick (1964). Problems in a homecare study for schizophrenia. *Arch. Gen. Psychiat.* 10, 143–154.

Schwartzman, A. E., and V. I. Douglas (1962). Intellectual loss in schizophrenia. *Canad. J. Psychol.* 16, 1–10.

Silverstein, M. L., and M. Harrow (1978) First rank symptoms in the postacute schizophrenic: A follow-up study. *Amer. J. Psychiat.* 135, 1481–1486.

Slater, E., and M. Roth (1969). *Clinical Psychiatry.* 3rd. ed. Williams & Wilkins, Baltimore.

Stephens, J. H., C. Astrup, and J. C. Mangrum (1966). Prognostic factors in recovered and deteriorated schizophrenics. *Amer. J. Psychiat.* 122, 1116–1121.

Strauss, J. S., and W. T. Carpenter (1974). The prediction of outcome in schizophrenia. II. *Arch. Gen. Psychiat.* 31, 37–42.

Strauss, J. S., W. T. Carpenter, and J. J. Bartko (1974). Speculation on the processes that underlie schizophrenic symptoms and signs. *Schizophrenia Bull.* 11, 61–73.

Tsuang, M. T., and G. Winokur (1974). Criteria for subtyping schizophrenia. *Arch. Gen. Psychiat.* 31, 43–47.

Tsuang, M. T., and R. F. Woolson (1978). Excess mortality in schizophrenia and affective disorder. *Arch. Gen. Psychiat.* 35, 1181–1185.

Tsuang, M. T., R. F. Woolson, and M. S. Fleming (1979). Long-term outcome of major psychosis. *Arch. Gen. Psychiat.* 36, 1295–1301.

Vaillant, G. E. (1964). Prospective prediction of schizophrenic remission, *Arch. Gen. Psychiat.* 11, 509–518.

Weinberger, D. R., E. F. Torrey, A. N. Neophytides, and J. Wyatt (1979). Lateral cerebral ventrical enlargement in chronic schizophrenia. *Arch. Gen. Psychiat.* 36, 735–739.

Wyatt, R. J., S. G. Potkin, J. E. Kleinman, D. R. Weinberger, D. J. Luchins, and D. V. Jeste (1981). The schizophrenia syndrome. *J. Nerv. Mental Dis.* 169, 100–112.

Wynne, R. D. (1963). The influence of hospitalization on the verbal behavior of chronic schizophrenia. *Brit. J. Psychiat.* 109, 380–389.

Zigler E., M. Glick, and A. March (1979). Premorbid social competence and outcome among schizophrenics and non-schizophrenic patients *J. Nerv. Mental Dis.* 167:478–483.

4 | Recent Genetic Research in Schizophrenia

RAYMOND R. CROWE

INTRODUCTION

This chapter will review recent progress in the genetics of schizophrenia, focusing on three issues. The first issue is the evidence supporting schizophrenia as a genetic disease. The second is the question of which diagnoses are related to the schizophrenia genotype. The third is the question of how schizophrenia is inherited. An additional line of research, stimulated by the genetic findings, involves work on individuals at high risk for developing schizophrenia in an effort to find a better phenotype than the disease itself. However, that issue is addressed elsewhere in this volume and will not be considered further here.

WHAT IS THE GENETIC EVIDENCE?

Schizophrenia is a familial disease. This fact is well illustrated by the family data reviewed by Zerbin-Rüdin (1972). Despite considerable heterogeneity in morbidity risks between studies, the averages make the point: compared with a 0.85% general population risk, the risk in every class of relative is increased. Among first-degree relatives, the morbidity risks are parents, 6.3%, children, 13.7%, and siblings, 10.4%; among second-degree relatives, grandchildren, 3.5%, nieces and nephews, 2.6%, aunts and uncles, 3.6%, grandparents, 1.6%, and half-siblings, 3.5%;

and among third-degree relatives, cousins 3.5%. Since this review, several large studies on a sizable number of relatives have appeared that support the earlier findings. Lindelius's (1970) study of 270 probands found morbidity risks for "confirmed schizophrenia" among first-degree relatives as siblings, 5.6%; children, 7.2%; and parents (who had died many years before the study), 0.59%. The risk for nieces and nephews was 3.9%. Bleuler (1978), in his investigation of 208 probands, found the following morbidity risks for "certain schizophrenia": siblings, 9.0%; children, 9.4%; rates for second-degree relatives were 2.4% for half-siblings and 3.8% for grandchildren. Karlsson's (1973) morbidity risks for the relatives of his 573 probands were lower: siblings, 3.5%; children, 3.1%; parents, 2.7%; grandparents, 1.5%; aunts and uncles, 2.0%; nieces and nephews, 2.9%; and first cousins, 1.1%. Although these figures are low compared to other studies, the category of "all functional psychoses" yields rates comparable to those previously cited. Böök, Wetterberg, and Modrzewska (1978) recently reported data on the first-degree relatives from a north Swedish isolate containing three extensive kindreds of schizophrenia, and these rates are 11% for parents, 8 to 13% for siblings (depending on whether a parent is affected or not), and 12% for children. Finally, the 200 schizophrenic families from the Iowa 500 material have not been completely analyzed, but the rate among pooled first-degree relatives is 5.5% (Tsuang, Winokur, and Crowe, 1980).

Two classes of relatives have especially high risks of developing schizophrenia; the first of these are offspring of two schizophrenic parents. Erlenmeyer-Kimling (1968) reviewed five studies providing data on these subjects. If the analysis is restricted to definite schizophrenia, the age-corrected morbidity risk from the pooled data is 39.2%. More recently, Böök's material yielded a morbidity risk of 28% among 31 offspring (Modrzeska, 1980).

A monozygotic (MZ) co-twin of a schizophrenic constitutes a second class of relative with an exceptionally high risk of developing schizophrenia. Recent studies are usually considered separately from earlier ones due to a number of methodological biases that plagued the earlier studies (Rosenthal, 1962). Gottesman and Shields (1976) reviewed the results of the five recent twin studies, finding proband-wise concordance rates for MZ twins ranging from 35 to 58%, compared with dizygotic (DZ) twin rates ranging from 9 to 26%. In every study the MZ concordance rate exceeded the DZ rate, but in no study did it approach 100%. These findings provide further evidence for schizophrenia as a genetic disease;

however, the MZ concordance rate of less than 100% indicates that genetic factors are not a complete explanation.

In short, the epidemiological data demonstrate that the risk of schizophrenia increases with the number of genes shared with a schizophrenic. The highest rates are found among MZ co-twins of schizophrenics who share 100% of their genes with a schizophrenic, followed by offspring of two schizophrenics, followed by first-, second-, and third-degree relatives, respectively. This fact has been known for over a generation, but it never received the credibility it deserved, since shared genes almost invariably meant shared environment. What was called for was an experimental design that would maintain shared genes, but eliminate shared environment. This led to adoption studies.

The first adoption study of schizophrenia was Heston's (1966) followup of 47 offspring born to schizophrenic mothers in state hospitals and separated from their mothers at birth. Personal interviews and multiple records collected on the index adoptees and 50 adopted controls at followup (mean age 36 years) led to a diagnosis of schizophrenia in five index adoptees, an age-corrected morbidity risk of 16.6%. This was significantly greater ($p < .025$) than the control adoptees, none of whom were diagnosed as schizophrenic.

Karlsson (1966, 1970) reported three samples of schizophrenics' relatives separated from their biological families in the first year of life and reared by non-relatives in foster homes. The first involved nine siblings reared in foster homes; three developed schizophrenia. In the second study, six of 29 biological siblings of foster-reared hospitalized schizophrenics were found to be schizophrenic. In the third group, three of 14 foster-reared children of hospitalized schizophrenic mothers had been hospitalized for schizophrenia. Combining the groups, one obtains an absolute schizophrenia rate of 23% among the 52 biological first-degree relatives at risk. This high rate may reflect the fact that many had two schizophrenic first-degree relatives, a factor known to increase the risk for schizophrenia.

The most thorough and convincing adoption studies have been the Danish investigations based on national adoption and psychiatric registers. Rosenthal et al. (1968, 1971) studied 76 adoptees of biological parents with what they termed the schizophrenia spectrum. This diagnosis included process schizophrenia diagnosed by all raters (30) or at least one (14), reactive (4) and borderline schizophrenia (4), manic depressive illness (7), and a residual of 17 parents for whom the diagnosis was unclear, but who were felt to belong in the schizophrenia spectrum. The 76 index and the 67 carefully matched control adoptees were placed in adoptive homes at a median age of six months and blindly interviewed at a mean age of 33 years. The main finding was that significantly more ($p < .05$) index adoptees (31.6%) were diagnosed as schizophrenia spectrum disorders than the control adoptees (17.8%). The former figure included three process and three borderline schizophrenics for a total schizophrenia rate of 14%—comparable to other studies, but not significantly higher than the control rate.

Using the same national registers, Kety et al. (1968, 1975) identified 33 schizophrenic adoptees (process, borderline, and reactive) and matched them with 33 control adoptees. The biological and adoptive relatives (parents, siblings, and half-siblings) of both groups were blindly interviewed and diagnosed by a consensus of investigators. Process or borderline schizophrenia was diagnosed in 6.4% of the 173 index biological relatives and another 7.5% were considered doubtful cases—a total schizophrenia rate of 13.9%. This was significantly higher ($p < .001$) than the rates found among the control biological relatives (3.4%). Among the adoptive relatives of both groups, the respective rates were 2.7% and 5.5%.

Two additional points about the Kety et al. study are worth mentioning. First, it can be argued that the proper experimental unit in a genetic study is the *family* and not the individual relative; thus, the proper analysis would be a comparison of the number of families positive for schizophrenia in the index and control groups. When this was done, 17 of 33 index families were positive compared with five of 34 controls ($p < .001$).

A second point makes the Kety et al. study especially convincing: namely, the schizophrenia rate found among the 63 biological paternal half-siblings (22%) was significantly higher ($p < .001$) than the 3% rate among the 64 control biological paternal half-siblings. This design eliminates the possibility of even a shared intrauterine environment influencing the outcome and leaves the genetic hypothesis as the only plausible explanation for the adoption study findings.

Another variation on the adoption theme was a cross-foster analysis in which offspring born to normal parents and reared by affected ones were compared with offspring born to affected parents and reared by normal ones (Wender et al., 1974). The first cross-fostered group consisted of 28 adoptees born to parents free of schizophrenia spectrum disorders and reared by adoptive parents, one of each pair falling in the schizophrenia spectrum (chronic or borderline schizophrenia, 13; doubtful schizophrenia or schizoid, 6; and acute schizophrenia or schizoaffective, 9). A second cross-fostered group consisted of 69 adoptees born to schizophrenia spectrum parents (chronic and borderline schizophrenia, 50; doubtful schizophrenia or schizoid, 9; acute schizophrenia or schizoaffective, 10) and reared by adoptive parents free of schizophrenia spectrum disorders. Finally, a group of adopted controls was included. The adoptees were evaluated blindly and rated on a scale of psychopathology. When the three groups were compared with respect to the percent falling into the most severe quartile of psychopathology (i.e., ranging from probable borderline to chronic schizophrenia), 18.8% of the adoptees of schizophrenia spectrum biological parents were diagnosed in this spectrum, despite being reared by non-spectrum adoptive parents, compared with 10.1% diagnosed among the adopted controls. However, the group of interest was the one born to non-spectrum parents, but reared by a spectrum adoptive parent; 10.7% of these adoptees were diagnosed in the spectrum, the percentage being almost identical to the adopted controls.

The major contribution of the adoption studies was the validation of the genetic hypothesis of schizophrenia. With this hypothesis generally accepted, attention then turned to other genetic issues that had been ignored because of distrust of the early genetic data. One of the more vexing of these was the question of a spectrum of psychopathology genetically related to schizophrenia, but milder in nature and shading into normal.

THE SCHIZOPHRENIA SPECTRUM

Many diverse conditions have been observed in the families of schizophrenics and would thus be candidates for inclusion in the schizophrenia spectrum. For the purpose of this review, they will be considered in three groups that appear to have some internal consistency. The first of these are disorders that have been considered variants of schizophrenia itself. These include borderline or latent schizophrenia, questionable and uncertain cases of schizoprrenia, acute schizophrenia, and schizoaffective illness. The second group consists of personality deviations frequently seen in relatives of schizophrenics, which are marked by traits that, in mild form, are suggestive of schizophrenia. These include paranoid qualities, eccentricities, lack of feeling, asociality, and anergia. Heston (1970) has referred to this group of disorders as "schizoidia." The third group of conditions are psychiatric disorders not usually thought of as variants of schizophrenia. These include alcoholism, affective disorder, and antisocial personality. The second and third group have been reviewed in detail by Shields, Heston, and Gottesman (1975).

Schizophrenia as a disease does not have a clear boundary, and a residual of borderline and doubtful cases is usually found. Bleuler (1978) tabulated the findings from the older literature as well as those from his 1972 publication and found that borderline cases, expressed as a percentage of total schizophrenics, varied from 10.5% in Bleuler's study to 35% in Kallmann's large Berlin sample. Similar findings have been reported in more recent family studies by Karlsson (1973), Lindelius (1970), and Stephens et al. (1975). Moreover, it will be recalled that in the recent twin studies, concordance rates have been considered to be more accurately expressed as a range, depending on whether borderline and questionable cases are included as schizophrenia.

Further support for the inclusion of borderline cases with process schizophrenia comes from the Danish adoption studies. In the Kety et al. (1975) study, schizophrenia was subdivided as either definite (chronic and latent) or doubtful (chronic and latent). The breakdown among the 173 index biological relatives was as follows: chronic schizophrenia, five; latent, six; and doubtful schizophrenia, 13. Among control biological relatives, the breakdown was chronic, none; latent, three; and doubtful, three. Although latent schizophrenia alone did not distinguish between the two groups at a statistically significant level, uncertain cases did ($p < .01$), and when chronic and latent cases were combined the difference was significant ($p < .001$). Furthermore, it is notable that when control adoptees with schizophrenia spectrum diagnoses were excluded, the number of latent and uncertain cases among their relatives fell from six to one. The adoptees study material (Rosenthal et al., 1971) is consistent with this finding, with more borderline and uncertain cases among the index adoptees (although the difference is not statistically significant) and the total schizophrenia spectrum significantly more frequent among index adoptees.

Turning to acute schizophrenia, the Danish adoption studies were remarkable in failing to find this disorder among the relatives of process schizophrenics, and conversely, failing to find process schizophrenia among the relatives of acute schizophrenics. Another way of approaching the question is to examine family studies of "acute schizophrenia." A recent review included 15 studies of this disorder with respect to the percent of probands with a family history of schizophrenia versus affective illness (Pope and Lipinski, 1978). In every study, affectively ill families outnumbered schizophrenic families, and moreover, in all nine studies comparing acute with process schizophrenics, there was a higher proportion of schizophrenic family histories among the process schizophrenics. A recent investigation of sib-pairs by Tsuang (1979), in which the index sib had schizophrenia, schizoaffective disorder, or affective disorder, revealed that schizophrenia paired with schizophrenia and affective disorder paired with affective disorder, but when the index sib had schizoaffective disorder, the other sibling tended to have either schizophrenia or affective disorder. Ödegaard's data (1972) demonstrate reactive and affective psychoses among relatives of schizophrenics and, conversely, schizophrenia among the relatives of reactive, atypical, and manic depressive psychotics. The proponderance of the data appears to support a separation between acute and process schizophrenia, although in some studies they overlap. Thus, the evidence is consistent in including borderline and latent schizophrenia in the spectrum, but suggests that "acute schizophrenia" is genetically related to other disorders.

The second group of disorders found among relatives of schizophrenics comprise character traits suggestive of schizophrenic symptoms in mild form. These include paranoid traits, eccentricities, lack of feeling, asociality, and anergia. In Kallman's (1938, 1946) data, approximately one-third of the first-degree relatives exhibited these traits. More recently, Alanen (1966) observed a group of conditions consisting of "schizoid and paranoid character, paranoid psychoses, jealousy paranoia, paranoid psychopath, psychotic personality and depressive psychosis" in 37 of the 109 (34%) first-degree relatives of schizophrenics he intensively studied, but none of these disorders appeared among 110 first-degree relatives of the neurotic patients studied. Bleuler (1978) commented on the frequency with which he observed what he termed "schizoid psychopathies and schizoid-psychopathological personality attitudes" among the siblings of his schizophrenic probands. Stephens et al. (1975) found a spectrum of "psychopathic, paranoid, and schizoid personality" in 28 of 111 (25%) first-degree relatives of schizophrenic probands compared with five of 69 (7%) first-degree relatives of non-schizophrenic psychiatric inpatients.

If this group of disorders is a valid entity, the highest rates should be found among MZ co-twins discordant for schizophrenia. Shields et al. (1975) have reviewed the twin data, finding among seven studies that could be reliably analyzed that the percent of non-schizophrenic disorders ranged from 7 to 29%. The percentage of "schizoid" conditions, the equivalent of the spectrum disorders under consideration here, ranged from 5 to 21% in the four studies in which they were so characterized. Finally, the percentage of normal co-twins ranged from 5 to 43%. The twin data are, therefore, consistent with the schizophrenia spectrum hypothesis; however, the frequency of normal co-twins indicates that the spectrum is not a marker for the schizophrenic genotype.

The adoption studies provide further support for the concept of a schizoid spectrum. Heston (1966) found "neurotic personality disorder" (various types of personality disorder and neurosis in which psychiatric disability was judged to be a significant handicap) in 13 of 47 index adoptees, significantly more than the seven cases among his 50 controls. (He also found more antisocial personality and mental deficiency among his index adoptees, but these disorders may be more relevant to those taken up in the next section.) The Kety et al. (1975) study blindly examined diagnoses of schizoid and inadequate personality among relatives of the adoptees. Although the consensus diagnoses failed to distinguish between index and control biological relatives with respect to this category, one of the raters did find a significant difference in the expected direction. Further support comes from Rosenthal et al. (1971), who found that schizophrenia spectrum disorder was significantly more frequent among the index adoptees than among the adopted controls. Inspection of the diagnoses of the ill adoptees reveals that most would fall within the concept of "schizoidia."

Rosenthal (1975) pointed out that the diagnosis of the co-parent must be taken into consideration before concluding that non-schizophrenic disorders in the offspring are genetically related to the diagnosis of the index parent. He divided the schizophrenia spectrum into a "hard spectrum" (chronic and borderline schizophrenia, definite and probable diagnoses) and a "soft spectrum" (similar to the concept of "schizoidia" presented above). Information was obtained on 54 co-parents who were blindly diagnosed as having or not having schizophrenia spectrum disorders. The assortative mating patterns were interesting in their own right. When the index parent was female, nine of 32 co-parents were diagnosed as having schizophrenia spectrum disorders and nine as having psychopathic disorders. When the index parent was male, 10 of 22 co-parents were diagnosed as having schizophrenia spectrum disorders and one as having a psychopathic disorder. Finally, there was a significant correlation between a schizophrenia spectrum diagnosis in the offspring and a similar diagnosis in the co-parent. Since only one of the co-parents fell into the "hard spectrum," this finding speaks for the influence of "soft spectrum" disorders in the non-schizophrenic co-parent on the outcome of the children. Thus, the Rosenthal et al. (1971) and Rosenthal (1975) data support the validity of the schizophrenia spectrum and clearly demonstrate the importance of positive assortative mating in schizophrenia.

The third group of conditions commonly encountered in families of schizophrenics consists of such better defined psychiatric syndromes as alcoholism and affective disorder, which are not ordinarily thought of as related to schizophrenia. Studies by Fowler and his associates (1975, 1977a,b) have helped to clarify the relationship of these disorders to process schizophrenia. In a study of offspring of schizophrenics, they found that 13 of 35 spouses were diagnosable by Feighner research criteria (1972) as follows: alcoholism, seven; antisocial personality, one; and undiagnosed illness, five. Ten of 28 offspring born to these 35 couples were also diagnosed mentally ill (five antisocial, two undiagnosed, and one diagnosis each of hysteria, anxiety neurosis, and schizophrenia). As in the Rosenthal (1975) study, there was a significant association between co-parent diagnosis and offspring illness. Fowler et al. combined their material (Fowler et al., 1974) with the Iowa 500 record study (Winokur et al., 1972) and determined which parental diagnoses were associated with a non-schizophrenic diagnosis in siblings of schizophrenic index cases. Three diagnoses found in the relatives frequently enough for statistical comparison were schizophrenia, alcoholism, and depression. The results demonstrated that a sibling diagnosis of schizophrenia was significantly associated only with a parental diagnosis of schizophrenia, a sibling diagnosis of alcoholism was associated only with a parental diagnosis of alcoholism, and a sibling diagnosis of depression was associated only with a parental diagnosis of "other" (which included depression). In short, none of the diagnoses increased the likelihood of any other diagnosis, as would be expected under a spectrum hypothesis. The question was further examined with data from two family studies (McCabe et al., 1971; Fowler et al., 1974). Non-schizophrenic diagnoses among the first-degree relatives were examined, since, if they were part of a schizophrenia spectrum, they should be encountered more frequently in families with secondary cases of schizophrenia. Contrary to this hypothesis, the most common diagnoses (affective disorder, alcoholism, antisocial personality, neurosis, and undiagnosed illness) were independent of a secondary case of schizophrenia. These studies indicate that major psychiatric syndromes other than schizophrenia appearing in the families of schizophrenics are not genetically related to process schizophrenia, but rather reflect the familial nature of the individual disorders entering the families through assortative mating.

An issue related to the problem of the schizophrenic spectrum is the question of subtype heterogeneity. The subtypes that have best stood the test of time are paranoid, hebephrenic, and catatonic. A body of genetic evidence supporting this has been reviewed by Tsuang (1975). One line of evidence comes from family and twin studies, in which subtype diagnoses between the index schizophrenic and the affected relatives are correlated. The family studies by Kallman (1938), Garrone (1962), and Ödegaard (1963) support such a subtype correlation, although the subtypes by no means "breed true." Turning to twin studies, Kringlen (1967) found subtype concordance in 13 of 14 concordant MZ pairs; Gottesman (1968) in nine of 11. A second line of evidence comes from studies indicating that the morbidity risk for schizophrenia is higher in hebephrenic than in paranoid families. This was true of the studies by Schulz (1932). Hallgren and Sjögren (1959), and Kallman (1938). Some recent data support these findings. Tsuang et al. (1974) pooled the data from family studies by McCabe et al. (1971) and by Fowler et al. (1974) to obtain 60 kindreds, 32 paranoid and 28 nonparanoid. The 13.9% morbidity risk for relatives of the nonparanoids was not significantly higher than the 7.2% found among relatives of the paranoids, but the difference was in the expected direction. Data from the Iowa 500 also support the idea of subtype specificity (Winokur et al., 1974). A blind family history assessment of hospital records led to the rather low morbidity risk of 2.75% in hebephrenic families, compared with 0.83% in paranoid families, again supporting the subtype distinction. These data lend some validity to subtyping schizophrenia along the lines of a paranoid–nonparanoid dichotomy, but more discriminating data than that afforded by present genetic approaches are required.

MODE OF TRANSMISSION

The last problem to be taken up is the question of how schizophrenia is inherited. Recent advances involve the application of complex mathematical models, a complete review of which is beyond the scope of this section. Nevertheless, brief consideration will be given to a review of what transmission models are and what can be learned from them.

A transmission model is basically a mathematical hypothesis, a set of predictions based on an assumption about the transmission of the disorder, which can be compared with observed data, and the fit of model to data tested statistically, so that the model is either accepted or rejected. Each model is defined by a set of parameters, such as the frequency of the trait in the population and its heritability. The parameters and the assumptions of the model comprise a mathematical formula, or set of formulas, that, for any set of parameter values, generate expected values of affected persons among various classes of relatives and the general population. Data collected on disease prevalence in the population and in these classes of relatives of affected persons provide the observed values against which the model is tested. The parameters are iterated over a series of values, successive values being substituted for each parameter in succession until the set of parameters giving the best fit of expected to observed values is obtained. This can be expressed as a Chi-square, which will be minimized for the best fitting parameter set, and if the probability level associated with the smallest Chi-square is greater than a predetermined criterion (say, .05), the model is said to provide a satisfactory fit to the data.

Alternatively, a pedigree analysis approach may be employed. For each model and parameter set, the probability of the observed numbers of affected and unaffected persons in each pedigree can be calculated, the product of these probabilities across pedigrees being expressed as a likelihood that is maximized by the best fitting parameter set. Goodness of fit can be tested under the likelihood approach to determine whether the model is or is not compatible with the observed data.

In interpreting the results of transmission model studies, it is important to remember that genetic transmission is a molecular concept and that what the epidemiologist sees may be many steps removed from the gene. Consequently, if a given model, say, a single gene model, provides a satisfactory fit to the data, this does not imply that single gene transmission has been proven. What it tells us is that the data are consistent with this hypothesis. The disease may later prove to be heterogeneous, consisting of two subtypes, each transmitted in a different manner than that originally predicted by the transmission model. Conversely, if a single gene model is rejected by the data, this does not imply that single gene transmission has been disproven, but only that the hypotheses about single gene transmission embodied in that transmission model do not fit the data. A different single gene model may fit. Finally, data sets in psychiatry often vary greatly from one investigation to another, and models fitting one data set may not fit another of the same disease.

With the genetic nature of schizophrenia established, the next question was how is the disease inherited, and attention logically turned to the application of genetic models. Although models with any number of loci and alleles may be proposed, the principle of parsimony dictates that one should begin with the two extremes of the continuum, namely, the single gene and the polygenic model, and in fact, most work has involved variations of these two models.

The earliest model to become widely accepted in psychiatric genetics was Slater's formulation of a single, incompletely penetrant gene (Slater, 1958; Slater and Cowie, 1971). The model is completely defined by the three parameters population prevalence of schizophrenia (0.085), the gene frequency (p), and the gene penetrance (m). The model was fit to data from the literature on children of one and two schizophrenic parents, siblings, and second- and third-degree relatives. The two parameters that gave the best fit to the observed data were a gene frequency of .03 and a penetrance of .13. Thus, the model predicted a relatively uncommon gene, which was predominantly recessive.

Slater (1966) developed a computational model based on the assumption that if a trait is transmitted as a single gene, then ancestral secondary cases should appear predominantly on one side of the pedigree (paternal or maternal), whereas in polygenic inheritance, they should appear on both sides more frequently than in single gene transmission. By using some simplifying assumptions, he arrived at the expectation that, in polygenic inheritance, pairs of ancestral cases should be unilaterally distributed approximately twice as frequently as bilaterally. Any deviation from this expected 2:1 ratio in the direction of excess unilateral pairs would be evidence for single gene transmission. Slater and Tsuang (1968) and Tsuang (1971) applied the model to two sets of kindreds, finding unilateral:bilateral ratios of 42:11 and 43:11, respectively. Both were significantly in excess ($p < .05$) of the 2:1 ratio predicted by polygenic inheritance.

The first polygenic formulation was Gottesman and Shields's (1967) application of the Falconer (1965) multifactorial threshold model to the data on schizophrenia. The model proposes a normal distribution of liability to schizophrenia that is both genetic and non-genetic, each factor of small effect and acting additively. The distribution encompasses a threshold such that persons whose liability values fall above the threshold manifest the illness and those below it do not. The model is defined by the population prevalence of schizophrenia (q) and its heritability (h^2). With q fixed, h^2 can be calculated from the correlation in prevalence between probands and any class of relatives. If the model fits, the heritabilities should be consistent across classes of relatives and indeed this was found. At a 1% prevalence, h^2 estimates on age-corrected data ranged from 79% among first-degree relatives to 106% for one set of twins. The consistency was acceptable, especially considering that the data came from five investigations in three countries. The calculations were subsequently revised by Kidd and Cavalli-Sforza (1973), using the tetrachoric correlation, and at a 1% population prevalence, the heritabilities ranged from 80 to 93%, substantiating the earlier analysis.

Heston (1970) proposed a variation of the single gene model that assumed complete penetrance of the gene. The model assumes that what is inherited is not only schizophrenia, but the entire spectrum of schizophrenia-like disorders referred to as "schizoidia." If the sum prevalence of schizophrenia and schizoidia is taken, in studies that record these data, the observed proportions of affected relatives comes surprisingly close to that predicted by simple autosomal dominance. For children, 49% are affected compared with the 50% expected, and the respective figures for siblings are 46% versus 50%; for parents, 44% versus 50%; for children of two schizophrenic parents, 66% versus 75%; and for monozygotic co-twins of schizophrenics, 88% versus 100%.

Kidd and Cavalli-Sforza (1973) developed a single locus threshold model that relates the liability-threshold concept of the multifactorial model to a single locus formulation. The model proposes a locus with two alleles Aa leading to the three genotypes AA, Aa, and aa, each having a mean liability around which environmental effects produce a liability distribution. The three liability distributions overlap to produce a continuous liability distribution. A threshold divides the distribution into affected and unaffected. The AA mean on the liability scale is arbitrarily set at 0 and the aa mean at 2.0, with the Aa mean falling between. The model is defined by four parameters: the gene frequency of the a allele (q), the environmental variance (ϵ^2), dominance, or the distance of the Aa mean from the AA mean (h'), and the threshold position (T). The model is fit to data on disease prevalence in the population and various classes of relatives by iterating values for the parameters and determining the best-fitting parameter set by the minimum Chi-square method. Because of the considerable heterogeneity of data between investigations, the model was fit to both a set of "low" and a set of "high" rates. It led to a number of parameter sets, all providing a suitable fit to the data. For illustration, one of the parameter sets will be described: $q = .10$, $e^2 = .36$, $h' = .25$, and $T = 1.6$. Since the AA mean is arbitrarily set at 0, the Aa mean is .25 (h'), and the aa mean 2.0, by convention. The liability scale can be standardized, using the standard deviation as a unit of measure, which in this case, is 0.6 (ϵ). The threshold ($T = 1.6$) lies 2.7 S.D. above the AA mean and 2.25 S.D. above the Aa mean. Thus, relatively few AA and Aa genotypes will exceed the threshold, and most persons with the disease will be aa, the mean of their liability distribution lying .67 S.D. above the threshold. Finally, the gene is a common one with frequency 0.10, meaning 19% of the population will carry it $[q^2 + 2q(1-q)]$.

Returning to the overall analysis, all parameter sets predicted a relatively common predominantly recessive gene as in the illustration. Although persons of the normal AA genotype had a small likelihood of developing schizophrenia, 16 to 25% of schizophrenics were AA, depending on the parameter set. (Although proportionally less AA are affected, they constitute the majority of the population and, thus, contribute a substantial number of cases.) The model, therefore, predicted a sizable proportion of sporadic cases. Another interesting finding was that the expected morbidity risk among siblings was higher than that for parents. This discrepancy, which is seen in most family studies of schizophrenia, is usually considered to be the result of a selection bias, but in fact, it is predicted by the single locus (and the polygenic) model. This is because siblings, unlike other first-degree relatives, can share *both* genes at a locus through common inheritance.

Matthysse and Kidd (1976) applied a single locus model to published schizophrenia data. The parameters of the model are the gene frequency of the pathogenic allele (q), the probability of a genetically normal individual becoming schizophrenic (f_0), the probability of the heterozygote becoming schizophrenic (f_1), and the probability of the genetically abnormal homozygote becoming schizophrenic (f_2). Applied to the published data, the model predicted a morbidity risk for MZ co-twins of schizophrenics and for offspring of dual schizophrenic matings that was unacceptably low (both 19.9%). However, for the population prevalence and for siblings and offspring of schizophrenics, a wide range of parameter sets were acceptable. The gene frequency varied between 0.3% and 2.2%, with the f_0, f_1, and f_2 parameters varying from a high of 0.5, 50.3, and 100% to a low of 0.0, 19.4, and 38.9%, respectively. The model also predicted a high rate of sporadic cases (61.2%), with 38.7% of schizophrenics being heterozygous and 0.1% homozygous.

The same authors tested a multifactorial model in which the population vulnerability to schizophrenia is considered to be normally distributed with a mean value of 100 and a standard deviation of 15 arbitrary units. The model assumes a cumulative normal (σ), a liability distribution that represents the probability that a person with a given vulnerability value will develop schizophrenia. The parameters of the model are the vulnerability value representing a 50% and that representing a 99% risk (i.e., the slope of the risk function and its position on the liability scale, respectively). When applied to the same data as their single locus model, the polygenic model estimated a 50% risk at 137 and a 99% risk at 148 units. Again, the model fit the data on population prevalence as well as first-degree relative prevalence, but led to unacceptably high risks for MZ co-twins (61%) and offspring of dual matings (54%). The authors calculated the proportion of schizophrenics with a liability of greater than 99% and came to the surprising conclusion that 9.1% would fall into this category. Thus, according to this model, nearly one schizophrenic in ten has a disease that is nearly 100% genetic. Although neither model fit the data in an acceptable fashion, both led to some common predictions. Both predicted a subgroup of schizophrenics with an extremely high genetic diathesis, the homozygotes in the single gene model and the high liability subgroup in the polygenic model. Both models also predicted environmental phenocopies, the normal homozygotes in the single gene model and the low liability subjects in the polygenic model.

Elston and his associates (Elston and Yelverton, 1975) have developed models for a limited number of loci. The simplest case is a single locus with two alleles A and a resulting in the three genotypes AA, Aa, and aa, with q the frequency of the A allele. The probability of being susceptible is represented by λ, which can be made to vary with genotype or to be independent of genotype. Age of onset is considered to be lognormally distributed with mean μ, which can vary with genotype or be independent of genotype. All age of onset distributions have the same standard deviation σ. The probability of transmitting the A allele is represented by τ, which is 1 for an AA parent, 0.5 for an Aa, and 0 for an aa. This "Mendelian model" can be contrasted with an "environmental model," which assumes that the three τs are equal, and therefore, the probability of transmitting the trait is independent of parental genotype. The goodness of fit of each model is determined by constructing a likelihood ratio with an "unrestricted model," in which the parameters are allowed to vary in order to give a perfect fit to the data.

Elston and his associates have analyzed a large sample of Kallman's (1938) kindreds, and the results of their most recent analysis (Elston et al., 1978) will be presented. The material included 178 pedigrees of probands with "nuclear" schizophrenia and 82 with paranoid and simple schizophrenia, referred to as the "peripheral" group. A trichotomous classification was employed to include "schizoidia" as a second affected state. The results ruled out the Mendelian and the environmental hypotheses in both data sets. However, the parameters of the unrestricted model were similar in the nuclear and peripheral groups, suggesting a similar pattern of transmission for both subtypes.

The most recent investigation comes from Stewart and associates (Stewart, 1980; Stewart, Debray, and Caillard, 1980a,b). In order to avoid the circularity involved in constructing a model and testing it on the same data, they tested a variety of 1, 2, and 4 locus models on published data on frequency of schizophrenia in the population (0.9%) and in siblings of schizophrenics (8%) and the frequency of the "schizophrenia spectrum" in the siblings of schizophrenics (15%). The best fitting 1, 2, and 4 locus models were then tested against 25 pedigrees collected by the authors. The data proved to be compatible with all three models, although the single locus model provided the best fit.

Studies employing genetic models have been unable to exclude either of the major hypotheses: single locus or polygenic. The reason for this failure undoubtedly lies in the diagnostic ambiguity of the data used by the models. In view of the problems in defining the schizophrenic phenotype already discussed, it should not be surprising to find that mathematical models have not clarified the mechanism of inheritance, and an answer to the question of how schizophrenia is inherited will most likely have to await the discovery of a more accurate phenotype than clinical diagnosis.

CONCLUSION

The past decade has been a period of active genetic research in schizophrenia and, looking back on this progress, a number of advances stand out and a number of problems remain. First, the question of "nature versus nurture" in schizophrenia has finally been settled with the demonstration that schizophrenia is indeed a genetic disease, but that the genetic determinism is not a complete explanation for its etiology and that non-genetic factors must also be considered. However, we have little information on what substrate the genes act through to produce the disease or what environmental factors are involved. Both are the subject of intense research, but remain to be elucidated.

The relationship of several subtypes of schizophrenia has been substantially clarified with the inclusion of borderline and latent schizophrenia in the same disease category as process schizophrenia. However, the preponderance of the data suggests that acute schizophrenia is a genetically unrelated illness. The place of the "schizoid" spectrum of disorders is less clear. The data support the inclusion of this group of disorders in the schizophrenia spectrum, but adoption studies have stressed the importance of assortative mating in leading to these conditions. To what extent they are related to process schizophrenia, and to what extent to the co-parent diagnosis, has still not been clearly defined. A major obstacle to progress in this area has been our inability to define or diagnose the "schizoid" (Shields, Heston, and Gottesman, 1975), and further progress in this area is likely to await a better definition. However, major psychiatric syndromes (e.g., depression and alcoholism) appearing in the families of schizophrenics are most likely the result of these same disorders entering the family through assortative mating and segregating independently of schizophrenia.

The application of mathematical models has not proven helpful in clarifying the mode of transmission. The data derived from family studies are inevitably ambiguous enough to fit most of the models tested, making it impossible to rule out any of the major transmission hypotheses.

From the geneticist's point of view, what is clearly needed is a phenotype that corresponds more closely with the genotype. Progress may come from better definitions of the spectrum disorders, such as the DSM-III definition of schizotypal personality. However, what is desperately needed is a biological marker of greater validity and reliability than clinical diagnosis. One hopes that the biological research discussed elsewhere in this symposium may bring us closer to such a marker and thus to a better understanding of the genetics of this disease.

REFERENCES

Alanen, Y. O. (1966). The family in the pathogenesis of schizophrenic and neurotic disorders. *Acta Psychiat. Scand. Suppl.* 189.

Bleuler, M. (1978). The schizophrenic disorders: Long-term patient and family studies. (S. M. Clemens, trans.) Yale University Press, New Haven.

Böök, J. A., L. Wetterberg, and K. Modrzewska (1978). Schizophrenia in a north Swedish geographical isolate, 1900–1977. Epidemiology, Genetics and Biochemistry, *Clin. Genet.* 14, 373–394.

Elston, R. C., and K. C. Yelverton (1975). General models for segregation analysis. *Amer. J. Human Genet.* 27, 31–45.

Elston, R. C., K. K. Namboodiri, M. A. Spence, and J. D. Rainer (1978). A genetic study of schizophrenia pedigrees. II. One-locus hypotheses. *Neuropsychobiology* 4, 193–206.

Erlenmeyer-Kimling, L. (1968). Studies on the offspring of two schizophrenic parents. In *The Transmission of Schizophrenia* (D. Rosenthal and S. S. Kety, eds.) *J. Psychiat. Res.* 6, Suppl. 1.

Falconer, D. S. (1965). The inheritance of liability to certain diseases, estimated from the incidence among relatives. *Ann. Human Genet.* (London) 29, 51–76.

Feighner, J. P., E. Robins, S. B. Guze, et al. (1972). Diagnostic criteria for use in psychiatric research. *Arch. Gen. Psychiat.* 26, 57–63.

Fowler, R. C., M. T. Tsuang, R. J. Cadoret, et al. (1974). A clinical and family comparison of paranoid and non-paranoid schizophrenia. *Brit. J. Psychiat.* 124, 346–351.

Fowler, R. C., M. T. Tsuang, R. J. Cadoret, and E. Monnelly (1975). Non-psychotic disorders in the families of process schizophrenics. *Acta Psychiat. Scand.* 51, 153–160.

Fowler, R. C., M. T. Tsuang, and R. J. Cadoret (1977a). Psychiatric illness in the offspring of schizophrenics. *Comp. Psychiat.* 18, 127–134.

Fowler, R. C., M. T. Tsuang, and R. J. Cadoret (1977b). Parental psychiatric illness associated with schizophrenia in the siblings of schizophrenics. *Comp. Psychiat.* 18, 271–275.

Garrone, G. (1962). Statistical and genetic study of schizophrenia in Geneva from 1901 to 1950. *J. Genet Humaine* 11, 89–219.

Gottesman, I. I. (1968). Severity/concordance and diagnostic refinement in the Maudsley-Bethlem schizophrenic twin study. In *The Transmission of Schizophrenia* (D. Rosenthal and S. S. Kety, eds.). Pergamon Press, New York.

Gottesman, I. I., and J. Shields (1967). A polygenic theory of schizophrenia. *Proc. Natl. Acad. Sci.* 58, 199–205.

Gottesman, I. I., and J. Shields (1976). A critical review of recent adoption, twin, and family studies of schizophrenia: Behavioral genetics perspectives. *Schizophrenia Bull.* 2, 360–401.

Hallgren, B., and T. Sjögren (1959). A clinical and genetical-statistical study of schizophrenia and low-grade mental deficiency in a large Swedish rural population. *Acta Psychiat. Scand. Suppl.* 140.

Heston, L. L. (1966). Psychiatric disorders in foster home reared children of schizophrenic mothers. *Brit. J. Psychiat.* 112, 819–825.

Heston, L. L. (1970). The genetics of schizophrenic and schizoid disease. *Science* 167, 249–256.

Kallman, F. J. (1938). *The Genetics of Schizophrenia.* Augustin, New York.

Kallman, F. J. (1946). The genetic theory of schizophrenia. *Amer. J. Psychiat.* 103, 309–322.

Karlsson, J. (1966). *The Biologic Basis of Schizophrenia.* Charles C. Thomas, Springfield, Ill.

Karlsson, J. (1970). The rate of schizophrenia in foster-reared close relatives of schizophrenic index cases. *Biol. Psychiat.* 2, 285–290.

Karlsson, J. L. (1973). An Icelandic family study of schizophrenia. *Brit. J. Psychiat.* 123, 549–554.

Kety, S. S., D. Rosenthal, P. H. Wender, and F. Schulsinger (1968). The types and prevalence of mental illness in the biological and adoptive families of adopted schizophrenics. In *The Transmission of Schizophrenia (D. Rosenthal and S. S. Kety, eds.). J. Psychiat. Res.* 6, Suppl. 1, pp. 345–362.

Kety, S. S., D. Rosenthal, P. H. Wender, F. Schulsinger, and B. Jacobsen (1975). Mental illness in the biological and adoptive families of adopted individuals who have become schizophrenic: A preliminary report based on psychiatric interviews. In *Genetic Research in Schizophrenia.* R. R. Fieve, D. Rosenthal, and H. Brill, eds.). Johns Hopkins University Press, Baltimore, pp. 147–165.

Kidd, K. K., and L. L. Cavalli-Sforza (1973). An analysis of the genetics of schizophrenia. *Soc. Biol.* 3, 254–265.

Kringlen, E. (1967). *Heredity and Environment in the Functional Psychoses.* William Heinemann, London.

Lindelius, R. (1970). A study of schizophrenia: A clinical prognostic, and family investigation. *Acta Psychiat. Scand., Suppl.* 216.

Matthysse, S. W., and K. K. Kidd (1976). Estimating the genetic contribution to schizophrenia. *Amer. J. Psychiat.* 133, 185–191.

McCabe, M. S., R. Fowler, R. Cadoret, and G. Winokur (1971). Familial differences in schizophrenia with good and poor prognosis. *Psychosom. Med.* 1, 326–332.

Modrzewska, K. (1980). The offspring of schizophrenic parents in a north Swedish isolate. *Clin. Genet.* 17, 191–202.

Ödegard, Ö. (1963). The psychiatric disease entities in the light of a genetic investigation. *Acta Psychiat, Scand., Suppl.* 169.

Ödegard, Ö. (1972). The multifactorial theory of inheritance in predisposition to schizophrenia. In *Genetic Factors in "Schizophrenia"* (A. R. Kaplan, ed.). Charles C. Thomas, Springfield, Ill.

Pope, H. G., and J. F. Lipinski (1978). Diagnosis in schizophrenia and manic-depressive illness. *Arch. Gen. Psychiat.* 35, 811–828.

Rosenthal, D. (1962). Problems of sampling and diagnosis in the major twin studies of schizophrenia. *J. Psychiat. Res.* 1, 116–134.

Rosenthal, D. (1975). The concept of sub-schizophrenic disorders. In *Genetic Research in Psychiatry* (R. R. Fieve, D. Rosenthal, and H. Brill, eds.). Johns Hopkins University Press, Baltimore, pp. 199–208.

Rosenthal, D., P. H. Wender, S. S. Kety, et al. (1968). Schizophrenics' offspring reared in adoptive homes. In *The Transmission of Schizophrenia* (D. Rosenthal and S. S. Kety, eds.) *J. Psychiat. Res.* 6, Suppl. 1.

Rosenthal, D., P. H. Wender, S. S. Kety, et al. (1971). The adopted-away offspring of schizophrenics. *Amer. J. Psychiat.* 128, 307–311.

Schulz, B. (1932). Zur erb pathologie der schizophrenie. *Z. Ges. Neurol. Psychiat.* 143, 175–293.

Shields, J., L. L. Heston, and I. I. Gottesman (1975). Schizophrenia and the schizoid: The problem for genetic analysis. In *Genetic Research in Psychiatry* (R. R. Fieve, D. Rosenthal, and H. Brill, eds.). Johns Hopkins University Press, Baltimore, pp. 167–197.

Slater, E. (1958). The monogenic theory of schizophrenia. *Acta Genetica* 8, 50–56.

Slater, E. (1966). Expectation of abnormality on paternal and maternal sides: A computational model. *J. Med. Genet.* 3, 159–161.

Slater, E., and V. Cowie (1971). *The Genetics of Mental Disorders.* Oxford University Press, London.

Slater, E., and M. T. Tsuang (1968). Abnormality on paternal and maternal sides: Observations in schizophrenia and manic-depression. *J. Med. Genet.* 5, 197–199.

Stephens, D. A., M. W. Atkinson, D. W. K. Kay, et al. (1975). Psychiatric morbidity in parents and sibs of schizophrenics and non-schizophrenics. *Brit. J. Psychiat.* 127, 97–108.

Stewart, J. (1980). Schizophrenia: The systematic construction of genetic models. *Amer. J. Human Genet.* 32, 47–54.

Stewart, J., Q. Debray, and V. Caillard (1980). Schizophrenia: The testing of genetic models by pedigree analysis. *Amer. J. Human Genet.* 32, 55–63.

Tsuang, M. T. (1971). Abnormality on paternal and maternal sides in Chinese schizophrenics. *Brit. J. Psychiat.* 118, 211–214.

Tsuang, M. T. (1975). Heterogeneity of schizophrenia. *Biol. Psychiat.* 10, 465–474.

Tsuang, M. T. (1979). "Schizoaffective disorder": Dead or alive? *Arch. Gen. Psychiat.* 36, 633–634.

Tsuang, M. T., R. C. Fowler, R. J. Cadoret, and E. Monnelly (1974). Schizophrenia among first-degree relatives of paranoid and non-paranoid schizophrenics. *Comp. Psychiat.* 15, 295–302.

Tsuang, M. T., G. Winokur, and R. R. Crowe (1980). Morbidity risks of schizophrenia and affective disorders among first-degree relatives of patients with schizophrenia, mania, depression and surgical conditions. *Brit. J. Psychiat.* 137, 497–504.

Wender, P. H., D. Rosenthal, S. S. Kety, et al. (1974). Crossfostering. *Arch. Gen. Psychiat.* 30, 121–128.

Winokur, G., J. Morrison, J. Clancy, et al. (1972). The Iowa 500. II. A blind family history comparison of mania, depression, and schizophrenia. *Arch. Gen. Psychiat.* 27, 462–464.

Winokur, G., J. Morrison, J. Clancy, et al. (1974). The Iowa 500: The clinical and genetic distinction of hebephrenic and paranoid schizophrenia. *J. Nerv. Ment. Dis.* 159, 12–19.

Zerbin-Rudin, E. (1972). Genetic research and the theory of schizophrenia. *Int. J. Ment. Health* 1, 42–62.

5 | Neurological, Electrophysiological, and Attentional Deviations in Children at Risk For Schizophrenia

L. ERLENMEYER-KIMLING,
BARBARA CORNBLATT, DAVID
FRIEDMAN, YVONNE MARCUSE,
JACQUES RUTSCHMANN, SAMUEL
SIMMENS, and SARALA DEVI

Although the dominant theme in American psychiatry for many years was nonbiological, data supporting the idea of schizophrenia as a brain disease have been accumulating since the beginning of this century. In the past two decades, in particular, acceptance of this idea has been strengthened by new evidence coming from genetic, neurochemical, and neurophysiological studies, among others. Moreover, as the several lines of evidence begin to converge, it is becoming possible to understand the relationships among the various aspects of behavior and biology that we know or postulate to be disturbed in schizophrenia.

Many questions remain to be answered, however. Among them is one concerned with the issue of antecedents versus consequences of the illness. Do dysfunctions that are observed in schizophrenic patients merely reflect the fact that these individuals are ill or do the same dysfunctions, perhaps in less pronounced degree, antedate the illness by many years? Because this is a question that can be answered only by studying schizophrenics before they become ill, a number of investigators have turned to the prospective study of populations that are at a higher than average statistical risk of developing a schizophrenic disorder at some time during their lives. Prospective examination and followup of such individuals should make it possible to determine whether deviations in behavioral and biological functions seen in schizophrenia occur prior to the onset of overt illness and may thus be used as indicators or "markers" of vulnerability to schizophrenia. Usually, but not always, the subjects of the prospective studies are children of schizophrenic parents because these children are known to have an elevated lifetime risk of developing schizophrenia. Compared to a risk of 1 to 2% in the general population, children of a schizophrenic mother or father have a lifetime risk of about 12% (Erlenmeyer-Kimling, 1977) and children of two schizophrenic parents have the exceptionally high risk of 35 to 46% (Erlenmeyer-Kimling, 1968; Slater, 1968).

Despite some major differences in the theoretical orientations of high-risk[1] researchers, several of their studies include assessments of biobehaviors that—when they are found to be disordered—point to dysfunctions of the central nervous system. Although all these biobehaviors are related, and deficits in them probably stem from the same central source, they can be considered under three separate categories: (1) neurological and motor functioning, (2) brain electrophysiology, i.e., electroencephalogram (EEG) and cortical event-related potentials, and (3) attentional processes. Table 5-1 lists the studies in which one or more of these categories of biobehaviors have been assessed. A few well-known studies do not appear in Table 5-1, as they either did not include any of the categories of assessment under consideration or have not, to our knowledge, yet reported data on them. Unfortunately, few of the studies have included more than one area of assessment, so that it is not possible, in most of the samples, to explore potential relationships among the different categories.

In our longitudinal study of children of one or two schizophrenic parents in New York, we have examined all three categories of func-

---

[1] The term "high risk" is used throughout this paper to refer to risk for schizophrenia or schizophrenia spectrum disorders and is applied to subjects who are considered to be at risk, usually by virtue of having schizophrenic parents.

TABLE 5-1.

SUMMARY OF ASSESSMENT CATEGORIES IN HIGH-RISK STUDIES

Study Code	Investigator(s)	Location	Assessments of Neuro-motor	Assessments of EEG/ERP	Attention
1	Fish	New York City	x		
2	Rosenthal/Marcus	Israel	x		
3	Schachter/Ragins (I)[a]	Pittsburgh	x		
	Schachter/Ragins (S)[b]	Pittsburgh	x		
4	Mednick et al.	Denmark	x		
	Itil/Saletu et al.	(Obstetric		x	
	Orvaschel et al.	sample)	x		x
5	Erlenmeyer-Kimling et al. (A)[c]	New York metro-politan	x	x	x
	Erlenmeyer/Kimling et al. (B)[d]	New York metro-politan	x	x	x
6	Garmezy et al.	Minnesota			x
7	Grunebaum et al.	Boston		x	x
8	Weintraub/Neale	Stony Brook (NY)			x
9	Hanson et al.	Minnesota (CPP)[e]	x		
10	Rieder/Rosenthal	Boston (CPP)[e]	x		
11	Marcuse/Erlenmeyer-Kimling	New York State (CPP)[e]	x		
12	McNeil/Kaij	Sweden	x		
13	Asarnow et al.	Waterloo, Canada			x
14	Marcus et al.	Israel	x		

[a] Schachter/Ragins (I), infant study
[b] Schachter/Ragins (S), school-age study
[c] Erlenmeyer-Kimling et al. (A), Sample A
[d] Erlenmeyer-Kimling et al. (B), Sample B
[e] CPP, Collaborative Perinatal Project sample

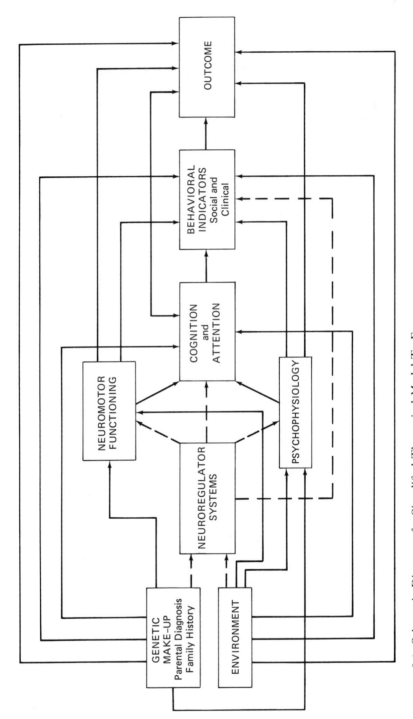

FIGURE 5-1. Schematic Diagram of a Simplified Theoretical Model To Explain Relationships among Variables Relating to Clinical Outcome

tioning because we had been led by the literature on adult schizophrenic patients to postulate that deviations in each area might be found as precursors of clinically defined schizophrenia and might, therefore, be the means by which we could identify those members of the group at high statistical risk who were at true genetic risk. The working model we have used in trying to understand risk for schizophrenia shares elements with Paul Meehl's (1972) outline of "conceptual chains in schizophrenia" and, like the theories of Meehl (1962, 1972) and Barbara Fish (1957), rests on the assumption that a neurointegrative defect is basic to a predisposition to the illness. More specifically, it is assumed that (1) in most cases, schizophrenia occurs in persons with a specific genetic predisposition, in interaction with nonspecific environmental stresses, (2) the genetic error (or errors) is mediated by disturbances in neuroregulatory systems, and (3) the latter are translated into a neurointegrative defect, which is expressed phenotypically as neuromotor, neurophysiological, and attentional-informational processing deviations that appear long before psychosocial and clinical disruptions emerge. A simplified schema of the model is presented in Fig. 5-1. Later on, we will discuss a preliminary analysis of some data in which we have begun to use the schema shown in Fig. 5-1 to examine relationships among different areas of functioning at early ages and their potential as predictors of development of psychopathology in late adolescence.

We will begin by reviewing the cumulative data from the 13 studies, including our own, in which neuromotor functioning, brain electrophysiology, and/or attentional processes have been examined, before considering our longitudinal study in more detail.

ASSESSMENTS OF NEUROMOTOR FUNCTIONING

Table 5-2 provides some descriptive information about the 10 studies that have included assessments of neuromotor functioning and that will be reviewed here.

The first study of children of schizophrenic parents specifically aimed at predicting vulnerability to schizophrenia from very young ages was undertaken by Barbara Fish (Fish, 1957; Fish and Alpert, 1963) and is still

TABLE 5-2.
DESCRIPTION OF STUDIES IN WHICH NEUROMOTOR ASSESSMENTS WERE MADE

Study Code	Investigator	Schizophrenic Parent	Normal Parent	Other Affected Parent [a]	Ages of Children at Assessment
1	Fish	12, mothers only	12, disadvantaged mothers	—	Birth; 3 days; 1, 2, 3, and 4 months; 2, 10, and 20 to 22 years
2	Rosenthal/Marcus	50, mothers or fathers	50, matched	—	7-0 years; half city-reared, half kibbutz-reared
3	Schachter/Ragins	14, mothers only	18, normal + other	—	3 or 4 to 8 months
		10, mothers only	10, normal + other	—	Some of above seen again at 12 to 19 months
		29, mothers only	28, normal + other	—	Elementary school
4	Mednick et al.	83, mothers or fathers	83, matched	83, matched mothers or fathers	Birth; 1 year
	Orvaschel et al.	72, mothers or fathers	72, matched	72, matched mothers or fathers	Pre- or early adolescence; same subjects as in Mednick et al.

5	Erlenmeyer-Kimling et al. (A)	80, mothers, fathers or both	100	25, mothers, fathers or both	7 to 12 years; subsequent examinations not applicable
	Erlenmeyer-Kimling et al. (B)	45, mothers, fathers or both	65, matched	40, mothers, fathers or both	7 to 12 years
9	Hanson et al.	33, mothers, fathers or both	33, matched 33, unmatched	36, mothers or fathers	Birth; 4 months; 1, 4, and 7 years
10	Rieder/Rosenthal	29, mothers or fathers; continuous schizophrenia	29, matched	—	Birth; 4 months; 1, 4, and 7 years; males only reported
		6, mothers or fathers; acute schizophrenia	6, matched 3630, total white Boston CPP	—	
11	Marcuse/Erlenmeyer-Kimling	17, mothers or fathers	88, matched	20, mothers or fathers	Birth; 4 months; 1 and 7 years
12	McNeil/Kaij	13, mothers only	71, matched	42, mothers only	4 days
14	Marcus et al.	17, mothers or fathers	18	19, mothers or fathers	3, 14 days; 4, 8, and 12 months

[a]Other affected parent: Code 4, character disorders; Code 5A and 5B, affective disorders; Code 9, various nonschizophrenic disorders; Code 11, affective disorders; Code 12, cycloid psychosis, manic-depressive and unipolar affective disorders, and nonendogenous psychoses; Code 14, affective disorders, personality disorders, and neurosis

ongoing. Fish (in press) was testing the hypothesis that "specific neurointegrative disorders in infancy predict vulnerability to later schizophrenia and schizophrenia-related psychopathology." Neurointegrative disorder in infancy—which Fish has called Pandevelopmental Retardation (PDR)—was hypothesized to be the antecedent primarily of early onset, poor premorbid, chronic schizophrenia, and childhood schizophrenia was thought to be the most severe variant of such cases. Criteria for measuring PDR were drawn from Lauretta Bender's histories of irregular development in the infancy of several childhood schizophrenics (Bender, 1947; Bender and Freedman, 1952). Diagnosis of PDR required both a lag in physical growth and a lag in gross motor and/or visual motor development. Predictions of vulnerability to schizophrenia consisted of ranking infants according to the severity of PDR between birth and two years. Eventual outcome was hypothesized to depend on an interaction between severity of PDR and environmental experiences (Fish, in press).

Seven of the 12 offspring of schizophrenic mothers examined by Fish from birth to ages 20 to 22 showed PDR in infancy, whereas only one of the 12 offspring of disadvantaged nonpsychotic mothers showed PDR. No fixed neurological defect occurred in these eight PDR infants, but they displayed a disorder of timing and integration of neurological maturation. In particular, Fish (in press) observed unusual fluctuations in the rate of development, with marked acceleration and retardation succeeding one another, and temporary losses of previously acquired abilities. Pandevelopmental Retardation was *not* related to obstetrical complications, sex of the infant, ethnic or racial background (i.e., black versus white), or socioeconomic status of the biological or rearing parents.

Pandevelopmental Retardation *was* related, however, to diagnoses of psychopathology at age 10 and ages 20 to 22. In blind evaluations at age 10, two high-risk children in whom PDR had been most extreme were diagnosed as schizophrenic. Soft neurological signs—consisting of perceptual disorders, poor fine motor coordination, and reading disabilities—occurred significantly more often in the high-risk children than in the controls at age 10 and tended to be related to PDR in infancy. The four instances of severe perceptual disorders at age 10 were in high-risk children who had shown PDR.

At ages 20 to 22, six of the 12 high-risk subjects were diagnosed by Fish, in nonblind evaluation, as having severe schizophrenia spectrum disorders (Fish, in press). Blind evaluations of MMPI data on these subjects by Irving Gottesman were largely in agreement with Fish's diagnoses. All six subjects had exhibited PDR in infancy.

Three of the 12 controls were diagnosed by Fish as depressive and two as having personality disorders. Gottesman's blind evaluation of MMPI data agreed in four cases, but the fifth case was classified as psychotic. The one control subject who had shown PDR was the only control subject not making an adequate vocational adjustment at ages 20 to 22.

Fish (1975, 1977, in press) observed other abnormal patterns in the first three months of life in some infants that she also considered to be of neurophysiological significance. An abnormally quiet state, with extreme underactivity and hypotonia, characterized four high-risk infants, three of whom displayed severe psychopathology at age 10. The abnormally quiet infants also showed extremely decreased nystagmus following caloric stimulation. Absent or decreased nystagmus was associated with the worst periods of PDR, "when physical growth was maximally retarded," suggesting to Fish (in press) that poor central nervous system integration was part of a continuing and profound process in these infants. Visual-motor performance was disturbed in several ways, but only failure of hand-to-hand integration has turned out to be related to later psychiatric impairment.

Fish recently concluded that a neurointegrative disorder was present in about one-half of the high-risk infants seen by her and that it was associated with later psychopathology. The integrative disorder affected many systems controlled by the central nervous system, including "physical growth, gross motor, visual-motor, and vestibular functioning, and possibly arousal" (Fish, in press). Fish has suggested that the pattern of these disorders points to a "dysregulation involving hypothalamic, neuroendocrine and reticular activating systems during the infancy of preschizophrenics." Whether such pervasive integrative deficiencies will be found to characterize the infancies of many preschizophrenics remains to be seen, however. Certainly the fact that one-sixth of Fish's high-risk subjects were diagnosed as schizophrenic and others had severe psychopathology at the age of 10 suggests that this was an unusual sample. In any event, Fish's work is of continuing interest because of its long-term nature and because of the promising leads that it offers.

Additional evidence of deviant neurological development in infancy among subjects at risk for schizophrenia comes from several other studies also, as can be seen from Table 5-3. Delays in motor development, which Fish (1977) had observed, have been reported by Mednick et al. (1971), who analyzed data from a large Danish birth cohort, by Ragins et al. (1975), in a study initiated by Joseph Schachter in Pittsburgh, and by Marcus et al. (in press), who found that 12 out of 17 high-risk infants

TABLE 5-3.

SUMMARY OF NEUROLOGICAL PROBLEMS REPORTED IN HIGH-RISK
SUBJECTS DURING INFANCY

Reported Problems	Study Code[a]					
Low birth weight		3(I),	4,	11,	12,	14
Fluctuations in physical growth	1,	3(I)				
Abnormally quiet state	1					
Decreased vestibular responses	1					
Delayed or poor motor development	1,	3(I),	4,			14
Delayed relex maturation or weak reflexes	1,	3(I),	4			
Poor fine motor abilities						14
Perceptual dysfunction		3(I)				
Atypical sleep patterns		3(I)				
Abnormal total exam score					12	
Negative findings		3(S),		9, 11		

[a] Study code: 1, Fish; 3(I), Schachter/Ragins infant study; 3(S), Schachter/Ragins school-age study; 4, Mednick et al.; 9, Hanson et al.; 11, Marcuse/Erlenmeyer-Kimling; 12, McNeil and Kaij; and 14, Marcus et al.

studied in Israel repeatedly performed poorly on motor and sensorimotor indicators on examinations from day 3 to one year, whereas very few of the infants of normal parents or of parents with other psychiatric problems did so. Slow motor development had previously been reported in follow-back studies of adult schizophrenics (Ricks and Nameche, 1966; Robins, 1966).

Like Fish, Ragins et al. (1975) noted sharp fluctuations in physical growth, perceptual dysfunctions, and a variety of atypical behaviors in their high-risk infants. These investigators found 40% (4/10) of the high-risk children, but none of their controls, to show delayed reflex maturation on examination between the ages of 12 and 19 months, with persistent positive Babinski responses and tonic neck reflexes. In the Danish sample studied by Mednick et al. (1971), weak or absent reflexes were the most common abnormalities found in children of schizophrenic parents on examination immediately after birth and five days later. Although both the offspring of schizophrenic parents and parents with other psychiatric disorders evinced more abnormalities than children of normal parents neonatally, the abnormalities tended to persist at day 5 only in the children of schizophrenic parents.

In five of the eight studies of infancy (see Table 5-3), the high-risk subjects tended to have lower birth weights or to be lighter for gestational age than the offspring of normal parents (Marcus et. al., in press; Marcuse and Cornblatt, in press; McNeil and Kaij, 1973; Mednick, Mura, Schulsinger & Mednick, 1971, 1973; Ragins et al., 1975). Mednick et al. (1971) and Marcus et al. (in press) have reported that, in their samples, low birth weight was associated with developmental difficulties in the high-risk children, but not in the controls. However, the difference in birth weights between high-risk children and controls is statistically significant in only one study (Mednick et al., 1973, a re-analysis of data presented in Mednick et al., 1971), and McNeil and Kaij (1978), reviewing the cumulative data on birth weight in the offspring of schizophrenics, have pointed out that even among the nonsignificant differences the direction of the difference is not always consistent. Moreover, Gottesman and Shields (1977) have conclusively demonstrated that, in monozygotic twins discordant for schizophrenia, the twin who later becomes schizophrenic is the lighter twin at birth in only about one-half the discordant pairs that have been studied. Thus a relationship between low birth weight and the occurrence of schizophrenia has not been demonstrated, and it is unclear what importance, if any, should be attached to the reports of an association between low birth weight and developmental difficulties in high-risk children.

Not all studies have shown clear-cut differences between high-risk infants and other infants with respect to neurological development and growth. For example, in blind examinations of infants born to schizophrenic women, women with other psychiatric disorders, and normal women, in Sweden, McNeil and Kaij (in press) found the highest rates of "clear neurological abnormality" in the babies of mothers with cycloid psychosis, followed by babies of mothers with other psychoses, normal control mothers (controls for the manic-depressive mothers), and schizophrenic mothers, in that order. Although the high-risk infants *did* have the poorest composite neurological deviation score based on total points for simple and complex reflexes, motor movements, activity level, and sentivity to touch, these infants did not appear to be much more deviant than those with mothers who had cycloid or other psychoses or than normal control mothers.

Ragins et al. (1975), who had noted developmental problems among high-risk infants and toddlers in direct, nonblind observations in the Pittsburgh study, found no significant differences between school-aged high-risk and control children with respect to their mothers' reports of infancy and developmental problems or age of achievement of developmental milestones. Whether the lack of difference between the reports of the schizophrenic and control women about their children's early development is entirely due to the retrospective nature of the reports or some other methodological consideration, or whether it represents a real absence of group differences in the Pittsburgh school-age sample, is not known.

In examining data on children of schizophrenic parents, children of parents with other psychiatric disorders, and children of normal parents who had participated in the Minnesota sample of the NINCDS Collaborative Perinatal Project (CPP), Hanson, Gottesman, and Heston (1976) found no consistent differences between high-risk children and the comparison groups on repeated measures of physical growth and repeated neurological examinations at birth, four months, one year, and seven years, although poor motor skills were found in 30% of the high-risk children at age four. Similar sets of data on the New York sample of the CPP have been examined in a study by Marcuse and Erlenmeyer-Kimling. Although some "soft" signs differences were found at ages four and seven, the high-risk children showed nonsignificantly superior fine and gross motor abilities at eight months and four years compared to control children of normal parents, and, starting at four months, "group differences in height, weight, and head circumference were not significant or even consistent in direction" (Marcuse and Cornblatt, in press).

Thus, of the eight separate samples of high-risk infants for which neurological and developmental data have been obtained, four (Fish, in press; Marcus et al., in press; Mednick et al., 1971; Ragins et al., 1975 infant study) give definite evidence of neurological abnormalities and delays, three (Hanson et al., 1976; Marcuse and Cornblatt, in press; Ragins et al., 1975 school-age study) do not, and one (McNeil and Kaij, in press) is inconclusive.

As shown in Table 5-4, however, all the studies examining neurological and/or motor functioning of high-risk subjects during childhood or early adolescence have shown some areas of dysfunction. Fish (Fish and Hagin, 1973) reported perceptual disabilities, poor fine motor coordination, and specific reading disabilities in her high-risk subjects at age 10. The same soft neurological signs, as well as deficient left-right orientation and poor auditory-visual integration, were seen in high-risk children in the project initiated by Rosenthal (1971) and carried out by Marcus (1974) in Israel. In that study, exactly one-half of the high-risk children

TABLE 5-4.
SUMMARY OF NEUROLOGICAL PROBLEMS REPORTED IN HIGH-RISK
SUBJECTS DURING CHILDHOOD AND EARLY ADOLESCENCE

Reported Problem				Study Code				
Poor gross motor abilities			4(b),	5A,	5B,	9		
Clumsy awkward behavior			4(b)					
Hyperactivity							10,	11
Deficient left-right orientation		2,		5A,	5B			
Poor fine motor abilities	1,	2,	4(b),	5A,	5B,	9,	10,	11
Perceptual dysfunctions	1,	2,		5A,	5B			
Reading disabilities	1,			5A,				11
Poor auditory-visual integration		2						
Heightened tactile sensitivity			4(b)					
Abnormal total exam score		2,					10,	11

[a] Study code: 1, Fish; 2, Rosenthal/Marcus; 4(b), Orvaschel et al.; 5A, Erlen-meyer-Kimling et al. (Sample A); 5B, Erlenmeyer-Kimling et al. (Sample B); 9, Hanson et al.; 10, Rieder/Rosenthal; and 11, Marcuse/Erlenmeyer-Kimling

below the age of 11 exhibited extremely poor neurological functioning, suggesting to the investigators that a single dominant gene hypothesis of schizophrenia might be supported by the data (Marcus, 1974; Rosenthal, 1974). The very poor performers were preponderantly male and city-reared (as opposed to kibbutz-reared).

In our longitudinal study in New York, high-risk subjects in each of the two independent samples showed deficiencies in gross and fine motor abilities—especially in the latter—and in perceptual abilities and left-right orientation (Erlenmeyer-Kimling, 1975; Marcuse, Cornblatt, and Erlenmeyer-Kimling, in preparation). When reading ability was tested in the first sample (Sample A), it, too, was found to be deficient in the high-risk subjects. Neuromotor deviations were most pronounced in high-risk boys below the age of 11 in both samples. Thus, the findings are consistent with those of Fish (Fish and Hagin, 1973) and of the Israeli study (Marcuse, 1974).

Difficulties in motor abilities among the children of schizophrenic parents were also seen in each of the three studies that used data from the NINCDS Collaborative Perinatal Project (Hanson, Gottesman, and Heston, 1976; Marcuse and Cornblatt, in press; Rieder and Nichols, 1979).

Hanson, Gottesman, and Heston (1976), using a motor abilities score that combined both gross and fine motor items in their examinations of the Minnesota CPP data, noted poor motor skills at age four in 30% of the high-risk subjects; but, more important, 17% of the high-risk subjects had poor motor skills combined with large intra-individual variability on psychological tests, and "schizoid" behavior—a pattern that was seen in none of the normal controls or in children of parents with other psychiatric disorders. Fine motor abilities were considered to be poor among the high-risk children in the study of the Boston CPP data initiated by Rosenthal and Rieder (cf., Rieder and Nichols, 1979) and in the study of the New York CPP data by Marcuse and Erlenmeyer-Kimling (Marcuse and Cornblatt, in press). High-risk subjects also scored relatively lower than children of normal parents on a neurological signs factor derived from an examination at age seven and on "hyperactivity" and immaturity factor scores based on behavioral ratings of the subjects. However, none of the three factors differed significantly between high-risk and control subjects in the New York CPP sample (Marcuse and Cornblatt, in press) or between female high-risk and control children in the Boston CPP sample (Rieder and Nichols, 1979), and the neurological signs factor showed no significance even among the males in the latter sample. Reading disabilities among the high-risk subjects in the New York CPP sample were thought to account for the subjects' poor school achievement (Marcuse and Cornblatt, in press).

Examining data collected in preadolescence or early adolescence on some of the subjects that Mednick et al. (1971) had extracted from a Danish birth cohort study, Orvaschel et al. (1979) found a nonsignificant trend toward neurological dysfunction in children of schizophrenic mothers or fathers in the areas of motor impersistence, associated movements, and posture or gait. Children of both schizophrenic mothers and mothers with other psychiatric disturbances were reported to have heightened tactile sensitivity and a greater degree of clumsy and awkward behaviors compared to children of schizophrenic fathers or fathers with other psychiatric disorders and children of normal parents. Orvaschel et al. (1979) have interpreted their finding of neurological dysfunction in the offspring of schizophrenic parents as reflecting delayed central nervous system maturation and their finding of heightened tactile sensitivity and clumsy behavior in children of psychiatrically disturbed mothers, regardless of diagnosis, as reflecting the results of being reared by a sick mother. With respect to the latter interpretation, however, it should be noted that the rearing status of the children in this sample was not reported. In another Danish sample studied by Mednick and Schulsinger (1968), a substantial number of children were found to have been separated from their schizophrenic mothers. If similar rates of separation applied to the children in the report by Orvaschel et al. (1979), the conclusion that neurological dysfunctions resulted from rearing by a sick mother would, of course, not be appropriate.

Taken all together, the studies of neuromotor functioning in children of schizophrenic parents indicate that various kinds of disruptions occur in these groups of subjects early in life. Although the reports on high-risk infants are mixed, ranging from the pervasive disorganization seen by Fish (in press) to complete failures to find any differences in neurological or motor development between high-risk and control infants in other studies (Hanson, Gottesman, and Heston, 1976; Marcuse and Cornblatt, in press; Ragins et al., 1975 school-age study), there is no disagreement that something is amiss in the neuromotor functioning of high-risk subjects during childhood. Impairment of fine motor coordination is the single sign reported by all investigators, and data on several of the signs suggest delays in motor development as well. Given that, at maximum, only 50%[2] of the children with one schizophrenic parent in any sample are expected to be at true genetic risk, it is not to be expected that all the high-risk children in these studies should show neuromotor abnormalities. Neurological dysfunctions were observed in more than one-half of the high-risk infants in Fish's study and in the infant study by Marcus et al. (in press) and in exactly one-half of the high-risk subjects under age 11 in the first Israeli study (Marcus, 1974). Other investigators, however, have usually not seen neuromotor disturbances in such high proportions of their subjects. Many of the results are not significant and merely show a trend toward greater dysfunction in a particular group of children with schizophrenic parents, suggesting that a subgroup of truly vulnerable children is nested with the main group. The test of the meaningfulness of the neuromotor findings in these studies lies in determining the extent to which dysfunctions observed at early ages relate to psychopathological outcome in later life. Thus far, only a few high risk re-

[2] According to a single dominant gene hypothesis, 50% of children with one schizophrenic parent would be expected to be at true risk, although the percentage actually manifesting schizophrenia might be (and, empirically, is known to be) lower owing to incomplete penetrance. According to polygenic threshold models, the percentage actually at risk would be well below 50%.

searchers have had an opportunity to do this, and, as noted earlier, Fish (in press) found Pandevelopmental Retardation in infancy to be related to both psychopathology and soft neurological signs at age 10 and to psychopathology at ages 20 to 22. In the Israeli school age study, the five children who have shown psychiatric "breakdowns" in adolescence also had signs of neuropsychological dysmaturation (Marcus, personal communication). In a later section, we will discuss preliminary indications that neuromotor difficulties in childhood are at least indirectly related to psychopathology in adolescence among the high-risk subjects in our longitudinal study.

ASSESSMENTS OF BRAIN ELECTROPHYSIOLOGY IN HIGH-RISK SUBJECTS

If the predisposition to schizophrenia is manifest in disorders of brain functioning, as is hypothesized, children at risk for schizophrenia may be expected to show deviations in brain electrophysiology. Electrical activity of the brain has been explored in numerous studies of schizophrenic patients (Buchsbaum, 1977; Itil, 1977; Roth, 1977; Shagass, 1977), but, thus far, such data have been reported from only three of the studies of high-risk children. Table 5-5 summarizes the main findings reported (1) by Itil et al. (1974) and Saletu et al. (1975) on subjects drawn by Mednick et al. (1971) from the Danish birth cohort study, (2) by Herman et al. (1977) on some of the children studied by Grunebaum et al. (1974) in Boston, and (3) by Friedman et al. (1979a,b, 1980) on subjects from the samples being followed by our group (cf., Erlenmeyer-Kimling et al., in press, a) in New York.

As can be seen in Table 5-5, EEG data have been reported from two of the investigating groups. Herman et al. (1977) found no EEG differences between children of schizophrenic mothers and children of normal mothers during performance of a task requiring sustained visual attention and a slight, nonsignificant tendency toward increased beta-1 activity in the left brain of the high-risk subjects during a resting period. Itil et al. (1974), however, reported that differences in several aspects of EEG activity (see Table 5-6) were observed in all eight EEG leads examined,

TABLE 5-5.

SUMMARY OF EEG AND EVENT-RELATED POTENTIAL FINDINGS IN
STUDIES OF CHILDREN OF SCHIZOPHRENIC PARENTS

Study Code	Investigator	Number of Subjects[a]		Age at Testing	Characteristic Reported to Occur More Frequently in High-Risk Subjects Than in Controls	Significance Level
		HR	NC			
					EEG	
4(a)	Itil et al.	31	50	10–12	More fast beta activity	
					Fewer fast alpha waves	Not
					More slow delta waves	reported
					Less average amplitude	
7	Herman et al.	6	6	7–10	More beta-1 activity, left side only, during resting but not during task	NS
					EVENT-RELATED POTENTIALS	
4(a)	Itil et al.	31	50	10–12	Shorter latencies ⎫ auditory	.05
					Lack of habituation ⎭	.05
4(a)	Saletu et al.[b]	62	63	12–14	Shorter latencies	.01–.05
					Greater intraindividual variability in latency in early components and less intraindividual variability in latency in late components ⎬ auditory	.05
7	Herman et al.	6	6	7–10	Larger amplitudes ⎫ visual	.001–NS
					Longer latencies ⎭	.001–NS
5A	Friedman et al.	20	20	8–14	Longer latencies auditory	.005–.01
5A	Friedman et al.	30	30	11–18	Smaller amplitude late positive components ⎬ visual	.02–.07
					Smaller amplitude early negativity	
5A 5B	Friedman et al.	28 13	28 17	11–18 10–12	Smaller amplitude late positive components ⎬ auditory	.05

[a] HR, high-risk; NC, normal control
[b] Subjects include those studied by Itil et al.

with computer evaluation of the data. The report is confusing because, although the computer evaluation indicated that high-risk subjects showed more fast beta activity, fewer fast alpha waves, and less average amplitude than the controls, visual (eyeball) inspection of the same data yielded opposite results—less fast beta activity, more fast alpha activity, and slightly higher average amplitudes in the high-risk children compared to the controls. Thus, the EEG data available thus far on children of schizophrenic parents are clearly not consistent and do not lend themselves to interpretation.

Findings with respect to event-related potentials (ERPs) are not consistent across the studies either. Itil et al. (1974), and later Saletu et al. (1975), working with a larger number of subjects from the same sample, reported that high-risk children showed shorter latencies of components after 100-msec post-stimulus than did control children in response to auditory stimulation, but both Friedman, Frosch, and Erlenmeyer-Kimling (1979a) and Herman et al. (1977) found longer latencies in their high-risk subjects, in the first case to auditory stimuli and in the second to visual stimuli.

Similar inconsistencies apply to the data on ERP amplitudes. Itil et al. (1974) and Saletu et al. (1975) saw no differences in amplitudes between their subject groups; Herman et al. (1977) found larger amplitudes in the high-risk subjects than in controls at 100- to 200-msec post-stimulus, and Friedman, Vaughan, and Erlenmeyer-Kimling (1980) and Friedman, Erlenmeyer-Kimling, and Vaughan (in press) observed smaller amplitudes in late positive components (P350 and P400) in the high-risk children in each of two independent samples using auditory stimuli. In a study of visual ERPs, Friedman, Vaughan, and Erlenmeyer-Kimling (1979b) found that four children out of a group of 30 high-risk and 30 normal comparison subjects showed very small differences in late positive component amplitudes between a simple and a more complex version of a task of sustained visual attention (the Continuous Performance Test). All four were children of schizophrenic parents. In normal comparison children and in the remainder of the high-risk group, the more complex visual task elicited larger amplitudes than the simpler task, suggesting that the four high-risk children may have differed from other subjects in the way in which they processed relevant information from the two tasks. Thus, the results from our group are in agreement for both auditory (Friedman, Erlenmeyer-Kimling and Vaughan (in press) and Friedman, Vaughan and Erlenmeyer-Kimling (1980) and visual (Friedman, Vaughan, and

Erlenmeyer-Kimling, 1979b) stimuli in showing reduced amplitude in late positive components among some of the high-risk children.

The finding of longer latencies in high-risk subjects by both Herman et al. (1977) and Friedman, Frosch, and Erlenmeyer-Kimling (1979a) may be indicative of deficient information-processing, as latency to peak of a given component has been used as a measure of the latency of a specific processing stage that is reflected by the particular component under study. The longer latencies observed in high-risk children are of interest also in the light of independent evidence that such children may suffer from attentional deficits (cf., Asarnow et al., 1978; Erlenmeyer-Kimling, 1968, 1975; Erlenmeyer-Kimling and Cornblatt, 1978; Rutschmann, Cornblatt, and Erlenmeyer-Kimling 1977), coupled with the report by Grunewald, Zuberbier-Grunewald, and Netz (1978) that children with poor concentration ability have longer latency ERP components than other children.

The observation of reduced amplitude in late positive components in each of the two samples in our longitudinal study (Friedman, Vaughan, and Erlenmeyer-Kimling, 1979b, 1980; Friedman, Erlenmeyer-Kimling, and Vaughan, in press) is of interest also because reduction of amplitude in late ERP components is one of the most consistent findings in research on adult schizophrenics (Roth, 1977; Shagass, 1976), and children with poor concentration ability also show smaller amplitudes in late components (Grunewald, Zuberbier-Grunewald, and Netz, 1978). Reduced amplitude in late positive components among high-risk children agrees well with the finding of cognitive deficits among such children, as both amplitude and latency of the late positive components have been shown to reflect the cognitive structure of the task during which they are recorded.

There is sufficient inconsistency among the published studies that more research on event-related potentials in high-risk subjects is warranted. The use of ERP methodology, which allows the recording of brain potentials known to reflect cognitive processing, is clearly called for, as both early and late ERPs can be recorded and related to the specific behavior (e.g., reaction time) under study, thereby allowing a more precise determination of psychophysiological relationships and their possible deficiencies in high-risk individuals.

ASSESSMENTS OF ATTENTIONAL PROCESSES IN HIGH-RISK SUBJECTS

Attentional dysfunctions in schizophrenia have been noted ever since Kraepelin (1919) classified and described the mental disorders. Many descriptions have been published (cf., Chapman and McGhie, 1962; Freedman and Chapman, 1973) on schizophrenic patients' experiences of stimulus swampage and loss of ability to attend, and numerous sytematic investigations of attentional processes have demonstrated that such processes are impaired in schizophrenics (see entire issue of *Schizophrenia Bulletin*, vol. 3, no. 3, 1977). Attentional deficits are present not only during psychotic states, but during remission, as well, in persons who have had a schizophrenic episode (Asarnow and MacCrimmon, 1978; Wohlberg and Kornetsky, 1973). Moreover, in a follow-back study, Ricks and Berry (1970) found that, along with various clearly neurological symptoms, impaired attention span was one of the characteristics reported in the records of a child guidance center (the Judge Baker Guidance Center) for individuals who later became chronic schizophrenics. Thus, the possibility that attentional deficits may reflect a central disorder in schizophrenia has received increasing support in recent years (cf., Garmezy, 1977; Matthysse, 1977).

Several of the studies of children of schizophrenic parents have included assessments of attentional processes in the search for possible early indicators of vulnerability to schizophrenia. Table 5-6 groups the attentional tests according to the underlying processes that they are purported to tap.

The test given most frequently in the high-risk studies is the Continuous Performance Test (CPT), which measures sustained visual attention. The CPT was initially developed by Rosvold et al. (1956) to assess brain damage, and various versions of the test have since been used in studies of schizophrenic patients (cf. Kornetsky and Mirsky, 1966; Orzack and Kornetsky, 1966). Discrepant results among the high-risk studies that have employed the CPT may be attributable to differences in levels of difficulty in different versions. In the studies by Grunebaum et al., children at the age of five or six (Cohler et al., 1977; Grunebaum et al., 1974) were instructed to respond to the color red when it appeared in a series of rapidly presented stimuli, whereas at older ages (Grunebaum et al., 1978; Herman et al., 1977) the target stimulus was a letter. Asarnow et al. (1978) used a digit as the target stimulus, as did we

TABLE 5-6.

ATTENTIONAL TESTS IN CHILDREN OF SCHIZOPHRENIC PARENTS, THE PROCESSES THEY REPRESENT

Name of Test (reported by the individual investigators)	Type of Process	Study Code [a]							
Continuous Performance Test	Sustained visual attention		5A1	5A3	5B	6	7[b]		13
Attention Span Task			5A1						
Digit Span	Short-term auditory or visual recall, with or without distraction							8	
WISC Digit Span			5A1		5B				
Visual-Aural Digit Span					5B				
Short-Term Memory Lag				5A3					
Dichotic listening	Selective auditory attention under overload conditions	4(b)							
Competing Voices									13
Information Overload				5A3	5B				
Embedded Figures Test	Detection of visual target stimuli or patterns from background stimuli						7[b]		
Visual Search								8	
Span of Apprehension									13
Concept Attainment									13
Stroop-Color-Word Test									13
Simple Reaction Time	Simple auditory or visual reaction time		5A1		5B	6			13
Signal Detection Task	Simple auditory stimulus detection	4(b)							

[a] Study code: 4(b), Orvaschel et al.; 5A1, Erlenmeyer-Kimling et al., Sample A, round 1 and 5A3 Erlenmeyer-Kimling et al., Sample A, round 3; 5B, Erlenmeyer-Kimling et al., Sample B; 6, Garmezy et al.; 7, Grunebaum et al.; 8, Weintraub/Neale; 13, Asarnow et al.
[b] Examinations given at several age bands

(Cornblatt and Erlenmeyer-Kimling, in press; Friedman, Vaughan, and Erlenmeyer-Kimling, 1979b) in one of the procedures administered in the third round of testing of our first sample (Sample A) and in the initial testing of the replicate sample (Sample B). In our first round of testing of Sample A, however, the subjects were instructed to respond when a stimulus—a slide of a playing card presented with or without auditory distraction—was identical to the one immediately preceding it (Erlenmeyer-Kimling, 1975; Erlenmeyer-Kimling and Cornblatt, 1978), and in one of the procedures given in subsequent examinations of Sample A and in the initial examination of Sample B, the subjects were told to respond to any pair of digits that was identical to the pair just before it (Cornblatt and Erlenmeyer-Kimling, in press; Friedman, Vaughan, and Erlenmeyer-Kimling, 1979b). Nuechterlein et al. (in press), in one of a series of studies of high-risk children directed by Garmezy, used our playing card version of the CPT in addition to five other adaptations to study high-risk children. Thus, there were differences in levels of difficulty introduced by the target stimuli and the subject's task in the several studies, as well as differences in rates of presentation and in instructions to the subjects regarding speed of response.

Asarnow et al. (1978) failed to find differences on the CPT between foster-reared children of schizophrenic mothers and children of normal parents, and several reports from the Grunebaum study also indicated that children of schizophrenic mothers performed no worse on the CPT than children of normal mothers. The Grunebaum study is confusing, however. Whereas Grunebaum et al. (1974) initially reported that five-year-old—but not six-year-old—children of schizophrenic mothers made more CPT errors than children of normal or nonschizophrenic psychotic mothers, Cohler et al. (1977), re-analyzing the data with some subtractions and additions of subjects, found no group differences. Upon followup testing of some of the subjects at older ages, the children of depressed mothers were reputed to make the greatest number of errors (Grunebaum et al., 1978; Herman et al., 1977). It is difficult to take the results of the followup testing seriously, however, as 59% of the mentally ill mothers from the sample that was small to begin with had dropped out, and there is some reason to believe that the drop-outs may have included the more disturbed mothers.

Both Asarnow et al. (1978) and Grunebaum et al. (Cohler et al., 1977; Grunebaum et al., 1974; Grunebaum et al., 1978; Herman et al., 1977) used relatively simple versions of the CPT. Using a simple version in which subjects were instructed to respond to the digit pair 08, we also found no differences between high-risk and normal comparison children at the ages of seven to 12 (Sample B) or 12 to 19 (Sample A, third round of testing). When more complex tasks were used, however, the expected differences in the direction of poorer performance among the high-risk subjects were found to be significant at the younger ages and to show a directional trend at older ages (i.e., in Sample A, round 3) (Cornblatt and Erlenmeyer-Kimling, in press; Erlenmeyer-Kimling et al., in press b). Distraction, consisting of a female voice reciting digits, may also have been more complex and therefore more effective in our study (Erlenmeyer-Kimling, 1975; Erlenmeyer-Kimling and Cornblatt, 1978; Rutschmann, Cornblatt, and Erlenmeyer-Kimling, 1977) than the 1000-cps tone used by Grunebaum et al. (1978) as a distractor. In our study, distraction (administered only to Sample A) lowered the performance level of the high-risk children to a greater extent than the performance of the normal comparison group, whereas Grunebaum et al. observed no distraction effect.

In addition to computing the number of correct and incorrect responses to CPT stimuli, we (Cornblatt and Erlenmeyer-Kimling, in press; Erlenmeyer-Kimling and Cornblatt, 1978; Rutschmann, Cornblatt, and Erlenmeyer-Kimling, 1977) obtained signal detection indices β, which is an index of response bias or caution, and d', which is an index of sensitivity or discriminability. No group differences were found with respect to β, which showed that other differences between high-risk and normal comparison subjects were not due to differences in test-taking attitudes. However, d' was significantly lower (indicating lower sensitivity) in the high-risk group in both samples on the first round of testing and non-significantly lower in later testing of Sample A (Erlenmeyer-Kimling et al., in press b). Moreover, d' appears to be a relatively good indicator of future psychopathology (Erlenmeyer-Kimling et al., in press a; Erlenmeyer-Kimling et al., in press b), as will be discussed in the following section. Low d' values in high-risk children relative to a stratified normal comparison sample were also found by Nuechterlein et al. (in press), who used more difficult versions of the CPT than did Grunebaum et al. (1978) or Asarnow et al. (1978). In Nuechterlein's sample, neither the children of mothers with other psychiatric disorders nor hyperactive children had low d' scores, but the hyperactive children had low β scores, indicating reduced response caution in such children as opposed to reduced sensitivity in the children at high risk for schizophrenia.

Thus, the results of the two studies (providing three independent samples) that have used more difficult task levels in testing sustained visual attention are in good agreement in showing poorer performance and lowered sensitivity in high-risk children.

Measures that call for short-term auditory or visual recall (see Table 5-6) have consistently discriminated between high-risk and normal comparison subjects in our samples (Erlenmeyer-Kimling and Cornblatt, 1978; Cornblatt and Erlenmeyer-Kimling, in press; Rutschmann, Cornblatt, and Erlenmeyer-Kimling, 1980), and in the study by Weintraub and Neale (in press), a measure that is very similar to our Attention Span Task also discriminates between high-risk and normal comparison subjects. However, Weintraub and Neal (in press) found no differences between children of schizophrenic and depressed parents in short-term auditory recall. In fact, Weintraub and Neale found very few differences between these two groups of subjects on a number of variables, whereas, in our study, there are differences between the groups on attentional variables, with the children of parents with affective disorders resembling children of normal parents more closely than the high-risk children.

A dichotic listening test administered to subjects from the Danish birth cohort study showed no differences between high-risk children and comparison children with normal or psychiatrically disturbed parents (Orvaschel et al., 1979). However, the dichotic listening test (Competing Voices task) used in the Waterloo study (Asarnow et al., 1978) yielded marginally significant differences between the small group of foster-care children of schizophrenic parents and normal comparison groups, and, in our study, another test of selective auditory attention under conditions of information overload (the Information Overload Test) discriminated well between high-risk and normal comparison subjects in both samples at different ages (Cornblatt and Erlenmeyer-Kimling, in press). It should be noted that the measure reported by Orvaschel et al. (1979) did not involve the subjects' participation in a task while the stimuli were being presented, as did the measures in both the other studies. The dichotic listening task used in the Danish study, as well as another attentional task (Signal Detection Task) that involved simple detection of auditory stimuli, may have been too easy for all subjects, thus obscuring attentional differences that might have emerged between high-risk and comparison subjects with more difficult tasks.

Although Asarnow et al. (1978) found tests that call for detection of visual target stimuli or patterns out of a background of irrelevant stimuli (the Span of Apprehension and Concept Attainment tests) to be among the best discriminators between children of schizophrenic and normal parents, Weintraub and Neale (in press) have reported that a test of this type (Visual Search) differentiated children of schizophrenic parents from children of normal parents, but not from children of depressed parents. Grunebaum et al. (1974) initially reported that five-year-old children of schizophrenic mothers performed poorly on the Embedded Figures Test, but re-analysis of the data by Cohler et al. (1977) and testing of some of the subjects at later ages (Grunebaum et al., 1978) showed the poorest performance on the part of children of depressed parents. Interpretation of the data across the three studies is complicated by several factors: (1) Numbers in the Waterloo (Asarnow et al., 1978) and Grunebaum (Grunebaum et al., 1974, 1978) studies were quite small. (2) Some subjects in the Grunebaum et al. (1974) report were subtracted in the Cohler et al. (1977) report and others were added, and subject attrition was high for the later testing reported by Grunebaum et al. (1978). (3) Unlike the other two studies, the study by Asarnow et al. (1978) had no children of depressed mothers for comparison. The usefulness of attentional measures of this type therefore remains to be further explored.

Simple reaction time, which has frequently been reported to be slower in schizophrenic patients than in normal control subjects, was initially found by L. Marcus (1972, directed by Garmezy) to be slower both in children of schizophrenic mothers and in acting-out (externalizing) children from a clinic group than in control subjects, but upon introduction of procedures designed to provide cognitive structure and motivational increments, the performance of the acting-out children came up to the level of their controls, while the performance of the children of schizophrenic mothers did not, suggesting that the latter showed a basic reaction time deficit, while the acting-out children's initially poor performance was due to lack of cooperation. In the Waterloo study (Asarnow et al., 1978), simple reaction time did not differ between fostered away children of schizophrenic mothers and children of normal parents. As Van Dyke, Rosenthal, and Rasmussen (1974) had previously reported that reaction time was slowed in the offspring of both schizophrenic and non-schizophrenic parents who were reared by a schizophrenic and was not slowed in adopted away offspring of schizophrenic parents, the difference between the findings in the two high-risk studies might be thought to be attributable to the difference in the rearing status of the children. But in our study, in which the children of schizophrenic parents were reared by their own parents, reaction times recorded during administration of the Continuous Performance Test consistently showed no differences between the high-risk and normal comparison subjects in either of two samples. It is possible that reasons for the differences among the studies lie not so much in differences in rearing status of the subjects as in differences in instructions and other methodological features.

Attempts have been made in the Waterloo study, as well as our own, to determine whether the same high-risk subjects contribute to group differences across more than one attentional task. Asarnow et al. (1978) used cluster analysis to detect subsets of children within the high-risk group who showed common patterns of performance across the tasks in their attentional battery. Four clusters were obtained, of which one contained four of the nine fostered away high-risk children and one fostered away child of normal parents; the subjects were reported to show differential impairment as a function of increase in the amount of information to be processed on a number of tasks, and the investigators (Asarnow et al., 1978) referred to an "overload" pattern of performance. Another cluster consisted solely of a high-risk child who showed impaired performance on all tasks in the battery. Thus, five out of nine high-risk subjects were identified as performing deficiently across a number of tasks (Asarnow et al., 1978).

In our study, several methods have been used to identify a subgroup of poor attentional performers within the high-risk group. For example, linear discriminant function analyses, using indices from the CPT in round one, combined with indices from the Bender-Gestalt Test and the Human Figure Drawing Test, identified 29% of the children with one schizophrenic parent and 25% of those with two schizophrenic parents in our first sample as having composite scores that were poorer than the cut-off score defining the worst 5% of the normal comparison group, while subjects whose parents had affective disorders were almost identical to the normal comparison group (Erlenmeyer-Kimling, Cornblatt, and Fleiss, 1979). The indices used in the discriminant function analysis were not exclusively attentional, but other analyses based only on the CPT and Attention Span Task (Erlenmeyer-Kimling and Cornblatt, 1978; Cornblatt and Erlenmeyer-Kimling, in press) have shown high-risk subjects to be deviant on a significantly larger number of indices than were comparison subjects: 30% of the high-risk subjects were deviant on four or more attentional indices opposed to only 3% of the normal comparison group (Cornblatt and Erlenmeyer-Kimling, in press). Cornblatt and Erlenmeyer-Kimling (in press) found that attentional deviance scores were significantly correlated ($r = .36$, $p< .01$) for high-risk subjects from test-ing round one to round three, but not for the normal comparison sub-jects ($r = .10$, ns), and concluded that although deviant performance ap-peared to be due to random fluctuation in the normal comparison group, the high-risk subjects who showed deviant performances tended to do so across a number of measures and over substantial intervals of time.

In summary, there is substantial evidence from several studies that points to the existence of attentional deficits in some children of schizo-phrenic parents long before the appearance of clear psychopathological symptoms. Results from the different studies are not entirely in agree-ment, however, concerning the kinds of attentional deviations that char-acterize these children, and two studies (Grunebaum et al., 1978 and Orvaschel et al., 1979) failed to find any attentional impairment in high-risk subjects, whereas a third (Weintraub and Neale, in press) found the same degree of impairment in children of depressed parents as in chil-dren of schizophrenic parents. Methodological differences or differences in the samples under examination may account for some or all of the variability across studies.

THE NEW YORK HIGH RISK PROJECT: EARLY MEASURES AND LATER PSYCHOPATHOLOGY

Since a major goal of high-risk research is to predict later clinical out-come on the basis of assessments made at early ages, it is of interest to consider how well some of the measures administered to subjects in the New York high-risk project at young ages predict to the current clinical status of these subjects in late adolescence.

DESCRIPTION OF THE STUDY

The New York high-risk project, described in detail elsewhere (Erlenmeyer-Kimling et al., 1979; in press b), includes two indepen-dently ascertained samples of high-risk and low-risk children. Sample A, recruited in 1971–72, consists of 80[3] high-risk subjects (children of one or two schizophrenic parents) and 125 low-risk subjects, of whom 100 have psychiatrically normal parents and 25 have one or two parents with affective disorders. Sample B, recruited during 1977 through 1979, consists of 45 children of one or two schizophrenic parents, 40 children of parents with affective disorders, and 65 children of normal parents.

Children in both samples were between the ages of seven and 12 years at the time of recruitment and were not in psychiatric treatment or otherwise considered to be psychiatrically disturbed. All subjects were white, English-speaking, and from intact families. Sample A has been re-examined twice since the initial examination, and Sample B has been examined twice. Between testing rounds, contact is maintained by telephone at 3- to 6-month intervals.

All three areas of biobehavioral functioning under consideration in this chapter have been found to be disturbed in some of the high-risk children in each of the two independent samples. These subjects showed neuromotor and attentional deviations, as well as unusual patterns of cortical event-related potentials, at relatively early ages.

Interim Assessment of Clinical Status

Subjects in Sample B are still quite young, and even the subjects in Sample A have thus far passed through only about 13% of their total life-time risk for schizophrenia,[4] so that ultimate determination of clinical outcomes in these subjects cannot be made until much later. However, interim assessments of the current clinical status of Sample A sub-

---

[3] Three subjects with a schizophrenic mother and manic-depressive father are not included here or in many of the analyses that have been published on this project.

[4] The calculation of the proportion of life-time risk passed through by Sample A at the average age of 17.5 years is based on life-time risk estimates derived from the distribution of ages at first hospitalization for schizophrenic patients (see Hanson et al., 1977). Data from our own study, from Mednick's Danish sample (Mednick et al., 1978), and from earlier studies of children of two schizophrenic parents as calculated by Dawes (1968), suggest, however, that onset ages may be earlier in children of schizophrenic parents than in schizophrenic patients generally (Erlenmeyer-Kimling, 1980).

jects do allow us to examine possible relationships between early deviance in the areas that we have used as indicators of brain dysfunction and psychopathology in adolescence.

Each of the subjects in Sample A has been rated on a five-point Behavioral Global Adjustment Scale (BGAS) as described by Cornblatt and Erlenmeyer-Kimling (in press). Ratings on the BGAS are made by raters who are blind with respect to the subject's parental group and take into account family relationships and the child's general level of development, peer relationships, and functioning in school or work. Scale point 1 on the BGAS applies to subjects who have been hospitalized for psychiatric reasons, and scale point 2 applies to subjects who have been in treatment or clearly warrant treatment for psychiatric problems. Scale point 3 indicates moderate difficulty in functioning in some areas, and scale points 4 and 5 refer to good and excellent functioning, respectively, in all areas.

Eight subjects have been hospitalized for psychiatric reasons and 15 have been or should have been in psychiatric treatment. The hospitalized subjects include five children of schizophrenic parents, two children of depressed parents, and one child of normal parents. The treated subjects include ten children of schizophrenic parents, four children of depressed parents, and one child of normal parents (see Erlenmeyer-Kimling et al., in press a).

RELATIONSHIP OF EARLY MEASURES TO CURRENT CLINICAL STATUS

The 15 high-risk subjects who have been hospitalized or in psychiatric treatment in adolescence scored more poorly than the remainder of the high-risk group on several of the measures that were administered in the first round of testing when the subjects were 7 to 12 years old (Erlenmeyer-Kimling et al., in press a).[5] The hospitalized and treated high-risk subjects had poorer neuromotor performance, lower IQ scores with a large Verbal IQ deficit relative to Performance IQ, and deviant performance on the attentional tasks compared to the remaining high-risk

[5] Since cortical event-related potentials were not recorded during the first round of testing, it is not possible to say whether or not they would have contributed to the pattern of early deficits seen in the high-risk subjects who are now classified as clinically deviant.

subjects or the groups of subjects with depressed or normal parents. Subjects from the latter two groups who have subsequently been hospitalized or in treatment did not show such a pattern of performance deviations on the measures from the first round of testing.

The relationship between some of the measures administered in the earlier testing and the subjects' current clinical status is depicted in Figure 5-2, which shows the preliminary results of applying path analysis[6] to a part of the schematic diagram of a model of risk that was shown in Fig. 5-1. In Fig. 5-2, "group" represents the subjects' parental background—either schizophrenic or normal parents—neuromotor and attentional functioning[7] are represented by measures from the first round of testing (1971–1972) and clinical status in 1979 is indicated by BGAS ratings carried out at that time. The purpose of the path analysis is to estimate the extent to which (1) group, that is, high-risk versus low-risk status, affects neuromotor and attentional functioning at ages 7–12 and clinical status in late adolescence; (2) neuromotor functioning affects attention and clinical status; and (3) attention affects clinical status.

In this analysis, the path coefficients, which are analogous to standardized regression weights, are all in the expected direction, and, as can be seen, high-risk status (group) is shown as affecting neuromotor functioning to an important degree and attention and current clinical status to a lesser, but still probably significant, degree. Neuromotor functioning, in

---

[6] Jöreskog and Sörbom's (1978) LISREL IV was used. The path analysis is based on a pair-wise deletion correlation matrix of the high-risk and normal subject data, with the sample sizes for the groups averaging to about $N = 164$. Variables, with the exception of BGAS, have been statistically residualized on age and sex. All variables and parameter estimates are standardized; BGAS scores are those determined in August 1979. Path coefficients in the causal diagram are interpreted analogously to standardized regression weights; larger numbers accordingly represent relatively greater estimated causal effects. The meaningfulness of the estimated path coefficients depends upon the validity of the causal assumptions represented in the diagram. Since this modal is mathematically just-identified, it is not possible to apply a statistical test of the overall causal model. (The measurement model is testable, though, and results indicate that the multiple indicator constructs—neuromotor functioning and attentional functioning—fit the data fairly well, with a Chi-square of 56.5 for 24 degrees of freedom.) The causal estimates can be checked as to their reasonableness, however, e.g., that the estimates have proper signs, positive error variances, etc. In this model, the path coefficients are all in the expected direction and error variances are positive.

[7] Event-related potentials are not available for inclusion in this analysis.

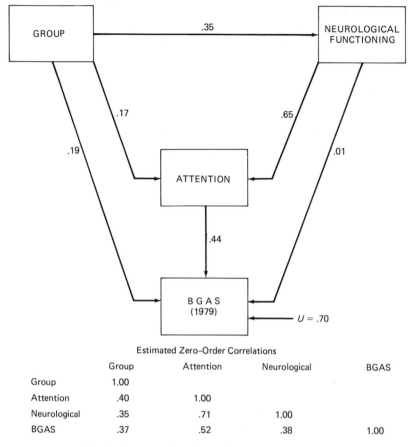

Estimated Zero-Order Correlations

	Group	Attention	Neurological	BGAS
Group	1.00			
Attention	.40	1.00		
Neurological	.35	.71	1.00	
BGAS	.37	.52	.38	1.00

FIGURE 5-2. Application of path analysis to round one neuromotor and attentional data and 1979 BGAS ratings for Sample A high-risk and normal comparison groups.

turn, is shown as having a large effect on attentional functioning, but little direct effect on current clinical status, whereas attentional functioning affects clinical status directly to an important degree. Zero-order correlations among the constructs, which are presented in the correlational matrix at the bottom of the figure, support the interpretations drawn from the path diagram. The symbol U represents the proportion of variance that is unaccounted for by the causally antecedent factors in the model. As shown here, $U = .7$, indicating that 30% of the variance in clinical status—BGAS ratings—is accounted for by group, neuromotor functioning, and attention. The results of the analysis thus lend support to at least part of our schematic model. Additional analyses incorporating psychophysiological and environmental variables will be of interest to explore the hypothesized relationships further. Application of path analysis to similar data on Sample B when the subjects reach late adolescence will serve as a test of the replicability of the results obtained on Sample A.

SUMMARY

Data from several high-risk studies, including ours (The New York High-Risk Project, Erlenmeyer-Kimling et al., 1979, in press b), strongly suggest that signs of brain dysfunction in the three areas discussed in this paper may be good indicators of vulnerability to schizophrenia. Fish (1957) and Meehl (1962, 1972) have postulated that neurointegrative defects lie at the core of the predisposition to develop schizophrenia, and the evidence now accumulating in high-risk studies indicates that such defects are to be found in subgroups of children of schizophrenic parents at young ages. Nevertheless, as noted in earlier sections, there remain a number of inconsistent findings across the studies that require clarification. Failure to find evidence of deviance among high-risk subjects in the biobehavioral areas under consideration may be attributable to methodological factors in some of the studies or even, with very small sample sizes in certain studies, to a chance absence of subjects who are at true genetic risk.

It is important to remember that very few of the subjects in these studies have passed through a large portion of the schizophrenia risk period. In Fish's study (in press), in which the subjects were evaluated in early adulthood, the ones who were found to be psychiatrically disturbed did appear to be showing schizophrenia or schizophrenia spectrum disorders, and in our study (Erlenmeyer-Kimling et al., in press a), the high-risk subjects who were hospitalized by late adolescence also appear to be schizophrenic. Diagnoses of the subjects in psychiatric treatment in our study are less clear, however, so that it is not yet possible to ascertain whether the deviations seen in childhood bear a predictive relationship specifically to schizophrenia or to psychopathology more generally. Early indicators that point to vulnerability to any type of psychopathology may be sufficient for intervention purposes because prevention is desirable no matter what form psychopathology takes. But, if a goal of high-risk research is to aid in unraveling etiology, then it must be possible to identify a complex of indicators that is specific to schizophrenia. It is not yet certain that we or other high-risk investigators have done the latter.

Two other kinds of problems may also trouble the high-risk studies at this stage. They are inclusion of false positives among the subjects predicted to be at true risk and of false negatives who are not identified as showing deviance on the indicators, but who later will become schizophrenic. Our expectation is that false negatives will prove to occur less frequently than false positives. False positives, however, may be important for further scrutiny because they may be genetically predisposed individuals who are fortunate enough to have environmental buffering that protects them from becoming ill. Such subjects might therefore provide a key to understanding environmental variables that help to produce a benign course in individuals with a "schizophrenic genotype."

Despite these uncertainties, which can only be clarified with followup of the samples of high-risk and comparison subjects, the finding of deviance in neuromotor functioning, cortical event-related potentials, and attentional processes, individually in several of the studies and jointly in our study, is most promising. The areas in which early disturbances are being reported in high-risk subjects are the same ones in which important disturbances have been observed in schizophrenic patients, and moreover, they are areas that fit a model of schizophrenia according to which a genetic and neuroregulatory disorder is mediated by biobehavioral functions that are directly controlled by the brain.

ACKNOWLEDGMENTS

The New York high-risk study is supported in part by USPHS grants #MH19560 and #MH30921, by a grant from the W. T. Grant Foundation, and by the Department of Mental Hygiene of New York State.

We thank Dr. Joseph Fleiss for statistical advice throughout the project and Dr. Donald Rock for guidance on path analysis models. We are grateful to the many members of our research team and to our several collaborators for their contributions. Thanks are due Anne Moscato and Noreen Dodge for typing the manuscript and Thomas Chin for preparing the figures.

REFERENCES

Asarnow, R. F., and D. J. MacCrimmon (1978). Residual performance deficit in clinically remitted schizophrenics: A marker of schizophrenia? *J. Abnorm. Psychol.* 87, 597–608.

Asarnow, R. F., D. J. MacCrimmon, J. Cleghorn, and R. A. Steffy (1978). The McMaster–Waterloo Project: An attentional and clinical assessment of foster children at risk for schizophrenia. In *The Nature and Origin of Schizophrenia: New Perspectives* (L. Wynne, R. Cromwell, J. Strauss, and S. Matthysse, eds.). John Wiley, New York.

Bender, L. (1947). Childhood schizophrenia. *Amer. J. Orthopsychiat.* 17, 40–56.

Bender, L., and A. M. Freedman (1952). A study of the first three years in the maturation of schizophrenic children. *Quart. J. Child Behav.* 1, 245–272.

Buchsbaum, M. S. (1977). The middle evoked response components and schizophrenia. *Schizophrenia Bull.* 3, 93–104.

Chapman, J., and A. McGhie (1962). A comparative study of disordered attention in schizophrenia. *J. Ment. Sci.* 108, 487–500.

Cohler, B. J., H. U. Grunebaum, J. L. Weiss, E. Gamer, and D. H. Gallant (1977). Disturbances of attention among schizophrenic, depressed and well mothers and their children. *J. Child Psychol. Psychiat.* 18, 115–135.

Cornblatt, B, and L. Erlenmeyer-Kimling (in press). Early attentional predictors of adolescent behavioral disturbances in children at risk for schizophrenia. In *Children at Risk for Schizophrenia: A Longitudinal Prospective* (N. Watt, E. J. Anthony, L. Wynne, and J. Rolf, eds.). Cambridge University Press, New York.

Dawes, R. M. (1968). An unexpected correlate of psychopathology among children of schizophrenic couples. *J. Psychiat. Res.* 6, 201–209.

Erlenmeyer-Kimling, L. (1968). Studies on the offspring of two schizophrenic parents. In *The Transmission of Schizophrenia* (D. Rosenthal and S. S. Kety, eds.). Pergamon Press, New York.

Erlenmeyer-Kimling, L. (1975). A prospective study of children at risk for schizophrenia: Methodological considerations and some preliminary findings. In *Life History Research in Psychopathology*, Vol. 4 (R. Wirt, G. Winokur, and M. Roff, eds.). University of Minnesota Press, Minneapolis.

Erlenmeyer-Kimling, L. (1977). Issues pertaining to prevention and interaction in genetic disorders affecting human behavior. In *Primary Prevention In Psychopathology* (G. W. Albee and J. M. Joffe, eds.). University Press of New England, Hanover, New Hampshire.

Erlenmeyer-Kimling, L., and B. Cornblatt (1978). Attentional measures in a study of children at high risk for schizophrenia. *J. Psychiat. Res.* 14, 93–98. Also in *The Nature and Origin of Schizophrenia: New Perspectives* (L. Wynne, R.

Cromwell, J. Strauss, and S. Matthysse, eds.). (1978) pp. 359–365. Wiley, New York.

Erlenmeyer-Kimling, L., B. Cornblatt, and J. Fleiss (1979). High-risk research in schizophrenia. *Psychiat. Ann.* 9, 79–111.

Erlenmeyer-Kimling, L., C. J. Kestenbaum, H. Bird, and U. Hilldoff (in press, a). Assessment of the New York high-risk project subjects in sample A who are now clinically deviant. In *Children at Risk for Schizophrenia: A Longitudinal Prospective* (N. Watt, E. J. Anthony, L. Wynne, and J. Rolf, eds.). Cambridge University Press, New York.

Erlenmeyer-Kimling, L., Y. Marcuse, B. Cornblatt, D. Friedman, J. D. Rainer, and J. Rutschmann (in press, b). The New York high-risk project. In *Children at Risk for Schizophrenia: A Longitudinal Prospective* (N. Watt, E. J. Anthony, L. Wynne, and J. Rolf, eds.). Cambridge University Press, New York.

Fish, B. (1957). The detection of schizophrenia in infancy. *J. Nerv. Ment. Dis.* 125, 1–24.

Fish, B. (1975). Biologic antecedents of psychosis in children. In *The Biology Of The Major Psychoses: A Comparative Analysis* (D. X. Freedman, ed.). Raven Press, New York.

Fish, B. (1977). Neurobiologic antecedents of schizophrenia in children: Evidence for an inherited, congenital neurointegrative defect. *Arch. Gen. Psychiat.* 34, 1297–1313.

Fish, B. (in press). Offspring of schizophrenics from birth to adulthood. In *Children at Risk for Schizophrenia: A Longitudinal Prospective* (N. Watt, E. J. Anthony, L. Wynne, and J. Rolf, eds.). Cambridge University Press, New York.

Fish, B., and M. Alpert (1963). Patterns of neurological development in infants born to schizophrenic mothers. In *Recent Advances in Biological Psychiatry*, Vol. 5 (J. Wortis, ed.). Plenum Press, New York.

Fish, B., and R. Hagin (1973). Visual-motor disorders in infants at risk for schizophrenia. *Arch. Gen. Psychiat.* 28, 900–904.

Freedman, B., and L. J. Chapman (1973). Early subjective experiences in schizophrenic episodes. *J. Abnorm. Psychol.* 82, 46–54.

Friedman, D., A. Frosch, and L. Erlenmeyer-Kimling (1979a). Auditory evoked potentials in children at high risk for schizophrenia. In *Evoked Brain Potentials and Behavior* (H. Begleiter, ed.). Plenum Press, New York.

Friedman, D., H. G. Vaughan, Jr., and L. Erlenmeyer-Kimling (1979b). Event-related potential investigations in children at high risk for schizophrenia. In *Event-Related Potentials in Man: Application and Problems* (D. Lehmann and E. Callaway, eds.). Plenum Press, New York.

Friedman, D., H. G. Vaughan, Jr., and L. Erlenmeyer-Kimling, (1980). The late positive complex to unpredictable auditory events in children at high risk for schizophrenia. *Psychophysiology* 17, 310–311.

Friedman, D., L. Erlenmeyer-Kimling, and H. G. Vaughan, Jr. (in press). ERP methodology in high risk research. In *Children at Risk for Schizophrenia: A Longitudinal Prospective* (N. Watt, E. J. Anthony, L. Wynne, and J. Rolf, eds.). Cambridge University Press, New York.

Garmezy, N. (1977). The psychology and psychopathology of attention. *Schizophrenia Bull.* 3, 360–369.

Gottesman, I. I., and J. Shields (1977). Obstetric complications and twin studies of schizophrenia: Clarifications and affirmations. *Schiz. Bull.* 3, 351–354.

Grunebaum, H., B. J. Cohler, C. Kauffman, and D. Gallant (1978). Children of depressed and schizophrenic mothers. *Child Psychiat. Human Develop.* 8, 219–228.

Grunebaum, H., J. Weiss, D. Gallant, and B. J. Cohler (1974). Attention in young children of psychotic mothers. *Amer. J. Psychiat.* 131, 887–891.

Grunewald, G., E. Zuberbier-Grunewald, and J. Netz (1978). Late components of average evoked potentials in children with different abilities to concentrate. *Electroenceph. Clin. Neurophysiol.* 44, 617–625.

Hanson, D. R., I. I. Gottesman, and L. L. Heston (1976). Some possible childhood indicators of adult schizophrenia from children of schizophrenics. *Brit. J. Psychiat.* 129, 142–154.

Hanson, D. R., I. I. Gottesman, and P. E. Meehl (1977). Genetic theories and the validation of psychiatric diagnoses: Implications for the study of children of schizophrenics. *J. Abnorm. Psychol.* 86, 575–588.

Herman, J., A. F. Mirsky, N. L. Ricks, and D. Gallant (1977). Behavioral and electrographic measures of attention in children at risk for schizophrenia *J. Abnorm. Psychol.* 86, 27–33.

Itil, T. M. (1977). Qualitative and quantitative EEG findings in schizophrenics. *Schizophrenia Bull.* 3, 61–79.

Itil, T. M., W. Hsu, B. Saletu, and S. Mednick (1974). Computer EEG and auditory evoked potential investigations in children at high risk for schizophrenia. *Amer. J. Psychiat.* 131, 892–900.

Jöreskog, K. G., and D. Sörbom (1978). LISREL, *IV: Analysis of Linear Structural Relationships by the Method of Maximum Likelihood—User's Guide*. National Educational Resources, Inc., Chicago.

Kornetsky, C., and A. Mirsky (1966). On certain psychopharmacological and physiological differences between schizophrenics and normal persons. *Psychopharmacologia* (Berl.) 8, 309.

Kraepelin, E. (1919). In *Dementia Praecox* (R. M. Barclay, trans). E. S. Livingston, Ltd., Edinburgh.

Marcus, L. M. (1972). Studies of attention in children vulnerable to psychopathology. Unpublished doctoral dissertation. University of Minnesota, Minneapolis.

Marcus, J. (1974). Cerebral functioning in offspring of schizophrenics: A possible genetic factor. *Int. J. Ment. Health* 3, 57–73.

Marcus, J., J. Auerbach, L. Wilkinson, S. Maeir, A. Mark, V. Peles, and C. M. Burack (in press). Infants at risk for schizophrenia: The Jerusalem infant development study. In *Children at Risk for Schizophrenia: A Longitudinal Prospective* (N. Watt, E. J. Anthony, L. Wynne and J. Rolf, eds.). Cambridge University Press, New York.

Marcuse, Y., and B. Cornblatt (in press). Children at high risk for schizophrenia: Predictions from infancy to childhood functioning. In *Life Span Research On*

The Prediction of Psychopathology (L. Erlenmeyer-Kimling, N. Miller, and B. S. Dohrenwend, eds.). Columbia University Press, New York.

Matthysse, S. (1977). The biology of attention. *Schizophrenia Bull.* 3, 370–372.

McNeil, T. F., and L. Kaij (1973). Obstetric complications and physical size of offspring of schizophrenic, schizophrenic like, and control mothers. *Brit. J. Psychiat.* 123, 341–348.

McNeil, T. F., and L. Kaij (1978). Obstetric factors in the development of schizophrenia: Complications in the births of preschizophrenics and in reproduction by schizophrenic parents. In *The Nature and Origin of Schizophrenia: New Perspectives* (L. Wynne, R. Cromwell, J. Strauss, and S. Matthysse, eds.). Wiley, New York.

McNeil, T. F., and L. Kaij (in press). Offspring of women with nonorganic psychoses: Progress Report. In *Children at Risk for Schizophrenia: A Longitudinal Prospective* (N. Watt, E. J. Anthony, L. Wynne, and J. Rolf, eds.). Cambridge University Press, New York.

Mednick, S. A., E. Mura, F. Schulsinger, and B. Mednick (1971). Perinatal conditions and infant development in children with schizophrenic parents. *Soc. Biol.* 18, S103–S113.

Mednick, S. A., E. Mura, F. Schulsinger, and B. Mednick (1973). Erratum and further analysis: "Perinatal conditions and infant development in children with schizophrenic parents." *Soc. Biol.* 20, 111–112.

Mednick, S. A., and F. Schulsinger (1968). Some premorbid characteristics related to breakdown in children with schizophrenic mothers. In *The Transmission of Schizophrenia* (D. Rosenthal and S. S. Kety, eds.). Pergamon Press, Oxford.

Mednick, S. A., F. Schulsinger, T. W. Teasdale, H. Schulsinger, P. H. Venables, and D. A. Rock (1978). Schizophrenia in high-risk children: Sex differences in predisposing factors. In *Cognitive Defects In The Development Of Mental Illness* (G. Serban, ed.). Brunner/Mazel, New York, pp. 169–197.

Meehl, P. E. (1962). Schizotaxia, schizotypy, schizophrenia. *Amer. Psychol.* 17, 827–838.

Meehl, P. E. (1972). Specific genetic etiology, psychodynamics and therapeutic nihilism. *Int. J. Ment. Health* (Spring/Summer) Vol. 1 pp. 10–27. Int. Arts & Sciences Press, New York.

Neuchterlein, K. H., S. Yonas-Phipps, R. Driscoll, and N. Garmezy (in press). Attentional functioning among children vulnerable to adult schizophrenia. In *Children at Risk for Schizophrenia: A Longitudinal Prospective* (N. Watt, E. J. Anthony, L. Wynne, and J. Rolf, eds.). Cambridge University Press, New York.

Orvaschel, H., S. Mednick, F. Schulsinger, and D. Rock (1979). The children of psychiatrically disturbed parents. *Arch. Gen. Psychiat.* 36, 691–695.

Orzack, M. H., and C. Kornetsky (1966). Attention dysfunction in chronic schizophrenia. *Arch. Gen. Psychol.* 14, 323.

Ragins, N., J. Schachter, E. Elmer, R. Preisman, A. E. Bowes, and V. Harway (1975). Infants and children at risk for schizophrenia. *J. Child Psychiat.* 14, 150–177.

Ricks, D. F., and J. C. Berry (1970). Family and symptom patterns that precede schizophrenia. In *Life History Research In Psychopathology*, Vol. I (M. Roff and D. F. Ricks, eds.). University of Minnesota Press, Minneapolis.

Ricks, D. F., and G. Nameche (1966). Symbiosis, sacrifice and schizophrenia. *Ment. Hyg.*, 50, 541–551.

Rieder, R. O., and P. L. Nichols (1979). Offspring of schizophrenics III. Hyperactivity and neurological soft signs. *Arch. Gen Psychiat.* 36, 665–674.

Robins, L. N. (1966). *Deviant Children Grow Up*. Williams & Wilkins, Baltimore.

Rosenthal, D. (1971). A program of research on heredity in schizophrenia. *Behav. Sci.* 16, 191–201.

Rosenthal, D. (1974). Issues in high-risk studies of schizophrenia. In *Life History Research In Psychopathology*, Vol. III (D. F. Ricks, A. Thomas, and M. Roff, eds.). University of Minnesota Press, Minneapolis.

Rosvold, H. E., A. Mirsky, J. Sarason, E. D. Bransome, Jr., and L. H. Beck (1956). A continuous performance test of brain damage. *J. Consult. Psychol.* 20, 343–350.

Roth, W. T. (1977). Late event-related potentials and psychopathology. *Schizophrenia Bull.* 3, 105–120.

Rutschmann, J., B. Cornblatt, and L. Erlenmeyer-Kimling (1977). Sustained attention in children at risk for schizophrenia: Report on a continuous performance test. *Arch. Gen. Psychiat.* 34, 571–575.

Rutschmann, J., B. Cornblatt, and L. Erlenmeyer-Kimling (1980). Auditory recognition memory in adolescents at risk for schizophrenia: Report on a verbal continuous recognition task. *Psychiat. Res.* 3, 151–161.

Saletu, B., M. Saletu, J. Marasa, S. Mednick, and F. Schulsinger (1975). Acoustic evoked potentials in offspring of schizophrenic mothers. ("high-risk" children for schizophrenia). *Clin. Electroenceph.* 6, 92–102.

Shagass, C. (1976). An electrophysiological view of schizophrenia. *Biol. Psychiat.* 11, 3–30.

Shagass, C. (1977). Early evoked potentials. *Schizophrenia Bull.* 3, 80–92.

Slater, E. (1968). A review of earlier evidence on genetic factors in schizophrenia. In *The Transmission of Schizophrenia* (D. Rosenthal and S. S. Kety, eds.). Pergamon Press, Oxford.

Spitzer, R. L., J. Endicott, and E. Robins (1975). Research Diagnostic Criteria (RDC) for a selected group of functional disorders. 2nd ed. November 23. Biometrics, New York.

Van Dyke, J. L., D. Rosenthal, and P. V. Rasmussen (1974). Electrodermal functioning in adopted-away offspring of schizophrenics. *J. Psychiat. Res.* 10, 199–215.

Weintraub, S., and J. M. Neale (in press). The Stony Brook high-risk project. In *Children at Risk for Schizophrenia: A Longitudinal Study* (N. Watt, E. J. Anthony, L. Wynne, and J. Rolf, eds.). Cambridge University Press, New York.

Wohlberg, G. W., and C. Kornetsky (1973). Sustained attention in remitted schizophrenia. *Arch. Gen. Psychiat.* 28, 533–537.

6 | The Relationship between Schizophrenic Language and the Aphasias

NANCY C. ANDREASEN

In their inception, psychiatry and neurology were sister disciplines. The great psychiatrists of the late nineteenth and the early twentieth century moved freely and comfortably between psychiatry and neurology. Many believed that the major psychiatric illnesses, and perhaps even the neuroses, derived from abnormalities in brain function. Even Freud (1966) spent part of his early scientific career studying in the laboratory of Meynert; he wrote a major scientific treatise on the subject of aphasia and hoped eventually to be able to relate his theoretical constructs to specific aspects of brain functioning or areas of the brain.

Most of the great descriptive psychiatrists responsible for the definition and delineation of schizophrenia viewed it as a brain disease. Kraepelin (1919) noted its similarity to the dementias and called attention to this by naming the disease "dementia praecox." Bleuler's (1950) emphasis on the characteristic disorders of thinking and the "disruption of associative threads" also suggests the importance of some type of brain dysfunction in schizophrenia. The most detailed attempt to relate schizophrenia to abnormal brain function was made by the Kleist-Leonhard school. Kleist (1960) described four major classes of schizophrenia: confused, paranoid, hebephrenic, and catatonic. Each of these major categories, or classes, was composed of several subtypes, which were thought to be localized in different areas of the brain. For example, confused schizophrenia was subdivided into speech-confused schizophrenia, characterized by sensory aphasic impairments and localized in the left temporal lobe; paralogical schizophrenia, characterized by ideational agnosia and localized in the occipital lobe; and incoherent schizophrenia, characterized by paralogical and paraphasic disturbances and localized in the diencephalon. Although most of Kleist's localizations are not likely to survive the test of time, he made a noteworthy contribution through his recognition that some forms of schizophrenia closely resemble the aphasias and his belief that careful study of specific clinical syndromes might aid in developing a more specific characterization of brain dysfunction in schizophrenia.

During recent years, interest in the search for brain dysfunction in schizophrenia has been renewed. The impetus for this derives from a variety of sources, such as studies of cerebral asymmetry, CAT scan abnormalities, and neurochemical studies. (Crow, 1980; Golden et al., 1980; Gruzelier and Flor-Henry, 1979; Snyder, Greenberg, and Yamamura, 1974; Van Praag, 1977; Weinberger et al., 1980a, b). One aspect that has captured considerable attention has been the relationship between disorganized schizophrenic language and the aphasias.

Chaika (1974) was the earliest among recent investigators to propose that some schizophrenic speakers suffer from an intermittent aphasia. She noted several features of schizophrenic language that were suggestive of aphasia, such as inappropriate use of phonological or semantic features of words, disrupted ability to apply rules of syntax and discourse, and production of sentences according to semantic and phonological features of previously uttered words rather than according to topic. Chaika's discussion, based on analysis of speech from only one patient, has led to considerable controversy. Fromkin (1975) has pointed out that many of the features noted also appear in the speech of normals. Lecours and Vanier-Clément (1976) have argued that the abnormalities in schizophrenic speech are due to an underlying cognitive abnormality rather than to a specific linguistic abnormality. Andreasen (1979a,b), Rochester and Martin (1979), and Gerson, Benson, and Frazier (1977) have all noted that disorganized speech occurs only in a small subset of schizophrenic patients and cannot be considered characteristic of schizophrenics as a whole.

The controversy over the relationship between schizophrenic language and aphasia raises several issues. How common is severely disorganized language in schizophrenia? Is the language abnormality due to a specific disruption in linguistic competence or is it due to an underlying cognitive abnormality that affects performance? If a defect in linguistic competence exists, is it in the syntactic, semantic, pragmatic, or discourse aspects of language? If a specific language deficit exists, can it be localized and mapped anatomically?

Unfortunately, most of the research to date on schizophrenic language and the aphasias has involved isolated studies of single cases or, at best, quite small samples. In our Iowa program for the study of abnormalities in language and communication, we have attempted to develop a comprehensive and systematic plan for defining and mapping these abnormalities. This plan has three phases:

> *Phase I:* Clinical description, involving definition of terms and determination of the frequency of disorganized language in a broad selection of psychotic patients.
>
> *Phase II:* Functional mapping of abnormalities in order to determine if specific deficits in linguistic competence occur.
>
> *Phase III:* Neurological and anatomical mapping in order to determine whether severely disorganized speech can be related to specific brain abnormalities.

PHASE I:
CLINICAL DESCRIPTION

In spite of decades of interest in "thought disorder" in schizophrenia, little emphasis has been placed on careful clinical description. Clinicians and researchers have used such traditional terms as "loose associations" in a relatively imprecise and nonstandarized way, making communication difficult and research nearly impossible. The first phase of our work thus involved the development of simple, but comprehensive definitions of terms or concepts commonly used to describe language abnormalities in the major psychoses. These are contained in the Scale for the Assessment of Thought, Language, and Communication (TLC), a 20-item scale containing definitions and instructions for rating such abnormalities as pressured speech, tangentiality, derailment (loose associations), incoherence, and neologisms.

The initial results of our work with this scale are summarized in Table 6-1. Contrary to traditional pessimism concerning the poor reliability of

TABLE 6-1.

RELIABILITY AND FREQUENCY OF TYPES OF THOUGHT-LANGUAGE-
COMMUNICATION DISORDER IN PSYCHIATRIC PATIENTS

TLC Disorder	Reliability (full scale weighted kappa) (n = 113)	Frequency (%)[a]		
		Manics (n = 32)	Depres- sives (n = 36)	Schizo- phrenics (n = 45)
Poverty of speech	.81	6	22	29
Poverty of content of speech	.77	19	17	40
Pressure of speech	.89	72	6	27
Distractible speech	.78	31	0	2
Tangentiality	.58	34	25	36
Derailment	.83	56	14	56
Incoherence	.88	16	0	16
Illogicality	.80	25	0	27
Clanging	.58	9	0	0
Neologisms	.39	3	0	2
Circumstantiality	.74	25	31	4
Loss of goal	.70	44	17	44
Perseveration	.74	34	6	24
Echolalia	.59	3	0	4
Blocking	.79	3	6	4
Global ratings		88	53	91

[a] Based on ratings > 1 on the TLC Scale.

rating thought and language, it was possible to achieve good to excellent reliability through careful definition of terms and an emphasis on empirical or behavioral observation. Several other findings are also notable. Derailment is equally common in mania and schizophrenia. Incoherence, or severely disorganized speech, which might be comparable to aphasia, is relatively uncommon, but does occur in 16% of both manics and schizophrenics. Longitudinal followup under way indicates, however, that the incoherence in these two groups has a different course, with nearly all manics returning to normal speech after recovery, whereas the abnormality persists in some schizophrenics, suggesting a different mechanism for the incoherence in these two groups of patients. Neologisms and blocking, sometimes described as common abnormalities in schizophrenia, are quite infrequent.

Although the data seemed to suggest initially that "thought disorder" or disorganized speech occurred in all three major psychoses, and therefore that it lacked diagnostic specificity, we were interested in determining whether specific patterns of abnormality were useful in diagnosis. We compared two different patterns in a multivariate analysis of variance. Pattern 1 gave an equal positive weighting to five common types of abnormality usually subsumed under the concent of loose associations: tangentiality, derailment, clanging, incoherence, and illogicality. No significant differences were found between the manics and schizophrenics when this pattern was applied. Pattern 2 involved dividing the abnormalities into two groups, positive symptoms and negative symptoms, which were given equal positive and negative weightings. Positive symptoms included pressured speech, tangentiality, incoherence, derailment, and illogicality, whereas negative symptoms included poverty of speech and poverty of content of speech. This pattern was quite useful in differentiating between manics and schizophrenics, yielding an F ratio significant at the .05 level. These results stress the importance of defining specific types of disorganized speech or "thought disorder," rather than simply using a global concept.

PHASE II:
MAPPING OF FUNCTIONAL ABNORMALITIES

Study of the psychology of language, or psycholinguistics, provides us with a set of terms and concepts that are quite useful for the investigation of language abnormalities in schizophrenia. These concepts can be used to divide language behavior into four components and are therefore of value for mapping the specific nature of language abnormalities.

> *The syntactic component:* The rules governing the ordering of words and the establishment of relationships between them (e.g., subject–verb–object).
> *The semantic component:* The rules governing the interpretation of the meaning of individual words.
> *The discourse component:* The set of rules governing the manner in

which sentences may be combined to construct an idea set or a story.

The pragmatic component: The set of rules governing the use of sentences to accomplish specific intents, such as to request or to inform, and the rules governing the use of sentences as a function of social interaction.

All these components are of interest in the study of schizophrenic language abnormalities. The semantic and syntactic components are easiest to study experimentally, but the discourse and pragmatic components are also of great interest.

Two additional aspects of language function are also quite important. One is the distinction between language perception and processing versus language production. As in some types of aphasia, it is quite possible that a speaker may be relatively competent in hearing and understanding language, but speak in a very disorganized manner. A second important aspect is the longitudinal observation of language abnormality, since abnormalities that are transient or reversible suggest a different mechanism than those that are chronic or irreversible.

Although our program is being applied to assess all aspects of language in schizophrenia, at the moment we have only preliminary data on some aspects. We have hypothesized that the schizophrenic is able to perceive and process language normally in terms of both the syntactic and semantic components. We predict that the major abnormality will be in language production, rather than perception and processing, and that this abnormality in production will include the semantic, discourse, and pragmatic components. We predict that the abnormalities will be reversible in some patients and irreversible in others, with irreversibility being correlated with greater disorganization at index evaluation. Our preliminary data confirm some of these hypotheses.

Our assessment of the syntactic and semantic components of language borrows two paradigms developed by psycholinguists to study language functions in normal individuals.

The Click Task is designed primarily to assess perception and processing of the syntactical components of language. Repeatedly, studies have indicated that normal individuals, when listening to sentences containing embedded clicks, tend to report hearing these clicks closer to syntactical boundaries than the clicks actually occur (Fodor and Bever, 1965). Subjects listen to sentences such as the following:

In order to catch the train, George rushed furiously to the station.

In this sentence, the syntactical boundary, or end of the clause, occurs after "train." A click might be embedded in the words "catch," "the," "rushed," or "furiously." Asked where they hear the click embedded, normal listeners are likely to report hearing it instead in the word "train," in the pause, or in the word "George." Psycholinguists believe that this phenomenon indicates that normal listeners tend to process language as syntactical units. Several previous studies have used this paradigm to study syntactical processing in schizophrenics and have demonstrated that schizophrenics are also prone to displace clicks to syntactical boundaries, which suggests that schizophrenics are competent in the syntactical processing of language (Carpenter, 1976; Rochester, Harris, and Seaman, 1973).

The Gist Task, designed to assess semantic aspects of language perception and processing, was also developed initially in order to study language functions in normal individuals (Bransford and Franks, 1971). This task requires that subjects listen to a series of sentences and later indicate whether they have heard them before. Sample sentences appear in Table 6-2. During the acquisition phase, subjects are never given sentences like the first sentence on the list, which contains four ideas. Instead, they are given sentences containing only one idea (such as those at the bottom of the table), two ideas, or three ideas. When later asked if they recognize sentences that they have heard previously, normal subjects typically report having heard the longer and more complete sentences containing four ideas, even though they did not actually hear them. This tendency to recognize and group together in memory a set of related concepts is called the Gist Effect.

These two tasks, the Click Task and the Gist Task, are useful methods for assessing syntactical and semantic aspects of language in schizophrenic patients. In administering these tasks, we introduced a useful innovation developed by Chapman and Chapman (1973), the Matched Task Design. Since the performance of schizophrenic patients in many cognitive tasks is often impaired because of inattentiveness, apathy, or other factors, they typically perform more poorly on most tasks than a matched control group. Chapman and Chapman's innovation involves matching tasks rather than subjects. When an experimental and a control task are matched psychometrically on level of difficulty and internal consistency (as measured by Cronbach's alpha), other extraneous cognitive factors, such as inattentiveness, are controlled for, and it is possible to determine whether a specific differential deficit in a given area occurs. In our studies of language, the Gist Task and the Click Task were treated

TABLE 6-2.
THE "GIST" TASK

FOUR:	The ants in the kitchen ate the sweet jelly which was on the table. (On Recognition Only)
THREES:	The ants ate the sweet jelly which was on the table (On Acquisition Only) The ants in the kitchen ate the jelly which was on the table. (On Acquisition Only) The ants in the kitchen ate the sweet jelly. (On Recognition Only)
TWOS:	The ants in the kitchen ate the jelly. (On Acquisition Only) The ants ate the sweet jelly. (On Both Acquisition and Recognition) The sweet jelly was on the table. (On Recognition Only) The ants ate the jelly which was on the table. (On Recognition Only)
ONES:	The ants were in the kitchen. (On Acquisition Only) The jelly was on the table. (On Acquisition Only) The jelly was sweet. (On Recognition Only) The ants ate the jelly. (On Recognition Only)

as experimental tasks and were matched with a digit span task that served as the control task.

Preliminary results from our testing of the first 54 subjects, reported as Z-scores, appear in Tables 6-2 and 6-3. Table 6-3 compares three patient groups, schizophrenics, manics, and schizoaffectives, on the Click Task and the control task. All three groups performed slightly better on the Click Task than on the control task, and the schizophrenics performed significantly better. This suggests that their ability to perceive and process language is syntactically intact. Table 6-4 compares the performance of the three patient groups on the Gist Task versus the control task. Again, the patient groups found the semantic memory tasks easier than the control task, and the schizophrenics and manics performed sig-

TABLE 6-3.

Z SCORES FOR CLICK AND CONTROL TASKS IN SCHIZOPHRENICS, MANICS, AND SCHIZOAFFECTIVES

	Click		Control			
	$\bar{x}$	S.D.	$\bar{x}$	S.D.	t	p
Schizophrenics (n = 24)	.180	1.561	−.562	.562	2.19	.05
Manics (n = 19)	.616	1.296	−.337	.764	−.825	NS
Schizoaffectives (n = 11)	.528	1.782	−.494	.678	1.75	NS

TABLE 6-4.

Z SCORES FOR GIST AND CONTROL TASKS IN MANICS, SCHIZOPHRENICS, AND SCHIZOAFFECTIVES

	Gist		Control			
	$\bar{x}$	S.D.	$\bar{x}$	S.D.	t	p
Schizophrenics (n = 24)	.282	1.268	−.754	.829	3.21	.01
Manics (n = 19)	.730	1.186	−.531	.873	3.51	.01
Schizoaffectives (n = 11)	.360	.913	−.478	1.180	1.60	NS

nificantly better on the Gist Task, suggesting that their semantic functions are intact. The implications of these findings will warrant further discussion when the full sample of 125 subjects is completed, since one wonders why schizophrenics consistently perform more poorly on the digit span task. Nevertheless, it is quite clear from these data that none of the patient groups has a specific differential deficit in syntactical or sematic aspects of language perception and processing. Each group finds language tasks easier to perform than non-language tasks.

The other major aspect of language function is language production. It is in this area that schizophrenics are probably most impaired. Unfortunately, this aspect of language is quite difficult to study experimentally or quantitatively. Nevertheless, several lines of evidence converge on the suggestion that language production is the major abnormality in schizophrenia. First, clinical ratings using the TLC Scale revealed many abnormalities in spontaneous speech, including poverty of speech, poverty of content, derailment, tangentiality, and incoherence. A review of the tape recordings and transcriptions of our extensive speech samples indicates that sentences were almost invariably syntactically well formed. Disturbances such as incoherence sometimes reflect an abnormality in semantic aspects of language use. Other abnormalities, such as derailment or tangentiality, suggest an abnormality in discourse or pragmatic aspects of language. Schizophrenic patients do not tie their sentences together cohesively, do not provide clues to the listener that they are changing topics, and do not answer the questions they are asked. In addition, Rochester and Martin (1979), who developed several methods for quantitatively measuring cohesion in discourse, found that a subset of schizophrenic patients had fewer cohesive ties, which further points to language production, and specifically to discourse, as a major area of abnormality in schizophrenia.

In summary, preliminary studies of functional mapping suggest several conclusions. Since schizophrenics tend to perform poorly on nearly all the tasks they are given, it is noteworthy that they are able to perform well on two tasks designed to measure their competence in processing language syntactically and semantically. These results confirm the common clinical impression that schizophrenic patients usually are able to understand what is said to them. On the other hand, in such patients, the production of language is often quite disorganized. We are still in the process of mapping the specific functions that are disorganized. Preliminary work suggests that semantic, discourse, and pragmatic aspects of language are the major areas of abnormality.

PHASE III:
NEUROLOGICAL AND ANATOMICAL MAPPING

The mapping of abnormalities of language function, as defined by psycholinguists, is a valuable descriptive exercise. Comparison of abnormalities in schizophrenic language with the aphasias also provides useful insights, since areas of anatomical abnormality have been at least partially mapped for the aphasias.

Although the classification and localization of the various aphasias is still a matter of controversy, six different disorders are usually recognized. *Broca's aphasia* is characterized by nonfluent speech that tends to be telegraphic, with a relatively well-preserved comprehension, greater ease in repetition than in spontaneous speech, phonemic paraphasias, and relatively well localized lesions in the third frontal convolution. *Wernicke's aphasia* is characterized by fluent speech, with many semantic paraphasias, impaired comprehension, impaired naming or word finding, and lesions in the posterior one-third of the superior temporal gyrus. *Anomic aphasia* is characterized by a relatively fluent speech that may show poverty of content, word finding difficulties, a deficit in naming, occasional semantic paraphasias, and a poorly localized but often small area of involvement of the posterior parietal and temporal regions. *Conduction aphasia* is characterized by speech that is variable in fluency, with good comprehension, markedly poor repetition, and lesions located between Wernicke's and Broca's areas. *Transcortical aphasia* is characterized by speech that tends to be variable in fluency, but typically echolalic, with repetition relatively better than all other language functions, poor comprehension, and a variable location of lesions. *Global aphasia* is characterized by marked impairment of all speech functions, with large diffuse lesions occurring in both the anterior and posterior language areas.

The speech of many schizophrenic patients tends to be relatively normal. Only a subset of patients shows abnormalities, and only a small group has abnormalities similar to the aphasias. Three types of language abnormalities tend to occur with relative frequency. Poverty of speech occurs in approximately 30% of patients and is characterized by a small output of speech that is syntactically and semantically intact. Although schizophrenic poverty of speech resembles Broca's aphasia because of impaired fluency, resemblances in other significant respects do not occur, making localization in Broca's area extremely unlikely. If one were to attempt to localize this syndrome, one would be more likely to think of lesions in the frontal region leading to symptoms of mutism, akinesis, and apathy. A subcortical localization is another possibility.

Approximately 40% of schizophrenic patients display impoverished content of speech, although in many cases it may be quite mild. This syndrome is reminiscent of transcortical aphasia. Patients with marked poverty of content display speech that is repetitive and stereotyped and that has an echolalic quality to it. They are typically quite fluent.

Only 16% of schizophrenic patients display incoherent speech, which may be highly reminiscent of Wernicke's aphasia. Such patients manifest fluent speech that is syntactically well formed, but that gives the overall impression of nonsensical jargon. The nonsensical impression is usually given by paraphasic-like semantic substitutions of words and phrases and a tendency to string words together on the basis of phonological or semantic relationships rather than topical relationships. These patients seem to show little awareness of their deficit.

Because language functions are relatively well localized in the brain, classification of schizophrenic patients based primarily on language abnormalities may be a useful method for studying brain dysfunction in schizophrenia. We are attempting to determine whether any of these syndromes of abnormal language behavior can be related to specific abnormalities on either neuropsychological tests or by CAT scanning.

ACKNOWLEDGMENTS

This research was supported in part by NIMH Grant MH 31593.

REFERENCES

Andreasen, N. C. (1979a). Thought, language, and communication disorders. I. Clinical assessment, definition of terms, and evaluation of their reliability. *Arch. Gen. Psychiat.* 36, 1315–1321.

Andreasen, N. C. (1979b). Thought, language, and communication disorders. II. Diagnostic significance. *Arch. Gen. Psychiat.* 36, 1325–1330.

Bleuler, E. (1950). *Dementia Praecox or the Group of Schizophrenia* (J. Zinkin, (trans). International Universities Press, New York.

Bransford, J. D., and J. J. Franks (1971). The abstraction of linguistic ideas. *Cognitive Psychol.* 2, 331–350.

Carpenter, M. D. (1976). Sensitivity to syntactic structure: Good versus poor premorbid schizophrenics. *J. Abnorm. Psychol.* 85, 41–50.

Chaika, E. (1974). A linguist looks at "schizophrenic" language. *Brain and Language* 1, 257–276.

Chapman, L. J., and J. P. Chapman (1973). Problems in the measurement of cognitive deficit. *Psychol. Bull.* 79, 380–385.

Crowe, T. J. (1980). Molecular pathology of schizophrenia: More than one disease process? *Brit. Med. J.* 280, 1–9.

Fodor, J. A., and T. G. Bever (1965). The psychological reality of linguistic segments. *J. Verbal Learning Verbal Behav.* 4, 414–420.

Fromkin, B. (1975). A linguist looks at "a linguist looks at 'schizophrenic' language." *Brain and Language* 2, 498–503.

Freud, S. (1966). *The Standard Edition of the Complete Psychological Works of Sigmund Freud*, Vol. I J. Strachey (trans. and ed.). London: The Hogarth Press, pp. 283–387.

Gerson, S. N., F. Benson and S. H. Frazier (1977). Diagnosis: Schizophrenia versus posterior aphasia. *Amer. J. Psychiat.* 134, 966–969.

Golden, C. J., J. A. Moses, P. Zelazowski, B. Graber, L. M. Zatz, T. B. Horvath, and P. A. Berger (1980). Cerebral ventricular size and neuropsychological impairment in young chronic schizophrenics. *Arch. Gen. Psychiat.* 37, 619–623.

Gruzelier, J., and P. Flor-Henry (eds.) (1979). *Hemisphere Asymmetries of Function in Psychopathology*. Elsevier/North Holland, Amsterdam.

Kleist, K. K. (1969). Schizophrenic symptoms and cerebral pathology. *J. Ment. Sci.* 106, 246–255.

Kraepelin, E. (1919). *Dementia Praecox and Paraphrenia* (R. M. Barclay trans. and ed.). E. & S. Livingstone, Edinburgh.

Le Cours, A. R., and M. Vanier-Clément (1976). Schizophasia and jargonaphasia. *Brain and Language* 3, 516–565.

Rochester, S. R., and J. R. Martin (1979). *Crazy Talk: A Study of the Discourse of Schizophrenic Speakers*. Plenum Press, New York.

Rochester, S. R., J. Harris and M. V. Seaman (1973). Sentence processing in schizophrenic listeners. *J. Abnorm. Psychol.* 82, 350–356.

Snyder, S. H., D. Greenberg, and M. I. Yamamura (1974). Antischizophrenic drugs and brain cholinergic receptors. *Arch. Gen. Psychiat.* 31, 58–61.

Van Praag, H. M. (1977). The significance of dopamine for motive action of neuroleptics and the pathogenesis of schizophrenia. *Brit. J. Psychiat.* 130, 463–474.

Weinberger, D. R., L. B. Bigelow, J. E. Kleinman, S. T. Klein, J. E. Rosenblatt and R. J. Wyatt (1980a). Cerebral ventricular enlargement in chronic schizophrenia. *Arch. Gen. Psxychiat.* 37, 11–13.

Weinberger, D. R., E. F. Torrey, A. N. Neophytides and R. J. Wyatt (1980b). Lateral cerebral ventricular enlargement in chronic schizophrenia. *Arch. Gen. Psychiat.* 36, 735–739.

7 | Neurology and Neuropathology of Schizophrenia

JANICE R. STEVENS

> It is uncontroversial that in the brain of schizophrenics have been found
> different kinds of histopathologic alterations; however these alterations
> cannot be considered rigorously specific of the disease but they are une-
> quivocal evidence of an ongoing organic process. Therefore, schizophrenia
> is not to be considered any more a psychodegenerative or psychogenic
> illness but a true organic disease of the nervous system.
>
> Longo (1952)

The success of modern pharmacological treatment of schizophrenia
supports Longo's conclusion. Clinical improvement of most patients with
schizophrenic psychoses following treatment with neuroleptic medication is similar to that achieved by medical treatment of many neurological disorders of unknown cause, e.g., Parkinson's disease and epilepsy.
Although still lacking a pathology, the clinical course and unequivocal
response of acute schizophrenic symptoms to a specific group of pharmacological agents suggest that a true encephalopathy underlies the disorder. The serious sequelae of the illness for at least one-half of those
affected stimulate efforts to understand the etiology of this common major mental illness. One aspect of that search is the attempt to determine
those essential characteristics of the schizophrenic syndrome that point
to possible cerebral substrates for the pathology and disturbed physiology. Study of the mental history, mental state, neurological history, and
behavior of individuals with schizophrenia allows a constellation of
symptoms and signs to emerge that direct attention to specific areas of
the brain subserving these functions. To assign the complex symptoms
and signs of schizophrenic illness to specific structures or regions may
seem both simplistic and premature. However, I ask the reader's indulg-

ence as we embark on such an effort, cast previous suppositions concerning etiology temporarily aside, and attempt to approach the schizophrenic psychoses as a direct neurological problem of cerebral localization. As in the focal epilepsies and other localized brain disorders, we may anticipate that by listening to the patient and closely observing his behavior we may determine where (but not why, as was the goal of conventional psychodynamic investigation) his illness arises.

PERCEPTUAL DISTURBANCES

Auditory, visual, olfactory, somatosensory, and visceral hallucinations, alterations in the signaling value of banal stimuli, and nameless fear or strangeness experienced by most schizophrenic patients are so frequently expressed in the auras of patients with temporal lobe epilepsy as to suggest involvement of similar limbic structures in both disorders. Disturbances in accurate signaling and interpretation of social cues and of social bonding follows removal of the entorhinal cortex and amygdala in free-living monkeys and leads to isolation and apathy, the description of which are strikingly reminiscent of the schizophrenic deficit state (Kling, Lancaster, and Benitone, 1970). Schizophrenics also report a variety of strange, often frightening, but occasionally pleasurable internal sensations, many of which have been elicited by stimulation of amygdala, septum, thalamic, and midbrain sites in man (Heath, 1954; Nashold, Wilson, and Slaughter, 1969a; Mark and Ervin, 1970; Stevens et al., 1969). Changes in sleep, appetite, menstrual cycle, and sexual perception early in the illness direct attention to the hypothalamus and other subcortical areas.

It appears that the pathology underlying the acute psychotic stages of schizophrenic illness allows a continuous barrage of auditory, visual, tactile, and even olfactory perceptions—symptoms associated with excitation of the temporal lobe and basal forebrain.

Case 1: A 19-year-old boy was admitted to the acute treatment ward by the police after threatening an officer who tried to question him. For several months he had been living alone in the woods. In the hospital, he appeared terrified and hid under the blankets. As we gained his confidence, he related hearing voices calling him "queer" and the "queen of Ulster" in a derogatory fashion. Neurological examination revealed absent glabellar reflex, frequent lateral glances, spontaneous paroxysmal blinking, occasional grimacing or *schnauzkrampf*, and asymmetrical plantar reflexes. Following four days' treatment with haloperidol, auditory hallucination, extraocular signs, and reflex asymmetry disappeared.

Both the frightening voices and the facial and ocular movements were abolished by the dopamine(DA)-blocking agent haloperidol, suggesting that these signs and symptoms are mediated by DA pathways modulating fear and the auditory and extraocular systems. Residual defects of will, social bonding, and cognitive abilities remained unchanged, suggesting fixed or non-DA-mediated pathology as a basis for these signs.

NEUROLOGICAL EXAMINATION

AUTOMATISMS AND STEREOTYPIES

Although neurological examination may reveal minor asymmetries of reflexes in schizophrenic patients, the conventional examination of patients with this disorder yields rather little if one depends on data obtained with the reflex hammer, ophthalmoscope, and tuning fork, the classic armamenteria of the neurologist. Unobtrusive observation yields much more. Patients with schizophrenia exhibit posturing; blinking; stillness and fixity of gaze; "checking"; circus movements; stereotyped automatisms of rubbing, rocking, and pacing; mirror pantomime; muttering; and ritual, many of which resemble the automatisms of psychomotor epilepsy. However, in sharp contrast to the latter, the staring and automatisms of schizophrenia can nearly always be interrupted, and there is neither amnesia for the motor act nor for words the examiner may direct to the patient during the abnormal behavior.

> Case 2: A 29-year-old native of the Virgin Islands, hospitalized since age 21 for catatonic schizophrenia, sat in the dayroom of his ward for hours mute, staring straight ahead, listening to continuous auditory hallucinations. At irregular intervals of 20 to 30 minutes he suddenly began to breathe rapidly and deeply, then blinked paroxysmally at rates up to three

per second for 10 to 15 seconds, muttered in Spanish, stood, threw his head back, and seemed to be praying. After 35 seconds he hitched up his belt, tucked his shirt more deeply in his trousers, took a deep breath, walked rapidly across the ward to the water fountain where he drank long and thirstily. Without looking to the right or left, he then returned to his accustomed chair in the dayroom and once again sat staring and mute until the next episode 20 to 30 minutes later. At any time during this elaborate ritual he could be interrupted, when he smiled gently and replied "nothing" to queries about what was going on. An electroencephalogram disclosed random spike activity over the right temporal lobe. Addition of diphenylhydantoin (300 mg a day) to his antipsychotic medications caused a decrease in the automatisms and blink rate, but a deterioration of his psychic condition. He lay on his bed mute and uncommunicative with bouts of talking to voices or bursts of high-pitched hyena-like laughter. When distracted from his preoccupation with internal stimuli, he was found to be oriented for person, place, and date. He replied to all other questions with "yes," "no," meaningless monosyllables, or mysterious hand signals. He was able to read, write, and follow one-step, but not two-step commands. He placed only three shapes in the Seguin formboard in one minute and would not attempt more complex tasks. Over a five-year period he showed little response to neuroleptics or efforts to engage him in social, industrial, and recreational activities on or off the hospital ward.

Although this patient's elaborate rituals or automatisms, which superficially resembled psychomotor seizures, decreased with anticonvulsant treatment, his general condition became worse. This has been our experience with other patients with clinical schizophrenia and suggest that if the EEG spike reflects pathological discharge, the neuronal structures involved are different than those responsible for epilepsy.

MOTOR DISTURBANCES

Catatonia

This curious state of waxy flexibility is usually accompanied by mutism, immobility, stupor, or excitement. Catatonia is not specific for schizophrenia, but is found in a number of recognized neurological entities with known pathology, as well as in manic-depressive illness. Not uncommon with von Economo's encephalitis, catatonia has also been reported in patients with other viral encephalitides that attack the basal ganglia and midbrain. Catatonia can be a manifestation of bilateral lesions of the globus pallidus (Mettler and Crandell, 1959) and is induced by several pharmacological agents, including amphetamine, bulbocapnine, and most recently, endorphins (de Jong, 1945; Powers, 1976; Bloom et al., 1976). As will be seen below, catatonic schizophrenia is associated with a more specific anatomical pathology than any other subtype, namely, neuronal loss in the globus pallidus.

Tics

Choreiform movements, particularly of the face, were described in dementia praecox by Kraepelin (1919) and others long before the era of phenothiazines and tardive dyskinesia. Yarden and Discipio (1971) noted that dyskinesias in young schizophrenic patients were associated with a progressive dementing course of the illness regardless of treatment. Facial dyskinesias prior to all treatment in the patient discussed above suggest involvement of rostro-medial regions of the extrapyramidal system or its projections. Pretreatment dyskinesias may thus be indicative of more extensive cerebral pathology or dysfunction than in schizophrenic syndromes free of these motor disturbances. The findings may thus relate to the poor prognosis reported for schizophrenia accompanied by ventricular dilation (Jacobi and Winkler, 1927; Johnstone et al., 1976; Weinberger et al. 1980). In contrast to the dementias accompanied by gross cerebral atrophy, patients with chronic schizophrenia often retain islands of more normal behavior, suggesting that elements of the intellect and affective life remain obscured or swamped by "cerebral noise," but are not altogether lacking.

Eye Signs

The most consistent neurological signs beyond the abnormalities of the mental state found in both early and late schizophrenia are in the domain of ocular movement. Since pseudo-Parkinsonism, induced by neuroleptic agents, and tardive dyskinesias following prolonged use or withdrawal of such agents may be associated with eye signs, neurological evaluation should precede initiation of drug treatment (Stevens, 1978). The signs noted below are not diagnostic of schizophrenia, but one or more of them can usually be found in nearly every case examined. For this reason they are useful in supporting the diagnosis and potentially useful for leading to a better understanding of the cerebral systems affected by this disorder.

Eye contact: Absence and avoidance of eye contact and *staring* for long periods into space are the most common ocular signs observed in schizophrenic patients. Similar staring is commonly observed as the very first indication of a seizure arising in the amygdala in man and animals, but may also be the only sign of petit mal epilepsy. In the latter, in contrast to amygdala seizures and schizophrenia, a characteristic cortical EEG discharge is always present.

Blink rate: Most normal adults blink six to 12 times per minute (Zametkin, Stevens, and Pittman, 1979). Nearly one-half of the patients with acute untreated schizophrenia have decreased, increased, or paroxysmal bouts of rapid blinking. In patients with chronic schizophrenia, steady rhythmic blinking at 60 to 80 times a minute is not uncommon. Such patients appear mute and preoccupied or distracted. In contrast to petit mal or psychomotor seizures, during which similar episodes of blinking may occur, such events can be readily interrupted in schizophrenic patients and the patient can retain information given during the episode (Stevens, 1978; Stevens et al., 1979).

Although cerebral centers responsible for maintenance or modulation of spontaneous blinking are not known, rhythmic blinking can be elicited by stimulation in the nucleus accumbens and the midbrain during kindled convulsions from the amygdala (Sato, 1977; Nashold, Slaughter, and Gill, 1969b; Herishanu, 1973) and following intravenous amphetamines (personal observations).

Glabellar reflex: This reflex is elicited while the examiner stands behind the subject so the tapping finger is not visible. The examiner taps the index or middle finger lightly on the patient's forehead just above the nasion. Most normal individuals blink in response to a light tap at the first stimulus. Repeated taps at intervals of about one per second elicit full blinks up to three to five successive taps, after which the reflex is extinguished. The blink reflex to even the first glabellar tap is often absent in acute untreated schizophrenics. In contrast, patients with central DA depletion (as in Parkinson's disease) or patients receiving neuroleptic DA-blocking agents, usually fail to habituate the glabellar reflex and display untiring blinks to repeated glabellar taps. Since persistence of the blink reflex (but decreased or absent spontaneous blinking) is usually an early index of DA depletion or blockade, absence of the glabellar reflex prior to treatment may be a sign of DA hypersensitivity or hyperactivity in systems inhibiting the blink reflex.

Episodic lateral deviation of the eyes: Repeated brief, sudden lateral deviation of the eyes to either side accompanied by arrest of speech or attention is a common sign in early schizophrenia. For several seconds, the eyes may remain sharply deviated laterally or laterally and downward. Deviation to the right is more common than to the left. Darting to-and-fro movements suggest searching behavior. In advanced chronic schizophrenia, these lateral head and eye movements may become an almost continual back-and-forth scanning. Similar eye movements are elicited in cats and monkeys by small amounts of amphetamine or apomorphine. These signs are usually the first to disappear following initiation of DA-blocking neuroleptic treatment, suggesting that they are mediated or activated by overactivity in a cerebral DA system. Both lateral glances and rapid horizontal movements of the eyes were observed in cats following placement of the GABA antagonist bicuculline in the ventral tegmental area of the mesencephalon, origin of the mesolimbic DA system (Stevens et al., 1974). Contraversive turning of the head and eyes also follows electrical stimulation of cortical area 8, the visual cortex (area 19), amygdala, substantia innominata, and midbrain tegmentum.

Paroxysmal saccadic eye movements: Episodic spontaneous lateral nystagmoid oscillations of the eyes are seen principally in untreated patients. As noted by Wallach and Wallach (1964), they may be accompanied by feelings of bodily disintegration.

> Case 3: A 26-year-old unmarried woman was admitted to hospital for long-standing isolation, autism, idleness, and sleeplessness. On admission she was mute, staring, fearful, suspicious, and hostile. Her eyes darted from side to side in a searching fashion. When they came to rest in mid-position, there were long pauses in speech during which there were coarse horizontal nystagmoid saccades. During one such episode the patient screamed that she was "falling apart" and begged someone to "hold me together." All these ocular signs rapidly disappeared following initiation of treatment with low doses of chlorpromazine, although suspiciousness, hostility, fearfulness, and isolation continued until more potent neuroleptics were used.

Interruption of smooth ocular pursuit movements: Jerky saccades during ocular pursuit were reported over 70 years ago in schizophrenic patients by Diefendorf and Dodge (1908). This sign has been investigated extensively by Holzman, Proctor, and Hughes (1973). Shagass, Amadeo, and Overton (1976) suggest that loss of smooth pursuit is closely related to a defect in attention. This sign is also found in neurological disorders affecting the midbrain tegmentum and basal ganglia, e.g., Parkinson's disease and multiple sclerosis.

Inability to move the eyes without moving the head: Commonly observed in patients with chronic schizophrenia, as well as in individuals with mental retardation, Parkinsonism, and dementia, this sign can often be overcome by repeated practice in all but the most chronic or deteriorated schizophrenic patients.

Inability to converge: Inability to converge with both eyes in the presence of intact adduction on lateral gaze is present in approximately one-quarter of patients with acute and one-half of patients with chronic schizophrenia. This was also the most common neurological sign observed among children with psychoses and is frequent in adults with post-encephalitic Parkinson's disease. To rule out a simple attention deficit, it is necessary to attempt to elicit convergence repeatedly and vigorously. To demonstrate intact muscle integrity and cooperation, the eyes must adduct during lateral gaze. To supplement visual cues with kinesthetic stimuli, the patient should be urged to converge on his own finger. Only when all these tests fail to elicit convergence is this sign considered positive and thus suggestive of abnormality of the mesencephalon near the midline, implicating the oculomotor convergence center just beneath the cerebral aqueduct.

Pupillary inequality: Kraepelin (1919) described both inequal and dilated pupils in patients with dementia praecox. In my experience, inequality is rare, but dilated pupils are common during acute psychosis. Pupils that respond poorly to light are common in both acute and chronic schizophrenia, implicating retino-tectal and sympathetic pathway involvement.

Elevation of the brows and horizontal creasing of the forehead: While not strictly an extraocular sign, this striking facial mannerism lends to the eyes an unusually wide-open protuberant appearance and gives the face an expression of extreme alertness or perplexity. Like pupillary dilation, this sign is associated with extreme arousal. In the monkey, a similar expression follows administration of amphetamine and is associated with excitement and threatening behavior.

Many of the ocular signs noted, but especially the stare, conjugate deviation of the eyes, and adversive movement of head and eyes are frequent accompaniments of psychomotor seizures and can be evoked by stimulation of the amygdala, nucleus accumbens, and substantia innominata (MacLean et al., 1955; Hunsperger and Bucher, 1967).

DISTURBANCES OF COGNITION, THOUGHT, AND DRIVE

Patients with long-standing chronic schizophrenia display striking deficits, including apathy, disordered attention, poor recent memory, inability to calculate, read, or do much more than eat, sleep, pace the room, and eliminate. There is often striking loss of judgment, logic, and abstract abilities; mumbled dysarthric speech, with loss of tone and cadence; garbled sentences; neologisms; jargon; or word salad. Late in the illness, chronic patients can become mute or respond only in mumbled incomprehensible monosyllables. More often, loss of all initiative and lack of interest in cleanliness or human interaction supervene, requiring supervision in order to meet daily needs of nutrition and hygiene.

The schizophrenic thought disorder, although often cited as the single pathognomonic element of the syndrome, shares with other dementias and organic brain syndromes the characteristics of concreteness and tangentiality. Neither these signs nor the typical loosening of associations speech disturbances or overinclusive thinking appear to have specific localizing value in our present state of ignorance, but are usually associated with loss of cerebral tissue, enlargement of the ventricles, and cortical atrophy (Johnstone et al. 1976; Weinberger et al. 1979).

ELECTROENCEPHALOGRAM STUDIES

Although Heath (1954) and others have reported subcortical spike activity from deep structures of the limbic forebrain, caudate nucleus, and amygdala in patients with active schizophrenia, the scalp EEG seldom demonstrates these events. During the past 10 years we have recorded several hundred EEGs from schizophrenic patients, many of whom were medication-free or had never received neuroleptic drugs. As in the studies of others (e.g., Hill, 1952), scalp EEGs were abnormal in 25 to 35% of schizophrenic patients. Asymmetrical theta and sharp or spike activity in the mid- or posterior temporal regions were the most common findings in abnormal records. Mild diffuse slowing was more frequent in catatonia. Occasionally paroxysmal, high voltage rhythmic alpha activity occurred over one temporal lobe, suggesting underlying hypersynchrony or deep spike activity (Fig. 7-1). Spectral analysis of the scalp EEG re-

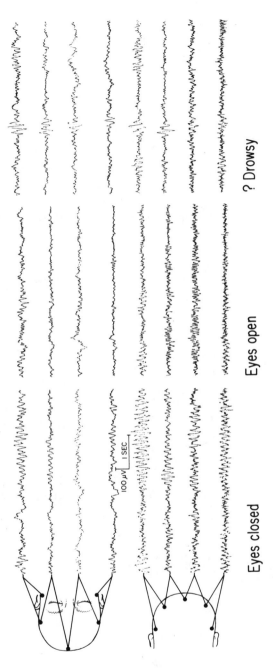

Eyes closed

Eyes open

? Drowsy

100 μV [1 SEC

FIGURE 7-1. Abnormal Brain Activity in Schizophrenics. Asymmetry of activity over the temporal regions is evident in the EEG of this 26-year-old woman (K. M.) with chronic paranoid schizophrenia who had not received neuroleptic medication at any time in the past. The amplitude of alpha activity over the left temporal region is three times higher than that over the right. When the eyes are open, left temporal activity becomes sharp and during drowsiness paroxysmal sharp and fast activity appears over the same regions. St. Elizabeth's Hospital (6/20/80)

121

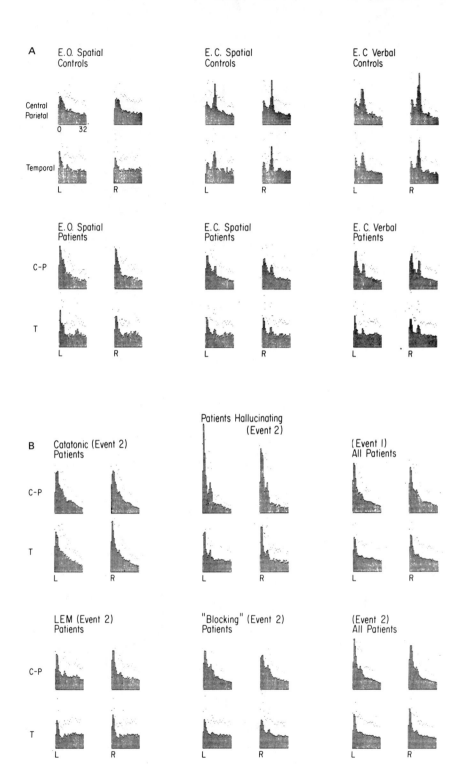

vealed more slow activity and less alpha activity in unmedicated schizophrenic subjects than in age-matched controls. Spectral analysis of telemetered EEGs recorded during hallucinated and catatonic episodes revealed a "ramp" spectrum, characterized by monotonic decline in power from the lowest to the highest frequency, a spectral profile similar to those obtained during remote spike activity in epileptic subjects (Stevens, 1976). This finding is consistent with Heath's observation and with limbic spike discharges recorded in animals with catatonia induced by opioids (Henriksen et al., 1978) (Fig. 7-2).

AN ANATOMY OF SCHIZOPHRENIA

The success of modern neuroleptic treatment of schizophrenia with DA-blocking agents led to the "dopamine hypothesis of schizophrenia" (Carlsson and Lindquist, 1963). Briefly stated, this hypothesis proposes that the symptoms of schizophrenia are related to hyperactivity or hypersensitivity of one or more DA systems of the brain (Horn and Snyder, 1971). In the brain, 85 to 95% of the DA axons terminate in the neostriatum and the limbic striatum. The similarity of many schizophrenic subjective symptoms and behaviors to the auras and automatisms of psychomotor epilepsy suggests that if there is pathological transmission in

FIGURE 7-2. Spectral Profiles in Schizophrenics. Pooled normalized average power spectra from central-parietal (C-P) and temporal (T) regions of the telemetered EEG are derived from 27 unmedicated schizophrenic patients during free behavior and during performance of visual and spatial tasks. (A) during verbal and spatial tasks for unmedicated schizophrenic and control subjects; (B) during abnormal behaviors of schizophrenics. Although delta peaks are generally prominent in both patient and control spectra, the ratio of delta to alpha activity is clearly larger for patients than controls and much larger for hallucinating patients than for any other group. This does not appear to be due to a greater blink or saccade predominance during hallucinations. *Ramp* spectra, characterized by the smooth decline of power from lowest to highest frequencies, associated with subcortical spike activity in epileptic animals and man, appear only during the catatonic state

cerebral DA systems in schizophrenia, it is most likely to occur in systems that receive projections from the amygdala and hippocampus, the most common foci for psychomotor epilepsy. As Walle Nauta (personal communications, 1971) first pointed out, there are striking parallels between the topographical projections of the neocortex to the caudate-putamen and of the amygdala, hippocampus, and pyriform cortex to the nucleus accumbens, olfactory tubercle, and bed nucleus of the stria terminalis, the major DA-receiving nuclei of the limbic striatum (Stevens, 1973). In further parallel, nuclei of the limbic striatum project both directly to the hypothalamus, thalamus, and midbrain and to a ventral pallidal region including the substantia innominata in a fashion analogous to the striatal projections to the thalamus, subthalamus, midbrain, and globus pallidus. In both striatal systems, there is a very high ratio of input (from widespread cortical and subcortical sites) to output. As a principal exit for the "DA-biased" limbic striatal "gate," the substantia innominata is of particular interest in the exploration of schizophrenic pathology.

The substantia innominata is a remarkable region, histologically, consisting of sheets of very large neurons (nucleus basalis), which in man appear much more numerous and are much more closely packed together than are the similar large neurons of the pallidum. The region is traversed by fiber projections between the entorhinal cortex-amygdala and the hypothalamus–septum–thalamus (the ventral amygdala–fugal pathway, diagonal band of Broca, lateral olfactory striae, and inferior thalamic peduncle). The substantia innominata also contains rostral fibers of the medial forebrain bundle, originating in the olfactory striae. Just as the neostriatum and the globus pallidus project to the ventral lateral thalamus, subthalamic nucleus, and substantia nigra, the substantia innominata neurons and fiber tracts project to the dorsal medial thalamus, hypothalamus, habenula, and ventral tegmentum (Heimer, 1978; Troiano and Siegel, 1978). Traversed or bounded by the major outflow pathways from the amygdala, hippocampus, and archicortex, the substantia innominata is a nodal point of converging information funneled from the wide sources of the limbic network to final paths of termination in the thalamus, frontal lobe, hypothalamus, and, ultimately, to the motor nuceli of the brainstem and spinal cord.

Bounded dorsally by the anterior commissure, globus pallidus, and ansa lenticularis, laterally by the junction of the amygdala and putamen, medially by the preoptic area of the hypothalamus, and inferiorally by the horizontal fibers of the olfactory striae and diagonal band that course unprotected by any cortical margin across the base of the forebrain, the substantia innominata merges anteriorally with the striatal-like structures of the olfactory tubercle in which lie the distinctive Islands of Calleja. Posteriorally the area merges into the interpeduncular fossa.

Kievit and Kuypers (1975) showed in the monkey that specific groups of large neurons in the substantia innominata project widely to all areas of the cerebral cortex. In the rat, Heimer (1978) has shown projections from individual groups of substantia innominata cells to the preoptic area, amygdala, and hippocampus, as well as a cholinergic projection to the entire cerebral mantle. Because of their strategic position at the apex of converging limbic inputs, the limbic striatum, the substantia innominata, and the hypothalamus are prime suspects in the investigation of the pathology of schizophrenia.

NEUROPATHOLOGICAL FINDINGS

By 1952, when many of the leading neuropathologists of the world met at the First International Congress of Neuropathology in Rome, more than 250 publications concerning the neuropathology of schizophrenia (or dementia praecox) had been published. However, the distinguished participants of the Congress reached no common agreement concerning pathological changes in the brain of schizophrenic patients. Indeed, there was a distinct difference of opinion between pathologists from Germany, France, and central Europe and those from the United States and the United Kingdom. The former group reported widespread degenerative neuronal changes in schizophrenic brains. These were generally relegated by American workers, and by Alfred Meyer of London, to agonal and postmortem effects or the results of aging. The Vogts (1952) reported on 35 brains studied by serial section. They found numerous changes (see Chapter 11). Meyer (1952) attributed many of the changes reported by the Vogts and their collaborators to nonspecific factors. Indeed, their studies, although monumental in scope and effort, are somewhat limited by their use of only Nissl and myelin stains. Recent histopathological studies from other laboratories, using other staining methods, add new information and redirect interest to the glial changes that caught the attention of a few early investigators. Nieto and Escobar (1972) found no important pathology in Nissl-stained sections of schizophrenic brains.

However, they reported that the silver carbonate stain for glia revealed diffuse gliosis in the diencephalon, septum, hypothalamus, and mesencephalic tegmentum of schizophrenic subjects. Also using other staining methods in addition to the Nissl, Fisman (1975) examined the brains of eight schizophrenic subjects (seven from patients over age 60; one age 42, but previously subjected to prefrontal lobotomy), 14 mental hospital controls (dementias and psychoses without hallucinations), and 10 brains from patients dying in a general hospital without nervous or mental disease. In his hands, the Nissl stain revealed cellular changes similar to those reported by the Vogts and their collaborators; these he considered due to aging. Using a glial stain, however, Fisman found multiple "glial knots" similar to those of viral encephalitis in the brainstem of six of eight schizophrenic brains examined and in only one mental hospital "control" subject. None of the brains from the general hospital patients showed similar changes.

The neuropathological study I have undertaken differs from those cited above because of the nature of the pathological material available and because clinical observations and pharmacological data led me to the hypothesis that the anatomical substrate of schizophrenia was probably closely related to the DA-receiving regions of the limbic forebrain or their projections. Accordingly, I have concentrated on examining pathological material from these regions. The hippocampus, amygdala, and pyriform cortex, sites of origin of most psychomotor seizures, and the corpus striatum and globus pallidus were also carefully scrutinized.

MATERIALS AND METHODS

Histological sections from 31 schizophrenic patients from 21 to 55 years of age, diagnosed, treated, and deceased at St. Elizabeth's Hospital, Washington, D.C., between 1955 and 1963 were examined. Material from six additional patients whose menal illness was diagnosed as schizophrenia, but who had a history of seizures, was also examined. Diagnosis of these patients was made by their ward physicians using the Kraepelinian subcategories of dementia praecox and DSM-I. Patients whose terminal illness or premorbid state included disorders that directly affect cerebral morphology (e.g., malignant hypertension, bacterial endocarditis, miliary tuberculosis, diabetes, uremia, lues, meningitis, or hepatic disease were excluded. Pathological sections from 13 nonschizophrenic patients hospitalized and deceased at Saint Elizabeth's Hospital during the same period, and ranging in age from 20 to 55 years, were intermingled with the schizophrenic material and examined by the author without knowledge of diagnosis. All sections examined were collected and previously described in routine autopsy reports and as part of an unpublished study of schizophrenia carried out by Meta Neuman, neuropathologist at the hospital from 1945 to 1979. In addition, Drs. Tom Kemper and Tom Gill, neuropathologists at Boston University and University of Oregon hospitals, also reported on this subject. The pathological findings reported in this chapter always include agreement between the observations of at least one of the above neuropathologists and the author.

Cases were included for this study only if sections of the basal ganglia, amygdala, thalamus, midbrain, hippocampus, and cerebellum were available. Hemotoxylin-eosin, myelin, Nissl, Holzer (glia), Bodian (axons, neuro-fibrillary changes) and PAS (Periodic-Acid-Schiff for mucopolysaccharide), and Perl's stain for iron were available for most cases. To determine the significance of findings observed or reported by other examiners, normal control material from three serially sectioned normal brains from individuals age 25, 32, and 45 years from the Yakovlev collection at the Armed Forces Institute of Pathology, Washington, D.C. was examined. Since the Yakovlev control brains are colloidin preparations, cut at 35μ and stained only by the Nissl and Weigert techniques, and since the St. Elizabeth's Hospital "control" brains were all from mentally ill individuals, further controls were prepared by obtaining sections of the basal ganglia, nucleus accumbens, amygdala, and hippocampus at levels identical to those from the St. Elizabeth's Hospital material from 20 consecutive autopsies of patients 10 to 55 years of age at the University of Oregon Health Sciences Center. An additional normal brain was contributed by Dr. Anthony d'Agostino of Good Samaritan Hospital, Portland, Oregon. These sections were stained with Nissl and hemotoxylin and eosin and by the PAS and Holzer techniques.

RESULTS

The data from examination of pathological material of 31 patients diagnosed as schizophrenic and six patients diagnosed as psychotic, schizophrenic, or paranoic, with epilepsy, were tabulated and analyzed according to the site and nature of the pathological findings and the

TABLE 7-1.
CLINICAL DIAGNOSTIC CATEGORIES FOR SEH[a] CASES

Catatonic
Conspicuous motor behavior either inhibitory (e.g., stupor) or excessive motor activity and excitement. May regress to a state of vegetation

Paranoid
Autistic, unrealistic thinking with mental content composed chiefly of ideas and delusions of persecution, grandeur, omnipotence, special ability, religiosity, and a prevailing mood of suspiciousness, hostility, or aggression

Hebephrenic
Shallow, inappropriate affect, unpredictable giggling, silly behavior, mannerisms, often somatic hallucinations and regressive behavior

Chronic Undifferentiated Schizophrenia
Mixed symptomatology, unclassifiable under one of the more specific categories above

---

[a] St. Elizabeth's Hospital classification 1925–1950. After Kraepelin (1919) and DSM-I.

Kraepelinian diagnostic subtype to which each patient was assigned by his physicians (Table 7-1).

Five general categories of pathology were identified in this material:

1. Cell (neuronal) loss
2. Beading or loss of myelin
3. Gliosis, as increase in number of astrocytes and/or glial fibrils
4. Infiltration of the corpora amylacea in unusual numbers or sites for age
5. Granular ependymitis, as formation of microscopic glial nodules on the surface of the ventricles or aqueduct with buried margin of ependymal epithelium beneath. Patches of denuded ependyma or glial nodules without buried ependymal cells are commonly found in the nonschizophrenic brains and were not included

Results of the pathological findings are summarized in Table 7-2 and Figure 7-3 and below.

Catatonics

As is evident from Table 7-1, in nearly one-half the patients diagnosed as catatonic schizophrenics, there was neuronal dropout, with axon or

TABLE 7-2.
NEUROPATHOLOGICAL FINDINGS IN SUBTYPES OF SCHIZOPHRENIA

Diagnosis	No.	Mean Age	Decreased Cell or Myelin, Fe				Gliosis						Ependyma		SI, GP, THAL, or MB	AMYG, HIP
			GP	SI	Acc	Cere	THAL	AMYG	HIP	MB	HT	SI	GRAN	GLiosis		
Catatonic	13	37.9	6[a]	5	4	5	3	4	4	5[a]	4[a]	4	3	10	10	6[a]
Catatonic/Paranoid	5	39.2	2	3	2	3	1	2	3	2[b]	2	3	2	4	5	4
Paranoid[c]	4	43.4						1			1		1	3	1	1
Hebephrenic	5	47.2	3[a]	2[a]		1	2		2	2	1	1	3	4	3	2
Chronic undifferentiated schizophrenia	4	54.3	1			1		1		1	1	1[d]	4	2	2	1
Epilepsy/Psychosis[c]	6	36	2[a]			5		1	5	3	1	1	2	5	4	5
Child schizophrenia	1	21								1[b]	1	1	1	1[d]		

[a] Mineral deposits only in one case.
[b] Pallor of substantia nigra in one case
[c] One case, cyst or malformation of the cingulate gyrus.
[d] Perivascular lymphocytes and macrophages

Key: Acc, nucleus accumbens (not available in every case); AMYG, amygdala; Cere, cerebellum; Fe, iron (?calcium); GP, globus pallidus; GRAN, ependymal granulations; HIP, hippocampus; HT, hypothalamus; MB, midbrain; SI, substantia innominata; THAL, thalamus

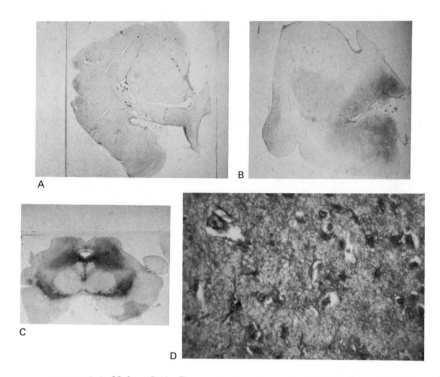

FIGURE 7-3. Holzer Stain Demonstrating Astroglia Cell Bodies and Fibrils.
A. Coronal section of the cerebral hemisphere at the level of the anterior
commissure of a 34-year-old male with postencephalitic Parkinson's disease
(PEPD). Note the homogeneous background stain, which was also found
in all non-mental hospital (i.e., Oregon) control brains. B. Coronal section
at the same level, with the same stain, and from the same laboratory, of a
29-year-old male with catatonic schizophrenia. Deep staining areas indicate
severe gliosis in the cortical medial and central amygdala nuclei, substantia
innominata, lateral hypothalamus, putamen, and external segment of globus pallidus (see Fig. 7-4 for anatomical detail). C. Coronal section through
the midbrain of a 32-year-old patient with postencephalitic Parkinson's disease. There is severe gliosis in the deeply stained regions surrounding the
acqueduct, dorsal tegmentum, tectum, and substantia nigra. D. Holzer
stain of gliotic region in case depicted in Fig. 7-3B, magnified 100 times,
shows an extensive proliferation of the astroglial fibrils.

myelin degeneration in the globus pallidus. Seventy-five percent had gliosis in the amygdala or hippocampus; 70% had gliosis in the midbrain or hypothalamus. When all patients presenting these changes in the basal ganglia, substantia innominata, midbrain, or thalamus were pooled, 10 of the 13 individuals with a diagnosis of catatonic schizophrenia (76%) had pathological changes in the globus pallidus, substantia innominata, midbrain, thalamus, or nucleus accumbens. (Dr. Tom Kemper, who examined material from many of the cases reported here, and Professor Walle Nauta, who examined the nucleus accumbens—olfactory tubercle region from one case, independently observed an apparent reduction in neurons in the nucleus accumbens in several brains from catatonic patients.) Unfortunately, accumbens sections were not available for every patient. Material from 10 of the 13 catatonic brains also displayed gliosis in the periventricular or periaqueductal region. There was fibrillary gliosis in the bed nucleus of the stria terminalis and adjacent pathways in the lateral wall of the anterior horn of the cerebral ventricles and/or at the origin of the stria terminalis at the junction of the corticomedial nucleus of the amygdala and substantia innominata in five cases (Fig. 7-4b).

Catatonic plus Paranoid

Of six patients with clinical diagnoses of both catatonic and paranoid schizophrenia, five (83%) displayed cell loss, myelin or axonal degeneration in the globus pallidus or the ventral (limbic) pallidum (three in the substantia innominata, two in the globus pallidus) and significant gliosis or cell loss in the hippocampus or amygdala. Three (50%) had a granular ependymitis.

Paranoid

Of the four patients diagnosed as paranoid schizophrenics, none had cell dropout or other pathological changes in the globus pallidus, thalamus, or midbrain; one had gliosis in the substantia innominata and supraoptic nucleus of the hypothalamus; one had a vascular anomaly of the cingulate gyrus; one had only granular ependymitis of the anterior horn, and one had gliosis of the hippocampus, amygdala, and mammillary body.

Hebephrenic

Three patients were diagnosed as hebephrenic schizophrenics and one patient was diagnosed as catatonic, with hebephrenia. Three of these four patients displayed granular ependymitis as above defined and peri-

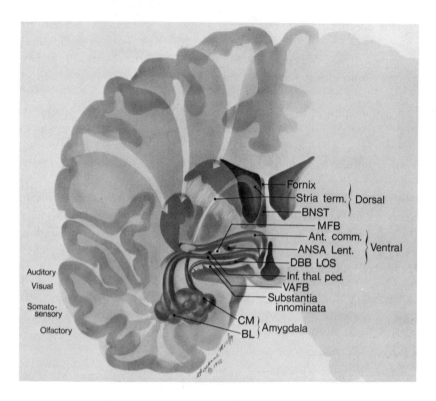

FIGURE 7-4. Anatomical Structures in Dorsal and Ventral *Carrefours* (Cross-roads) of the Limbic Forebrain. BNST, bed nucleus of the stria terminalis; DBB, diagonal band of Broca; LOS, lateral olfactory stria; VAFP, ventral amygdala–fugal pathway; CM, cortico medial nucleus; BL, basal lateral nucleus; INF THAL PED, inferior thalamic peduncle. (Adapted from Klinger and Gloor, 1960.)

ventricular or periaqueductal gliosis. Only one (the patient diagnosed catatonic with hebephrenia) had significant cell loss in the globus pallidus. Gliosis of the midbrain tegmentum was prominent in a second and gliosis of thalamus and preoptic-tuberal area of hypothalamus in a third.

Chronic Undifferentiated Schizophrenia

Of the four patients so diagnosed, all were 54 to 55 years of age at death. In contrast to the catatonics, who in only three (of 13) cases had a granular ependymitis (23%), all the patients with chronic undifferentiated schizophrenia presented granular nodular ependymal changes. Beyond the ependymal changes, these patients presented diverse pathologies. One had old healed infarcts of the caudate nucleus, another decreased pigmentation and cell dropout in the substantia nigra, and a third extensive gliosis in the supraoptic nucleus, bed nucleus of the stria terminalis, olfactory tubercle, dorsal amygdala, and interpeduncular fossa. The fourth demonstrated massive infiltration of the corpora amylacea in both the dorsal and ventral *carrefour* (crossroad) zones (the amygdala–substantia innominata junction; the bed nucleus of the stria terminalis–fornix–striae medullaris junction) and the medial hypothalamus and thickening of basal meninges.

Epilepsy and Psychosis

Of the six patients with this diagnosis, five had significant pathology in the hippocampus and cell loss in the dentate nucleus or cortex of the cerebellum. Three had gliosis in the subcortical nuclei of the basal ganglia or mesencephalon, three granular ependymitis, and one sclerosis of the amygdala and an old infarct of the cingulate gyrus.

Childhood Schizophrenia

A 21-year-old schizophrenic patient (diagnosed childhood schizophrenia) displayed striking gliosis and ependymal granulations in addition to lymphocytic and macrophage accumulations around vessels and gliotic changes in the midbrain tegmentum. Accumulations of corpora amylacea were abundant for so young an individual and were collected in perivascular zones in the deep regions of the amygdala, hippocampus, and substantia innominata.

Controls

Histological sections similar to those derived for the schizophrenic brains were examined from 13 nonschizophrenic St. Elizabeth's Hospital patients, aged 35 to 55 years, hospitalized during the same period as the index cases. Their diagnoses were Huntington's chorea (2), Alzheimer's disease (1), inclusion body encephalitis (1), postencephalitic Parkinsonism (4), general paresis (1), Korsakoff's psychosis (1), Pick's disease (1), "chronic brain syndrome" (1), and mania (1). The pathology of the first 12 cases was in each instance typical of the disorder, with the exception of the Alzheimer patient (diagnosed catatonic during life), who presented Lewy bodies and loss of substantia nigra cells in addition to typical neurofibrillary changes and senile plaques. Five patients had granular ependymitis, including both the Huntington's chorea patients. Three patients had periaqueductal gliosis (Korsakoff's, postencephalitic Parkinsonism) (Fig. 7-3c); one had amygdala gliosis (Pick's), two had mineral deposits in the basal ganglia (Pick's, Korsakoff's). Three had gliosis in the thalamus and substantia nigra (postencephalitic Parkinsonism) and two had gliosis in the mesencephalic tegmentum (Pick's postenaphalitic Parkinsonism); there was no gliosis in the hypothalamus or the substantia innominata in any case. The manic patient had neuronal loss in the globus pallidus.

The diagnoses for the non-mental hospital control patients were leukemia (4), carcinoma (3), pulmonary embolus (1), rheumatic heart disease (1), moving vehicle accident (1), drowning (1), kidney transplant rejection and infection (1), and a miscellany of other disorders (8). Sections from the basal ganglia, midbrain, and limbic forebrain regions corresponding to the schizophrenic material, and stained with the Holzer method for glial fibrils, did not display gliosis similar to that seen in the schizophrenic brains in a single case. Corpora amylacea were abundant in the brains of these control patients over the age of 37. However, essentially none were found in the brains of younger patients, with the exception of a 27-year-old male with a kidney transplant rejection who expired following widespread infection secondary to vigorous immunosuppressive therapy. This man, who had had long-standing uremia and renal dialysis, had extensive corpora amylacea deposits in the bed nucleus of the stria terminalis and other subependymal sites.

DISCUSSION

The clinical history, mental status, and neurological examination of patients with schizophrenia suggest an encephalopathy involving regions of the brain that modulate, mediate, and integrate attention, affective response, continuity of thought, and significance of perceptions, as well as sleep, certain ocular movements, and facial expressions, social bonding, and defense. Experimental studies in animals and clinical–pathological correlations in humans indicate that the regions most likely to induce changes in these functions are the hypothalamus, upper brainstem, septum, amygdala, hippocampus, and related subcortical nuclei of the limbic system. The normal or nonspecific scalp EEG accompanying the schizophrenic syndrome and normal or slightly dilated ventricular systems support the clinical evidence of a predominant subcortical position for the pathology of this group of disorders. Rapid relief of the early symptoms of schizophrenia by pharmacological agents that block DA receptors in the brain initially suggested to me that the pathological substrate of this disorder should lie in areas of the limbic system in which DA receptors terminate. As noted above, cell loss in the nucleus accumbens was discerned in several cases by Walle Nauta and Tom Kemper. This important observation is being followed up by quantitative cell counts, comparing schizophrenic and age-matched control material. Gliosis, the predominant pathology, was found in the dorsomedial thalamus, brainstem, hypothalamus, and periventricular–periaqueductal regions. Cell dropout was most evident in the globus pallidus in catatonics. These areas share the property of being direct recipients or projection systems from the DA-receiving nuclei of the neostriatum and limbic striatum.

All the patients studied in this report had been ill and hospitalized for more than seven years, and some were first diagnosed and institutionalized 20 to 30 years prior to death. Only one, the childhood schizophrenic, age 21 at death, displayed any signs of active inflammatory reaction in the brain (perivascular lymphocytes and macrophages). Thus the pathology viewed in this material was generally healed, old, quiescent, or slowly progressive.

The gliosis and focal neuronal dropout observed coincide closely with the areas of gliosis reported in schizophrenic brains by Nieto and Escobar (1972). Since these patients had received a variety of treatments during their hospitalization, the question may reasonably arise as to whether the gliosis observed is not the result of treatment rather than of the primary disease process. All the patients in this study, save one, were treated with either neuroleptics or reserpine and/or by electroconvulsive therapies (ECT). Drug dosages were generally modest by today's standards. Gliosis in the brainstem was found in all patients receiving ECT, and in one-half the patients for whom there was no record of such treatment. Of six patients without gliosis of the brain, none had received ECT. The data suggest that ECT may contribute to gliosis, but does not appear to account for gliosis in 50% of those affected. The relationship found between catatonia and loss of neurons in the globus pallidus has been reported by many other investigators (Josephy, 1930; Buscaino, 1920; Hopf, 1952; Vogt and Vogt, 1952) and is consistent with clinical and experimental neurological observations that bilateral infarction of the globus pallidus induces catatonic symptoms (Mettler and Crandell, 1959).

Loss of Purkinje cells, granule cells, or neurons of the dentate nucleus in catatonics and in the epileptic psychoses is consistent with recent radiological and post-mortem data showing anterior vermis atrophy in a percentage of chronic schizophrenic patients (Weinberger et al., 1980). The distribution of subcortical gliosis or cell loss in patients with psychosis and epilepsy includes most of the subcortical sites affected in the psychoses, but there is much more frequent pathological change in the hippocampus than in psychosis alone. As in the series of institutionalized epileptics reported by Margerison and Corsellis (1966), autopsy material permits detection of numerous scattered subcortical lesions that are not appreciated in the surgical pathologies available from an excised temporal lobe. The data presented, however, are from a limited number of sections and do not represent every area of the brain. Not surprisingly, involvement of the seizure-prone hippocampus in the pathological process distinguishes the epileptic psychoses from the non-epileptic psychotics in this series. Gliosis in the amygdala, basal ganglia, midbrain, and hypothalamus in patients with epilepsy and psychosis is similar to the distribution of lesions in the schizophrenic patients and may thus relate to the psychotic process in both groups.

The *corpora amylacea*, homogeneous polyglucosan bodies, are so common in the brains of middle-aged and older patients who are free of neurological or mental disease that they are generally regarded as part of the normal aging process of the brain. However, as every neuropathologist recognizes, corpora amylacea also tend to accumulate in regions of neuronal loss or matrix degeneration. Bodies of similar composition are present in neurons of patients with La Fora body disease and the glycogen storage disorders of the brain, but are rarely found in the brains of children or young adults in the absence of a degenerative disease, focal injury, or infection (Alder, 1953; Robitaille et al., 1980). The sites of predilection for accumulation of corpora amylacea in these schizophrenic brains coincides with their distribution in otherwise normal middle-aged and older adults, namely, the dorsal amygdala, the adjacent substantia innominata, the region of the bed nucleus of the stria terminalis, and the anterior perforated space (Austin and Sakai, 1976). However, the abundance of corpora amylacea in the brains of young schizophrenic patients in this series raises the possibility of a premature degenerative or destructive process in specific regions.

Ependymal granulations are a ubiquitous and striking finding in the ventricles of individuals who survive chronic meningitides of tuberculosis or lues. The presence of a few small ependymal excrescences composed of astroglia in individuals without a history of these or of any other central nervous system infection is so common that their importance in these schizophrenic brains may well be doubted. Ependymal granulation were found in 43% of the schizophrenics, 50% of the St. Elizabeth's Hospital "controls," and 33% of the general medical patients. There was a difference, however, in the character, frequency, and locus of ependymal granules in schizophrenic patients, compared with both groups of controls. When the granulations were scored 1 to 4$^+$, based on the number per histological section and size and distribution in more than one ventricular site (e.g., aqueductal, III, IV, anterior horn, inferior horn), 11 schizophrenic brains, one St. Elizabeth's Hospital "control" brain, and one general medical brain received more than a 1$^+$ rating, whereas 15 of the schizophrenic or epilepsy psychotic brains did so. Johnson and Johnson (1972), who reported granular ependymal excrescences in 65% of routine autopsied brains (but did not require buried ependymal epithelial cells for this diagnosis), considered them to be probably residuae of childhood viral infections of the central nervous system. The greater number, larger size, and wider distribution of ependymal granulations found in the schizophrenic brains in this study lends support to other evidence for a healed inflammatory encephalopathy. It must be noted, however, that our "control" brains were derived from an Oregon university hospital population of generally low income Portland residents, whereas the schizophrenic brains were collected from a mostly urban, lower socioeconomic class population of Washington, D.C.

Gliosis, the most ubiquitous abnormality found in these schizophrenic brains, is usually a response to neuronal loss or damage. The gliosis in these brains is maximum in subependymal and basal forebrain regions at the sites of major pathways and junctions (*carrefours*) of the limbic system [e.g., origin and terminus of the stria terminalis and ventral amygdala fugal pathway, fornix, inferior thalamic peduncle, striae medullaris (septo-habenular tract), diagonal band of Broca, and lateral olfactory tract]. Of the pathways involved, the consequences of lesions in the stria terminalis and ventral amygdala-fugal pathway, the major projection bundles between the amygdala and the basal forebrain, have received the most attention in the experimental laboratory.

The *stria terminalis* originate in the corticomedial and central nuclei located on the dorsal border of each amygdala, close to the tail of the caudate nucleus. Following the medial border of the caudate as it curves posteriorly and then forward again around the inferior horn and body of the lateral ventricle, the paired striae, like the fornices, lie throughout their entire course just below the ependymal lining of the inferior horn, body, and anterior horn of the lateral ventricle. They are thus in a vulnerable position with respect to the periventricular gliosis observed in these brains. At their several termini, the stria terminalis fasicles synapse in nuclei of the limbic striatum (the nucleus accumbens, lateral septum, and bed nucleus of the stria terminalis), anterior preoptic area, and posterior and ventral-medial hypothalamus (Fig. 7-4).

The second major output system of the amygdala, the ventral amygdala–fugal pathway, arises from the more lateral amygdala nuclei and sweeps medially and posteriorally through the substantia innominata beneath the anterior commissure to terminate in the medial frontal cortex, nucleus accumbens, olfactory tubercle, and preoptic areas as well as in the medial hypothalamus where its terminals partly overlap with the terminals of the stria terminalis (De Olmos, 1972; Dreifuss, 1972). These two pathways establish reciprocal control of individual units of the ventral medial nucleus of the hypothalamus, a major control center for mediation of predatory, defense, feeding, and sexual activity (Murphy, Dreifuss, Gloor, 1968).

In general, the dorsal amygdala projections through the stria terminals inhibit firing of the ventral medial neurons, whereas stimulation of the ventral amygdala–fugal pathway is at least initially excitatory. This reciprocity at the neuronal level also extends to certain behaviors elicited by direct stimulation of the ventral medial nucleus, as was shown for attack behavior in the cat in the classic experiments of Egger and Flynn (1967). Interruption of this pathway abolishes mouse-killing behavior in rats (Kaada, 1972). In contrast, lesions of the cortical medial nuclei or stria terminalis interfere with reproductive behavior in rats (Elwers and Critchlow, 1961).

The amygdala receives extensive input from cortical and subcortical sites representing all the sensory systems (auditory, visual, olfactory, and somatosensory). The production of a galaxy of complex perceptual and affective sensations by amygdala stimulation in humans suggests that specialized regions of amygdala serve as a switching center for incoming polysensory information. The *déja-vu* sensation, or its reciprocal, the uncanny sense of strangeness reported by some individuals with temporal lobe epilepsy and many patients with schizophrenia, can be elicited from stimulation of the hippocampus as well as the amygdala in humans. This suggests that sensory stimuli arriving in the amygdala may be relayed to the hippocampus to discern familiarity or novelty. From both the amygdala and the hippocampus, information is then sent directly, or via limbic striatal "filters" (e.g., the nucleus accumbens, bed nucleus of stria terminalis, and lateral septum), to a "final common path" for action via the hypothalamus, brainstem, and spinal cord and to the frontal lobe via the dorsal medial and anterior thalamus. Experimental studies suggest that social behavior and feeding and attack, defense, lactation, copulatory, and other responses essential to individual and species survival are relayed to and from the amygdala by the two major pathways described above. Compromised or "shorted" circuits in this intricately designed dual control system could result from the pathology observed in these schizophrenic brains and may contribute to the bizarre and troubling subjective disturbances, perceptual distortions, and unpredictable and maladaptive responses in social behavior. An extreme example of disturbance in this system occurs in the amygdalectomized free-living primate described by Kling, Lancaster, and Benitone (1970). In contrast to the well-known Kluver-Bucy syndrome of caged amygdalectomized primates, animals released to their former habitat following amygdalectomy avoid members of their family and tribe, are inactive, fearful, and isolative and withdraw from friendly gestures and appear unable to respond appropriately to social communication and environmental cues. Failing to follow the group or to forage successfully for food, most such animals disappear, presumably to starve or to succumb to predator attack.

There are estrogen and testosterone receptors in several regions of the amygdala complex, in the limbic striatal nuclei and the hypothalamus (Pfaff, 1968). Gonadal steroids potentiate or inhibit transmission of evoked potentials from the amygdala through the bed nucleus of the stria terminalis to the hypothalamus (Kendrick and Drewett, 1979), thus influencing approach or defense behavior. The effect of gonadal steroids on the latency and sign of electrical potentials and on the behavior elicited by amygdala stimulation may explain, at least in part, why gliosis in the amygdala projection pathways in schizophrenic brains might occur in early life, but subsequently may only be associated with important clinical consequences during and following the rise of the hormonal tides of puberty and pregnancy. Lesions in the projections to and from the amygdala, hippocampus, and related structures of the ventral forebrain prior to puberty may have little behavioral effect before these systems are put to use in the service of social recognition, pair-bonding, reproduction, and independent life. Alternatively, sexual maturity, with the binding of gonadal steroids in specific regions of the amygdala, nucleus accumbens, olfactory tubercle, and substantia innominata may increase the vulnerability of units in these regions to whatever causative agent or agents induce the neuropathological changes observed.

Uhl and Snyder (1979) recently reported that the stria terminalis carries fibers containing the tridecapeptide *neurotensin* from the amygdala to the bed nucleus of the stria terminalis. *Enkephalin* and *vasoactive intestinal peptide* also traverse this pathway (Roberts et al., 1980). Striatal *enkephalin*, and *neurotensin* are increased following treatment with neuroleptics, with a particularly striking chronic elevation of *neurotensin* in the nucleus accumbens (Hong et al., 1978; Govoni et al., 1980). Nemeroff (1980) proposed that *neurotensin*, which has many of the properties of antipsychotic agents (including the capacity to inhibit amphetamine-induced locomotor behavior, a putative measure of mesolimbic DA excitability) may be an endogenous neuroleptic. Gliosis of the stria terminalis and its bed nucleus could mean interference with the transmission of *neurotensin* and other peptides to crucial forebrain structures. Damage in this pathway could also induce compensatory innervation by catecholamine terminals in the affected termination sites (as was shown by Raisman, 1969, in the fornico-septal pathway) or DA-receptor supersensitivity (as has been demonstrated by Crow and others; see this volume).

Although this discussion has been limited to the two major amygdala-fugal pathways (which, as noted, are actually two-way streets), many other tracts coursing through the dorsal and ventral *carrefour* zones connect the various limbic substations with one another and with the cerebral cortex and the neostriatal and thalamic systems. Although the chemistry and physiology of these pathways have been less thoroughly investigated than the stria terminalis and ventral amygdala-fugal pathway, they may be of equal importance in producing psychiatric and physiological disturbances in patients with gliosis in the periventricular region and ventral substantia innominata. If functional in modulating neuronal activity, the intriguing discovery of DA receptors on astroglia, described by Henn in this volume, could provide yet another source of abnormal DA activity in the pathologically gliosed regions of these schizophrenic brains.

ETIOLOGY

The cause or causes of schizophrenia are, of course, unknown. The *decursus morbi* of this syndrome bears a striking likeness to that of multiple sclerosis. Both disorders display three principal modes of progression: (1) attacks with remissions and exacerbations with or without residual deficit; (2) recurrent attacks with partial remission, but increasing deficit; (3) insidious onset, with steady relentless progression for months or years and permanent, usually severe, deficit. Russian nosology, emphasizing the pattern of progression rather than the presenting phenomenology, recognizes these types by their clinical classification of *periodic*, *shift*, and *progressive* (relentless) schizophrenia. These modes of progression are suggestive of an infectious or an autoimmune process.

The pathological material described here is consistent with a healed inflammatory process. Several epidemiological factors support the clinical and pathological evidence for an infectious origin of the disorder. The incidence of schizophrenia is higher and the disorder more malignant in temperate and northern climates than in the tropics. There is a seasonal variation in the births of individuals who eventually manifest schizophrenia and a distinct predilection for lower socioeconomic groups living under crowded and deprived conditions (Torrey and Peterson, 1976; Torrey, Torrey, and Peterson, 1977; Kohn, 1973). Persistent virus infections of the nervous system in man, such as Jacob Creutzfeldt disease, demonstrate slow, steady progression or, as in the case of herpes virus, recurrence under conditions of altered immunity. Reported cytopathic factors in schizophrenic serum (Sukhorukova, 1966; Heath and Krupp, 1967), lymphocytes that do not respond to T mitogens in schizophrenic patients (Liedeman and Prilipko, 1976), detection of a transferable virus-like agent in the cerebrospinal fluid (Crow et al., 1979), if confirmed, would lend further support to the evidence of an inflammatory, perhaps viral etiology of the illness. Albrecht et al. (1980) found a depressed serum: cerebrospinal fluid ratio for the cytomegalovirus antibody in a significant number of patients with chronic schizophrenia. However, attempts to transfer an infective agent by direct cerebral inoculation of fresh schizophrenia brain into animals, tissue culture, or viral genome hybridization probes have not demonstrated an infectious agent.

Cytomegalovirus (CMV) is a particularly attractive candidate for inducing the pathological lesions described in these schizophrenic brains. More than 65% of the adult population harbors antibodies to the virus, indicating previous infection. Cytomegalovirus is asymptomatic in most adults and children, but like other members of the herpes virus family, it persists in dormant latent form in tissues and is activated under conditions of altered immunity. The most common antecedents recognized to date are pregnancy, during which virus is activated and excreted in the urine of approximately 10% of expectant mothers in the United States and the United Kingdom, and in transplant patients following treatment with immunosuppressive agents where it has become a major cause of mortality (Stern, 1969). Congenital infection is common and induces a widespread systemic reaction including destructive periventricular lesions and gliosis in the fetal brain. Congenitally acquired CMV infection can persist in a latent form, and lead to mental retardation and deafness. Genetically transmitted hypoimmunity to a virus, immune suppression during the hormonal tides of adolescence, pregnancy, and stress, and transmission from parents, especially from mother to infant, could account for the peculiar pattern of familial transmission of observed schizophrenias.

Fred Plum (1972) has called schizophrenia the "graveyard of neuropathologists." Given this risk, and the fact that this study does not include serial sections or even all regions of the brain, there nevertheless appears to be some support for the conclusions of many others who have reported that schizophrenia is associated with an anatomical pathology, the uniformity and ubiquity of which lies not in a unique histopathological change, but rather in the occurrence in young adulthood and middle life of "degenerative changes usually reserved for senility" (Vogt and Vogt, 1952). Subjective symptoms and neurological signs associated with schizophrenic illnesses strongly resemble experimental and clinical disorders of the limbic forebrain. The pathology described points to gliotic and degenerative changes that are maximum in subependymal regions and at the origin and terminus of major pathways between the amygdala and the basal forebrain and in the hypothalamus, globus pallidus, medial thalamus, and midbrain. Meticulous attention to phenomenological manifestations of the illness and pursuit of pathological findings with recently developed immunological techniques, as well as conventional neuropathology, could lead to a classification of the "functional psychoses" similar to that developed for epilepsy, i.e., based on specific signs that correspond to the site and nature of anatomical substrates, and, ultimately, on the etiological factors that predispose to the pathological changes.

ACKNOWLEDGMENTS

I am grateful to Meta Neuman, director of the neuropathology laboratory at St. Elizabeth's Hospital, Washington, D.C., 1945 to 1979, from whose excellent collection of historical and histological material the neuropathological studies in this report are derived, and to Dr. James Solomon, Director of the Blackburn Laboratory, St. Elizabeth's Hospital, who made the collection available to me. Drs. Tom Kemper, Tom Gill, and Nathan Blank examined much of the histological material, but are not responsible for the interpretations offered here. Dr. Lou Bigelow generously contributed historical data. Dr. Colin Buchan, neuropathologist at the University of Oregon Health Sciences Center, generously provided control material; Mrs. Lesta Godfrey prepared this material for histological examination. Drs. Vernon Armbrustmacher and Paul Yakovlev and Mr. Mohammed Haleem, at the Armed Forces Institute of Pathology, Washington, D.C., provided extraordinary assistance. Mrs. Rexine M. Hayes contributed substantially to the editing, and also typed the manuscript. Finally, I am grateful to Drs. Paul MacLean and Walle Nauta who provided inspiration and information that guided many aspects of these clinical and neuropathological studies.

REFERENCES

Albrecht, P., E. F. Torrey, E. Boone, J. T. Hicks, and N. Daniel (1980). Elevation of cytomegalovirus antibody in the cerebrospinal fluid of schizophrenic patients. *Lancet* (in press).
Alder, N. (1953). On the nature, origin and distribution of the corpora amylacea of the brain with observations on some new staining reactions. *J. Ment. Sci.* 99, 689–697.
Austin, J., and M. Sakai (1976). Disorders of glycogen and related macromolecules in the nervous system. In *Handbook of Clinical Neurology* (P. J. Vinken and G. W. Bruyn, eds.). North-Holland Publishing Co., Oxford, England.

Bloom, F., D. Segal, N. Ling, and R. Guillemin (1976). Profound behavioral effects in rats suggest new etiological factors in mental illness. *Science* 194, 630–632.

Buscaino, V. M. (1920). Le cause anatomo-pathologiche della manifestazione schizofrenica nella demenza precoce. *Rivista di patologia nervosa e mentale* 25.

Carlsson, A., and M. Lindquist (1963). Effect of chloropromazine or haloperidol on the formation of 3-methoxytyramine and normetanephrine in mouse brain. *Acta Pharmacol. Toxicol.* 20, 140–144.

Crow, T. J., E. C. Johnstone, D. G. C. Owens, I. N. Ferrier, J. F. Macmillan, R. P. Parry, and D. A. J. Tyrrell (1979). Characteristics of patients with schizophrenia or neurological disorder and virus-like agent in cerebrospinal fluid. *Lancet* 1, 842–844.

De Jong, H. H. (1945). *Experimental Catatonia*. Williams & Wilkins Co., Baltimore.

De Olmos, J. S. (1972). The amygdaloid projection field in the rat as studied with the cupric-silver method. In *Advances in Behavioral Biology*, Vol. 2 (B. E. Eleftheriou, ed.), Plenum Press, New York, pp. 145–204.

Diefendorf, A. R., and R. Dodge (1908). An experimental study of the ocular reactions of the insane from photographic records. *Brain* 31, 451.

Dreifuss, J. J. (1972). Effects of electrical stimulation of the amygdaloid complex on the ventromedial hypothalamus. In *Advances in Behavioral Biology*, Vol. 2 (B. E. Eleftheriou, ed.), pp. 295–317. Plenum Press, New York.

Egger, M. D., and J. P. Flynn (1967). Further studies on the effects of amygdaloid stimulation and ablation on hypothalamically elicited attack behavior in cats. In *Progress in Brain Research*, Vol. 27 (W. R. Adey and T. Tokizane, eds.). *Structure and Function of the Limbic System*, pp. 165–182. Elsevier Publishing Co., Amsterdam.

Elwers, M., and V. Critchlow (1961). Precocious ovarian stimulation following interruption of stria terminalis. *Amer. J. Physiol.* 201, 281.

Fisman, M. (1975). The brain stem in psychosis. *Brit. J. Psychiat.* 126, 414–422.

Govoni, S., J. S. Hong, H. U. T. Yang, and E. Costa (1980). Increase of neurotensin content elicited by neuroleptics in nucleus accumbens. *J. Pharmacol. Exp. Ther.* (in press).

Heath, R. G. (1954). *Studies in Schizophrenia*. Harvard University Press, Cambridge.

Heath, R. G., and I. M. Krupp (1967). Schizophrenia as an immunologic disorder. I. Demonstration of antibrain globulins by fluorescent antibody techniques. *Arch. Gen. Psychiat.* 16, 1–9.

Heimer, L. (1978). The olfactory cortex and the ventral striatum. In *Limbic Mechanisms: The Continuing Evolution of the Limbic System Concept* (K. E. Livingston and O. Hornykiewicz, eds.), pp. 95–188. Plenum Press, New York.

Henriksen, S. J., F. E. Bloom, F. McCoy, N. Ling, and R. Guilllemin (1978). Beta endorphin induces non-convulsive limbic seizures. *Proc. Natl. Acad. Sci. (U.S.A.)* 75, 5221–5225.

Herishanu, Y. (1973). On a lower brain stem localization of the center of periodic blinking. *Confin. Neurol.* 35, 90–93.

Hill, D. (1952). EEG in episodic psychotic and psychopathic behavior. *Electroencephalogr. Clin. Neurophysiol.* 4, 419–442.

Holzman, P. S., L. R. Proctor, and D. W. Hughes (1973). Eye-tracking performance in schizophrenia. *Science* 181, 179–181.

Hong, J. S., H. U. T. Yang, W. Fratta, and E. Costa (1978). Rat striatal methionine-enkephalin content after chronic treatment with cataleptogenic and non-cataleptogenic antischizophrenic drugs. *J. Pharmacol. Exp. Ther.* 205, 141–147.

Hopf, A. (1952). Über histopathologische veranderungen im pallidum und striatum bei schizophrenie. In *Proceedings of the International Congress of Neuropathology*, Vol. terzo, pp. 629–635. Rosenberg & Sellier, Torino, Italy.

Horn, A. S., and S. H. Snyder (1971). Chlorpromazine and dopamine: Conformational similarities that correlate with the antischizophrenic activity of phenothiazine drugs. *Proc. Natl. Acad. Sci.* (U.S.A.) 68, 2325–2328.

Hunsperger, R. W., and V. M. Bucher (1967). Affective behaviour produced by electrical stimulation in the forebrain and brain stem of the cat. In *Progress in Brain Research*, Vol. 27 (W. R. Adey and T. Tokizane, eds.) *Structure and Function of the Limbic System*, pp. 103–12. Elsevier Publishing Co., New York.

Jacobi, W., and H. Winkler (1927). Encephalographische studien an chronisch schizophrenen. *Arch. Psychiat. Nervenkr.* 81, 299–332.

Johnson, K. P., and R. T. Johnson (1972). Granular ependymitis. Occurrence in myxovirus infected rodents and prevalence in man. *Amer. J. Pathol.* 67, 511–521.

Johnstone, E. C., T. J. Crow, C. D. Frith, J. Husband, and L. Kreel (1976). Cerebral ventricular size and cognitive impairment in chronic schizophrenia. *Lancet* 2, 924–926.

Josephy, H. (1930). Dementia praecox (Schizophrenie). In *Die Anatomie der Psychosen* (O. Bumke, ed.), p. 763, Handb. d. Geisteskrankh. 11 (spez. Teil VII). Julius Springer, Berlin.

Kaada, B. R. (1972). Stimulation and regional ablation of the amygdaloid complex with reference to functional representations. In *Advances in Behavioral Biology*, Vol. 2 (B. E. Eleftheriou, ed.), *The Neurobiology of the Amygdala*, pp. 205–281. Plenum Press, New York.

Kendrick, K. M., and R. F. Drewett (1979). Testosterone reduces refractory period of stria terminalis neurons in the rat brain. *Science* 204, 877–879.

Kievit, J., and H. G. J. M. Kuypers (1975). Basal forebrain and hypothalamic connections to frontal and parietal cortex in the rhesus monkey. *Science* 187, 660–662.

Kling, A., J. Lancaster, and J. Benitone (1970). Amygdalectomy in the free ranging vervet (cercopithecus aethiops). *J. Psychiatr. Res.* 7, 191–199.

Klinger, J., and P. Gloor (1960). The connections of the amygdala and the anterior temporal cortex. *J. Comp. Neurol.* 115, 333–369.

Kohn, M. L. (1973). Social class and schizophrenia: A critial review and a reformulation. *Schizophrenia Bull.* (No. 7, Winter), 60–76.

Kraepelin, E. (1919). *Dementia Praecox and Paraphrenia*. E. & S. Livingstone, Edinburgh.

Liedeman, R. R., and L. L. Prilipko (1976). The behavior of T lymphocytes in schizophrenia. In *Neurochemical and Immunologic Components in Schizophrenia* (D. Bergsma and A. Goldstein, eds.), pp. 365–377. Alan R. Liss, Inc., New York.

Longo, V. (1952). Discussion. In *Proceedings of the First International Congress of Neuropathology*, Vol. primo, pp. 584–591. Rosenberg & Sellier, Torino, Italy.

MacLean, P. D., S. Flanigan, J. P. Flynn, C. Kim, and J. R. Stevens (1955). Hippocampal functions: Tentative correlations of conditioning, EEG, drug, and radioautographic studies. *Yale J. Biol. Med.* 27, 380–395.

Margerison, J. H., and J. A. N. Corsellis (1966). Epilepsy and the temporal lobes. *Brain* 89, 499–529.

Mark, V. H., and F. R. Ervin (1970). *Violence and the Brain.* Harper & Row, New York.

Mettler, F. A., and A. Crandell (1959). Relation between Parkinsonism and psychiatric disorder. *J. Nerv. Ment. Dis.* 129, 551.

Meyer, A. (1952). Critical evaluation of histopathological findings in schizophrenia. In *Proceedings of the First International Congress of Neuropathology*, Vol. primo, pp. 649–666. Rosenberg & Sellier, Torino, Italy.

Murphy, J. T., J. J. Dreifuss, and P. Gloor (1968). Responses of hypothalamic neurons to repetitive amygdaloid stimulation. *Brain Res.* 8, 153–166.

Nashold, B. S. Jr., W. P. Wilson, and D. G. Slaughter (1969a). Sensations evoked by stimulation in the midbrain of man. *J. Neurosurg.* 30, 14–24.

Nashold, B. S. Jr., D. G. Slaughter, and J. P. Gills (1969b). Ocular reactions in man from deep cerebellar stimulation and lesions. *Arch. Ophthalmol.* 81, 538–543.

Nemeroff, C. B. (1980). Neurotensin: Perchance an endogenous neuroleptic? *Biol. Psychiat.* 15, 283–302.

Nieto, D., and A. Escobar (1972). Major psychoses. In *Pathology of the Nervous System* Vol. 3 (J. Minckler, ed.) McGraw-Hill, New York.

Pfaff, D. W. (1968). Autoradiographic localization of radioactivity in rat brain after injection of tritiated sex hormones. *Science* 161, 1355–1356.

Plum, F. (1972). Prospects for research on schizophrenia. 3. Neurophysiology. Neuropathological findings. *Neurosci. Res. Program Bull.* 10, 384–388.

Powers, P. S. (1976). Hyperpyrexia in catatonic states and the multiple causes of catatonia. *Dis. Nerv. Syst.* 164, 358–361.

Raisman, G. (1969). Neuronal plasticity in the septal nuclei of the adult rat. *Brain Res.* 14, 25–48.

Roberts, G. W., P. L. Woodhams, T. J. Crow, and J. M. Polak (1980). Loss of immunoreactive VIP in the bed nucleus following lesions of the stria terminalis. *Brain Res.* 195, 471–475.

Robitaille, Y., S. Carpenter, G. Karpati, and S. Dimauro (1980). A distinct form of adult polyglucosan body disease with massive involvement of central and peripheral neuronal processes and astrocytes. *Brain* 103, 315–336.

Sato, M. (1977). Functional changes in the caudate and accumbens nuclei during amygdaloid and hippocampal seizure development in kindled cats. *Folia Psychiatr. Neurol. Jpn.* 31, 501–512.

Shagass, C., M. Amadeo, and D. A. Overton (1976). Eye tracking performance and engagement of attention. *Arch. Gen. Psychiat.* 33, 121–125.

Stern, H. (1969). Cytomegalovirus: A cause of persistent latent infection. *J. Clin. Pathol. (Suppl.)* 25, 34–38.

Stevens, J. R. (1973). An anatomy of schizophrenia? *Arch. Gen. Psychiat.* 29, 177–189.

Stevens, J. R. (1976). Computer analysis of the telemetered EEG in the study of epilepsy and schizophrenia. *Acta. Neurochir. (Suppl.)* 23, 71–84.

Stevens, J. R. (1978). Disturbances of ocular movements and blinking in schizophrenia. *J. Neurol. Neurosurg, Psychiat.* 41, 1024–1030.

Stevens, J. R., V. H. Mark, F. Ervin, P. Pacheco, and K. Suematsu (1969). Deep temporal stimulation in man. *Arch. Neurol.* 21, 157–169.

Stevens, J. R., K. Wilson, and W. Foote (1974). EEG and schizophrenia: Experimental activation of the mesolimbic dopamine pathway. *Electroencephalogr. Clin. Neurophysiol.* 37, 201.

Stevens, J. R., L. Bigelow, D. Denney, J. Lipkin, A. Livermore, Jr., F. Rauscher, and R. J. Wyatt (1979). Telemetered EEG–EOG during psychotic behaviors of schizophrenia. *Arch. Gen. Psychiat.* 36, 251–262.

Sukhorukova, L. E. (1966). Changes in neuroglia in continuous schizophrenia. *Zhurnal Neuropatol Psikh.* 66, 1408–1416.

Torrey, E. F., and M. R. Peterson (1976). The viral hypothesis of schizophrenia. *Schizophrenia Bull.* 2, 136–146.

Torrey, E. F., B. B. Torrey, and M. R. Peterson (1977). Seasonality of schizophrenic births in the United States. *Arch. Gen. Psychiat.* 34, 1065–1070.

Troiano, R., and A. Siegel (1978). Efferent connections of the basal forebrain in the cat: The substantia innominata. *Exp. Neurol.* 61, 198–213.

Uhl, G. R., and S. H. Snyder (1979). Neurotensin: Neuronal pathway projecting from amygdala through stria terminalis. *Brain Res.* 161, 522–526.

Vogt, C., and O. Vogt (1952). Alterations anatomiques de la schizophrenie et d'autres psychoses dites fonctionelles. In *Proceedings of the First International Congress of Neuropathology*, Vol. primo. Rosenberg & Sellier, Torino, Italy.

Wallach, M. B., and S. S. Wallach (1964). Involuntary eye movements in schizophrenia. *Arch. Gen. Psychiat.* 11, 71–73.

Weinberger, D. R., E. Fuller Torrey, A. N. Neophytides, and R. J. Wyatt (1979). Lateral cerebral ventricular enlargement in chronic schizophrenia. *Arch. Gen. Psychiat.* 36, 735–739.

Weinberger, D. R., J. E. Kleinman, D. J. Luchins, L. B. Bigelow, and R. J. Wyatt (1980). Cerebellar pathology in schizophrenia: A controlled postmortem study. *Amer. J. Psychiat.* 137, 359–361.

Yarden, P. E., and W. J. Discipio (1971). Abnormal movements and prognosis in schizophrenia. *Amer. J. Psychiat.* 128, 317–323.

Zametkin, A., J. R. Stevens, and R. Pittman (1979). Ontogeny of spontaneous blinking and of habituation of the blink reflex. *Ann. Neurol.* 5, 453–457.

8 | Brain Morphology in Schizophrenia: *In Vivo* Studies

DANIEL R. WEINBERGER and
RICHARD JED WYATT

Prior to the relatively recent emergence of the neurochemical and neuropharmacological hypotheses of schizophrenia, it was widely believed that the disorder had a neuroanatomical basis. The search for morphological abnormalities of the brain has involved primarily two approaches: microscopic examination of postmortem specimens, using traditional histological methods, and radiological study of gross cerebral structure in living patients. The former approach was enthusiastically pursued for most of the first half of the century, only to lose momentum in the early 1950s because of what seemed to be insoluble methodological problems and unresolvable controversy. The latter approach, although productive of some of the most consistently replicated findings in the annals of schizophrenia research, never gained momentum primarily because the method used [pneumoencephalography (PEG)] was poorly suited for the study of psychotic patients.

In the past decade, the advent of a revolutionary radiological technique, computed axial tomography (CAT), has renewed interest in the study of cerebral morphology in living schizophrenics. Studies using this new method have confirmed and extended the findings described with pneumoencephalography and have reopened the issue of whether morphological abnormalities of the brain are relevant to schizophrenia. In this chapter, we will review the results of the *in vivo* approaches to this issue.

PNEUMOENCEPHALOGRAPHY STUDIES

In 1919, Dandy described a technique for demonstrating the contours of the brain in living patients. He showed that air injected into the lumbar subarachnoid space found its way into the ventricles and over the convexities of the brain where it served as a contrast medium for x-rays transmitted through the skull. Distortion of the normal appearance of the air-filled spaces indicated cerebral pathology. This pneumoencephalographic technique soon became one of the major diagnostic tools in clinical neuroradiology.

Eight years after Dandy's report, Jacobi and Winkler (1927) published their PEG findings in 19 chronic schizophrenic patients, most of whom were under 40 years old. They found "unquestionable" internal hydrocephalus in 18 cases. Since Jacobi and Winkler's initial report, over 30 PEG studies of schizophrenic patients have appeared, the vast majority of which also found enlarged cerebral ventricles or other evidence of cerebral atrophy in a considerable percentage of patients. Not surprisingly, most of these studies would not meet today's more rigorous requirements for scientific objectivity. Few of the studies employed adequate controls; most used poorly defined diagnostic criteria; and the pneumoencephalographic procedure varied from study to study. Despite these methological problems, some of these reports merit a second look. We have culled from the literature six studies that fulfill at least marginal standards for objectivity. In each, either an objective, quantitative interpretation of the pneumoencephalograms was used or a control population was included. Some also provided a description of diagnostic methods, as well as an indication of how patients were selected. Table 8-1 summarizes the findings in these six reports.

Of the six studies, Lempke's (1935), from Germany, is the weakest. He studied 100 chronic schizophrenics, considered "unmistakable schizophrenic," based on the consensus of the hospital staff. Most of these patients were under 50 years old. The pneumoencephalograms of the patients were compared with those of 42 similarly aged controls, being patients with epilepsy, migraine, "psychopathy," and "hysteria." The scans were scored on a five-point scale corresponding to increasing grades of atrophy. He found evidence of atrophy in 85% of the schizophrenic patients, 50% of whom had enlarged ventricles. Only five of the controls had ventricles of equivalent size. Lempke made two other interesting observations. The degree of ventricular enlargement appeared to be re-

TABLE 8-1.

PNEUMOENCEPHALOGRAPHIC (PEG) STUDIES

Study	Sample	Results
1. Lempke (1935)	100 chronic schizophrenics 42 controls	Fifty percent of schizophrenics had enlarged ventricles compared with 20% of controls
2. Huber (1957)	195 randomly selected schizophrenics	Severe *defekt* patients: 82% had enlarged ventricles No *defekt* patients: 17% had enlarged ventricles
3. Haug (1962)	101 chronic schizophrenics 63 other psychiatric patients	Schizophrenics' ventricular size larger than controls ($p <$ .05)
4. Nagy (1963)	260 schizophrenics 133 manic-depressives	Atrophy in 58% of schizophrenics, 28% of manic-depressives
5. Storey (1966)	18 schizophrenics 18 neurological controls	No differences
6. Asano (1967)	32 "nuclear" schizophrenics 21 "peripheral" schizophrenics	Ventricular enlargement: nuclear 42%; peripheral 25%; severe 78%; mild 10%

lated to the degree of personality disintegration. Also, six of his patients had been studied earlier by Jacobi and Winkler and their repeat PEGs were unchanged. This led Lempke to conclude that the atrophic changes were not progressive, but reflected a congenital anomaly. Lempke also provided pictures of many of the PEGs to illustrate the magnitude of the abnormalities. Unfortunately, his diagnostic criteria were vague, the films were not evaluated blindly, and his comments, which echoed the political rhetoric of his time, raise doubts about his objectivity.

Huber (1957), in an extensive monograph, reported the results of PEGs of 195 randomly selected schizophrenic patients all treated in the same clinic in Heidelberg and diagnosed according to the principles of Kurt Schneider. Most of his sample was under 50 years old and had never received somatic therapy. In addition, he excluded patients with serious medical illnesses or with clinical evidence of brain damage. A standardized air insufflation procedure and linear measurements of the ventricular system (ventricular indices) were used. Although Huber did not include a control group per se, he divided his sample in terms of the degree of clinical *defekt*, defined by a social competance scale and by clinical assessment of completeness of remissions. The ventricles of 69% of the entire sample were outside the accepted normal range for ventricular indices. Eighty-two percent of the severe defect patients had enlarged ventricles, as compared with 17% of the no-defect patients. Huber noted that the degree of abnormality was less than is usually found in degenerative brain diseases and that it corresponded to the degree of clinical deterioration. He commented on the possible relevance of somatic treatment. The majority of his patients had never had ECT or other somatic therapies, and those that had were not any more abnormal than the other patients. He also studied 11 similarly aged patients with affective disorders and found enlarged ventricles in only two cases. It is of note that these two cases were the only patients in this group with unremitting illnesses. Huber included numerous pictures of PEGs of patients with varying degrees of atrophy and *defekt*. He concluded that the findings in schizophrenia probably represented a congenital defect or "hypoplasia." Huber's study suffers primarily from the lack of a normal control group, the failure to measure the films blindly, and the absence of statistical analysis. He was in a unique position, however, to follow prospectively many of his sample for up to 20 years. He has recently reported (Huber, Gross, and Schutter, 1975) that patients who had enlarged ventricles early in the course of their illness had a poor outcome. This is strong support for his contention that ventricular enlargement has prognostic significance.

The most exhaustive and objective PEG study was conducted by Haug (1962). He avoided most of the methodological pitfalls of earlier studies, but he did not have access to a normal control group. Another problem with his study was that patients were not randomly selected, but had been referred for PEG either because of diagnostic uncertainty or clinical suspicion of "organicity." Haug collected his patient sample entirely from the chronic wards of the Dikemark Hospital in Oslo. He excluded patients with a history of alcohol abuse or head trauma. Diagnoses were said to be consistent with standard practice in Scandinavian mental hospitals, and in the case of schizophrenia, followed the principles of Bleuler and Langfeldt. Clinical diagnosis and PEG evaluation proceeded independently, and the same neuroradiologist examined all the films using standardized linear measurements. In addition, a uniform air insufflation procedure was followed in each case.

Comparing the diameter of the bodies of the lateral ventricles of 101 schizophrenics (mean age 41, age range 20 to 60) with those of 63 "non-organic" mental disorders (mean age 50, age range 20 to 70), Haug found that the ventricles of the schizophrenic group were significantly larger ($p < .05$). He also observed more cases of cortical atrophy among the schizophrenics. Although he found a substantial number of abnormal PEGs in the non-schizophrenic patients, he stated, "both in point of frequency of pathological findings and in point of extent of atrophic changes, the schizophrenic group is in between the definitely organic and the believed non-organic disorders" (p. 34).

Haug's study was so comprehensive that several additional observations are worth mentioning. Like his predecessors, he correlated the degree of atrophy with the degree of clinical deterioration. He viewed enlarged ventricles as a poor prognostic sign, whether in patients with schizophrenia or in patients with other mental disorders. He also could not correlate the abnormalities with prior somatic treatment. Thirty-one patients had repeated PEGs after an interval of from two months to four and one-half years (mean two and one-half years). Twenty-seven of these repeat studies were unchanged, irrespective of a change in clinical status. None of the repeat PEGs showed an improved picture. Four cases had progressive atrophy, and in each of these the clinical state had deteriorated. Haug even provided autopsy findings on three schizophrenic patients he had previously studied by PEG. In each case the brain was considered grossly and microscopically normal, even though two of these patients had clearly abnormal PEGs. Haug considered these cases examples of the generally accepted fact that subtle forms of atrophy are more easily observed *in vivo* than at postmortem examination. He included in his monograph ample photographic evidence of the morphological abnormalities he described.

In his last of a series of reports from Austria, Nagy (1963) summarized his findings in 260 schizophrenic patients and 133 "manic-depressives," all women under 50 years of age. Nagy's study is noteworthy for the size of his sample; however, his methods are vague. He did not discuss his diagnostic or selection criteria, and his PEG procedure was not uniform. Nevertheless, using the same linear measurements as Huber and the same system for subgrouping patients according to degree of *defekt*, he found pathological PEGs in 58% of the schizophrenics as compared with 23% of the "manic-depressives." Nagy also found a strong relationship between atrophy and *defekt* in both groups of patients.

The only study to rival Haug's for rigorous design was that of Storey (1966). In fact, his is the only "controlled" study in which no difference was found between schizophrenic patients and control subjects. He compared the PEGs of 18 young chronic schizophrenic patients (all under 45 years old) to those of 18 similarly aged "normal" controls. His patients were diagnosed by consensus of the author and a consultant and had no clinical evidence of brain damage. Selection criteria were not described. Controls came from the radiological department at Saint George's Hospital, London and consisted of individuals studied for epilepsy, "giddiness," and "severe migraine." The controls were believed to be free of "serious intracranial disease." Using standard linear measurements made by two neuroradiologists who were unaware of the clinical diagnoses, he found no statistically significant differences between the two groups. Seven of the patients and four of the controls, however, were considered by at least one of the neuroradiologists to have an abnormal PEG. Thus, as Storey acknowledged in his comment, although he found no differences between these groups, he had not answered the question of whether his patients had abnormal PEGs. His control group may well have had larger ventricles than those of asymptomatic healthy individuals.

Finally, Asano (1967), in Osaka, studied 53 schizophrenic patients (mean age 29), none of whom had "neurological signs" or a history of cerebral trauma or encephalitis. The patients were divided into a "nuclear" and "peripheral" group ("Mitsuda's classification") and these groups were further subdivided into two grades of clinical "deterioration." These classifications were determined prior to PEG. A standard PEG procedure was followed, and linear measurements similar to those of Huber and Nagy were used to evaluate the size of the ventricles. Asano found that 35% of his patients had enlarged ventricles. Of the patients in the nuclear, severe deterioration category, however, 94% had enlarged ventricles in contrast to only 10% of the patients in the peripheral, mildest deterioration category ($p < .001$). Asano felt that since the findings were not correlated with age, they might represent a congenital defect.

In light of these six studies and numerous others with similar results, albeit less rigorous designs, it is difficult to explain why the PEG findings have received such little attention (Bliss, 1976). The studies described can be criticized for the reasons already mentioned. In addition, none of them included a control group of asymptomatic individuals (virtually impossible considering the nature of the PEG procedure) necessary to establish the normative range. None of the studies used rigorous diagnostic criteria and in only one were the patients selected randomly. In addition, the PEG procedure itself may introduce an artifact because air has been shown to occasionally increase the size of the ventricular space (LeMay, 1967).

It is important to emphasize that the PEG studies did not find enlarged ventricles or evidence of atrophy in every patient. They found that only some individuals have these abnormalities, apparently a more severely affected, poor-prognosis subgroup. Haug's concluding comments were prophetic. "The results of the present study and of several similar studies establish that morphological cerebral changes are present in many schizophrenics. This is a most important finding in itself, which, regardless of how it is interpreted, cannot but influence our conception of schizophrenia and future research into schizophrenia."

ECHOENCEPHALOGRAPHY STUDIES

Although not a radiological technique, echoencephalography can provide information about intracerebral structure in living patients. The method involves transmitting ultrasonic frequencies through the skull and recording echoes on an oscilloscope. The pattern of echoes reflects the position of midline structures, such as the third ventricle. Two echoencephalographic studies of psychiatric patients have been reported. The results support the PEG findings. Holden et al. (1973) assessed the width of the third ventricle in 79 chronic schizophrenic patients and 79 normal volunteers matched for age and gender. Although there was no overall difference between these groups, they found a significant inverse relationship between ventricular size in the patients and response to treatment. Similar results were reported by Daum et al. (1976) in a study of 100 consecutive psychiatric admissions of various diagnoses to an acute treatment ward. They found that third ventricular size was a significant predictor of length of hospital stay, regardless of diagnosis. Huber (1979) recently reported that, as part of his long-term prospective study, some patients received echoencephalograms. The methodology was not described, but he claims that third ventricular width correlated inversely with outcome, a finding similar to his results with PEG.

These studies have not been repeated, primarily because echoencephalography is a limited technique. The ventricular echoes are often unclear and are affected by other factors, such as skull thickness.

COMPUTERIZED AXIAL TOMOGRAPHIC STUDIES

Computed axial tomography (CAT) is a unique radiological technique for visualizing the internal contents of the human body. The only similarity between it and traditional methods, such as PEG, is that both utilize x-rays. In a CAT scan, x-rays transmitted through the body strike scintillation crystals, generating voltages that are amplified and stored in digital form. The magnitude of the voltages is proportional to the degree to which the radiation has been attenuated in its pass through the body. A tomographic scanning procedure is used. For brain scanning, this involves an x-ray source that rotates in a specified plane around the circumference of a thin cross section (usually horizontal) of the head. As the source rotates, voltages are computed for x-ray paths transversing the brain from various angles. The voltage readings are mathematically reconstructed into an image that represents the distribution of densities within that tissue plane ("slice"). Since several contiguous slices are scanned, the complete series approximates a three-dimensional reconstruction. In processing literally hundreds of thousands of readings, the system can show soft tissue structure in astounding detail. The resolution of today's so-called "fourth-generation" scanners is approximately 0.3 mm.

In this section, we will review the application of CAT to the study of schizophrenia. First we will describe the evidence that CAT abnormalities exist in schizophrenic patients and then we will consider their clinical and biological implications.

TABLE 8-2.
CAT FINDINGS IN SCHIZOPHRENIC PATIENTS

Study	Sample	Findings
1. Johnstone et al. (1976)	17 chronic schizophrenics 8 normal controls	Larger cerebral ventricles in schizophrenics than in controls ($p < .01$)
2. Weinberger et al. (1979a)	58 chronic schizophrenics 56 normal controls	Ventricles in patients larger than controls ($p < .0001$)
3. Weinberger et al. (1979b)	60 chronic schizophrenics 62 normal controls	Wider cortical sulci in patients than in controls ($p < .05$)
4. Weinberger et al. (in press)	10 chronic schizophrenics 12 non-schizophrenic controls (all siblings of the patients)	No abnormalities in siblings, ventricles of patients significantly larger ($p < .01$)
5. Rieder et al. (1979)	17 schizophrenic outpatients	Four with cortical atrophy
6. Rieder et al. (in press)	68 research patients 29 chronic schizophrenics 24 affective disorders	Schizophrenics and affective patients had larger ventricles than literature controls ($p < .001$), only schizophrenics had cortical atrophy
7. Famuyiwa et al. (1979)	45 chronic schizophrenics	Thirty-one had abnormal scans
8. Golden et al. (1980a)	42 chronic schizophrenics	Sixty percent exceeded normal ventricular size drawn from the literature
9. Trimble and Kingsley (1978)	11 schizophrenic patients	Seven with early or questionable ventricular enlargement
10. Campbell et al. (1979)	35 schizophrenic outpatients	Six had "cortical atrophy"; one patient had ventricular enlargement
11. Weinberger et al. (1979c)	75 psychiatric patients 60 chronic schizophrenics	Ten schizophrenic patients with atrophy of the anterior cerebellar vermis
12. Heath et al. (1979)	85 schizophrenic patients	Thirty-four had vermian atrophy

Study	Sample	Findings
13. Luchins et al. (in press)	66 right-handed chronic schizophrenics 100 neurological controls	Patients without atrophy had increased reversals of the usual asymmetry of the frontal and occipital lobes
14. Naeser et al. (in press)	17 chronic schizophrenics	Reversed occipital asymmetry three times more frequent than normal
15. Golden et al. (1980b)	24 chronic schizophrenics 22 "normal" controls	Reduced CAT numbers in several brain regions in the schizophrenics

COMPUTERIZED AXIAL TOMOGRAPHIC FINDINGS IN SCHIZOPHRENIA

In virtually every CAT study of schizophrenia, some patients had evidence of cerebral atrophy—usually enlarged ventricles or dilated cortical fissures and sulci. These studies are summarized in Table 8-2. The first study was reported by Johnstone et al. (1976). They compared the size of the lateral ventricles, determined quantitatively, of 17 chronic schizophrenic patients [diagnosed by Feighner et al. (1972) criteria, mean age 58] with those of eight, similarly aged normal volunteers. The schizophrenic patients had significantly larger ventricles ($p < .01$).

In an attempt to replicate Johnstone's finding, we blindly compared the ventricular size of 58 chronic schizophrenic patients diagnosed prior to CAT scanning by Research Diagnostic Criteria (Spitzer, Endicott, and Robins, 1977) with that of 56, similarly aged, asymptomatic, healthy volunteers (Weinberger et al., 1979a). All subjects were under 50 years old (mean age of both groups, 30). Ventricular size was measured by planimetry, as described by Synek and Reuben (1976). This method involves measuring the area of the lateral ventricles in the CAT slice that shows them at their largest and then expressing this area as a percentage of the intracranial space in the same slice [ventricular brain ratio (VBR)]. This method is highly reliable and correlates extremely well with computer-derived ventricular volume (Penn, Belanger, and Yasnoff, 1978; Jacobs et al., 1978). The patients had significantly larger ventricles ($p < .0001$). In addition, 40% of the patients exceeded the control range, whereas 53% were outside two standard deviations of the control mean. Despite the considerable difference in ventricular size between these groups, the magnitude of ventricular enlargement was relatively subtle. Less than one-half the patients with ventricles larger than the largest control had CAT scans that were interpreted subjectively by a neuroradiologist as abnormal; these were usually read as showing "mild enlargement" or "generous" ventricles. The VBRs were considerably less than have been reported in patients with dementia or hydrocephalus (Synek and Reuben, 1976; Jacobs and Kinkel, 1976). In fact, the mean VBR (8.7) for the schizophrenic patients is similar to the VBR reported for normal individuals 70 years of age (Barron, Jacob, and Kinkel, 1976; Earnest et al., 1979).

In the same patient and control samples, we also measured blindly the widths of the Sylvian fissures and the interhemispheric fissure and the mean width of the three broadest cortical sulci (Weinberger et al., 1979b). The patients had a significantly broader distribution of widths for each of these structures. Furthermore, approximately one-third of the patients had at least one structure width that exceeded the widest control.

Since these original studies, we have increased the size of our samples. To date, we have examined 80 chronic schizophrenic patients and 66 asymptomatic control subjects (mean age of both groups 29, age range 20 to 49). Figure 8-1 shows the size of the lateral ventricles (in (VBR units) of the subjects in these groups. It is apparent that the ventricles of the patients are significantly larger and that approximately one-third of them are outside the control range. In our expanded series, the distribution of widths for cortical structures is still significantly different between the groups, although the percentage of patients with a cortical structure wider than the control limit has dropped to 18.

In a related study, we compared the CAT scans of 10 young, chronic schizophrenic patients with those of a novel control group, 12 of their discordant siblings (Weinberger et al. 1981). The purpose of this study was twofold: to control for possible socioeconomic and cultural effects on ventricular size and to explore the possibility that the CAT findings might be coincidental familial traits. In each sibship, the schizophrenic patient had the largest ventricles. Although seven of the patients exceeded the previously defined normal range, all the siblings were well

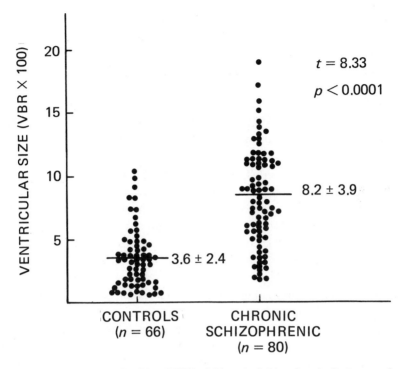

FIGURE 8-1. Ventricular Size (VBR) of Chronic Schizophrenic Patients and Healthy Control Subjects

within this range. Three patients had an abnormally dilated cortical structure; none of the siblings showed cortical abnormalities. The results of this study suggested that at least in these sibships the CAT abnormalities were in fact markers of the illness and not coincidental familiar traits.

Rieder et al. (1979) reported the results of CAT scans in 17 randomly selected, chronic schizophrenic outpatients (RDC diagnosis) between the ages of 20 and 35. Four of the patients had mildly or moderately prominent cortical sulci as judged by two neuroradiologists. There were no controls and ventricular measurements were not made.

In another study, Rieder et al. (1981) reported the CAT scan results of 68 psychiatric inpatients of various diagnoses on the clinical research wards of the NIMH. Ventricular size was evaluated blindly by the VBR method and sulcal size was graded visually on a four-point scale. Using normal values from the literature as a control group, Rieder et al. found that the 29 patients with chronic schizophrenia had significantly larger ventricles ($p < .001$). Furthermore, the size of the ventricles of these patients was not significantly different from the chronic schizophrenic patients studied by Weinberger et al. (1979a). Mild to moderate sulcal dilation was found in five patients, but a normal control group was not used to validate whether this was, in fact, abnormal.

Famuyiwa et al. (1979) studied 45 "long-stay" chronic schizophrenic patients under age 60 (mean age, 48), all of whom fulfilled Feighner et al. (1972) diagnostic criteria. Thirty-one of the scans were considered abnormal, showing either ventricular enlargement defined by linear ventricular indices or cortical atrophy evaluated subjectively. Twenty-four of the 37 cases in which ventricular measurements were made exceeded the normal limits drawn from the literature.

Golden et al. (1980a) studied 42 chronic schizophrenic patients (DSM-III diagnostic criteria) between the ages of 20 and 40. Selection criteria were unclear, but 22 patients had been referred for suspicion of "brain dysfunction." Using published normal values for comparison, they found that the VBRs of 60% of their patients exceeded the normal limit. The mean VBR of their sample was approximately 50% larger than that of the samples of Weinberger et al. and Rieder et al. and more than three times the mean of the normal subjects studied by Weinberger et al.

In two reports, no CAT abnormalities were found in schizophrenic patients. Trimble and Kingsley (1978) studied 11 patients (mean age 34, unspecified diagnostic criteria) referred to exclude organic disease. Using Evans ratio (Evans, 1942), a linear index of frontal horn span, they found that the ventricular size of all the patients fell within the normal range. Their findings, however, are questionable for several reasons. Evans ratio was originally designed for evaluating ventricular size on antero-posterior views of PEGs. It assesses only frontal horn span. On CAT scans, linear frontal horn measurements do not correlate well with actual ventricular volume (Penn, Belanger, and Yasnoff, 1978), particularly when the volume is small. Measuring only the frontal horns also involves an assumption that enlargement will be diffuse. Despite these methodological problems, our re-examination of Trimble and Kingley's published data reveals that seven of their 11 patients fell into the range that Evans considered indicative of early or questionable ventricular enlargement.

Campbell et al. (1979) performed CAT scans on 35 outpatients (mean age 37) "described as schizophrenic" by two psychiatrists. The cerebral cortex was assessed subjectively, and ventricular size was determined by

Huckman's measure (Huckman, Fox, and Topel, 1975), another frontal horn span index. A control sample was not included. Six patients had evidence of cortical atrophy, and one patient exceeded Huckman's normal limit. Campbell et al. dismissed their findings as being nonspecific and inconsistent.

In addition to ventricular enlargement and cortical atrophy, three other abnormalities have been observed on CAT scans of schizophrenic patients. Three reports describe apparent atrophy of the anterior cerebellar vermis. Weinberger et al. (1979c) found that 10 of 60 chronic schizophrenic patients had this finding, defined by the presence of three vermian gyri (Allen, Martin, and McLain, 1979). None of the 15 patients with other psychiatric diagnoses had evidence of cerebellar atrophy. The sibling study mentioned above included three of the patients with vermian atrophy. Cerebellar atrophy was not found in any of the siblings (Weinberger et al. 1981). Heath, Franklin, and Shraberg (1979) found atrophy of the vermis in 34 of 85 (40%) schizophrenic patients. Rieder et al. (1981) observed this finding in only two of 28 schizophrenic patients under age 50.

Another finding concerns asymmetries of the frontal and occipital lobes. It has long been known that the human brain is not a perfectly symmetrical organ. Several anatomical asymmetries have been documented, some of which may relate to lateralized cerebral functions, such as language (LeMay, 1976). On CAT scans, asymmetries of the frontal and occipital lobes can be observed; normal right-handed individuals tend to have wider right frontal and left occipital lobes (LeMay, 1976; LeMay and Kido, 1978). This normal asymmetric pattern has recently been shown in postmortem histological preparations to correspond with actual differences in the volume of these lobes, present as early as 20 weeks of gestation (Weinberger et al., 1982). Reversals of the normal occipital lobe asymmetry have been observed in CAT studies of patients with autism (Hier et al., 1978a), developmental dyslexia (Heir, LeMay, and Rosenberger, 1978b), and verbal intellectual deficits (Rosenberger and Hier, 1980). It also appears that reversals are more frequent in schizophrenic patients. Luchins, Weinberger, and Wyatt (in press) compared the frontal and occipital asymmetries of 66, right-handed, chronic schizophrenic patients with those of 100 randomly selected CAT scans from the NIH neuroradiology files (excluding only patients with space-occupying lesions or trauma). The groups differed significantly in the frequency of reversals of both the expected frontal (p <.01) and occipital (p <.01) asymmetry. An equally interesting finding from this study was that schizophrenic patients with evidence of atrophy (either ventricular enlargement or cortical atrophy) did not differ from the control subjects. The patients who had otherwise quantitatively normal CAT scans had the high frequency of reversals. One other study has looked for lobar asymmetries in schizophrenic patients. Naeser et al. (1981) measured the CAT scans of 17 schizophrenic patients, all of whom had prefrontal leukotomies performed 25 years earlier. They found reversed occipital asymmetry (right wider than left) to be three times more frequent in their patient sample than in the normal subjects studied by LeMay (1976).

Finally, Golden et al. (1980b) compared the actual "CAT numbers" from several regions of the brain of 24 schizophrenic patients and 22 controls evaluated for various symptomatic complaints, but ultimately considered normal. Their method involved randomly selecting CAT numbers from the computer printout of several CAT slices. The printout is a numerical map of the relative densities contained within that slice. They found several regions to be significantly less dense in the schizophrenic patients as compared with the controls. The left frontal region showed the greatest difference. This exciting new method provides a means of comparing differences in brain parenchyma that is not possible from the reconstructed visual images. The Golden et al. study, however, does not conclusively establish a deficit in parenchymal density in the schizophrenic patients. In their random selection of CAT numbers, they did not exclude sampling from within the ventricular space. Thus the difference they found may be simply the result of larger ventricles in the patients causing a greater representation of low density (water) numbers in the computer printout. There are also a number of artifacts inherent in using CAT numbers, such as variation in radiation energy, skull thickness and size, and various machine artifacts, that will have to be minimized before this method can be used with confidence (Zatz and Alvarey, 1977; McCullough, 1977).

SUMMARY OF CAT FINDINGS

The CAT studies confirm earlier PEG findings and indicate evidence of brain atrophy in some patients with a diagnosis of chronic schizophrenia. The most frequent finding is mild ventricular enlargement. Atrophy of the cortex and cerebellar vermis occur to a lesser degree. When those patients with atrophy are segregated out, an additional group with CAT abnormalities, those with reversed asymmetries of the frontal and occipital lobes, can be identified. Clearly, these findings cannot be considered pathognomonic, since many patients, probably the majority, have normal CAT scans. Nevertheless, the conclusion that some of these patients have a structural brain abnormality is unavoidable. The questions that must be considered include: Are these findings the result of treatment?; If they are not, are they relevant to the pathogenesis of the schizophrenic syndrome?; Do they define a more homogeneous subtype of this disorder?, and finally, What is their etiology?

THE ROLE OF TREATMENT

Since none of the CAT studies mentioned involved "first-break" patients, it is possible that the findings are the result of treatment. Neuroleptic drug therapy, ECT, and the impact of chronic institutionalization might, at least theoretically, produce brain atrophy. Although this possibility cannot be definitively dismissed, the available evidence weighs heavily against it. To begin with, several of the PEG studies included patients who had never received somatic therapy (Huber, 1957; Nagy, 1963). Others (Haug, 1962; Asano, 1967) found no relationship between somatic therapy (neuroleptic drugs and ECT) and PEG findings. Johnstone et al. (1976) included in their CAT study four patients who had never been treated with either neuroleptics or by ECT. The ventricles of these four patients were as large as those of the rest of the group. None of the other CAT studies could demonstrate a relationship between treatment and the abnormalities (Weinberger et al., 1979a; Weinberger et al., 1979b; Golden et al., 1980a; Rieder et al. 1981; Golden et al., 1980b). Patients with evidence of atrophy had not been treated longer with drugs or more frequently by ECT or been institutionalized longer than patients with normal CAT scans. Furthermore, in these studies there was no correlation between the magnitude of the abnormalities and the duration or frequency of treatment.

Another approach to the possible impact of treatment is to study older patients who have been continuously hospitalized and treated with neuroleptic drugs for extended periods. We recently examined 24 chronic schizophrenic patients between the age of 50 and 80 and compared them with a group of normal volunteers of similar age (Weinberger, Jeste, and Wyatt, unpublished data). The patients had been hospitalized for an average of 30 years and had received drug therapy for most of this period. Although the patients had significantly larger ventricles than did the controls, they were quantitatively less abnormal relative to their control group than were the younger patients (Weinberger et al., 1979a) relative to theirs. The degree of cortical atrophy in the older patients (common in this age range) did not differ from that in the controls. These results suggest that the difference between the older and younger patients, in spite of 20 more years of hospitalization and drug therapy, is consistent simply with the effects of aging. Preliminary results from a study of first-break patients indicate that enlarged ventricles exist in some patients prior to any treatment (Weinberger et al., unpublished data).

THE QUESTION OF SPECIFICITY

In considering whether the CAT findings might be related to the pathogenesis of the schizophrenic syndrome, we should note that none of the findings are in themselves specific. Ventricular enlargement and dilated cortical sulci can occur in any degenerative brain disease and are concomitants of normal aging (Barron, Jacobs, and Kinkel, 1976; Haug, 1977). They have also been described in alcoholics (Lee et al., 1979) and in patients with chronic severe migraine headaches (Hungerford, duBoulay, and Zilkha, 1976). Cerebellar atrophy is also a nonspecific finding, particularly common among alcoholics (Haubek and Lee, 1979). The lobar asymmetries, as noted, were first described in individuals with other disorders.

Some patients with other psychiatric disorders also have evidence of atrophy. This was demonstrated in PEG studies (Haug 1962; Nagy, 1963) and more recently in a CAT study (Rieder et al., 1981). In the PEG studies, it was found that patients with unremitting illnesses were especially likely to have enlarged ventricles and cortical atrophy. The study by Rieder et al. appears to replicate this. Included in this study, in addition to the schizophrenic patients, were 24 significantly older patients with affective disorders. Since age is an important factor affecting ventricular size, the schizophrenic and affective patients could not be directly compared. Nevertheless, after a statistical age correction procedure (which may not be valid, since age and ventricular size do not correlate linearly), no difference in ventricular size was found between these patient groups. The affective patients under age 50, however, did not have cortical or cerebellar abnormalities. In interpreting these results, we should point out that the affective disorder patients in this study were probably atypical. All of them were research volunteers who had failed to respond to conventional therapy. Another atypical aspect of this sample was the magnitude of the VBRs. The mean for the affective group aged 50 to 60 was within the range reported for patients with dementia. Nevertheless, this study appears to confirm earlier PEG findings, showing that at least some patients with affective disorders have CAT abnormalities. A recent study of a more typical sample of elderly depressed patients found no significant difference between their CAT scans and those of a normal control group (Jacoby and Levy, 1980). This latter report did note, however, that nine of the 40 depressed patients as well as 10 of the 50 controls had "enlarged ventricles."

In the history of psychiatry research, many of the biological findings that have been observed in schizophrenic patients are also found in other psychiatric patients. Examples include reduced platelet MAO activity and elevated serum CPK activity. The biological and pathogenic significance of such abnormalities are justifiably questioned once they are shown to be nonspecific.

In the case of cerebral atrophy, however, the argument is somewhat different. First of all, the finding is not a peripheral or indirect clue to a putative abnormality of the brain. It is an abnormality of the brain. Second, ventricular enlargement per se is not a neuropathological process, but the result of one. As such, it is only a marker for a process that may or may not be specific. The etiology and clinical significance of ventricular enlargement may be entirely different in schizophrenic patients than in other psychiatric patients. There is some evidence to support this. In the study by Rieder et al., age was a significant determinant of CAT abnormalities for the affective disorder patients, but not for the schizophrenics. This suggests that the abnormalities in the former group may have had a different etiology, perhaps related to aging or to factors secondary to being depressed. The finding that age or length of illness in the case of the schizophrenics does not correlate with ventricular size has also been found by others (Weinberger et al., 1979a; Golden et al., 1980a) suggesting that in this group ventricular enlargement reflects a more static condition. An alternative possibility is that the process or processes underlying cerebral atrophy in schizophrenia are nonspecific, but relevant because of interactions with other pathogenic factors.

It is not uncommon in medicine for nonspecific findings to be unimportant in one clinical setting, and crucial in another. Thus, enlarged ventricles can be overlooked in a well-functioning 75-year-old individual, but they dare not be in someone who is incontinent and has a gait disturbance. In the latter case, they serve as a marker for a pathological process affecting cerebrospinal fluid (CSF) circulation. Similarly, enlarged ventricles in a 25-year-old schizophrenic patient may have specific implications, despite the "nonspecificity" of the finding.

In this discussion we have assumed that, except for the reversed asymmetries, the CAT findings represent brain atrophy. Atrophy, itself a nonspecific finding, is a histopathological diagnosis that in the brain indicates irreversible degeneration. It is inferred from a CAT scan that shows enlarged CSF spaces (ventricles, sulci, and cisterns) in the absence of obstruction of CSF circulation. Several recent reports have suggested, however, that all that is "atrophy" on a CAT scan is not atrophy of the brain. From cases of "reversible atrophy" on a CAT image that have been described (Heinz, Martinez, and Haenggeli, 1977; Rodeck and Campbell, 1979; Carlen et al., 1978; Deonna and Voumard, 1979), it appears that changes in the size of the CSF spaces may reflect alterations in fluid, electrolyte, and nutritional status.

We have explored the possibility that the CAT findings in our patients reflect changes other than atrophy. No abnormalities of CSF dynamics or evidence of reversibility have been found. The CSF pressure at lumbar puncture has been within normal limits in all examined cases (43). Three of the patients with large ventricles underwent radionuclide cisternography, which showed no evidence of impaired CSF absorption. Five patients with abnormal scans have been re-scanned after a two- to three-year period. In each case, the repeat scans were the same as the originals. As mentioned, in several PEG studies followup examinations were done, in no instance was improvement seen.

It appears, therefore, that the CAT findings in schizophrenia reflect fixed structural abnormalities of the brain. The nature of the abnormalities is probably atrophy, although a congenital defect or dysplastic process cannot be excluded. All these possibilities are as nonspecific as the

CAT findings. Their etiologies may be diverse. Nevertheless, if the CAT findings are relevant to the schizophrenic syndrome, then patients who have them should be different in some meaningful way from patients who lack them.

CLINICAL AND BIOLOGICAL SIGNIFICANCE OF CAT FINDINGS IN SCHIZOPHRENIA

Cerebral atrophy is usually associated with impaired performance on neuropsychological tests. Several studies have explored the possibility that schizophrenic patients with atrophy on CAT scans are a more neuropsychologically impaired subgroup. Johnstone et al. (1978) found that intellectual impairment, as measured on the Withers and Hinton test battery, correlated ($r = -.70$; $p < .01$) with ventricular size. Furthermore, they could not relate this to the presence of prominent hallucinations or delusions, since test performance was poorer in patients with primarily negative symptoms (affective flattening, retardation, and poverty of speech). Famuyiwa et al. (1979) found a significant ($p < .05$), but less impressive correlation ($r = .36$), between performance on the paired associative learning test and the neuroradiologists' score of degree of atrophy. They did not find a significant correlation for performance on the Withers and Hinton battery.

Three studies have found a relationship between impairment on the Halsted Reitan Battery (HRB) and CAT evidence of atrophy. Rieder et al. (1979) compared their four patients with sulcal dilation to four, clinically similar aged-matched patients with normal CAT scans. The HRB was administered by the same examiner who was blind to the CAT findings. Each of the four patients with sulcal prominence scored in the impaired range, as compared with only one of the patients with a normal CAT scan. In a similar study, Donnelly et al. (1980) compared eight patients with atrophy to seven patients with normal scans. Again, they found greater impairment in the former group. Since the Donnelly et al. study, we have expanded our sample to 23 patients. The 11 patients with atrophy had significantly worse scores on the average impairment rating (AIR) (mean + S.D. 2.7 ± .7) than did the patients with normal scans (1.7 ± 8; $p <. 005$). Furthermore, 10 of the former group scored in the "organically" impaired range ($AIR > 1.55$), as compared with only five of the normal patients ($p = .03$). Adams et al. (1980) administered the HRB to 60 schizophrenic patients, some of whom had atrophy. They found a small correlation ($r = -.38$, $p < .01$) between the Halsted Impairment index and ventricular size. They also found that patients with atrophy were more likely to score in the impaired range. Golden et al. (1980a) found an association between ventricular enlargement and impairment on the Luria-Nebraska Neuropsychological battery. Eight of the 14 subscales correlated significantly with VBR; overall, they found a multiple correlation of 0.72 for VBR and Luria Scores.

Taken together, these studies lend strong support to the notion that CAT abnormalities are associated with neuropsychological impairment. Adams et al. (1980) cautioned that such group findings should not be used to suggest that an individual schizophrenic patient with neuropsychological impairment has brain damage. Clearly, many patients with normal scans will score poorly on these tests. What stands out, however, is that patients with CAT abnormalities are more likely to perform poorly and that as a group their performance will be more homogeneous.

We recently studied the relationship of atrophy to several other neurological abnormalities frequently found in schizophrenic patients (Weinberger et al., submitted a). Patients were examined on an inventory of non-focal ("soft") signs, completed a pendulum eye-tracking protocol, and had scalp EEGs. In each case, the tests were administered and interpreted without knowledge of the CAT results. Twenty patients with atrophy had significantly more non-focal signs than did 20 clinically similar patients with normal scans. Also, pendulum eye tracking, graded qualitatively from oculographic recordings, was significantly more disordered in the 12 patients with atrophy who were able to complete the test than in 18 patients without atrophy. The EEG results were somewhat surprising. Of the 44 patients who had EEGs, 29 were abnormal, with the abnormality usually consisting of excess theta activity. The frequency of abnormality was not different for patients on drugs and for those who had been drug-free for several weeks. Eighty percent of the patients with abnormal EEGs had normal CAT scans. In other words, patients with atrophy were much more likely to have a normal EEG, perhaps reflecting the subcortical location of ventricular enlargement. Although the meaning of this finding is unclear, it again illustrates that patients with atrophy are a different population.

Another clinical parameter that appears to correlate with atrophy is premorbid adjustment. In a study of 51 patients, the 21 with atrophy had significantly poorer school and social adjustment than did the patients with normal scans (Weinberger et al., 1980b). The difference was particularly striking during childhood. This finding raises the possibility that the CAT abnormalities relate to a pathological process that occurs early in development.

All the correlations mentioned above have been associated with poor prognosis. Since the PEG studies demonstrated an inverse relationship between atrophy and prognosis, the CAT findings also might be expected to have prognostic significance. We investigated the response of 20 chronic schizophrenic patients (10 with enlarged ventricles, 10 without) to eight weeks of standard neuroleptic drug therapy (Weinberger et al., 1980a). The patients with enlarged ventricles had a significantly poorer response, despite similar dosages and serum drug concentrations.

The implication of this latter study is that dopamine blockade is less likely to reduce psychopathology in patients with atrophy. Stated another way, dopaminergic hyperactivity (the "dopamine hypothesis") may not be relevant to the psychopathology of these patients. Two recent studies have provided further evidence for this. Kleinman et al. (in press) found that, in drug-free patients, serum prolactin concentrations, an indirect measure of central nervous system dopaminergic activity, correlates inversely with psychopathology in patients with normal CAT scans, but not in those with enlarged ventricles. In a related study, Karson et al. (in press) found that spontaneous blink rates, a possible indicator of mesencephalic dopaminergic activity, were higher in patients with normal scans. Furthermore, they found that drug treatment significantly reduced blink rates, but again only in those patients with normal scans.

The clinical and biological significance of the CAT abnormalities other than cerebral atrophy have been less thoroughly pursued. Franklyn et al. (1980) studied 12 patients with vermian atrophy and 12 age-matched patients with normal scans. They found that the former group had a more insidious onset and a poorer response to drugs and ECT. Luchins, Weinberger, and Wyatt (in press) reported the WAIS scores of 24 patients, eight of whom had reversals of the expected lobar asymmetries. The group with reversals were significantly more likely to have poorer verbal than performance IQs. Luchins et al. (in press a) have also found that the frequency of HLA-A2 is increased in patients with lobar reversals.

Finally, the CAT findings do not appear to correlate with any of several catecholeamine parameters believed relevant to schizophrenia, including platelet MAO activity, serum dopamine-β-hydroxylase activity, and urinary phenylethylamine excretion (Jeste et al., 1982). DeLisi et al (1981), however, found that patients with CAT atrophy had higher whole blood serotonin concentrations than did clinically similar patients with normal scans and that ventricular size and serotonin concentration were significantly correlated ($r = .55$, $p < .03$). This finding, although intriguing, is difficult to interpret.

CONCLUSIONS

1. Studies of cerebral structure in living patients, including pneumoencephalographic, echoencephalographic, and computed axial tomographic scans all show that some patients with the diagnosis of chronic schizophrenia have subtle structural abnormalities of the brain.

2. The most frequent finding is mild ventricular enlargement. Dilation of cortical sulci and fissures are less common. Together, these abnormalities probably represent brain atrophy. They may also correspond to developmental defects or dysplastic processes. Atrophy of the anterior cerebellar vermis has been found in a small percentage of patients. Patients without atrophy have an increased frequency of reversals of the normal frontal and occipital lobe asymmetries.

3. The findings do not appear to be the result of treatment, either institutional or somatic.

4. The etiology of the abnormalities is unknown. The results of a study of premorbid adjustment suggest that atrophy may predate the onset of the typical syndrome in late adolescence.

5. Despite the nonspecificity of cerebral atrophy, it appears to be clinically and biologically relevant in schizophrenic patients. Individuals with this finding are a more homogeneous population. They tend to have the following characteristics: negative symptoms, neuropsychological deficits, non-focal neurological signs, disordered

smooth pursuit eye movements, less frequent EEG abnormalities, poor premorbid adjustment, and poor response to drug treatment. These patients may comprise a group for whom dopaminergic hyperactivity is not an important pathogenic factor.

REFERENCES

Adams, K. M., J. Jacism, G. G. Brown, and R. Boulos (1980). Neurobehavioral and CT deficit in schizophrenics. Presented at the 133rd Annual APA Meeting, San Francisco.

Allen, J. H., J. T. Martin, and L. W. McLain (1979). Computed tomography in cerebellar atrophic processes. *Radiology* 130, 379–382.

Asano, N. (1967). Pneumoencephalographic study of schizophrenia. In *Clinical Genetics in Psychiatry. Problems in Nosological Classification* (H. Mitsuda, ed.). Igaku Shoin Ltd, Tokyo, pp. 209–219.

Barron, S. A., L. Jacobs, and W. R. Kinkel (1976). Changes in size of normal lateral ventricles during aging determined by computed tomography. *Neurology* 26, 1011–1013.

Bliss, E. L. (1976). Neurological features of schizophrenic syndromes. In *The Biology of the Schizophrenic Process* (S. Wolfe and B. B. Berle, eds.) Plenum Press, New York, pp. 40–45.

Campbell, R., P. Hays, D. B. Russel, and D. J. Zacks (1979). CT scan variants and genetic heterogeneity in schizophrenia. *Amer. J. Psychiat.* 136, 722–723.

Carlen, P. L., G. Wortzman, R. C. Holgate, et al. (1978). Reversible cerebral atrophy in recently abstinent chronic alcoholics measured by computed tomography scans. *Science* 200, 1076–1078.

Dandy, W. E. (1919). Roentgenography of the brain after the injection of air into the spinal cord. *Ann. Surg.* 70, 397–403.

Daum, C. H., W. M. McKinney, R. C. Proctor, et al. (1976). Echoencephalographs of 100 consecutive acute psychiatric admissions. *J. Clin. Ultrasound* 4, 329–333.

DeLisi, L. E., L. M. Neckers, D. R. Weinberger, and R. J. Wyatt (in press). Increased whole blood serotonin concentrations in chronic schizophrenic patients. *Arch. Gen. Psychiat.*

Deonna, T., and C. Voumard (1979). Reversible cerebral atrophy and cortico-trophin. *Lancet* ii, 207.

Donnelly, E. F., D. R. Weinberger, I. N. Waldman, and R. J. Wyatt (1980). Cognitive impairment associated with morphological brain abnormalities on computed tomography in chronic schizophrenic patients. *J. Nerv. Ment. Dis.* 168, 305–308.

Earnest, M. P., R. K. Heaton, W. E. Wilkinson, and W. F. Manke (1979).

Cortical atrophy, ventricular enlargement and intellectual impairment in the aged. *Neurology* 29, 1138–1143.

Evans, W. A. (1942). An encephalographic ratio for estimating ventricular enlargement and cerebral atrophy. *Arch. Neurol. Psychiat.* 47, 931–937.

Famuyiwa, O. O., D. Eccleston, A. A. Donaldson, and R. F. Garside (1979). Tardive dyskinesia and dementia. *Brit. J. Psychiat.* 135, 500–504.

Feighner, J. P., E. Robins, S. B. Guze, et al. (1972). Diagnostic criteria for psychiatric research. *Arch. Gen. Psychiat.* 26, 57–63.

Franklyn, D. E., R. G. Heath, F-T. Kung, and R. E. Garey (1980). Comparison of schizophrenic patients with and without cerebellar vermis atrophy. Presented at the 35th Annual Meeting of the Society of Biological Psychiatry, Boston.

Golden, C. J., J. A. Moses, M. A. Zelazowski, et al. (1980a). Cerebral ventricular size and neuropsychochological impairment in young chronic schizophrenics. *Arch. Gen. Psychiat.* 37, 619–623.

Golden, C. J., G. Grabe, J. Coffman et al. (1980b). Brain density deficits in chronic schizophrenia. Presented at the 133rd Annual APA Meeting, San Francisco.

Haubek, A., and KV. Lee (1979). Computed tomography in alcoholic cerebellar atrophy. *Neuroradiology* 18, 77–79.

Haug, G. (1977). Age and sex dependence of the size of the normal ventricles on computed tomography. *Neuroradiology* 14, 201–204.

Haug, J. O. (1962). Pneumoencephalographic studies in mental disease. *Acta Psychiat. Scand.* (Suppl. 165) 38, 1–114.

Heath, R. G., D. E. Frankyln, and D. Shraberg (1979). Gross pathology of the cerebellum in patients diagnosed and treated as functional psychiatric disorders. *J. Nerv. Ment. Dis.* 167, 585–592.

Heinz, R., J. Martinez, and A. Haenggli (1977). Reversibility of cerebral atrophy in anorexia nervosa and Cushing's syndrome. *J. Comp. Asst. Tomog.* 1, 415–418.

Hier, D. B., M. LeMay, P. B. Rosenberger, and V. P. Perlo (1978a). Developmental dyslexia: Evidence for a sub-group with reversal of cerebral asymmetry. *Arch. Neurol.* 35, 90–92.

Hier, D. B., M. LeMay, and P. B. Rosenberger (1978b). Autism: Association with reversed cerebral asymmetry. *Neurology* 28, 348–349.

Holden, J. M. C., G. Forno, T. Itil, and W. H. Hsu (1973). Echoencephalographic patterns in chronic schizophrenia (relationship to therapy resistance). *Biol. Psychiat.* 6, 129–141.

Huber, G. (1957). *Pneumoencephalographische und Psychopathologische Bilder Bei Endogen Psychosen.* Springer-Verlag, Berlin.

Huber, G., G. Gross, and R. Schutter (1975). A long-term follow-up study of schizophrenia: Psychiatric course of illness and prognosis. *Acta Psychiat. Scand.* 52, 49–57.

Huber, G. (1979). Pure defect and its meaning for a somatosis hypothesis of schizophrenia. In *Biological Psychiatry Today* (J. Obiols, C. Ballus, E. Gonzales, and J. Pugol, eds.) Elsevier North Holland, Amsterdam pp. 345–350.

Huckman, M. S., J. Fox, and J. Topel (1975). The validity of criteria for the evaluation of cerebral atrophy by computed tomography. *Radiology* 116, 85–92.

Hungerford, G. D., G. H. duBoulay, and K. J. Zilkha (1976). Computerized axial tomography in patients with severe migraine: A preliminary report. *J. Neurol., Neurosurg Psychiat.* 39, 990–994.

Jacobi, W., and H. Winkler (1927). Encephalographische studien au chronisch schizophrenen. *Arch. Psychiat. Nervenkr.* 81, 299–332.

Jacobs, L., and W. Kinkel (1976). Computerized axial transverse tomography in normal pressure hydrocephalus. *Neurology* 26, 501–507.

Jacobs, L., W. R. Kinkel, F. Painter, *et al.* (1978). Computerized tomography in dementia with special reference to changes in size of normal ventricles during aging and normal pressure hydrocephalus. In *Alzheimer's Disease: Senile Dementia and Related Disorders.* (R. Katzman, R. D. Terry, and K. L. Bick, eds.). Raven Press, New York, pp. 241–260.

Jacoby, R. J., and R. Levy (1980). Computed tomography in the elderly. 3. Affective disorder. *Brit. J. Psychiat.* 136, 270–275.

Jeste, D. V., J. E. Kleinman, S. G. Potkin, D. J. Luchins, and D. R. Weinberger (1981). *Ex Uno Multe:* Subtyping the schizophrenic syndrome. *Biol. Psychiat.* 17: 199–222.

Johnstone, E. C., T. J. Crow, C. D. Frith, et al. (1976). Cerebral ventricular size and cognitive impairment in chronic schizophrenia. *Lancet* 11, 924–926.

Johnstone, E. C., T. J. Crow, C. D. Frith, M. Stevens, L. Kreel, and J. Husband (1978). The dementia of dementia praecox. *Acta Psychiat. Scand.* 57, 305–324.

Karson, C., L. B. Bigelow, J. E. Kleinman, D. R. Weinberger, and R. J. Wyatt (in press). Halopindol-induced changes in blink rates correlate with changes in BPRS scores. *Brit. J. Psychiat.*

Kleinman, J. E., D. R. Weinberger, A. D. Rogol, et al. (in press). Relationship between plasma prolactin concentrations and psychopathology in chronic schizophrenia. Arch. Gen. Psychiat.

Lee, K., L. Moller, H. Finn, *et al.* (1979). Alcohol induced brain damage and liver damage in young males. *Lancet* ii, 759–761.

LeMay, M. (1967). Changes in ventricular size during and after pneumoencephalography. *Radiology* 88, 57–63.

LeMay, M. (1976). Morphological cerebral asymmetries of modern man, fossil man and non-human primates. *Ann. N. Y. Acad. Sci.* 280, 349–366.

LeMay, M., and D. K. Kido (1978). Asymmetries of cerebral hemispheres on computed tomograms. *J. Comp. Asst. Tomogr.* 2, 470–476.

Lempke, R. (1935). Untersuchungen uber die soziale Prognose der schizophrenic unter besonderer Berucksichtigung des encephalographischen Befundes. *Arch. Psychiat. Nervenkr.* 104, 89–136.

Luchins, D. J., D. R. Weinberger, E. F. Torrey, *et al.* (1981). HLA-A₂ increased in schizophrenic patients with reversed cerebral asymmetry. *Brit. J. Psychiat.*

Luchins, D. J., D. R. Weinberger, and R. J. Wyatt (in press). Cerebral asymmetry in schizophrenia as determined by computed tomography. *Amer. J. Psychiat.*

McCullough, E. C. (1977). Factors affecting the use of quantitative information from a CT scanner. *Radiology* 124, 99–107.

Naeser, M. A., H. L. Levine, D. F. Benson, et al. (1981). Frontal leukotomy size and hemispheric asymmetries on CT scans of schizophrenics with variable recovery. *Arch. Neuro.* 38: 30–37.

Nagy, K. (1963). Pneumoencephalographische befunde bei endogen psychosen. *Nervenarzt* 34, 543–548.

Penn, R. D., M. G. Belanger, and W. A. Yasnoff (1978). Ventricular volume in man computed from CAT scans. *Ann. Neurol.* 3, 216–223.

Rieder, R. O., E. F. Donnelly, J. R. Herdt, and I. N. Waldman (1979). Sulcal prominence in young chronic schizophrenic patients: CT scan findings associated with impairment on neuropsychological tests. *Psychiat. Res.* 1, 1–8.

Rieder, R. O., L. S. Mann, D. R. Weinberger, D. P. van Kammen, and R. M. Post (1981). CAT-scans in patients with schizophrenia, schizoaffective disorder and affective disorder, presented at APA Annual Meeting New Orleans.

Rodeck, C. H., and S. Campbell (1979). Reversible cerebral atrophy caused by corticotrophin. *Lancet* i, 1246–1247.

Rosenberger, P. B., and D. B., Hier (1980). Cerebral asymmetry and verbal intellectual deficits. *Ann. Neurol.* 8, 300–304.

Spitzer, R. L., J. Endicott, and E. Robins (1977). *Research Diagnostic Criteria (RDC) for a Selected Group of Functional Disorders.* 3rd ed. Biometrics, New York.

Storey, P. B. (1966). Lumbar air encephalography in chronic schizophrenia: A controlled experiment. *Brit. J. Psychiat.* 112, 135–144.

Synek, V., and J. R. Reuben (1976). The ventricular-brain ratio using planimetric measurement of EMI scans. *Brit. J. Radiol.* 49, 233–237.

Trimble, M., and D. Kingsley (1978). Cerebral ventricular size in chronic schizophrenia. *Lancet* i, 278.

Weinberger, D. R., E. F. Torrey, A. Neophytides, and R. J. Wyatt (1979a). Lateral cerebral ventricular enlargement in chronic schizophrenia. *Arch. Gen. Psych.* 36, 735–739.

Weinberger, D. R., E. F. Torrey, A. Neophytides, and R. J. Wyatt (1979b). Structural abnormalities of the cerebral cortex in chronic schizophrenia. *Arch. Gen. Psychia.* 36, 935–939.

Weinberger, D. R., E. F. Torrey, and R. J. Wyatt (1979c). Cerebellar atrophy in chronic schizophrenia. *Lancet,* 1, 718–719.

Weinberger, D. R., L. B. Bigelow, J. E. Kleinman, S. T. Klein, J. E. Rosenblatt, and R. J. Wyatt (1980a). Cerebral ventricular enlargement in chronic schizophrenia: Association with poor response to treatment. *Arch. Gen. Psychiat.* 37, 11–14.

Weinberger, D. R., E. Cannon-Spoor, S. G. Potkin, and R. J. Wyatt (1980b). Poor premorbid adjustment and CT scan abnormalities in chronic schizophrenia. *Amer. J. Psychiat.* 137, 1410–1413.

Weinberger, D. R., L. E. DeLisi, A. N. Neophytides, and R. J. Wyatt (1981). Familial aspects of CT abnormalities in chronic schizophrenic patients. *Psychiat. Res.* 4, 65–71.

Weinberger, D. R., L. E. DeLisi, S. Targum et al. (unpublished data).

Weinberger, D. R., D. J. Luchins, J. Morihisa, and R. J. Wyatt (1982). Asymmetric volumes of the right and left frontal and occipital lobes of the human brain. *Ann. Neurol.* 11: 97–100.

Weinberger, D. R., R. L. Wagner, J. R. Stevens, et al. (submitted, a). Neurological abnormalities in chronic schizophrenia.

Weinberger, D. R., D. V. Jeste, and R. J. Wyatt (unpublished data).

Zatz, L. M., and R. E. Alvarez (1977). An inaccuracy in computed tomography: The energy dependence of CT values. *Radiology* 124, 91–97.

9 | Dopamine: A Role in Psychosis or Schizophrenia

FRITZ A. HENN

Hypotheses about biological mechanisms that may go awry in schizophrenia have come in large part from pharmacological data. In this case, the cure was thought to point to the cause. Unfortunately, the "cure" in the form of drugs is, at best, a suppression of symptoms. Nonetheless, this strategy has been successful in directing research. I wish to consider the historical development of the principal biological theory of schizophrenia, the dopamine hypothesis, the evidence for and against it, the etiological implications of this theory, and recent evidence that may pave the way for a new, more inclusive hypothesis about biochemical malfunctions, which could play a role in the production of schizophrenic symptoms.

Pharmacological investigations into schizophrenia took their current direction from the discovery of neuroleptic drugs. The word neuroleptic was coined by Delay and Deniker (1957) to emphasize similar actions of two very different drugs, reserpine and chlorpromazine. These drugs both appeared to have antipsychotic activity and also to cause disturbances in motor functions analogous to those seen in Parkinsonism. It was known that reserpine depleted monoamines and Carlsson et al. (1965) showed that DOPA could reverse the effects of reserpine. DOPA could have served as a precursor to both dopamine (DA) and norepinephrine (NE), but at concentrations that reversed the effects of reserpine, only DA was restored. Thus, attention was centered on the role of DA in both schizophrenia and Parkinson's disease. Ehringer and Hornykiwicz (1960) were soon able to demonstrate that Parkinsonism resulted in an almost complete loss of DA from the striatum.

Since neuroleptic drugs, such as chlorpromazine and haloperidol, appeared to cause Parkinsonian symptoms, but did not lower DA levels, alternative explanations for their actions were sought. Carlsson and Lindquist (1963) examined the effect of chlorpromazine and haloperidol on the accumulation of metabolites of DA and NE. They found an increased concentration of metabolites and suggested that this implied an increased rate of synthesis of DA and NE. This could occur if the DA signal were blocked, these investigators hypothesized, this being the first suggestion that neuroleptics block DA receptors.

Thus, there was evidence that neuroleptics act by reducing DA activity. Soon this led to the early formulations of the DA hypothesis of schizophrenia (Van Rossen, 1966). In its simplest form, the hypothesis states that schizophrenia may be associated with an overactivity of DA synapses (Mattysse, 1973; Snyder et al., 1974). Data from studies of neuroleptic effects and of model psychosis have been used to support this hypothesis.

One approach has been the study of toxic psychosis. The rationale is that if a drug-induced psychosis can mimic schizophrenic symptoms, an understanding of the central effect of the drug may aid in understanding schizophrenia. Initially, hallucinogens were thought to provide a model psychosis, but early on it was shown that the psychosis produced by these compounds was quite different from that seen in schizophrenia (Hollister, 1962). This is in contrast to amphetamine psychosis, which can be misdiagnosed as acute paranoid schizophrenia unless a history of drug abuse is obtained (Connell, 1958). The amphetamine psychosis that mimics paranoid psychosis is usually found in a chronic amphetamine user, but no delirium is seen. Other reactions to amphetamines are acute and toxic, showing a psychosis with confusion and disorientation; this is not an illness that models schizophrenia. Chronic administration of *d*-amphetamine can produce a paranoid psychosis in healthy volunteers that resembles paranoid schizophrenia (Randrup and Munkvad, 1972). The mechanism by which amphetamine causes such a psychosis could involve either NE or DA, since amphetamines interact with both neurotransmitter systems centrally. However, since the NE molecule is asymmetric and has stereoisomers, whereas DA does not, a study using both the *d* and *l* forms of amphetamine should differentiate between these two possibilities. The *d*-amphetamine isomer is a more potent NE uptake inhibitor, whereas both *d* and *l* forms are equally potent in blocking DA uptake (J. Coyle and S. Snyder, 1969). This, plus numerous lesion studies, suggests that *d*-amphetamine interacts preferentially with NE systems, whereas both isomers interact equally effectively with DA systems. Angrist, Shopsin, and Gershon (1971) studied the ability of the two isomers of amphetamine to mimic paranoid psychosis in healthy volunteers. In general, their conclusions suggest that *d*- and *l*-amphetamine are nearly equipotent in eliciting psychotic symptoms. Thus, amphetamine psychosis suggests that dopaminergic systems may be involved in symptom production.

Evidence that suggests that DA overactivity caused by amphetamines might relate to schizophrenia comes from the work of Janowsky and his colleagues. They reported that symptoms in schizophrenic patients given a stimulant, methylphenidate, worsened (1973). Since methylphenidate is not as effective in stimulating motor activity as amphetamines, it is of interest to compare the effect of these drugs in schizophrenic patients. Such a study has been done, and it demonstrated that the amphetamines were less potent in activating existing psychotic symptoms (Janowsky and Davis, 1976). Studies with stimulants were seen as generally consistent with the DA hypothesis, though the reason for the higher potency of methylphenidate compared to *d*-amphetamine remains to be elucidated.

The strongest support of the DA hypothesis has come from a study of neuroleptic drug activity in the last decade. These studies encompass functional studies of behavior, electophysiological studies on DA-rich areas, the action of neuroleptics on DA-sensitive adenylate cyclase, and the ability of neuroleptics to effect DA release and to compete for DA receptor sites directly.

The connection between specific behaviors and DA in animals has been demonstrated by the administration of DA, the precursor DOPA, and such DA agonist drugs as apomorphine and amphetamines. One such study illustrated that rats showed deficient discrimination after DA stimulation. This effect was reversed by neuroleptics (Ahlenius and Engel, 1975). Neuroleptics, at doses that cause a return to normal behavior in DA-stimulated rats, completely inhibit the behavior of normal rats. Thus, there appears to be a competition between neuroleptics and DA for some receptor site.

Electrophysiological studies have also demonstrated a competition between neuroleptic drugs and iontophoretically administered DA. These studies suggest that DA inhibits cells in the rat caudate nucleus and that this inhibition is reversed by neuroleptics (Bunney et al., 1973; G. Aghajanian and Bunney, 1977; Bunney, 1978). An interesting series of experiments was carried out on cells of the substantia nigra zona compacta. These cells were identified by means of lesions and fluorescent staining, following the injection of L-DOPA, as dopaminergic cells (Aghajanian and Bunney, 1977). Direct microiontophoresis of either NE or DA on these cells inhibited them. The use of α or β antagonists was without an effect; neuroleptic drugs, however, are able to block the effect of DA. This suggests that the receptor is specifically dopaminergic and that it is located on DA-containing neurons, namely, it is an autoreceptor. Thus, electrophysiological studies support at least two different types of DA receptor, one assumed to be postsynaptic, the other presynaptic. Although there is a clear indication that neuroleptics antagonize DA in electrophysiological studies, there is some dispute as to whether DA is excitatory or inhibitory (York, 1978; Siggins, 1978). It may turn out that DA is primarily a modulator of other inputs (Berger et al., 1978). This clearly is the case in the mammalian superior cervical ganglion (Libet, 1979).

The antagonism between neuroleptic drugs and DA shown at both the behavioral level and the cellular level using electrophysiological techniques has been explored on the enzymatic level using biochemical techniques. Kebabian and Greengard (1971) described a DA-sensitive adenylate cyclase in striatal tissue. This enzyme appeared more sensitive to DA than NE and was not inhibited by α or β blockers. It was found to be sensitive to inhibition by a variety of neuroleptics (Clement-Cormier et al., 1974; Iversen, 1975). Inhibition was proportional to the clinical potency of the neuroleptic drugs, with one exception. The butyrophenones, such as haloperidol, which are very potent clinical agents, inhibited the DA-stimulated adenylate cyclase at concentrations comparable to those found effective for chlorpromazine (Iverson, 1975), a drug that is much less potent clinically. Within the class of butyrophenones, there is a good correlation with clinical potency (Miller, Horn, and Iverson, 1974). Thus, in general, neuroleptic drugs antagonize DA effects at the enzymatic level. One proposal suggests that DA mediates its effects through adenylate cyclase by stimulating protein phosphorylation by $3'5'$ cAMP (Greengard, 1976). The incongruity between the potency of neuroleptics in treating psychosis and in inhibiting DA-stimulated adenylate cyclase was resolved by the finding of multiple DA receptors.

This was first postulated from studies of DA turnover, and subsequently suggested by electrophysiological studies, but it was only recently directly demonstrated by receptor-binding studies. The measurement of DA receptors began when Seeman and his coworkers developed a receptor assay using butyrophenones (Seeman et al., 1975). They found that neuroleptics inhibited butyrophenone binding in the same rank order as the clinical potency of these drugs. This work was confirmed in Snyder's laboratory (Creese, Burt, and Snyder, 1976). Initially, there was some debate over the interpretation of the finding that inhibition of adenylate cyclase and haloperidol binding by neuroleptics followed different patterns, since it could represent two forms of the same receptor or reflect multiple receptors. But, as mentioned earlier, the electrophysiological evidence suggested multiple receptors, as did the biochemical studies. For example, it has been shown that DA synthesis in synaptic fractions is inhibited by DA agonists (Goldstein, Anagnosti, and Shirron, 1973; Christiansen and Squires, 1974) and that this effect is reversed by neuroleptics. This may take place on the presynaptic element of the synapse where DA synthesis presumably takes place. Thus, a variety of evidence pointed to presynaptic receptors. More evidence had come from binding studies. Two ligands, apomorphine (Seeman et al., 1976) and ADTN (2 amino-6,7-dihydroxy-1,2,3,4 tetrahydronaphthalene) (Creese and Snyder, 1978), were found to have binding patterns and biochemical activity that suggested that they labeled different receptors than those labeled by the butyrophenones. This was first clearly stated by Kebabian, who proposed two classes of DA receptor: those linked to adenylate cyclase, D_1, and those not linked to this enzyme, D_2 (Kebabian and Calne, 1979). Thus, at least two distinct DA receptors have been demonstrated by binding studies. The relationship of the D_1 receptor to the autoreceptor has been postulated, but not established. Lesion studies involving cortical ablation demonstrate a reduction in D_2 type receptors in the striatum, and this accounts for 30 to 40% of the spiroperidol-binding sites (Garau et al., 1978; Schwarz et al., 1978). These are the sites thought to play a role in neuroleptic activity.

STUDIES OF THE DOPAMINE SYSTEM IN SCHIZOPHRENIC PATIENTS

The first approach in the search for dopaminergic overactivity in the central nervous system (CNS) has been to study prolactin blood levels in normal controls compared to schizophrenics. The rationale is that since prolactin secretion is inhibited by DA, central overactivity might result in lower prolactin levels. Careful studies of prolactin levels failed to find any consistent difference between schizophrenic patients and controls (Meltzer, Goode, and Fang, 1978).

Next, the occurrence of DA metabolites was determined in the cerebrospinal fluid (CSF). If there was overproduction of DA, DA metabolite levels might be expected to be increased in schizophrenic patients. The principal metabolite for DA centrally is homovanillic acid (HVA). Concentrations of HVA were measured in several studies (Persson and Roos, 1969; Bowers, 1974; Berger, et al., 1980), with and without probinacid, an agent that blocks the transport of acidic metabolites from the CSF. These studies indicate normal or perhaps lower values of HVA in the CSF of schizophrenics.

Measurement of the enzymes involved in the synthesis and degradation of DA has been attempted in autopsy material from schizophrenic brains. This work is still incomplete and fraught wih difficulties. However, to date no significant differences have been reported (Barchas, Elliott, and Berger, 1977). It should be noted that although the controversy persists over whether platelet MAO activity is lowered in schizophrenics, lowering is not a consistent finding in brain autopsy material.

The DA receptors have been determined directly by several laboratories in autopsy samples of schizophrenic and control brains. Lee and Seeman (1980) suggest a difference of over 90% in the binding of haloperidol with caudate tissue from schizophrenic patients, showing 85.6 fmol/mg binding compared to control tissues showing 44.5 fmol/mg binding. The binding for spiroperidol was also elevated by 50% in this study. These results are similar to those reported by Crow's group (Owen et al., 1979; see Chapter 10), but differ from the results of Mackay et al. (1980), who found no difference. They must be evaluated in light of the inside of neuroleptics and the ability of these drugs to increase receptor binding. The induction of supersensitivity appears to be the basis of tardive dyskinesia, and animal studies confirm an increase in neuroleptic binding following administration of the drug over long periods (Clow et al., 1980). Thus, it would be important to look at untreated schizophrenic patients in whom the diagnosis was clearly established and from whom autopsy samples of the mesolimbic DA tract were available. Such studies have not been made; however, some samples from unmedicated patients have been studied. These amount to approximately seven patients, whose histories are not detailed, but who were stated to have been drug-free. Binding studies on these patients showed a 50% increase in DA receptors. Thus, it is suggested that the number of DA receptors may increase in schizophrenia, apart from any drug effect. This is disputed by the recent work of Mackay et al. (1980), who found no differences in samples from patients who had been off drugs for at least one month prior to their death. This finding is the only biological evidence of DA overactivity in schizophrenic patients.

Since interest in neuroleptic drug activity has focused attention on the DA system, an examination of the location of central DA pathways is appropriate. Central DA neuron systems have been mapped, using formaldehyde and glyoxylic acid fluorescence histochemistry. These methods reveal seven distinct DA systems, three of which are of particular interest in reference to the neuroleptic drugs. The first of these is the neostriatal system involving cell bodies in the substantia nigra projecting to the caudate and putamen. There appears to be a topographical relationship between cells in the substantia nigra and their termination. In other words, cells in the lateral substantia nigra project to lateral portions of the caudate nucleus. This tract appears to be involved in fine motor control and is the one most seriously affected in Parkinson's disease.

The second DA system originates in the ventromedial tegmental area, with one exception, which orginates in the substantia nigra, and terminates in limbic and cortical areas. These fibers innervate the nucleus accumbens, olfactory tubercle, and septal areas, and send projections to the frontal cortex, especially the anteromedial portion. This system is thought to be involved in the manifestations of psychosis. The final DA system, which clearly interacts with neuroleptics, is the tubrohypophyseal system. The cell bodies are located in the arcuate nucleus of the hypothalamus, terminating in the median eminence. This system is involved in the control of prolactin secretion; thus, peripheral measures of prolactin can serve as a window into at least one DA system in the CNS. There are four more restricted DA systems that do not play an obvious role in the action of neuroleptics. These systems include neurons in the olfactory bulb and retina, along with cells in the periaqueductal gray region and a pathway in the zona incerta connecting the hypothalamus and septum (see Lindvall, 1979, for more detail).

The fine structure of all the catecholamine pathways provide a surprise when studied in detail. Though DA is the least thoroughly studied catecholamine, published reports of its structure correspond to the findings for NE (Decarries, Watkins, and Lapierre, 1977) and serotonin (Decarries, Beaudet, and Watkins, 1975; Chan-Palay, 1976). Hokfelt (1968) carried out the first study on the striatum of rats, using the false transmitter 5-hydroxydopamine to visualize DA storage sites. He found that about 15% of the presynaptic areas identified in his sections contained DA. Very few of the boutons containing DA appeared to make contact with postsynaptic neurons. Tennyson and her coworkers (1974) carried out a more quantitative study on rabbit striatum, using 5-hydroxydopamine to visualize DA storage granules. She found that about 9% of the striatal boutons in rabbit appear to be dopaminergic boutons. Of these, very few were found to make contact with a clearly defined postsynaptic membrane. Though problems in the angle of sectioning may obscure some postsynaptic profiles, it is unlikely that 98% would be missed. In addition, there was a much higher proportion of complete synaptic profiles in non-dopaminergic boutons. This points to an anatomical structure that is more apt to secrete a neuromodulator than a neurotransmitter.

SUMMARY OF EVIDENCE AGAINST DOPAMINE HYPOTHESIS

This overview of the role of dopaminergic systems suggests two things: (1) Neuroleptic drugs almost certainly act at least in part through their effect on DA systems; (2) data on schizophrenic patients do not provide a solid basis for the DA hypothesis. Recalling that neuroleptic drugs show no specificity for schizophrenia, but rather are effective in mania, certain toxic psychoses, and psychotic depressions (Baldessarini, 1977), we conclude that they are correctly labeled antipsychotic. What this implies is that they are active against such positive psychotic symptoms as delusions and hallucinations, without having any specific effect against the negative symptoms of schizophrenia, such as lack of motivation, negativism, and anhedonia. In view of the natural history of schizophrenia and the inability of Schniederian symptoms, taken as a measure of psychosis, to predict a chronic schizophrenic course, I would suggest that these negative symptoms constitute the unique core of schizophrenia, whereas delusions and hallucinations are symptoms that also occur in the acute stage of a variety of other psychiatric illnesses. Thus a DA hypothesis regarding the expression of hallucinations and delusions appears viable, whereas the view that a derangement of DA systems is fundamental in schizophrenia has not been proven.

A critique of the DA hypothesis begins with the pharmacological evidence. This is relatively consistent, if indirect, in pointing to DA. Questions arise both with regard to neuroleptic specificity and to new drug classes. For example, clozapine, an antipsychotic with virtually no extrapyramidyl side effects, has binding characteristics that suggest a muscarinic component. This has been used to explain its unusual properties, which are not entirely consistent with action at a dopaminergic receptor. The activity of clozapine is clearly not accounted for by a simple combination of its anticholinergic and antidopaminergic properties (Ljungberg and Ungerstedt, 1979). Its pharmacological profile suggests an alternative action to a simple DA receptor blockade (Burki et al., 1975), although it does compete very weakly with haloperidol at DA-binding sites. It resembles metaclopramide in binding studies, a drug that appears to have limited antipsychotic properties (Nakra, Bond, and Lader, 1975). Studies on patients reveal that amphetamines, which would be predicted to have universally disastrous results in schizophrenia, at times cause improvement (Van Kammen et al., 1977). The lack of more pronounced psychotic reactions in patients on L-DOPA therapy is surprising, as is the worsening of some patients on α methyl para tyrosine (Gershon et al., 1967), a tyrosine hydroxylase inhibitor. The failure to find changes in patients that indicate DA hyperactivity, such as changes in prolactin levels in blood or in HVA levels in CSF, bring the DA hypothesis into question.

The DA hypothesis is remarkable for its ability to predict pharmacological responses, especially considering that schizophrenia is probably a heterogeneous group of illnesses with regard to etiology. In this situation a relatively simple hypothesis that assumes one defect, namely overactivity of DA systems, might be thought to have limited predictive power. That this is not the case implies that this defect plays a role in the production of psychotic symptoms. Since our only pharmacological tools act to dampen psychotic symptoms, this hypothesis has been robust enough to withstand most of the pharmacological tests performed. When we consider psychotic symptoms that can involve hallucinations in all sensory modalities, as well as disordered thinking, and recall the limited anatomical distribution of the DA neurons, it appears that DA systems must modulate transmission through a number of other CNS tracts. This modulatory role may utilize several different DA receptors; in fact, the catecholamines all appear to act through a number of distinct receptors in the CNS (Snyder and Goodman, 1980).

DOPAMINE RECEPTORS AND ASTROGLIA

One approach to defining these various receptors is to use different binding ligands. In the case of DA receptors, no ligand, either a DA agonist or antagonist, defines a single homogeneous population of receptors. In our laboratory, we have taken a different approach in looking at multiple receptors. Rather than defining the DA receptor by using a variety of ligands, we attempted to isolate various binding sites, using cellular and subcellular fractionation techniques. The first study was an examination of the localization of the haloperidol-binding site in subcellular fractions and in cellular fractions prepared from bovine caudate (Henn, Anderson, and Sellstrom, 1977). Synaptosomes showed a 70% enrichment of receptor after isolation of a synaptosomal fraction. However, caudate fraction enriched over 70% in astroglia showed over a 400% enrichment in haloperiodol-binding sites. This suggests that a binding site might be localized on glia. The next question involved the biochemical activity of such a receptor. An examination of the DA-sensitive adenylate cylcase also showed a fourfold enrichment in the glial cell fraction, although the functional relationship between adenylate cylcase and the DA receptor remains to be established.

Binding studies using bulk isolated fractions are critically dependent on the purity of the fraction. Unfortunately, the techniques of subcellular fraction and cellular isolation are only able to provide enriched fractions, not pure fractions. Synaptic fractions appear to contain approximately 50% synaptic membranes and 50% contaminating material (Henn, Anderson, and Rustad, 1976). Astrological fractions prepared without tryspin appear to contain 50 to 70% astroglial material and 30 to 50% contaminating material, depending on the preparation. The use of trypsin allows the preparation of astrocytic fractions containing over 80%

TABLE 9-1.

ENZYMATIC MARKERS AND SPIROPERIDOL BINDING OF CNS FRACTIONS

	Glutamine synthetase[a] (nmole/mg prot./hr)	Glutamic acid decarboxylase (nmole/mg prot./hr)	Spiroperidol binding (fmol/mg prot.)
Cortical homogenate	0.837	0.829	76.3
Cortical synaptosomes	0.413	1.370	86.9
Cortical astroglia	0.923	0.527	142.5

[a] Conditions chosen to maximize glutamine synthetase activity.

astroglia by weight (Farooq and Norton, 1978). This treatment, however, decreases receptor binding by 58%. Nonetheless, there is still an astroglia enrichment in spiroperidol binding by this technique (Henn, Deering, and Anderson, 1980).

Enzyme markers are used to monitor the purity of the preparations. Recently, several well-defined markers of astroglial cells have been discovered. Glautamine synthesase, an enzyme involved in the glial metabolism of glutamate, has been localized exclusively in astroglia (Norenberg and Martinez-Hernandez, 1979), using immunocytochemical methods. This enzyme was chosen as a glial marker. Glutamate decarboxylase, the GABA-synthesizing enzyme, was chosen as a marker of synaptic areas, since it has also been localized in synapses with immunocytochemical methods. Table 9-1 illustrates the degree of enrichment in spiroperidol binding and of marker enzymes found in bulk isolated astroglial cell fractions and synaptosomes. These results suggest that contamination cannot account for the observed binding in the glial cell fraction, since the enrichment in both the glial marker and neuroleptic receptor occurs in the glial fraction, but not in the synaptosomal preparation. This suggests that there are not enough receptors in the synaptic fraction to account for the binding seen in the glial cell fraction.

These binding studies demonstrate a neuroleptic receptor on a fraction of astroglial cells. Since some DA receptors are coupled to an adenylate cyclase, whereas others appear to be independent of this enzyme, we investigated the astroglial adenylate cylcase. This enzyme was found to be enriched in parallel with the neuroleptic receptor. Furthermore, the enzyme was stimulated by DA. To look at the role NE might have in activating the glial enzyme, α and β blockers were used. The results suggest that the enzyme is most sensitive to activation by DA. The enzyme requires guanine nucleotides, and its activity is stabilized by the non-metabolized GTP analog GTpp NHp, which also protected the enzyme against a variety of inhibitors. Among the most interesting inhibitors of glial adenylate cylcase are the neuroleptic drugs. The ability of a series of phenothiazines and butyrophenones to inhibit adenylate cycyclase was determined. Table 9-2 shows the rank order of these compounds in inhibiting the glial enzyme's activity. This shows that, unlike the results obtained with caudate homogenates, inhibition by these compounds correlated completely with the rank order of their clinical potency. In contrast, astroglia isolated from neocortex did not show receptor enrichment or a DA-sensitive adenylate cyclase. This suggests that a glial receptor coupled to adenylate cyclase is a specialized feature of areas rich in dopaminergic innervation.

The function of the second messenger system in synaptic activity has been extensively studied. Currently, there is considerable dispute over the direct role of this system in synaptic activation. A hypothesis based

TABLE 9-2.

COMPARISON OF RANK ORDER OF CLINICAL DOSAGE AND ADENYL-CYCLASE INHIBITION BY NEUROLEPTIC DRUGS

Neuroleptic Drug	Equivalent Daily Dose[a]	Caudate Glial Cell (IC_{50} $\mu mol/l$)[b]
Aliphatic phenothiazine (chlorpromazine)	100	38.8
Piperidine phenothiazine (mesoridazine)	50	5.2
Piperazine phenothiazine (trifluoperzaine)	5	2.0
Butyrophenone (haloperidol)	2	2.9

[a] Equivalent daily dose with chlorpromazine arbitrarily taken as 100.

[b] Caudate glia assayed in media containing 1 $\mu mol/l$ Gpp(NH)p, which protects against neuroleptic inhibition; brain homogenate inhibition of enzyme assayed in this manner by chlorpromazine has an IC_{50} of approximately 30 $\mu mol/l$.

TABLE 9-3.

PROTEIN KINASE ACTIVITY OF CNS FRACTIONS

| | $-cAMP$ | $+cAMP$ | Increase |
	(pmol PO_4/mg prot./min)		(%)
Astroglia	519 ± 53	836 ± 66	61
Synaptosomes	414 ± 64	624 ± 44	50

primarily on work in the laboratories of Greengard (Beam and Green-gard, 1975) and Bloom (1975), is that cAMP is formed postsynaptically following neurotransmitter stimulation of an adenylate cyclase. This, in turn, stimulates the phosphorylation of a specific protein through activation of a protein kinase. The phosphoprotein alters the membrane potential and is inactivated by a phosphoprotein phosphatase, whereas cAMP is removed by a phosphodiesterase.

In order to determine whether caudate astroglia respond to liberated DA, the protein phosphorylation system in bulk isolated caudate astroglia was investigated. We began by examining astroglia for protein kinases. Table 9-3 shows the results of measuring protein phosphorylation in the presence and absence of 3'-5' cAMP in fractions of caudate homogenate, synaptosomes, and astroglial cells. These results clearly demonstrated the presence of a protein kinase sensitive to 3'-5' cAMP in astroglia. The specific activity of the protein kinase was highest in the fraction of isolated astroglial cells. The kinases were also most responsive to stimulation by cAMP. Purified astroglia membranes were isolated to examine the nature of the natural substrates (Henn and Hamberger, 1976) and used to measure protein phosphorylation. The proteins phosphorylated specifically in the presence of cAMP were determined by SDS polyacrylamide gel electrophoresis. Multiple bands were revealed, which appeared to be quite similar to those reported for phosphorylation of synaptic membrane proteins. Again, the specific activity of the phosphorylated proteins was highest in the isolated astroglial cell fractions. This is difficult to reconcile with the recent studies on the immunocytochemical localization of protein II, a phosphorylated protein claimed to be exclusively neuronal (Bloom et al., 1979).

This demonstration of a neuroleptic receptor on astroglia coupled to the second messenger system and resulting in protein phosphorylation suggests that neurons may communicate directly with glia. Such communication would appear to be regulated by neuromodulatory compounds secreted by neurons, analogous to the release of neurotransmitters, but the target would be different. The catecholamines appear to be the best candidates for such a neuromodulatory role. The results obtained thus far also suggest that the response the neurons elicit is primarily metabolic, and we would suggest that a possible end result of neuronal communication with glia is alteration of the neuronal environment and thus regulation of the level of information flow through the neuronal system. Some examples of the ability of catecholamines to interact with glia include the activation of glycogen breakdown and the induction of specific enzyes. In the CNS, the area for glycogen storage is primarily the astrocyte. The stimulation of receptors activates glycogen breakdown in most brain areas (Nahorski, Rodgers, and Edward, 1975). For some time, it has been known that NE increased the concentration of cAMP in glioma cells through stimulation of a β receptor can be directly demonstrated in C_6 and primary astroglial cultures, using the binding ligand dihydroalprenol. Norepinephrine can also cause the breakdown of glycogen in the CNS, presumably through activation of this receptor system in astrocytes.

Our discovery of a caudate glial adenylate cyclase that is preferentially activated by DA and is not blocked by propranolol may also point to a metabolic regulatory role. This is suggested by the report of Anchors and Garcia-Rill (1977) that DA regulates glycogen breakdown in the caudate nucleus. This must occur through activation of an astroglial DA-sensitive system, since glycogen in the striatal area appears exclusively in astroglial cells. Thus, functional studies of energy metabolism point to direct neuronal–glial communication through specialized DA receptors.

If DA functions as a general modulator of CNS activity, how does this relate to the more specific derangements that might occur in schizophrenia. One of the oldest ideas is that of a toxin or toxins produced by aberrant metabolic pathways. This idea received its impetus from the observation of Osmond and Smythies (1952) that methylated forms of catecholamine metabolites are hallucinogens. This led to the analysis of vast quantities of urine and some information on dietary influence determining the nature of excretion products. However, no toxin was identified. One experiment, which was carried out in an investigation of the methylation hypothesis (Pollen, Cardon, and Kety, 1961), involved the use of methyl donors to exacerbate certain schizophrenic symptoms. This exacerbation of schizophrenic symptoms following methionine loading has been demonstrated in several laboratories, and it is known that methionine serves as a precursor for a variety of methylation reactions via the formation of 5-adenosyl-L-methionine. Recently, it has been proposed that phospholipid methylation may act to transduce biological signals through cell membranes (Hirata and Axelrod, 1980). In general, it appears many receptors are coupled to two methyltransferase enzymes that sequentially methylate phosphotidyl ethanolamine to phosphotidyl choline. These reactions distribute membrane phospholipids asymmetrically with choline head groups on the outer membrane surface and ethanolamine on the inner surface. Such changes in membranes appear to increase their fluidity (Hirata, Strittmatter, and Axelrod, 1979). This, in turn, can facilitate the coupling of some receptors to adenylate cyclase. This sequence of events has been suggested for the coupling of the β receptor of the rat reticulocyte to adenylate cyclase. Since some neurotransmitters are at least partially coupled to adenylate cyclase in the CNS, we were interested to see if such a reaction takes place in CNS tissue.

Since methionine loading would act to facilitate phosphatidyl ethanolamine conversion to phosphatidyl choline, we might expect an increase in membrane fluidity and increased coupling of adenylate cyclase to the DA receptor in striatal and limbic tissue. Thus, methionine loading would be analogous to increasing dopaminergic activity in the CNS, if phospholipid methylation were stimulated by DA. This would account for the exacerbation of psychotic symptoms with methionine loading, in spite of our inability to isolate specific toxins. In fact, such a sequence of reactions would suggest that methionine and amphetamine might increase psychotic symptomatology in a similar fashion. Thus, the results of methionine loading are explicable in terms of the DA theory of psychosis without invoking any other mechanism. We thus examined the effect of DA on methylation reactions in striatal tissue slices in order to see if there is experimental support for the scheme outlined above.

It appears that there is a DA-sensitive methylation of phospholipids in caudate tissue. This stimulation was linear over 30 minutes when caudate slices were used and was maximal in our hands with approximately $5 \times 10^{-6} M$ DA. After this symposium, an abstract appeared that supports this finding. Boehme and Ciaranello (1980) reported that with purified rat striatal synaptosomes they found a linear increase in DA-stimulated methylation. They found maximal stimulation at $3 \times 10^{-4} M$ DA, and an analysis of their lipid products revealed that phosphatidyl choline was the predominant product of this reaction. Interestingly, they only reported a partial inhibition of methylation by neuroleptic drugs. Thus, some evidence is accumulating that suggests that catecholamines may, in part, be acting via methylation of membrane lipids.

The data presented above suggest that DA is involved in a variety of psychotic symptoms, regardless of their origin, and that little, if any, evidence directly links a disorder in the DA system of schizophrenic patients with the etiology of their illness. If such a link exists, it is most likely to involve an etiological factor in the subgroup of schizophrenic patients who do not go on to develop chronic negative symptoms (see Chapter 10 by Crow). Neuroleptic drugs do appear to block some DA receptors. There are multiple classes of DA receptors, some of which may reside on astroglial cells, and these receptors may act, at least in part, by stimulating phospholipid methylation. Changes in phospholipid methylation may account for the exacerbation of some schizophrenic patient symptoms, following methionine loading. Thus, it appears that the liberation of DA and its action on a variety of receptors modulate the expression of delusions and hallucinations, rather than regulating the central features of any specific illness.

REFERENCES

Aghajanian, G. K., and B. S. Bunney (1977). Dopamine astoreceptors: Pharmacological characterization by microiontophoretic single cell recording studies. Naunyn Schmiedebergs Arch. Pharmacol. 297, 1–8.

Ahlenius, S., and J. Engel (1975). Antagonism by haloperidol of the L-DOPA induced disruption of a successive discrimination in the rats. J. Neural Transmiss. 36, 43–49.

Ancors, W., and J. Garcia-Rill (1977). Dopamine, a modulator of carbohydrate metabolism in caudate nucleus. Brain Res. 133, 183–189.

Angrist, B., B. Shopsin, and S. Gershon (1971). The comparative psychotominetric effects of stereoisomers of amphetamine. Nature 234, 152–154.

Baldessarini, R. (1977). Chemotherapy in Psychiatry. Harvard University Press, Cambridge, Mass. pp. 13–56.

Barchas, J., G. R. Elliott, and P. Berger (1977). Second Rochester Int. Conf. Schizophrenia. (R. Cromwell and L. Wynne, eds.). Wiley, New York.

Beam, K. and P. Greengard (1975). Cyclic nucleotides, protein phosphorylation and synaptic function. Cold Spring Harbor Symp. Quant. Biol. 40, 157–168.

Berger, P., F. Faull, J. Kilkowski, P. Anderson, H. Kraemer, K. Davis, and J. Barchas (1980). CSF monoamine metabolites in depression and schizophrenia. *Am. J. Psychol.* 137, 174–180.

Bloom, F. E. (1975). The role of cyclic nucleotides in central synaptic function. *Rev. Physiol. Biochem. Pharm.* 74, 1–103.

Bloom, F., T. Veda, E. Battenberg, and P. Greengard (1979). Immunocytochemical localization in synapses of Protein II, an endogenous substrate for protein kinases in mammalian brain. *Proc. Natl. Acad. Sci. (U.S.A.)* 76, 5982–5986.

Boehme, R., and R. Ciaranello (1980). Abstracts Society for Neuroscience 10th Annual Meeting 82.6 p. 215.

Bowers, M. G., Jr. (1974). Central dopamine turnover in sxhizophrenic syndromes. *Arch. Gen. Psychol.* 31, 50–54.

Bunney, B. S. (1978). The electrophysiological pharmacology of midbrain dopaminergic systems. In *The Neurobiology of Dopamine* (A. Horn, J. Korf, and B. Westerink, eds.). Academic Press, New York, pp. 417–452.

Bunney, B., J. R. Walters, R. H. Roth, and G. Aghajanian (1973). Dopaminergic neurons: Effect of antipsychotic drugs and amphetamine on single cell activity. *J. Pharmacol. Expl. Therap.* 185, 560–571.

Burki, H., R. Eichenberger, A. Sayers, and T. G. White (1975). Clozapine and the dopamine hypothesis of schizphrenia, a critical appraisal. *Pharmakopsychiat. Neuropsychopharmacol.* 8, 115–121.

Carlsson, A. (1965). Drugs which block the storage of 5-hydroxytryptamine and related amines. *Hdbk. Exper. Pharmakol.* 19, 529–592.

Carlsson, A., and M. Lindqvist (1963). Effect of chlorpromazine or haloperidol on formation of 3 methoxytyramine and normetanephrine in mouse brain. *Acta Pharmacol.* 20, 140–144.

Chan-Palay, V. (1976). Seritonin axons in the supra and subependymal plexuses and in the leptomeninges; their roles in local alterations of cerebrospinal fluid and vasomotor activity. *Brain Res.* 102, 103–130.

Christiansen, J., and R. F. Squires (1974). Antagonistic effects of apomorphine and haloperidol on rat striatal synaptosomal tyrosine hydroxylase. *J. Pharm. Pharmacol.* 26, 367–368.

Clement-Cormier, Y., J. W. Kebabian, G. Petzold, and P. Greengard (1974). Dopamine sensitive adenylate cyclase in mammalian brain: A possible site of action of antipsychotic drugs. *Proc. Natl. Acad. Sci. (U.S.A.)* 71, 1113–1171.

Clow, A., A. Theodorow, P. Jenner, and C. Marsden (1980). Changes in rat striatal dopamine turnover and receptor activity during one year's neuroleptic administration. *Eur. J. Pharmacol.* 63, 135–144.

Connell, P. H. (1958). *Amphetamine Psychosis.* Chapman and Hall, London.

Coyle, J. and S. H. Snyder (1969). Catecholamine uptake by synaptosomes in homogenates of rat brain: Stereo-specificity in different areas. *J. Pharmacol. Exptl. Ther.* 170, 221–231.

Creese I., D. Burt, and S. H. Snyder (1976). Dopamine receptor binding predicts clinical and pharmacological potencies of anti schizophrenic drugs. *Science* 192, 471–483.

Creese, I., and S. H. Snyder (1978). Dopamine receptor binding of ^{3}H-ADTN regulated by guanyl nucleotides. *Eur. J. Pharmacol.* 50, 459–461.

Delay, J., and P. Deniker (1957). Caracteristiques psychophysiologiques des medicaments neuroleptiques. In *The Psychotropic Drugs* (S. Garattini and V. Ghetti, eds.). Elsevier Amsterdam, pp. 485–501.

Descarries, L., A. Beaudet, and K. C. Watkins (1975). Seritonin nerve terminals in adult rat neocortex. *Brain Res.* 100, 563–588.

Descarries, L., K. Watkins, and Y. Lapierre (1977) Noradrenergic axon terminals in the cerebral cortex of rat III, topometric structural analysis. *Brain Res.* 133, 197–222.

Ehringer, H., and O. Hornykiewicz (1960). Distribution of noradrenaline and dopamine in the human brain and their behavior in diseases of the extrapyramidal system. *Klin. Wschr.* 38, 1236–1239.

Farooq, M., and W. T. Norton (1978). A modified procedure for isolation of astrocyte and neuron enriched fractions from rat brain. *J. Neurochem.* 31, 887–894.

Garau, L., S. Govoni, E. Stefanini, M. Trabucchi, and P. Spano (1978). Dopamine receptors: Pharmacological and anatomical evidence indicate that two distinct dopamine receptor populations are present in rat striatum. *Life Sci.* 23, 1745–1750.

Gershon, S., L. Heikimian, A. Floyd, Jr., and L. Hollister (1967). Methyl p tyrosine in schizophrenia. *Physchopharmacologia* 11, 189–194.

Gilman, A., and M. Nirenberg (1971). Effect of catecholamines on the adenosine $3'–5'$ monophosphate concentrations of clonal satellite cells of neurons. *Proc. Natl. Acad. Sci. (U.S.A.)* 68, 2165–2168.

Goldstein, M., B. Anagnosti, and C. Shirron (1973). The effect of trivastal, haloperidol and debrityrl cyclic AMP on ^{14}C dopamine synthesis in rat striatum. *J. Pharm. Pharmacol.* 25, 348–351.

Greengard, P. (1976). Possible role for cyclic nucleotides and phosphorylated membranes in postsynaptic actions of neurotransmitters. *Nature* 260, 101–108.

Henn, F. and A. Hamberger (1976). Preparation of glial plasma membrane from a cell fraction enriched in astrocytes. *Neurochem. Res.* 1, 261–273.

Henn, F., D. Anderson, and D. Rustad (1976). Glial contamination of synaptosomal fractions. *Brain Res.* 101, 341–344.

Henn, F. A., D. J. Anderson, and A. Sellstrom (1977). Possible relationship between glial cells, dopamine and the effects of antipsychotic drugs. *Nature* 266, 637–638.

Henn, F. A., J. Deering, and P. Anderson (1980). Receptor studies on isolated astroglial cell fractions prepared with and without trypsin. *Neurochem. Res.* 5, 459–464.

Hirata, F., and J. Axelrod (1980). Phospholipid methylation and biological signal transmission. *Science* 209, 1082–1090.

Hirata, F., W. Strittmatter, and J. Axelrod (1979). β-adrenergic receptor agonists increase phospholipid methylation membrane fluidity and adrenergic receptor–adenylate cyclase coupling. *Proc. Natl. Acad. Sci. (U.S.A.)* 76, 368–372.

Hokfelt, T. (1968). *In vitro* studies on central and peripheral monoamine neurons at the ultrastructural level. *Z. Zellforsch.* 91, 1–74.

Hollister, L. E. (1962). Drug induced psychosis and schizophrenic reactions, a critical comparison. *Ann. N.Y. Acad. Sci.* 96, 80–88.

Iversen, L. L. (1975). Dopamine receptors in brain. *Science* 188, 1084–1089.

Janowsky, D., and J. Davis (1976). Methyphenidate, dextroamphetamine, and levamphetamine: Effects on schizophrenic symptoms. *Arch. Gen. Psych.* 33, 304–308.

Janowsky, D., M. El-Yousel, J. Davis, and H. Sekerke (1973). Provocation of schizophrenic symptoms by intravenous methylphenidate. *Arch. Gen. Psych.* 28, 185–191.

Kebabian, J. and D. Calne (1979). Multiple receptors for dopamine. *Nature* 277, 92–96.

Kebabian, J., and P. Greengard (1971). Dopamine sensitive adenyl cyclase: Possible role in synaptic transmission. *Science* 174, 1346–1349.

Lee, T., and P. Seeman (1980). Elevation of brain neuroleptic dopamine receptors in schizophrenia. *Amer. J. Psychol.* 137, 191–197.

Libet, B. (1979). Which postsynaptic action of dopamine is mediated by cAMP. *Life Sci.* 24, 1043–1058.

Lindvall, O. (1979). Dopamine pathways in the rat brain. In *The Neurobiology of Dopamine* (A. S. Horn, J. Korf, and B. H. C. Westerink, eds.). Academic Press, New York, pp. 319–342.

Ljungberg, T., and U. Ungerstedt (1979). Evidence that the different properties of haloperidol and clozapine are not explained by differences in anticholinergic potency. *Psychopharmacology* 60, 303–307.

Mackay, A., E. Bird, E. Spokes, M. Rossor, L. Iversen, I. Cresse, and S. H. Snyder (1980). Dopamine receptors and schizophrenia drug effect on illness? *Lancet* ii, 915–916.

Mattysse, S. (1973). Antipsychotic drug actions: A clue to the neuropathology of schizophrenia. *Fed. Proc.* 32, 200–205.

Meltzer, H., D. Goode, and V. Fang (1978). *The Effect of Psychotropic Drugs on Endocrine Function I Neuroleptics, Precursors and Agonists in Psychopharmacology: A Generation of Progress* (M. Lipton, A. DiMascia, and K. Killam, eds.). Raven Press, New York, pp. 509–529.

Miller, R J., A. S. Horn, and L. L. Iversen (1974). The action of neuroleptic drugs on dopamine stimulated adenosine cyclic 3'–5' monophosphate production in rat neostriatum and limbic forebrain. *Mol. Pharmacol.* 10, 759–766.

Nahorski, S. R., K J. Rodgers, and C. Edward (1975). Cerebral glycogenolysis and stimulation of adrenoreceptors and histamine H_2 receptors. *Brain Res.* 92, 529–533.

Nakra, B., A. J. Bond, and H. Lader (1975). Comparative psychotropic effects of metoclopramide and prochlorperazine in normal subjects. *J. Clin. Pharm.* 15, 449–455.

Norenberg, M., and A. Mortinez-Hernandez (1979). Fine structural localization of glutamine synthetase in astrocytes of rat brain. *Brain Res.* 161, 303–310.

Osmond, H. and J. R. Smythies (1952). Schizophrenia: A new approach. *J. Ment. Sci.* 98, 309–315.

Owen, F., T. J. Crow, M. Poulter, A. J. Cross, A. Longden, and G. Riley (1979). Increased dopamine receptor sensitivity in schizophrenia. *Lancet* ii, 223–225.

Persson, T., and B. E. Roos (1969). Acid metabolites from monoamines in CSF of chronic schizophrenics. *Brit. J. Psychol.* 115, 95–98.

Pollen, W., P. V. Cardon, and S. S. Kety (1961). Effects of amino acid feeding in schizophrenic patients treated with iproniazid. *Science* 133, 104–106.

Randrup, A., and I. Munkvad (1972). Influence of amphetamines on animal behavior: Stereotypy, functional impairment and possible animal-human correlations. *Psychol. Neurol. Neurochem.* 75, 193–202.

Schwarz, R., I. Cresse, J. Coyle, and S. H. Snyder (1978). Dopamine receptors localized on cerebral cortical afferents to rat corpus striatum. *Nature* 271, 766–768.

Seeman, P., M. Chaw-Wong, J. Tedesco, and K. Wong (1975). Brain receptors for antipsychotic drugs and dopamine: Direct loading assays. *Proc. Natl. Acad. Sci. (U.S.A.)* 72, 4376–4380.

Seeman, P., T. Lee, M. Chaw-Wong, J. Tedesco, and K. Wong (1976). Dopamine receptors in human and calf brain using ^{3}H apomorphine and an antipsychotic drug. *Proc. Natl. Acad. Sci. (U.S.A.)* 73, 4354–4358.

Siggins, G. R. (1978). The electrophysiological role of dopamine in striatum: Excitatory or inhibitory? In *Physchopharmacology: A Generation of Progress* (M. Lipton, A. Di Mascio, and K. F. Killam, eds.). Raven Press, New York, pp. 143–157.

Snyder, S. H., and R. R. Goodman (1980). Multiple neurotransmitter receptors. *J. Neurochem.* 35, 5–15.

Snyder, S., S. Banerju, H. Yamamura, and D. Greenberg (1974). Drugs, neurotransmitters and schizophrenia. *Science* 184, 1243–1253.

Tennyson, V., R. Herkkila, C. Mytilineou, L. Cote, and G. Cohen (1974). 5-Hydroxydopamine "tagged" neuronal boutons in rabbit neostriatum: Interrelationship between vesicles and axonal membrane. *Brain Res.* 82, 341–348.

Von Kammen, D., W. Bunney, J. Dorcherty, D. Jemirson, R. Post, S. Siris, M. Ebert, and J. Gillin (1977). *Adv. Biochem. Psychopharmacol.* 16, 655–659.

Van Rossen, J. M. (1966). The significance of dopamine receptor blockade for the mechanism of action of neuroleptic drugs. *Arch. Int. Pharmacodyn. Ther.* 160, 492–494.

York, D. (1978). The neurophysiology of dopamine receptors. In *The Neurobiology of Dopamine* (A. Horn, J. Korf, and B. Westerink, eds.). Academic Press, New York, pp. 395–415.

10 | Two Syndromes in Schizophrenia and Their Pathogenesis

T. J. CROW, A. J. CROSS,

EVE C. JOHNSTONE, and F. OWEN

Schizophrenia is an elusive concept. Both Kraepelin and, with greater emphasis, Bleuler believed that the diseases they had grouped together could be distinguished from the organic psychoses. Kraepelin (1919) wrote that in dementia praecox "memory is comparatively little disordered. The patients are able, when they like, to give a correct detailed account of their past life, and often know accurately to a day how long they have been in hospital." Bleuler (1950) stated that "in contrast to the organic psychoses, we find in schizophrenia . . . that orientation, memory, consciousness and motility are not directly disturbed," and "consciousness is not altered in the chronic conditions of schizophrenia. In this respect the schizophrenics behave as do the healthy." Recent research casts doubt on the view that these statements can always be sustained, and suggests rather that there is a group of patients with chronic schizophrenia whose psychological impairments closely resemble those seen in dementia. Bonhoeffer (1909) had put forward the view that the psychoses induced by drugs and other toxins (the "exogenous psychoses") had in common disturbances of consciousness and that in this respect they could be distinguished from the functional psychoses. Yet descriptions of the amphetamine psychosis (Connell, 1958; Ellinwood, 1967) makes it apparent that there is at least one exogenous psychosis in which disturbance of consciousness (in Bonhoeffer's sense, which resembles conventional psychiatric usage) is not prominent and that the features of this psychosis closely resemble those of acute paranoid schizophrenia.

Thus, organic states induced by a specific toxin can resemble acute schizophrenia both in the presence of characteristic types of delusion and hallucination and in the lack of a disturbance of consciousness, whereas in some chronic conditions of schizophrenia, there is an intellectual impairment that, at present, is indistinguishable from that seen in dementia.

These issues may well be relevant to the problem of definition. It is generally agreed (e.g., World Health Organization, 1975) that neither Kraepelin nor Bleuler arrived at an operational definition that can be reliably adopted by other workers. Bleuler believed that he had identified certain fundamental symptoms, but these are not so well defined that they can be incorporated into rules for diagnosis; Schneider's first-rank symptoms, on the other hand, can be used in this way (Wing, Cooper, and Sartorius, 1974). Such symptoms, therefore, define a core syndrome of "nuclear schizophrenia," and although many illnesses commonly considered schizophrenia," will not be included in this definition, this is an advance. However, it is already apparent (Brockington, Kendell, and Leff, 1978; Bland and Orn, 1980) that the presence of such symptoms does not predict poor long-term outcome. Since the latter is the criterion by which Kraepelin distinguished dementia praecox from schizophrenia, such a procedure can hardly be said to validate the concept according to its historical development.

The view to be advanced here is that recent research on the neurochemical disturbance in schizophrenia and the nature of the defect in some chronic schizophrenic illnesses is relevant to the problem of predicting long-term outcome and response to neuroleptic drug treatment. Specifically, it is suggested that there is sufficient evidence to distinguish two separate pathological processes, and insofar as these processes can be related to specific clinical syndromes, the problem of diagnosis and prediction of outcome can be clarified.

NEUROHUMORAL HYPOTHESES

Johann Thudichum, the father of neurochemistry, once remarked that only when the chemistry of the brain is known "in the minutest detail" might it be possible to understand the chemical bases of mental disorders. Since the former objective is far from our reach, it might be thought premature to discuss the chemistry of schizophrenia. Yet there is a feeling that there has been progress in understanding the chemistry of some psychiatric and neurological diseases, even if many aspects of neurochemistry remain obscure. This optimism arises in part from the advance of the neurohumoral theory. The recognition that nerves act by releasing chemical substances and the identification of an increasing number of these transmitters provide a conceptual tool for understanding the brain and its dysfunctions. Many centrally acting drugs affect neurohumors. Some of these drugs can improve or exacerbate the symptoms of schizophrenia and it is plausible that these effects occur as a result of interactions with specific transmitters.

The first neurohumoral hypothesis (Table 10-1) was formulated independently by Gaddum (1954) and by Woolley and Shaw (1954). It was argued that since hallucinations follow LSD administration, and since LSD can antagonize serotonin, the hallucinations and other psychotic phenomena that occur in schizophrenia may be due to a functional deficiency of serotonin in the brain. Randrup and Munkvad (1965, 1972) advanced a similar argument, focusing on amphetamine psychosis as a model and proposing that increased dopaminergic transmission was the fundamental disorder. Amphetamine hallucinosis, probably more closely than LSD psychosis, resembles acute paranoid schizophrenia (Connell, 1958; Ellinwood, 1967), and at least some of the central actions of the amphetamines are due to dopamine (DA) release (Randrup and Munkvad, 1966; Creese and Iversen, 1975). Moreover, the behavioral effects of amphetamine (Randrup and Munkvad, 1965), like the symptoms of the amphetamine psychosis (Angrist, Lee and Gershon, 1974; Gunne, Angåard, and Jönsson, 1972), are reversed by drugs that have antipsychotic effects in schizophrenia. Such drugs selectively increase DA turnover (Carlsson and Lindquist, 1963), an effect that, it is suggested, is a feedback response to blockade of DA receptors. Thus it is plausible that by impairing dopaminergic transmission these drugs induce a functional Parkinsonism comparable to the DA depletion that occurs in idiopathic Parkinsonism (Hornykiewicz, 1966). According to the DA hypothesis of schizophrenia, this action accounts not only for the extrapyramidal, but also for the therapeutic effects of neuroleptic drugs. This theory alone explains both the phenomena of the amphetamine psychosis and the efficacy of neuroleptic drugs.

A quite different hypothesis proposed by Stein and Wise (1971), that there is a selective loss of norepinephrine (NE) neurons, has the potential

TABLE 10-1.
NEUROHUMORAL HYPOTHESIS OF SCHIZOPHRENIA

Authors	Theory	Principal Arguments
Gaddum (1954) Woolley and Shaw (1954)	Serotonin deficiency	LSD psychosis resembles schizophrenia; LSD blocks serotonin receptors
Randrup and Munkvad (1965)	DA overactivity	Amphetamine psychosis resembles acute paranoid schizophrenia; amphetamines increase DA release; antipsychotic drugs block DA receptors
Stein and Wise (1971)	Norepinephrine neuron degeneration	Reward processes are mediated by central norepinephrinergic systems; anhedonia is a core feature of chronic schizophrenia
Murphy and Wyatt (1972)	MAO deficiency	Platelet MAO activity is reduced in some schizophrenic patients
Roberts (1972)	GABA deficiency	

for explaining some features of the defect state. There is a fairly strong case (Crow, Spear, and Arbuthnott, 1972; Ritter and Stein, 1973) that the NE-containing neurons of the locus coeruleus system, which innervate the neo-, pallio-, and cerebellar cortices as well as the hippocampus and some other structures, function as a reward system, since activation of this system through implanted electrodes in animal experiments will support "self-stimulation," lever-pressing behavior. Moreover such behavior is associated with increased NE turnover in the ipsilateral cerebral cortex (Anlezark et al., 1975). Stein and Wise argued that dysfunction of the system could lead to the "anhedonia" or impaired affective responsivity, which is so characteristic of the clinical picture in some chronic schizophrenic states.

From the finding that the activity of the enzyme MAO is reduced in platelets in some patients with schizophrenia (Murphy and Wyatt, 1972) it might be suggested that this change is but a reflection of a similar deficiency of enzymatic activity in the central nervous system. Such a change, if it were sufficiently large to affect monoamine metabolism, would presumably lead to increased biological effectiveness of the amines. Thus such a defect might be compatible with the DA theory.

Other theories also have a relationship to this hypothesis. Thus, it might be argued that the efficacy of neuroleptic drugs is due, not to an absolute, but rather to a relative excess of DA with respect to other transmitters interacting with dopaminergic systems. One such transmitter is GABA, postulated by Roberts (1972) to be deficient not only in Huntington's chorea, but also in schizophrenia. An alternative possibility suggested by Bowers (1974) and Crow, Deakin, Johnstone, and Longden (1976) is that the disorder lies not in the DA neuron itself, but rather in the postsynaptic receptor and constitutes an increase in number or responsiveness of this structure.

Each of these hypotheses has been tested in the postmortem brain, as has the DA hypothesis regarding the mechanism of action of neuroleptic drugs.

MECHANISM OF THE ANTIPSYCHOTIC EFFECT

The DA hypothesis derived substantial support from two studies (Miller, Horn, and Iversen, 1974; Clement-Cornier, Kebabian, Petzold, and Greengard, 1974) demonstrating a strong positive correlation between clinical potency of individual neuroleptic drugs and their ability to inhibit stimulation by DA of the DA-sensitive adenylate cyclase, an enzyme located in the corpus striatum and assumed to be closely related to the DA receptor. However, it was recognized that the potency of the butyrophenones in this system was less than would be predicted from their clinical effectiveness.

The discrepancy was explained following the development of the butyrophenone-binding technique for studying DA receptors. Haloperidol, like some other butyrophenone drugs, can be used as a ligand for one type of DA receptor, and in this system the potency of the butyrophenones as a class falls into line with that of the other major classes of neuroleptics, the phenothiazines and thiaxanthenes (Creese, Burt, and Snyder, 1976; Seeman, Lee, Chau-Wong, and Wong, 1976). Thus an objection to the hypothesis was removed.

A second objection was the apparent lack of correlation between extrapyramidal side effects and antipsychotic effectiveness. It was long ago argued (e.g. Deniker, 1960; Flügel, 1953) that extrapyramidal activity was necessary for the therapeutic effect, but this view was apparently contradicted by the observation that there are some drugs (e.g., thioridazine) that are antipsychotic, but that also have been shown to have a lower incidence of side effects than such drugs as chlorpromazine and fluphenazine (National Institute of Mental Health, 1964). In animal models of dopaminergic activity, such as turning behavior in unilaterally lesioned rats after amphetamine administration, thioridazine is apparently much less effective than chlorpromazine (Crow and Gillbe, 1973, 1974). However, a factor that must be taken into account is muscarinic cholinergic antagonist activity. Neuroleptic drugs with a low incidence of extrapyramidal effects have relatively high anticholinergic activity (Miller and Hiley, 1974; Snyder, Greenberg, and Yamamura, 1974). It seems they have their own "in-built" anti-Parkinsonian activity. Moreover, the inhibitory effects of standard neuroleptic drugs (e.g., chlorpromazine) in animal behavioral models of dopaminergic transmission can be diminished by administration of muscarinic antagonists (Muller and Seeman, 1974).

It can be argued from these findings that if both antipsychotic and extrapyramidal effects are due to DA-receptor blockade, they cannot be occurring at the same site in the brain. For if they were, the antipsychotic as well as the Parkinsonian effects would be reversed by anticholinergic drugs, and this is generally assumed not to be the case (but see below). Andén (1972) suggested that the antipsychotic effect might be due to receptor blockade in the mesolimbic system (which includes the nucleus accumbens) and presented evidence that the interaction between DA and acetylcholine in this area differs from that in the corpus striatum. There is some evidence (e.g., Crow, Deakin, and Longden, 1977) that the therapeutic effects of neuroleptic drugs correlate better with their actions on dopaminergic mechanisms in the nucleus accumbens than in the striatum; with chronic administration, there is less adaptative change in this region and when it occurs it has a slower time-course (Bowers and Rozitis, 1976; Scatton, Glowinski, and Julou, 1976).

Thus the DA hypothesis has survived several challenges, and receptor blockade, particularly within the mesolimbic system, appears a plausible explanation of the antipsychotic effect. However, much of the evidence on which the hypothesis rests comes from animal experiments, and it appeared possible that a circular procedure might be developing. Drugs that are effective in schizophrenia had been found to block DA receptors and dopaminergic transmission in animal models, and these tests were being used as the only predictors of new therapeutic agents to be tried in humans. A more direct test of the hypothesis in patients appeared desirable and this was made possible by the discovery (Miller, Horn, and Iversen, 1974) that for the thiaxanthenes, DA-receptor antagonist activity is stereo-selective. This group of compounds possesses a geometric isomerism dependent upon a carbon–carbon double bond at the root of the side chain on the b ring (Fig. 10-1).

The *cis* (α) isomers are substantially more active as DA antagonists than the *trans* or β forms, the ratio between the activities of the two isomers being more than a 1000-fold in the adenylate cyclase system (Miller, Horn, and Iversen, 1974) and approximately 50-fold in the butyrophenone-binding assay (Enna, et al., 1976). Both forms are included in the standard oral preparation, and a trial (Johnstone et al., 1978a) was conducted to compare the two isomers with placebo in the treatment of patients with acute schizophrenia (diagnosed by the presence of nuclear symptoms).

The findings (Fig. 10-2) demonstrate that although in this situation (shortly following admission to hospital) there are substantial reductions in symptoms in patients on placebo, a significant drug effect does occur, but is limited to the *cis* (α) isomer. This result is consistent with the possibility that DA-receptor antagonism is the only necessary component for the therapeutic effect. Some other possible mechanisms of action (e.g., NE or opiate antagonism) are excluded by this result, since both isomers are equally active on these receptors. The α isomer is a more effective serotonin antagonist than is the β isomer (Enna et al., 1976), but serotonin antagonism is a poor predictor of therapeutic efficacy of neuroleptic drugs (Bennett and Snyder, 1975) and trials of serotonin antagonists in schizophrenia have been negative (Holden, Itil, Keskiner, and Gannon, 1971). Thus the DA hypothesis of neuroleptic action has survived a rather stringent test and no other known pharmacological action predicts thereapeutic efficacy.

An interesting aspect of this clinical trial was that the therapeutic effect emerged rather slowly, significant differences between the treatments appearing only in the third and the fourth week of treatment. Serum prolactin concentrations were assessed during the trial (Cotes et al., 1978) and were elevated in patients on α-flupenthixol within the first week. Since this effect presumably reflects blockade of DA receptors in the pituitary, it was argued that the discrepancy between the time-course

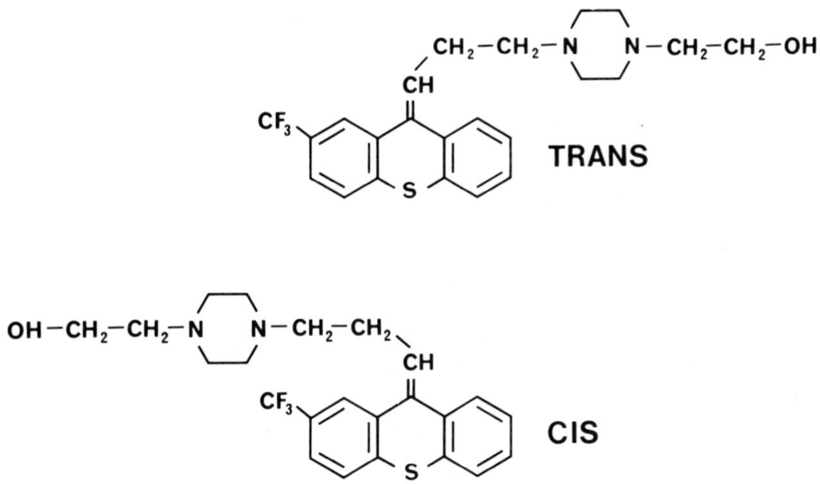

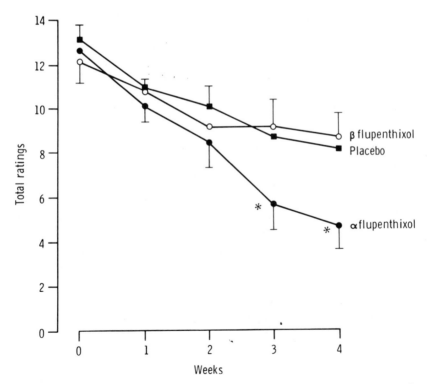

FIGURE 10-1. The Stereoisomers of Flupenthixol

FIGURE 10-2. Symptom Change in Patients on the *Cis* (α) and *Trans* (β) Isomers of Flupenthixol

of receptor blockade and the emergence of the therapeutic effect suggests that DA-receptor blockade is necessary only for some other process with a slower time-course to bring about the change in symptoms. However, recent findings cast doubt on this conclusion and suggest rather that the slow time-course is an effect of the anticholinergic medication that all the patients in this trial were receiving. The new findings (Crow, Frith, Johnstone, and Owens, 1980) are that (contrary to most expectations) anticholinergic medication does tend to diminish the therapeutic effect of neuroleptic drugs and may slow the time-course of improvement. Without anticholinergic medication, the time-course of the therapeutic effect parallels the development of the extrapyramidal effects. Thus DA-receptor blockade by itself may be a sufficient explanation of the therapeutic effect. The recent findings also suggest a rather subtle interaction between cholinergic and dopaminergic systems in the production of symptoms and cast some doubt on the argument advanced above for localizing the therapeutic effect exclusively in the mesolimbic system.

A further important finding of the trial of the flupenthixol isomers was that the antipsychotic effect was limited to positive symptoms—such features of the clinical state, as delusions, hallucinations, and thought disorder—that are pathological by their presence. Negative symptoms—normal functions that are diminished or absent—changed little during the trial and showed no differential response to active medication (Fig. 10-3).

It has previously been susggested (Goldberg, Klerman, and Cole, 1965) that most schizophrenic symptoms respond to medication, but this assertion is based upon behavioral ratings rather than clinical interviews. Thus it appears that negative behavioral *features*, such as "lack of self-care" and "social withdrawal," may be secondary to positive symptoms, such as delusions and hallucinations. Although the above findings are based on small numbers, they do suggest that negative symptoms assessed in a clinical interview are not improved by neuroleptic medication.

NEUROCHEMICAL STUDIES ON POSTMORTEM BRAIN

All current neurohumoral hypotheses (Table 10-1) have been assessed in postmortem brain studies. This approach depends on the assumption

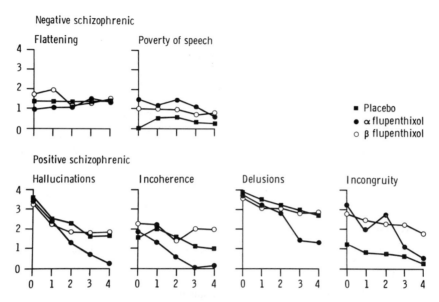

FIGURE 10-3. Changes in Positive and Negative Schizophrenic symptoms on α- and β-Flupenthixol and Placebo

that whatever disturbance underlies the initial illness persists until death, but it is apparent that many patients continue to have symptoms (both positive and negative). Moreover, many aspects of neurohumoral transmission (e.g., ligand-binding capacities, enzyme activities) are well preserved after death and the strategy thus provides the most direct approach to the neurochemistry of the disease.

A study of DA-β-hydroxylase activity (Cross et al., 1978) did not demonstrate a deficit of this enzyme in a series of 12 schizophrenic patients and 12 control subjects (Table 10-2).

The findings do not support the hypothesis of Stein and Wise (1971), but the numbers involved are rather small. A more extensive study, with particular attention to features of the premortem clinical state, will be required to exclude the possibility that there is a subgroup of patients with specific adrenergic transmission deficits. It is of some interest that such deficits have been demonstrated in some patients suffering from Alzheimer's disease (Cross et al., 1980).

Similarly, no evidence has been obtained for abnormalities of MAO activity, although this was examined with four substrates (5-HT and benzylamine as substrates for the types A and B, respectively, of the

TABLE 10-2.
DBH ACTIVITY IN POSTMORTEM BRAINS OF TWELVE SCHIZOPHRENICS
AND TWELVE CONTROLS (MEAN ± S.D.)[a]

| Brain Area | DBH Activity[b] | | "t" | p |
	Controls	Schizophrenics		
Hypothalamus	131 ± 41	156 ± 55	1.32	NS
Hippocampus	24 ± 8	25 ± 9	0.22	NS
Parietal cortex	25 ± 7	21 ± 8	1.36	NS
Frontal cortex	24 ± 7	27 ± 9	0.86	NS
Occipital cortex	27 ± 8	24 ± 7	0.96	NS
Temporal cortex	24 ± 6	25 ± 6	0.40	NS

[a] From Cross et al. (1978).

[b] Expressed as n mol product formed/g tissue/hr.

enzyme, tyramine, since it was used in some previous studies of the plate-let, and DA, since it was suggested there might be a specific form of the enzyme for this amine) in 14 different areas of the brain (Table 10-3).

These findings do not support the view that MAO activity is reduced in the brains of some schizophrenics, and indeed earlier studies (e.g., Owen et al., 1976) had failed to replicate the finding of reduced platelet enzyme activity in a series of 56 drug-free chronic schizophrenics. It seems possible that the findings in platelets, which have been controver-sial, are a secondary (but perhaps slow) effect of neuroleptic medication.

Other enzymes that have been examined and found unchanged in schizophrenic brain include tyrosine hydroxylase (Cross et al., 1978), DOPA decarboxylase (McGeer and McGeer, 1977; Wyatt et al., 1978), glutamic acid decarboxylase (Cross and Owen, 1979), and choline ace-tyltransferase (Cross and Owen, 1979). Although some of these enzymes have sometimes been reported to show abnormal levels of activity in schizophrenic brain (e.g., Bird et al., 1977), the findings have not been consistent. No abnormalities were found in our series of brains.

Particular interest attaches to assessments of dopaminergic function. In a brain series (43 schizophrenics and 44 controls) collected in collab-oration with workers in Cambridge, we examined concentrations of DA

TABLE 10-3.
MAO ACTIVITIES IN POSTMORTEM BRAINS FROM TEN CONTROLS AND NINE SCHIZOPHRENICS[a,b]

Brain Region	5-HT		Benzylamine		Tyramine		Dopamine	
	Controls	Schizophrenics	Controls	Schizophrenics	Controls	Schizophrenics	Controls	Schizophrenics
Temporal cortex	36± 5	41±10	43± 6	40± 5	100±22	94±19	15± 3	14± 3
Parietal cortex	37± 5	41± 6	30± 5	31± 8	97±15	89±12	18± 5	21± 6
Frontal cortex	44± 5	45± 4	41± 6	42± 6	121±28	112±14	28± 6	25± 4
Occipital cortex	56±16	49±10	46±11	40± 9	98±25	91±14	30±10	26± 4
Cingulate cortex	53±16	54±16	68±19	67±16	193±61	211±25	19±10	20± 6
Hypothalamus	82±21	70±13	131±32	117±19	214±45	183±36	34± 8	32±10
Hippocampus	69±14	75±13	82±15	89±13	134±20	142±17	32± 6	28± 4
Caudate	47± 6	47± 5	86±15	92± 8	145±27	145±17	30± 4	28± 5
Putamen	44± 4	43± 6	85±12	75±12	137±34	133±22	17± 5	20± 7
Accumbens	68± 7	74± 7	130±24	145±31	189±23	195±35	51± 5	51±10
Thalamus	51± 4	48± 8	59±12	60±10	112±16	113±13	28± 5	27± 4
Substantia nigra	56± 7	59±16	58±12	63±10	113±18	133±28	14± 4	15± 4
Cerebellum	25± 8	31± 7	16± 5	14± 6	38± 6	35± 5	4± 1	4± 1
Amygdala	71±11	72± 9	76±10	71±10	196±23	183±26	19± 3	21± 2

[a] From Cross et al. (1977).

[b] p is nonsignificant for any comparison between controls and schizophrenics.

TABLE 10-4.
DOPAMINE (DA) HOMOVANILLIC ACID (HVA), AND 3,4-
DIHYDROXYPHENYLACETIC ACID (DOPAC) IN POSTMORTEM BRAINS
ASSAYED BY GAS CHROMATOGRAPHY[a,b]

Study	Controls (mean ± sem) (n = 19)	Schizophrenics[c] (mean ± sem) (n = 18)
CRC		
Caudate		
DA	1.6 ± 0.3	2.5 ± 0.3*
HVA	5.4 ± 0.3	3.8 ± 0.5**
DOPAC	1.3 ± 0.18	0.8 ± 0.13
Accumbens		
DA	0.9 ± 0.3	0.7 ± 0.1
HVA	4.7 ± 0.5	5.5 ± 0.5
DOPAC	1.5 ± 0.02	1.1 ± 0.15
Cambridge	n = 25	n = 25
Caudate		
DA	1.7 ± 0.2	2.0 ± 0.2
HVA	4.3 ± 0.4	5.6 ± 0.8
DOPAC	0.8 ± 0.10	0.5 ± 0.10
Accumbens		
DA	1.4 ± 0.1	2.0 ± 0.1***
HVA	4.4 ± 0.3	4.9 ± 0.6
DOPAC	0.4 ± 0.04	0.4 ± 0.05

[a] From Bird et al. (1979).

[b] In μg/g of tissue.

[c] Probabilities: $*p < 0.05$; $**p < 0.02$; $***p < 0.01$.

and its metabolites homovanillic acid (HVA) and dihydroxyphenylacetic acid (DOPAC) in the corpus striatum and nucleus accumbens (Bird et al., 1979; Table 10-4).

Although there are some differences between schizophrenics and controls (e.g., DA is increased in some areas in the former), these are not consistent in the two series. Moreover there is no evidence of an increase in turnover as indicated by concentrations of the metabolites, the only significant difference being a decrease in HVA in the caudate nucleus in the schizophrenic group in the CRC series of brains. Thus, the findings do not support the view that DA neurons are overactive, and in this they are consistent with some earlier cerebrospinal fluid studies (Bowers, 1974; Post, Fink, Carpenter, and Goodwin, 1975). However, DA turnover was not measured in the frontal cortex, and evidence of an increase in DA metabolites in this area (possibly as a consequence of neuroleptic administration) has been reported (Bacoupolos, Spokes, Bird, and Roth, 1978).

One parameter of dopaminergic transmission, however, does show changes in the brains of many schizophrenic patients. This is the DA receptor as studied by butyrophenone-binding techniques. With spiroperidol as ligand, at a concentration of 0.8 nm, a mean increase in binding was found in 19 schizophrenics as compared to 19 control brains in the corpus striatum, putamen, and nucleus accumbens (Owen, et al., 1978; Fig. 10-4).

Significant differences ($p < 0.01$) were found in each of the dopaminergically innervated areas. However it is possible that the amount of this difference is diminished by the presence in the brains of many patients of neuroleptic administered in life. Some neuroleptic remains in the brain; it cannot readily be washed out and it interferes competitively with ligand binding (Owen, Cross, Poulter, and Waddington, 1979). This

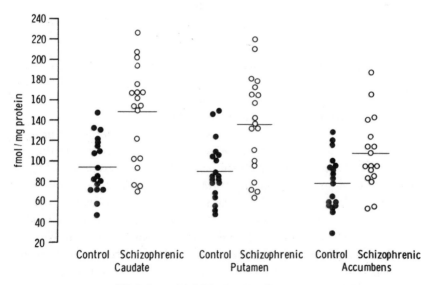

FIGURE 10-4. ^{3}H-Spiroperidol Binding in Three Areas of Schizophrenic and Control Brain with a 0.8 nm Concentration of Ligand

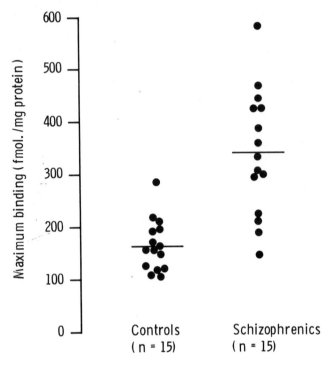

FIGURE 10-5. Maximum Spiroperidol Binding in the Caudate Nucleus

effect can best be circumvented by deriving maximum binding capacity from a saturation (Scatchard) analysis. When this was done in the caudate nucleus in 15 schizophrenics and 15 controls, a mean increase of 100% in the patient group was obtained (Fig. 10-5).

However it is interesting that the scatter in the schizophrenic group is wide and that approximately one-third of the values are within the normal range. These findings with spiroperidol as ligand are in broad agreement with those of Lee, et al. (1978), who used haloperidol values. In our series, the influence of residual neuroleptic was to increase the dissociation constant (K_D) presumably as a result of inhibition of the binding of the labeled ligand at low ligand concentrations. In patients who had not received neuroleptics before death (there were five patients in our original series who, from a careful scrutiny of all available case records, had been drug-free for at least one year before death), the K_D was closely similar to the values observed in controls. Thus, the change in the schiz-

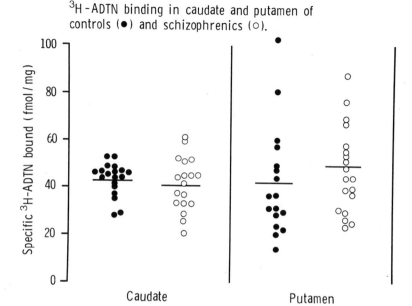

^{3}H-ADTN binding in caudate and putamen of controls (●) and schizophrenics (○).

FIGURE 10-6. Binding of the DA Agonist ADTN in Postmortem Brain of Controls (●) and Schizophrenics (○)

ophrenic group appears to be an increase in the number or the density of the butyrophenone-binding sites.

Different types of DA receptor have been distinguished and the change in schizophrenic brain is selective to one type. Thus binding of the DA agonist ADTN (an amino-tetralin derivative) is not increased (Fig. 10-6).

These findings again are in agreement with those of Lee et al. (1978) in which apomorphine (with binding characteristics resembling those of ADTN) was used as the agonist ligand. It has been claimed (Titeler, List, and Seeman, 1979) that these ligands bind selectively to a presynaptic ("D$_3$") DA receptor, and if this is the case, the above findings suggest that, in schizophrenia, the changes occur at sites other than those of the presynaptic DA neuron.

Kebabian and Calne (1979) distinguished two DA receptors according to their association with an adenylate cyclase mechanism. The D$_1$ receptor is associated with adenylate cyclase, whereas the D$_2$ receptor is not. Butyrophenones are relatively specific ligands for the D$_2$ receptor, whereas such thiaxanthes as flupenthixol have an affinity for the D$_1$ receptor, although they also label the D_2 receptor. In an attempt to determine whether the change in schizophrenic brain is selective to one receptor, we studied the binding of flupenthixol (Cross, Crow, and Owen, 1981).

Flupenthixol binding can be demonstrated to be partly displaceable by domperidone, a butyrophenone that is a selective D_2 receptor ligand, and in this way the D_1 and D_2 components of flupenthixol binding can be distinguished. Maximum flupenthixol binding in schizophrenic brain was increased and, as with spiroperidol binding, there was an apparent increase in K_D in patients who were receiving neuroleptics at the time of their death. However, when the domperidone-displaceable component was distinguished, the increase in binding appeared to be largely limited to this (i.e., the D_2) component (Table 10-5).

There is evidence that the D_1 receptor is localized mainly on intrinsic striatal cell bodies, whereas some D_2 receptors are associated with cortico-striatal afferents. The evidence thus is compatible with the view that the change in schizophrenia is in a D_2 receptor, which is located on the terminals of a system projecting from the cerebral cortex to the striatum (and perhaps also from hippocampus and limbic lobe structures to the nucleus accumbens).

The question of whether the changes in the D_2 receptor are associated with the disease process or are secondary to drug treatment, in other words whether neuroleptic drugs cause a long-term increase in numbers of receptors, is critical. Three considerations suggest that the changes may be at least partly associated with the disease process.

> 1. In a series of five patients, careful examination of all available case records revealed no evidence of neuroleptic drug administration for one year before death. In these five patients, maximum spiroperidol binding was increased 49% by comparison with controls ($p < 0.05$). Two of these patients, who apparently had never had neuroleptic drugs, had a mean increase of 77% by comparison with controls.
> 2. In tissue samples from 12 brains of patients with Huntington's chorea who had received neuroleptic drugs, spiroperidol binding was not significantly increased by comparison with four patients who had not received medication (^{3}H-spiroperidol binding at 0.8 nm, on drugs, 85.5 ± 36; off drugs, 76.4 ± 30).
> 3. In some animal studies of the effects of chronic neuroleptic drug administration, increases have been observed in agonist binding (Muller and Seeman, 1977) and adenylate cyclase activity (the D_1

TABLE 10-5.

DOMPERIDONE DISPLACEMENT OF ^{3}H-FLUPENTHIXOL BINDING IN
POSTMORTEM BRAIN[a]

	D_1 Component	D_2 Component
Controls	104 ± 16	57 ± 9
Schizophrenics	133 ± 11	109 ± 16[b]

[a] Results as fmol/mg protein.
[b] $p < 0.02$.

receptor) (Marsden and Jenner, 1980). Therefore the fact that such changes are not seen in postmortem brain in schizophrenia suggests that the changes observed in the D_2 receptor may not be due to drugs, but rather may be related to the disease process. However, further evidence on this question is required.

A number of other receptors have been assayed in the postmortem brain and the values in schizophrenia have been found to be comparable to those seen in controls. These include LSD and 5HT binding (LSD binding being assessed in both the corpus striatum and the frontal cortex), GABA and benzodiazepine binding, and binding of the muscarinic cholinergic ligand quinuclidinyl benzilate and the adrenergic compound WB-4101. The enzymes, receptors, transmitters, and transmitter metabolites that have been found to be comparable in schizophrenic and control brain are listed in Table 10-6.

TABLE 10-6.

SUBSTANCES FOUND TO BE COMPARABLE IN SCHIZOPHRENIC AND
CONTROL BRAIN SAMPLES

Enzymes	Ligand Binding	Transmitters	Transmitter Precursors and Metabolites
Tyrosine hydroxylase	LSD	Dopamine	5-HIAA
DOPA decarboxylase	5-HT	Norepinephrine	Kynurenine
Dopamine-β-hydroxylase	GABA	Serotonin	Tryptophan
Monoamine oxidase	Diazepam	GABA	HVA
Choline acetyltransferase	QNB		DOPAC
Glutamic acid decarboxylase	ADTN		

Thus the binding of butyrophenones to the D_2 receptor stands out as the single chemical characteristic that distinguishes schizophrenic brains as a group from those of controls.

STRUCTURAL CHANGES IN THE BRAIN

Contrary to the views expressed by Bleuler, it now is clear that a proportion of patients with illnesses that by traditional criteria would be considered schizophrenic have psychological impairments of an "organic" type. Thus approximately 25% of long-stay inpatient populations have been found to have "age disorientation," and most of these patients underestimate their own ages (Crow and Mitchell, 1975; Stevens, Crow, Bowman, and Coles, 1978). These patients also make errors in stating what year it is and in estimating the duration of their hospital stay that are consistent with their own view of their age. The findings suggest that for these patients "time stands still" in that from a certain point in the course of their illness they have ceased to record the passage of time (Crow and Stevens, 1978). Thus, some chronic schizophrenic patients suffer from a constellation of psychological deficits of an "organic" type that, according to conventional psychiatric concepts, would suggest the presence either of structural changes in the brain or gross disturbance of brain metabolism. Yet there seems to be little as yet to indicate that this group of patients suffers from atypical types of schizophrenic illness. Moreover, past experience of somatic therapies, including insulin coma, ECT, and neuroleptic drugs, was not more extensive in the group of patients with "age disorientation" than in those without it.

Using a discrepancy of five years between true and subjective age as a criterion, approximately 25% of three separate inpatient populations with chronic schizophrenia have been found to show age disorientation (Crow and Mitchell, 1975; Stevens, Crow, Bowman, and Coles, 1978; Smith and Oswald, 1976). Thus "organic" type psychological changes for which no ready explanation is available appear to be common in the long-stay inpatient, chronic schizophrenia population.

A radiological study of a group of chronic schizophrenic patients using computerized axial tomography (CAT) revealed that structural brain

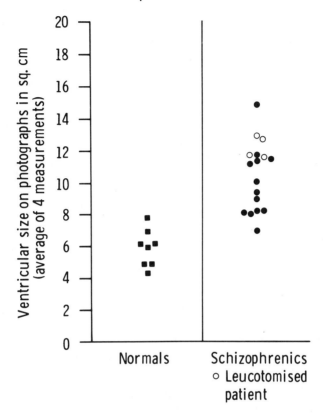

FIGURE 10-7. Mean Ventricular Size Assessed From CAT Scans in a Group of Chronic Institutionalized Schizophrenics and Controls

changes may also be present in a proportion of these patients (Johnstone et al., 1976; Johnstone et al., 1978b). Mean ventricular size (assessed with a planimeter from consecutive pairs of brain sections) was significantly increased in the schizophrenic group by comparison with an age- and premorbid occupation-matched control group (Fig. 10-7). In this study there was no evidence of increased cortical sulcal width.

Some earlier radiological studies suggested that structural changes may be present in some schizophrenic patients. For example, both Haug (1962), who studied a series of over 90 schizophrenic patients aged under 60 years, and Asano (1967), who studied 53 schizophrenic patients of mean age 29 years, found that pneumonencephalographic abnormalities

TABLE 10-7.
PNEUMOENCEPHALOGRAPHIC CHANGES IN SCHIZOPHRENIA

Author	Number of Patients	Age (years)	Subgroups	Pneumoencephalogram Normal	Abnormal
Haug (1962)	91	Under 60	Without deterioration	39	6
			With deterioration	9	37 (p < .001)
Asano (1967)	53	Mean 29	"Peripheral" (n = 21)	12	9
			"Nuclear" (n = 32)	7	25 (p < .01)

were related to certain clinical characteristics. Thus, Haug found abnormal air encephalograms to be significantly more common in patients with deterioration as assessed clinically and Asano found such changes to be more common in patients with "nuclear" as compared to "peripheral" types of illness when subdivided according to Mitsuda's classification (Table 10-7).

By demonstrating a relationship between structural brain changes and certain clinical characteristics within groups of patients, these studies have avoided the problem of many pneumoencephalographic studies—the absence of a normal control group. Thus a number of earlier workers (e.g., Jacobi and Winkler, 1928; Lemke, 1935; Moore, Nathan, Elliott, and Laubach, 1933; Huber, 1964; Bratfos and Sagedal, 1960; Fröshaug and Retterstöl, 1956; Young and Crampton, 1974) have reported sometimes severe ventricular abnormalities in some patients with schizophrenia. However, interest in these findings was diminished by the study of Storey (1966), who found no excess of abnormalities in 18 chronic schizophrenics by comparison with a control group investigated for neurological disease and judged to have no structural brain changes. Two further studies examined the size of the third ventricle. In a pneumoencephalographic investigation (Peltonen, 1962), there was no change in ventricular width, but in an echoencephalographic study (Holden et al., 1973), there was evidence of an increase, in the schizophrenic group.

More recent CAT scan studies have extended the earlier findings

(Johnstone et al., 1976, 1978b). Weinberger, Torrey, Neophytides, and Wyatt (1979) also found a substantial increase in the ventricle/brain ratio in a group of 56 chronic schizophrenics, compared with an age-matched control group, and found that this difference was present in patients in their 20s and 30s as well as in older patients. By contrast with the earlier findings, this group of workers also found some patients with evidence of cortical changes, although these changes were unrelated to lateral ventricular abnormalities (Weinberger, Torrey, Neophytides, and Wyatt, 1979b).

In the first CAT scan study (Johnstone et al., 1976, 1978b), increased ventricular size was found to be related to evidence of intellectual impairment (Table 10-8).

This finding was confirmed in three later studies. Thus Rieder et al. (1979), in a small study of outpatients, found evidence of cerebral atrophy in some cases; in those patients in whom it was present, there was also evidence of intellectual impairment. Donnelly et al. (1980) found lateral ventricular enlargement in inpatients to be related to poor performance on the Halstead-Reitan test battery, and recently Golden and colleagues (1980) have shown such changes to be related to impairments on a wide variety of the component tests of the Luria Battery. The finding of a relationship between intellectual impairment and structural changes in the brain is relevant to the issue of whether intellectual impairments observed in chronic schizophrenic patients can be attributed to poor mo-

TABLE 10-8.

CORRELATIONS BETWEEN COGNITIVE FUNCTION AND MEASURES OF BRAIN SIZE WITHIN THE GROUP OF PATIENTS WITH SCHIZOPHRENIA

Comparison	Correlation Coefficient	Number of Patients	Significance
Withers and Hinton v. ventricular area	0.70	13	$p < .01$
Withers and Hinton v. ventricular area as percent of brain area	0.64	13	$p < .05$
Withers and Hinton v. brain area as percent of skull area	0.51	13	$p < .10$ ($p < .05$, 1-tailed)

tivation and to lack of cooperation in testing. If such impairments are regularly associated with brain changes, it seems that a purely motivational explanation may be incorrect.

Again in the first CAT scan study (Johnstone et al., 1976, 1978b), increased ventricular size and intellectual impairment were also found to be significantly related to the presence of the negative schizophrenic symptoms—flattening of affect and poverty of speech. By contrast, intellectual impairment and increased ventricular size were apparently unrelated to the presence of positive schizophrenic symptoms.

TWO SYNDROMES

On the basis of the recent CAT scan and the earlier pneumoencephalographic studies, there is a rather strong case that some patients with chronic schizophrenia have structural brain changes; from pharmacological and neurochemical studies, there is a case that part of the disturbance in schizophrenia is related to a change in dopaminergic transmission. The question obviously arises as to the relationship between these two changes. It has been suggested (Crow, 1980a; Crow et al., 1980) that these changes reflect two separate dimensions of pathology and are associated, respectively, with negative and positive symptoms (Table 10-9).

The significance of this distinction is that it appears that positive symptoms define the drug-responsive component as indicated by the findings of the trial of the isomers of flupenthixol. This is the reversible component of the illness. By contrast, the type II syndrome (negative symptoms), which is not present in many patients, indicates a component of irreversibility and therefore predicts poor long-term outcome. It appears that the type II, but not the type I syndrome is associated with intellectual impairment. It is suggested that the type I syndrome reflects a disturbance of dopaminergic transmission, perhaps an increase in numbers of D_2 receptors, whereas the type II syndrome is related to structural changes, presumably reflecting cell loss, at some as yet undefined site in the brain.

Although the two syndromes may represent separate dimensions of pathology, it is clear that they do not constitute separate diseases. They

TABLE 10-9.
TWO SYNDROMES IN SCHIZOPHRENIA

	Type I	Type II
Symptoms	Delusions, hallucinations, thought disorder (positive symptoms)	Flattening of affect, poverty of speech, loss of drive (negative symptoms)
Type of illness in which most commonly seen	Acute schizophrenia	Chronic schizophrenia (the "defect state")
Response to neuroleptics	Good	Poor
Outcome	Reversible	? Irreversible
Intellectual impairment	Absent	Sometimes present
Postulated pathological process	? Increased DA receptors	Cell loss and structural changes in the brain

commonly occur together as in classical or Kraepelinian schizophrenia, in which episodes of positive symptoms are gradually followed by the development of the type II syndrome or defect state. On the other hand, the two syndromes can occur separately. Thus psychoses from which complete recovery occurs, sometimes referred to as "good-prognosis schizophrenia," or "reactive" or "psychogenic" psychoses, correspond to the pure type I syndrome. A type II syndrome developing insidiously without episodes of positive symptoms corresponds to simple schizophrenia (Fig. 10-8).

Traditional subdivisions of the disease can be related to the presence or absence of the two syndromes. Thus some paranoid illnesses are chronic type I syndromes. Hebephrenic illnesses typically combine features of both syndromes, and "simple schizophrenia" describes the development of the type II syndrome without the prior occurrence of the type I syndrome.

Changes with time can also be accommodated within this schema (Fig. 10-8). Thus, patients with the pure type I syndrome may develop type II features. Some patients with type I and type II symptoms may lose the former, and develop the "pure defect state," and some patients in this latter category may re-experience positive symptoms. What seems to be a very unusual occurrence, however, is to lose the features of the

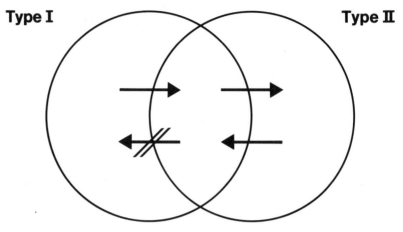

Type I   **Type II**

Paranoid schizophrenia   Hebephrenic   Simple schizophrenia
'Good-prognosis' schizophrenia   schizophrenia   The 'defect state'
Schizophreniform psychosis
Reactive schizophrenia

FIGURE 10-8. The Type I and Type II Syndromes of Schizophrenics and Their Interrelation

type II syndrome—once present, negative symptoms appear to persist. If, as suggested above, these symptoms are closely related to structural changes in the brain, their persistence can be readily understood.

The distinction between two syndromes is supported by a number of recent findings. Thus Angrist, Rotrosen, and Gershon (1980a) found that patients whose symptoms were made worse by amphetamine were likely to respond to chlorpromazine, a finding to be expected from the DA hypothesis. Symptoms were assessed with the Brief Psychiatric Rating Scale (BPRS) and subsequent re-analysis (Angrist, Rotrosen, and Gershon, 1980b), according to the positive versus negative symptom dichotomy indicated that negative symptoms were only moderately worsened by amphetamine and showed no response to chlorpromazine (Table 10-10).

Indeed when emotional withdrawal (which these authors argue may sometimes be secondary to positive symptoms) was excluded, the remaining negative symptoms on the BPRS scale ("motor retardation" and "blunted affect") were not influenced by either drug. By contrast there was an increase in positive symptoms on amphetamine and a decrease on chlorpromazine, both changes being highly significant. Amphetamine

TABLE 10-10.

CHANGES IN POSITIVE AND NEGATIVE SYMPTOM RATINGS ON THE BPRS
SCALE IN 21 SCHIZOPHRENIC PATIENTS IN RESPONSE TO 0.5 MG/KG OF
d-AMPHETAMINE AND NEUROLEPTIC MEDICATION[a]

	Base line	Post-amphetamine[b]	Post-neuroleptic[b]
Positive Symptoms	21.3	26.6***	15.4***
Negative Symptoms			
Total	8.1	8.9*	7.7
Emotional withdrawal	3.5	4.4***	2.9**
Motor retardation and blunted affect	4.7	4.5	4.9

[a] Adapted from Angrist, Rotrosen, and Gershon (1980).
[b] Probabilities: *$p < .05$; **$p < .02$; ***$p < .001$.

administration and neuroleptic administration define the dopaminergic component. Therefore, these findings provide rather strong support for the view that the type I syndrome is the dopaminergic component and that changes in dopaminergic transmission are not directly relevant to the type II syndrome.

The recent study of Weinberger et al. (1980) established that drug responsiveness is related to the presence or absence of evidence of cerebral ventricular changes. Patients with definite evidence of increased ventricular size showed little improvement when placed on neuroleptic medication, whereas BPRS ratings were significantly diminished in those with normal ventricles. Thus the presence of the structural changes, which are significantly associated with the type II syndrome, predicts poor response to neuroleptic drugs.

Holden, Stock, Holden, and Itil (submitted) have also shown that a group of patients who were carefully selected for non-responsiveness to neuroleptic drugs could be distinguished from responders by their poor performance on tests of intellectual function.

In their recent survey of long-stay inpatients meeting the Feighner criteria for a diagnosis of schizophrenia, Owens and Johnstone (1980) obtained findings that were compatible with the concept of the two syndromes (Table 10-11). Thus in this group of patients, negative symptoms were significantly correlated with the presence of intellectual impairment

TABLE 10-11.

RELATIONSHIP[a] AMONG POSITIVE AND NEGATIVE SYMPTOMS AND OTHER
NEUROLOGICAL, COGNITIVE, AND BEHAVIORAL FEATURES IN A GROUP OF
500 FEIGHNER-POSITIVE SCHIZOPHRENIC PATIENTS IN THE LONG-STAY
WARDS OF A MENTAL HOSPITAL

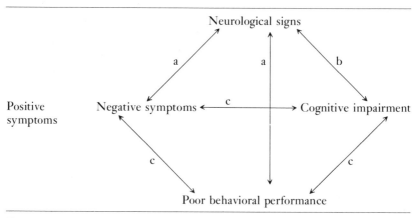

From Owens and Johnstone (1980).

[a] Key to relationships: a, $p < .02$; b, $p < .01$; c, $p < .001$.

and poor behavioral performance (and also the presence of neurological, mostly extrapyramidal signs). None of these features was significantly related to the presence of positive symptoms, and interestingly, neither the positive symptoms nor the negative symptoms or their correlates were related to recent or past history of neuroleptic medication (Owens and Johnstone, 1980).

Thus this study supports the concept that positive and negative symptoms reflect separate dimensions of pathology and that the negative symptoms are related to the more incapacitating behavioral and and cognitive impairments of the defect state.

The distinction between the two syndromes may be relevant to recent controversies concerning the criteria for diagnosing schizophrenia. It is already apparent that those nuclear (Schneiderian first-rank) symptoms, which are regarded by some as the most reliable criteria for diagnosing the illness, are not good predictors of long-term outcome (Brockington, Kendell, and Leff, 1978; Bland and Orn, 1980). Conversely, criteria such as those of Feighner and the DSM-III system, which require the presence of illness for a continuous interval of six months, are more successful (Kendell, 1980). Persistence of illness for six months presumably selects those patients with an irreversible component. On the other hand, nuclear symptoms, among other positive symptoms, may respond well to neuroleptic drugs. Therefore, it seems worth testing the proposition that the negative symptoms (because they are associated with the irreversible component) predict poor long-term outcome, whereas the positive symptoms predict potential response to neuroleptics. The separation of the two components may improve prediction of outcome and identify that group of schizophrenic illnesses that, from the outset, are likely to follow a deteriorating course.

It is also relevant that the early presence of "organic" psychological changes may be associated with poor outcome. In a recent study of the Iowa 500 group, Tsuang (Chapter 2) has found that the presence of disorientation at the time of the index illness was significantly associated with poor outcome at a 30-year followup.

THE NATURE OF THE DISEASE PROCESS

The genetic contribution to the disease is well established from twin and adoption studies. However, the limitations of a simple genetic view are now also apparent. Concordance in monozygotic twins is probably no more than 50%, and in many cases there is a well-defined time of onset in early, middle, or sometimes even late adult life. The disease cannot be a simple inherited disorder of metabolism.

Recent interest in life events and family environment as possible precipitants of hospitalization (Vaughn and Leff, 1976) has encouraged the view that the genetic component may involve a special vulnerability to specific types of stress and that, in the presence of stress, the disease is expressed. However, such an account fails to distinguish the functional psychoses from the personality disorders, to which genetic predisposition is also relevant (Slater and Cowie, 1971); it also overlooks Jaspers's point that in the functional psychoses we are dealing with a significant change that has an onset at a particular point in time, a change that cannot be understood as a personality development and that can only be accounted for if it is assumed that "a process has intervened in the biological happenings and irreversibly and incurably altered the psychic life by interrupting the course of biological events" (Jaspers, 1963, p. 702).

It has been suggested (Crow, 1980b,c) that the types of process that could account for such a change are more circumscribed than is often thought. Thus, although toxins or dietary deficiencies are sometimes considered as pathogenetic factors in the psychoses, they would have to be selective for those with a particular genetic disposition and to be active in those individuals only from a particular point in time. These constraints make it difficult to devise a plausible toxic or dietary hypothesis.

An immunological (i.e., autoimmune) or infective (e.g., viral) process could account for these characteristics. Susceptibility to viral infections is often genetically determined, as also are known autoimmune diseases. These latter, moreover, are sometimes considered to be initiated by viral infection (Lewis, 1974).

EVIDENCE FOR A VIRAL ETIOLOGY

That schizophrenic symptoms may sometimes result from viral infection is suggested by reports of schizophrenia-like illnesses as sequelae of the influenza epidemic of 1918 (Menninger, 1926) and of the later epidemic of encephalitis lethargica (Jelliffe, 1927; Hendrick, 1928; McCowan and Cook, 1928). The influenza virus of 1918 is presumably no longer with us and the encephalitis lethargica agent was never detected, but it seems possible that both diseases were due to a virus that in vulnerable people could attack the neuronal systems. Vilyuisk encephalitis can occur in acute and chronic forms, sometimes with acute exacerbations that lead to progressive impairment (Petrov, 1970). The disease may take several forms among which meningoencephalitis and amyotrophic lateral sclerosis are frequent, but a schizophrenia-like syndrome is also common and this progresses to dementia.

Thus, there are some precedents for the view that schizophrenic symptoms may be a consequence of viral infection (Torrey and Peterson, 1976; Crow, 1978).

On the basis of these considerations, a search was recently initiated with cell culture techniques for evidence of viral infection in patients with acute episodes of psychosis (Tyrrell et al., 1979; Crow et al., 1979). Viruses were found in the throats of a number of patients, but were commonly found species. No identifiable viruses were detected in cerebrospinal fluid (CSF) specimens, but in 18 of 47 patients with schizophrenia, a cytopathic effect was detected in stationary MRC 5 human embryonic fibroblast cell cultures. These 18 patients included a number with nuclear schizophrenic symptoms, but they were similar to those patients in whom no such effect was obtained, except there was a tendency for the finding to be associated with poor outcome (Crow et al., 1979).

Occasionally the cytopathic effect persisted through one or two cell culture passages, but regular passage never occurred. Therefore, it could not be demonstrated that the effect was due to the presence of a virus. However, the results of pretreating the CSF before inoculation into cell culture were compatible with this possibility, since the cytopathic effect was abolished by passing CSF through filters of 50-nm and sometimes 100-nm pore size. The agent was resistant to treatment with chloroform and was also stable on heating to 56°C for one hour (Table 10-12). It was unaffected by pretreatment with the DNA synthesis inhibitor bromodeoxyuridine (BUDR).

Thus the findings are compatible with the possibility that the agent present in CSF is a smallish RNA virus. However, such an agent (or agents) was also found in some patients with Huntington's chorea, one or two patients with multiple sclerosis, and some patients with neurological symptoms of obscure origin. Therefore, association with a specific disease process has not been demonstrated.

TABLE 10-12.

CHARACTERISTICS OF "VIRUS-LIKE AGENT" IN CEREBROSPINAL FLUID FROM PATIENTS WITH SCHIZOPHRENIA OR OTHER NEUROLOGICAL DISORDER (E.G., HUNTINGTON'S CHOREA)

Size: 50–100 nm

Resistant to heat at 56 °C for 1 hour; resistant to chloroform

Not inhibited by bromodeoxyuridine (a DNA synthesis inhibitor)

Three interpretations of these findings are possible at the present time.

1. The presence of the agent is unrelated to disease of the nervous system.
2. The presence of the agent is a secondary consequence of central nervous system disease, reflecting release of toxic or perhaps infective material from damaged neural tissue.
3. The agent is in some way causally related to the presence of the psychiatric and neurological disease.

Evidence for a significant association with central nervous system disease (Tyrrell et al., 1979) does not support interpretation 1, and the heterogeneity of the diseases in question would appear to make interpretation 3 implausible. Thus the second interpretation, that the effects observed are in some way secondary to the disease process, would appear the most likely explanation of the association. However, the possibility that an agent that is relatively widely distributed in the community has specific neuropathogenic effects in genetically predisposed individuals or that a class of such agents interacting with particular genetic substrates causes a range of neuropsychiatric disease should not be dismissed. For this reason, we are continuing transmission experiments in a variety of animal species.

CONCLUSIONS

It is suggested that two syndromes can be distinguished in illnesses presently described as schizophrenic and that these may reflect separate dimensions of pathology. Patients with the type I syndrome characterized by the presence of positive symptoms (delusions, hallucinations, and thought disorder) may respond to neuroleptic drugs. The therapeutic effects of these drugs are closely associated with their ability to block dopamine (DA) receptors, and this raises the question of whether there is a disturbance of dopaminergic transmission. Cerebrospinal fluid and postmortem studies have revealed no increase in DA neuron activity, but in about two-thirds of the brains studied, there was evidence of increased numbers of DA (specifically D_2) receptors. It is argued that this change may not be a secondary effect of neuroleptic medication, but rather may be associated with the disease process.

Patients with the type II syndrome characterized by the presence of negative symptoms (flattening of affect, poverty of speech, and loss of drive) appear not to respond to neuroleptic medication. The syndrome is associated with intellectual impairment and, according to some earlier air encephalographic and recent computerized axial tomographic investigations, with increased ventricular size. The type II syndrome thus corresponds to the schizophrenic "defect state." It is argued that this syndrome, by contrast with the type I syndrome, may be an irreversible result of a qualitatively different pathological process. Thus, although the type I syndrome predicts potential response to neuroleptic drugs, the type II syndrome predicts poor long-term outcome.

The two syndromes do not represent separate diseases, since many patients have both classes of symptom either simultaneously or at different points in time. Thus, in some patients, acute episodes of delusional psychosis are followed by the gradual development of type II syndrome, and in some of these patients positive symptoms are lost with the passage of time, although they may reappear, with further psychotic exacerbations. What appears to be exceptional however, if it occurs at all, is for patients who have once developed negative symptoms to lose them. This may be because such symptoms are associated with structural changes in the brain.

Whereas the two syndromes commonly are associated, they may also occur separately. Thus, the type I syndrome when it occurs alone may be followed by complete recovery. In this case, it may represent those illnesses that are sometimes referred to as "reactive" or "psychogenic" psychoses or "good-prognosis" schizophrenia. However, the type I syndrome also includes some chronic paranoid syndromes. The type II syndrome sometimes develops insidiously without episodes of positive symptoms ("simple schizophrenia"). The diagnosis in this case may be difficult, since it is difficult to assess negative symptoms clinically.

It is argued that neither genetic nor presently identified environmental factors are sufficient to explain the etiology of schizophrenia, but rather a specific pathogenic agent remains to be identified. This could be a virus to which genetically predisposed subpopulations are susceptible. Such a virus might induce a neurohumoral disturbance in some individuals and a more diffuse encephalitic process in others, the particular pathology perhaps depending upon genetic predisposition. Some evidence for the presence of a virus-like agent in the CSF of some patients with schizophrenia has been presented, but the viral nature of this agent has not been established and its etiological relationship to the disease remains to be clarified.

References

Anden, N. E. (1972). Dopamine turnover in the corpus striatum and the limbic system after treatment with neuroleptic and antiacetylcholine drugs. *J. Pharm. Pharmacol.* 24, 905–906.

Angrist, B., H. K. Lee, and S. Gershon (1974). The antagonism of amphetamine-induced symptomatology by a neuroleptic. *Amer. J. Psychiat.* 131, 817–819.

Angrist, B., J. Rotrosen, and S. Gershon (1980a). Responses to apomorphine, amphetamine and neuroleptics in schizophrenic subjects. *Psychopharmacology* 67, 31–38.

Angrist, B., J. Rotrosen, and S. Gershon (1980b). Positive and negative symptoms in schizophrenia—differential response to amphetamine and neuroleptics. *Psychopharmacology* 72, 17–19.

Anlezark, G. M., D. S. Walter, G. W. Arbuthnott, T. J. Crow, and D. Eccleston (1975). The relationship between noradrenaline turnover in cerebral cortex and electrical self-stimulation through electrodes in the region of locus coeruleus. *J. Neurochem.* 24, 677–681.

Asano, N. (1967). Pneumoencephalographic study of schizophrenia. In *Clinical Genetics in Psychiatry* (H. Mitsuda, ed.) Igaku-Shoin, Tokyo, pp. 209–219.

Bacopoulos, N. C., E. G. Spokes, E. D. Bird, and R. H. Roth (1978). Antipsychotic drug action in schizophrenic patients: Effects on cortical dopamine metabolism after long-term treatment. *Science* 205, 1405–1407.

Bennett, J. P., and S. H. Snyder (1975). Stereospecific binding of D-lysergic acid diethylamide (LSD) to brain membranes; Relationship to serotonin receptors. *Brain Research* 94, 523–544.

Bird, E. D., T. J. Crow, C. C. Iversen, A. Longden, A. V. P. Mackay, G. J. Riley, and E. G. Spokes (1979). Dopamine and homovanillic acid concentrations in the post-mortem brain in schizophrenia. *J. Physiol. Lond.* 293, 36–37p.

Bird, E. D., E. G. Spokes, J. Barnes, A. V. P. Mackay, L. L. Iversen, and M. Shepherd (1977). Increased brain dopamine and reduced glutamic acid decarboxylase and choline acetyltransferase activity in schizophrenia and related psychoses. *Lancet* ii, 1157–1159.

Bland, R. C., and H. Orn (1980). Schizophrenia: Schneider's first rank symptoms and outcome. *Brit. J. Psychiat.* 137, 63–68.

Bleuler, E. (1950). Dementia Proaecox or the Group of Schizophrenia. International Universities Press, New York.

Bonhoeffer, K. (1909). 'Zur Frage der exogenen Psychosen.' Zentbl. Nervenheilk 32, 499–505. Translated and reprinted in Themes and Variations in European Psychiatry (S. R. Hirsch and M. Shepherd, eds.) John Wright, Bristol (1974).

Bowers, M. B. (1974). Central dopamine turnover in schizophrenic syndromes. Arch. Gen. Psychiat. 31, 50–54.

Bowers, M. B., and A. Rozitis (1976). Brain homovanillic acid: Regional changes over time with antipsychotic drugs. Europ. J. Pharmacol. 39, 109–115.

Bratfos, O., and E. Sagedal (1960). Luftencephalografiske undersøkelsar nos pasienter innlagt i sinusykehus. Nord. Med. 64, 1606–1609.

Brockington, I. F., R. E. Kendell, and J. P. Leff (1978). Definitions of schizophrenia: Concordance and prediction of outcome. Psychol. Med. 8, 387–398.

Carlsson, A., and M. Lindqvist (1963). Effect of chlorpromazine and haloperidol on formation of 3-methoxy-tyramine and normetanephrine in mouse brain. Acta Pharmac. Toxicol. 20, 140–144.

Clement-Cormier, Y. C., J. W. Kebabian, G. L. Petzold, and P. Greengard (1974). Dopamine-sensitive adenylate cyclase in mammalian brain: A possible site of action of antipsychotic drugs. Proc. Natl. Acad. Sci. (U.S.A.) 71, 1113–1117.

Connell, P. H. (1958). Amphetamine Psychosis. Maudsley Monograph No.5. Chapman and Hall, London.

Cotes, P. M., T. J. Crow, E. C. Johnstone, W. Bartlett, and R. C. Bourne (1978). Neuroendocrine changes in acute schizophrenia as a function of clinical state and neuroleptic medication. Psychol. Med. 8, 657–665.

Creese, I., D. R. Burt, and S. H. Snyder (1976). Dopamine receptor binding predicts clinical and pharmacological potencies of antischizophrenic drugs. Science 192, 481–483.

Creese, I., and S. D. Iversen (1975). The pharmacological and anatomical substrates of the amphetamine response in the rat. Brain Res. 83, 419–436.

Cross, A. J., T. J. Crow, V. Glover, R. Lofthouse, F. Owen, and G. J. Riley (1977). Monoamine oxidase activity in post-mortem brains of schizophrenics and controls. Brit. J. Clin. Pharmacol. 4, P719.

Cross, A. J., T. J. Crow, W. S. Killpack, A. Longden, F. Owen, and G. J. Riley (1978). The activities of dopamine-β-hydroxylase and catechol-o-methyl-transferase in schizophrenics and controls. Psychopharmacology 51, 117–121.

Cross, A. J., T. J. Crow, and F. Owen (1979). Gamma-aminobutyric acid in the brain in schizophrenia. Lancet i, 560–561.

Cross, A. J., T. J. Crow, and F. Owen (1981). ³H-flupenthixol binding in post-mortem brains of schizophrenics: Evidence for a selective increase in dopamine D-2 receptors. Psychopharmacology 74, 122–124.

Cross, A. J., T. J. Crow, E. K. Perry, R. H. Perry, G. Blessed, and B. H. Tomlinson (1981). Reduced dopamine-β-hydroxylase activity in Alzheimer's Disease. Brit. Med. J. 232, 93–94.

Cross, A. J., and F. Owen (1979). The activities of glutamic acid decarboxylase and choline acetyl transferase in post-mortem brains of schizophrenics and controls. *Biochem. Soc. Trans.* 7, 145–146.

Crow T. J. (1978). Viral causes of psychiatric disease. *Postgrad. Med. J.* 54, 763–767.

Crow, T. J. (1980a). Molecular pathology of schizophrenia: More than one disease process? *Brit. Med. J.* 280, 66–68.

Crow, T. J. (1980b). The search for an environmental agent in schizophrenia. *Trends in Neurosciences 3*, XIII–XIV.

Crow T. J. (1980c). Advances in drug treatment or an understanding of the disease process which comes first? Priorities for research on the causation of schizophrenia and manic-depressive psychosis. *Priorities in Psychiatric Research* (M. H. Lader, ed.). Wiley, Chichester, pp. 148–162.

Crow, T. J., J. F. W. Deakin, E. C. Johnstone, and A. Longden (1976). Dopamine and schizophrenia. *Lancet* ii, 563–566.

Crow, T. J., J. F. W. Deakin, and A. Longden (1977). The nucleus accumbens: Possible site of antipsychotic action of neuroleptic drugs? *Psychol. Med.* 7, 213–221.

Crow, T. J., I. N. Ferrier, E. C. Johnstone, J. F. Macmillan, D. G. C. Owens, R. P. Parry, and D. A. J. Tyrrell. (1979). Characteristics of patients with schizophrenia or neurological disorder and virus-like agent in cerebrospinal fluid. *Lancet* i, 842–844.

Crow, T. J., C. D. Frith, E. C. Johnstone, and D. G. C. Owens (1980). Schizophrenia and cerebral atrophy. *Lancet* i, 1129–1130.

Crow, T. J., and C. Gillbe (1973). Dopamine antagonism and antischizophrenic potency of neuroleptic drugs. *Nature* 245, 27–28.

Crow, T. J., and C. Gillbe (1974). Brain dopamine and behaviour. A critical analysis of the relationship between dopamine antagonism and therapeutic efficacy of neuroleptic drugs. *J. Psychiat. Res.* 11, 163–172.

Crow, T. J., and W. S. Mitchell (1975). Subjective age in chronic schizophrenia: Evidence for a sub-group of patients with defective learning capacity? *Brit. J. Psychiat.* 126, 360–363.

Crow, T. J., P. J. Spear, and G. W. Arbuthnott (1972). Intracranial self-stimulation with electrodes in the region of the locus coeruleus. *Brain Res.* 36, 275–287.

Crow, T. J., and M. Stevens (1978). Age disorientation in chronic schizophrenia: The nature of the cognitive deficit. *Brit. J. Psychiat.* 133, 137–142.

Deniker, P. (1960). Experimental neurological syndromes and the new drug therapies in psychiatry. *Comp. Psychiat.* 1, 92–102.

Donnelly, E. F., D. R. Weinberger, I. N. Waldman, and R. J. Wyatt (1980). Cognitive impairment associated with morphological brain abnormalities on computed tomography in chronic schizophrenic patients. *J. Nerv. Ment. Dis.* 168, 305–308.

Ellinwood, E. H. (1967). Amphetamine psychosis: I. Description of the individuals and process. *J. Nerv. Ment. Dis.* 144, 274–283.

Enna, S. J., J. P. Bennett, D. R. Burt, I., Creese, and S. H. Snyder (1976). Stereospecificity of interaction of neuroleptic drugs with neurotransmitters and correlation with clinical potency. *Nature (Lond.)* 263, 338–347.

Flügel, F. (1953). Therapeutique par medication neuroleptic obtenue en realisant systematiquement des états Parkinsoniformes. *L'Encephale* 45, 1090–1092.

Fröshaug A., and N. Retterstöl (1956). Clinical and pneumoencephalographic studies on cerebral atrophies of middle age. *Acta Psychiat. Scand, Suppl.* 106, 83–102.

Gaddum, J. H. (1954). *Ciba Foundations Symposium on Hypertension.* (G. W. Wolstenholme, ed.). Little, Brown, Boston, pp. 75–77.

Golden, C. J., J. A. Moses, R. Zelazowski, B. Graber, L. M. Zatz, T. B. Horvath, and P. A. Berger (1980). Cerebral ventricular size and neurophysiological impairment in young chronic schizophrenics. *Arch. Gen. Psychiat.* 37, 619–623.

Goldberg, S. C., G. L. Klerman, and J. O. Cole (1965). Changes in schizophrenic psychopathology and ward behaviour as a function of phenothiazine treatment. *Brit. J. Psychiat.* 111, 120–133.

Gunne, L. M., E. Angåard, and L. E. Jönsson (1972). Clinical trials with amphetamine blocking drugs. *Psychiat. Neurol. Neurochir. (Amsterdam)* 75, 225–226.

Haug, J. O. (1962). Pneumoencephalographic studies in mental disease. *Acta Psychiat Scand* 38, Suppl. 165.

Hendrick, I. (1928). Encephalitis lethargica and the interpretation of mental disease. *Amer. J. Psychiat.* 84, 989–1014.

Holden, J. M. C., T. Itil, A. Keskiner, and P. Gannon (1971). A clinical trial of antiserotonin compound, cinanserin in chronic schizophrenia. *J. Clin. Pharmacol.* 11, 220–226.

Holden, J. M. C., M. J. Stock, U. P. Holden, and I. M. Itil (1982). Profile patterns of therapy resistant schizophrenia. Manuscript submitted.

Holden, J. M. C., G. Forno, T. Itil, and W. Hsu (1973). Echoencephalographic patterns in chronic schizophrenia (relationship to therapy resistance). *Biol. Psychiat.* 6, 129–141.

Hornykiewicz, O. (1966). Dopamine (3-hydroxytyramine) and brain function. *Pharm. Revs.* 18, 925–964.

Huber, G. (1964). Neuroradiologie und Psychiatrie. In *Psychiatrie der Gegenwart, Forschung und Praxis Vol 1/1B Grundlagenforschung zur Psychiatrie Part B* (H. W. Gruhle, R. Jung, W. Mayer-Gross, and M. Muller, eds.) Springer-Verlag, Berlin.

Jacobi W., and H. Winkler (1928). Encephalographische studien an schizophrenen. *Arch. Psychiat. Nervenkr.* 84, 208–226.

Jaspers, K. (1963). *General Psychopathology* (J. Hoenig and M. W. Hamilton, trans.). Manchester University Press, Manchester.

Jelliffe, S. E. (1927). The mental picture in schizophrenia and epidemic encephalitis. *Amer. J. Psychiat.* 6, 413–465.

Johnstone, E. C., T. J. Crow, C. D. Frith, J. Husband, and L. Kreel (1976). Cerebral ventricular size and cognitive impairment in chronic schizophrenia. *Lancet* ii, 924–926.

Johnstone, E. C., T. J. Crow, C. D. Frith, M. W. P. Carney, and J. S. Price (1978a). Mechanism of the antipsychotic effect in the treatment of acute schizophrenia. *Lancet* i, 848–851.

Johnstone, E. C., T. J. Crow, C. D. Frith, M. Stevens, L. Kreel, and J. Husband (1978b). The dementia of dementia praecox. *Acta Psychiat. Scand.* 57, 305–324.

Kebabian, J. W., and D. B. Calne (1979). Multiple receptors for dopamine *Nature* 277, 197.

Kendell, R. E. (1980). The outcome of Feighner and DSM III schizophrenia. Paper presented to the Schizophrenia Group, November 1980. The Wellcome Foundation.

Kraepelin, E. (1919). Dementia Praecox (R. M. Barclay, trans.). Fascimile edition published by R. E. Krieger, New York (1971).

Lee, T., P. Seeman, W. W. Tourtelotte, I. J. Farley, and O. Hornykiewicz (1978). Binding of ^{3}H-neuroleptics and ^{3}H-apomorphine in schizophrenic brains. *Nature* 274, 897–899.

Lemke, R. (1955). Neurologische bei schizophrenie. *Psychiatr. Neurol. Med. Psychol.* 7, 226–229.

Lewis, R. M. (1974). Spontaneous autoimmune diseases of domestic animals. *Intl. Rev. Exptl. Pathol.* 13, 55–82.

Marsden, C., and P. Jenner (1980). The pathophysiology of extra-pyramidal side effects of neuroleptic drugs. *Psychol. Med.* 10, 55–72.

McCowan, P. K., and L. C. Cook. (1928). The mental aspect of chronic epidemic encephalitis. *Lancet* i, 1316–1320.

McGeer, P. L., and E. D. McGeer (1977). Possible changes in striatal and limbic cholinergic systems in schizophrenia. *Arch. Gen. Psychiat.* 34, 1319–1323.

Menninger K. A. (1926). Influenza and schizophrenia. An analysis of post-influenzal "dementia praecox" as of 1918, and 5 years later. *Amer. J. Psychiat.* 5, 469–529.

Miller, R. J., and C. R. Hiley (1974). Antimuscarinic properties of neuroleptics and drug-induced Parkinsonism. *Nature (Lond.)* 248, 596–597.

Miller, R. J., A. S. Horn, and L. L. Iversen (1974). The action of neuroleptic drugs on dopamine-stimulated adenosine cyclic 3', 5'-monophosphate production in neostriatum and limbic forebrain. *Mol. Pharmac.* 10, 759–766.

Moore, N. T., D. Nathan, A. R. Elliott, and C. Laubach (1933). Encephalographic studies in schizophrenia (dementia praecox) a report of sixty cases. *Amer. J. Psychiat.* 12, 801–810.

Muller, P., and P. Seeman (1974). Neuroleptics: Relation between cateleptic and anti-turning actions, and role of the cholinergic system. *J. Pharm. Pharmac.* 26, 981–984.

Muller, P., and P. Seeman (1977). Brain neurotransmitter receptors after long-term haloperidol: Dopamine, acetylcholine, serotonin, β-noradrenergic and naloxone receptors. *Life Sci.* 21, 1751–1758.

Murphy, D. L. and R. J. Wyatt (1972). Reduced MAO activity in blood platelets from schizophrenic patients. *Nature* 238, 225–226.

National Institute of Mental Health, Psychopharmacology Service Centre, Collaborative Study Group (1964). Phenothiazine treatment in acute schizophrenia. *Arch. Gen. Psychiat.* 10, 246–261.

Owen, F., R. C. Bourne, T. J. Crow, E. C. Johnstone, A. R. Bailey, and H. I.

Hershon (1976). Platelet monoamine oxidase in schizophrenia: An investigation in drug-free chronic hospitalised patients. *Arch. Gen. Psychiat.* 33, 1370–1373.

Owen, F., A. J. Cross, T. J. Crow, A. Longden, M. Poulter, and G. J. Riley (1978). Increased dopamine receptor sensitivity in schizophrenia. *Lancet* ii, 223–226.

Owen, F., A. J. Cross, M. Poulter, and J. L. Waddington (1979). Change in the characteristics of ³H-spiperone binding to rat striatal membranes after acute chlorpromazine administration: effects of buffer washing of membranes. *Life Sci.* 25, 385–390.

Owens, D. G. C., and E. C. Johnstone (1980). The disabilities of chronic schizophrenia: Their nature and the factors contributing to their development. *Brit. J. Psychiat.* 136, 384–395.

Peltonen, L. (1962). Pneumoencephalographic studies on the third ventricle of 644 neuropsychiatric patients. *Acta Psychiat. Scand.* 38, 15–34.

Petrov, P. A. (1970). Vilyuisk encephalitis in the Yakut Republic (USSR) *Amer. J. Trop. Med. Sci.* 19, 146–150.

Perry, E. K., and R. H. Perry (1980). The cholinergic system in Alzheimer's disease. In *Biochemistry of Dementia* (P. J. Roberts, ed.). Wiley, Chichester, pp. 135–183.

Post, R. M., E. Fink, W. T. Carpenter, and F. K. Goodwin (1975). Cerebospinal fluid amine metabolites in acute schizophrenia. *Arch. Gen. Psychiat.* 32, 1013–1069.

Randrup, A., and I. Munkvad (1965). Special antagonism of amphetamine-induced abnormal behaviour. Inhibition of stereotyped activity with increase of some normal activities. *Psychopharmacologia* 7, 416–422.

Randrup, A., and I. Munkvad (1966). On the role of catecholamines in the amphetamine excitatory response. *Nature (Lond.)* 211, 540.

Randrup, A., and I. Munkvad (1972). Evidence indicating an association between schizophrenia and dopaminergic hyperactivity in the brain. *Orthomol. Psychiat.* 1, 2–7.

Rieder, R. O., E. F. Donnelly, J. R. Herdt, and I. N. Waldman (1979). Sulcal prominence in young chronic schizophrenic patients: C.T. Scan findings associated with impairment on neuropsychological tests. *Psychiat. Res.* 1, 1–8.

Ritter, S., and L. Stein (1973). Self-stimulation of noradrenergic cell group (A6) in the locus coeruleus of rats. *J. Comp. Physiol. Psychol.* 85, 443–452.

Roberts, E. (1972). An hypothesis suggesting that there is a defect in the GABA system in schizophrenia. *Neurosci. Res. Prog. Bull.* 10, 468–482.

Scatton, B., J. Glowinski, and L. Julou (1976). Dopamine metabolism in the mesolimbic and mesocortical dopaminergic systems after single or repeated administrations of neuroleptics. *Brain Res.* 109, 184–189.

Seeman, P., T. Lee, M. Chan-Wong, and K. Wong (1976). Antipsychotic drug doses and neuroleptic/dopamine receptors. *Nature (Lond.)* 261, 717–719.

Slater, E., and V. Cowie (1971). *The Genetics of Mental Disorders.* Oxford University Press, London.

Smith, J. M., and W. T. Oswald (1976). Subjective age in chronic schizophrenia. *Brit. J. Psychiat.* 128, 100.

Snyder, S. H., D. Greenberg, and H. I. Yamamura (1974). Antischizophrenic drugs and brain cholinergic receptors. *Arch. Gen. Psychiat.* 31, 58–61.

Stein, L., and C. D. Wise (1971). Possible aetiology of schizophrenia: Progressive damage to the noradrenergic reward system by 6-hydroxydopamine. *Science* 171, 1032–1036.

Stevens, M., T. J. Crow, M. Bowman, and E. C. Coles (1978). Age disorientation in chronic schizophrenia: A constant prevalence of 25% in a mental hospital population? *Brit. J. Psychiat.* 133, 130–136.

Storey, P. B. (1966). Lumbar air encephalography in chronic schizophrenia: A controlled experiment. *Brit. J. Psychiat.* 112, 135–144.

Titeler, M., S. List, and P. Seeman (1979). High affinity dopamine receptors (D_3) in rat brain. *Comm. Psychopharmacol.* 3, 411–420.

Torrey, E. F., and M.. R. Peterson (1976). The viral hypothesis of schizophrenia. *Schizophrenia Bull* 2, 136–146.

Tyrrell, D. A. J., T. J. Crow, R. P. Parry, E. C. Johnstone, and I. N. Ferrier (1979). Possible virus in schizophrenia and some neurological disorders. *Lancet* i, 839–841.

Vaughn, C. E., and J. P. Leff (1976). The influence of family and social factors on the course of psychiatric illness. *Brit. J. Psychiat.* 129, 125–137.

Weinberger, D. R., L. I. B. Bigelow, J. E. Kleinman, S. T. Klein, J. E. Rosenblatt, and R. J. Wyatt (1980). Cerebral ventricular enlargement in chronic schizophrenia: An association with poor response to treatment. *Arch. Gen. Psychiat.* 37, 11–13.

Weinberger, D. R., E. F. Torrey, A. N. Neophytides, and R. J. Wyatt (1979a). Lateral cerebral ventricular enlargement in chronic schizophrenia. *Arch. Gen. Psychiat.* 36, 735–739.

Weinberger, D. R., E. F. Torrey, A. N. Neophytides, and R. J. Wyatt (1979b). Structural abnormalities in the cerebral cortex of chronic schizophrenic patients. *Arch. Gen. Psychiat.* 36, 935–939.

Wing, J. K., J. E. Cooper, and N. Sartorius (1974). *The Measurement and Classification of Psychiatric Symptoms.* Cambridge University Press., London.

Woolley, D. W., and E. Shaw (1954). A biochemical and pharmacological suggestion about certain mental disorders. *Proc. Natl. Acad. Sci. (U.S.A.)* 40, 228–231.

World Health Organization (1975). Schizophrenia: A Multinational Study. W.H.O. Public Health Paper No. 63, Geneva.

Wyatt, R. J., E. Erdelyi, M. A. Schwartz, M. Herman, and J. D. Barchas (1978). Difficulties in comparing catecholamine-related enzymes from the brains of schizophrenia and controls. *Biol. Psychiat.* 13, 317–333.

Young, I. J., and A. B. Crampton (1974). Cerebrospinal fluid uric acid levels in cerebral atrophy occurring in psychiatric and neurological patients. *Biol. Psychiat.* 8, 281–292.

11 | New Visions of the Schizophrenic Brain: Regional Differences in Electrophysiology, Blood Flow, and Cerebral Glucose Use

M. S. BUCHSBAUM and

D. H. INGVAR

INTRODUCTION

A biological test for schizophrenia has so far eluded investigators. Each new neurohormone, each new putative neurotransmitter becomes a candidate—could its deficiency or excess be the cause of or at least a marker for schizophrenia? Each new electrophysiological test similarly raises the possibilities of the ultimate diagnostic test. The schizotiters or schizowaves are tested on small populations of subjects with excitement, but few receive any widespread support. After a time, even their own developers move on to new transmitters and recordings, abandoning the techniques in the storm of neuroscientific progress. This state of our scientific progress may be related to two important types of heterogeneity—diagnostic and anatomical.

Diagnostic Heterogeneity

In order to establish a biological measure, today's researcher typically compares values from a group of schizophrenics and controls. Such a strategy is intended to reveal salient biological differences between the groups studied. Schizophrenia is diagnosed on the basis of current and past symptoms. Researchers often assume that the more refined, rigorous, or strict the diagnostic criteria, the more homogeneous the diagnostic groupings and consequently the higher the t-test values for between-group comparisons of their biological measure, but this assumption may not be heuristic. Schizophrenia may be a heterogeneous syndrome without a single etiology; such group comparisons may reflect biological differences found in only a portion of the population (Goldman, 1977; Buchsbaum and Rieder, 1979). Further, the group comparison technique is not precisely the strategy followed in neurology or internal medicine. Psychoses associated with vitamin B deficiency, lupus, syphilis, or other biological factors are poorly distinguished on behavioral grounds—drug responses or the immunological tests make the diagnosis. Davidson and Bagley (1969) review this problem elsewhere. By following the biological measure, far greater etiological homogeneity may be attained, genetic association shown, and course and treatment response predicted (Buchsbaum and Rieder, 1979).

Anatomical Heterogeneity

Even if we were to achieve diagnostic homogeneity, the problem of anatomical heterogeneity remains. The brain is not the same from area to area as is, for example, the liver. Each liver cell, whether it is in the top left or bottom right, carries on the same function as its neighbor, and abnormalities in function can be assessed by examining metabolic products in the urine, enzyme levels in the blood, or liver tissue by biopsy. But in the brain, cells in each lobe, nucleus, or layer have specialized functions, with specific local neurochemistry. Local abnormalities of metabolism may not be reflected in the total cerebrospinal fluid pool—and even less in the blood or urine (Meltzer, 1976). Examination of local metabolic function may thus be crucial for identifying metabolic markers or functional deficits of any kind.

LOCAL FUNCTIONAL APPROACHES

Neurologists and neuropsychologists have traditionally examined patients by looking for "localizing" signs—deficits unequivocally linked to a specific central nervous system region or regions. This has been easier in the case of simple reflexes or certain isolated and well-characterized, highly trained cognitive skills, such as reading. However, simple spinal reflexes, basic motor functions, and sensory acuity are little disturbed in schizophrenia. It is the higher level of perceptual, cognitive, and social behavior that is characteristically abnormal—suggesting the need for a search in the cerebral cortex. But deficits in mood regulation, social contact, and appropriate behavior are harder to characterize or to quantify than reflexes, and they interact with cognitive deficits to such an extent that their localization has been extremely difficult. A functional rather than a gross neuroanatomical basis for deficits may further complicate the research. Until now, no major and specific morphological change has been demonstrated at autopsy in the brains of chronic schizophrenics. Dynamic techniques for the study of local function, sufficiently non-invasive to allow repeated testing in normal individuals and patients, are necessary.

Advances in electroencephalographic (EEG), blood flow, and most recently, positron emission tomographic (PET) techniques have made available methods to assess not only cortical, but subcortical structures in a non-invasive way. In this chapter we review these methods, with emphasis on the techniques and possibilities—since this is a newly opened field.

ELECTROENCEPHALOGRAPHY AND LOCAL CORTICAL FUNCTION

From the earliest psychiatric studies of the EEG, Berger and Lerrere (see Itil, 1977) noted that schizophrenics had low amplitude irregular waves within a frequency of over 16-cps (beta rhythm) and a relative reduction of the higher amplitude regular 10-cps (alpha rhythm). This has been widely confirmed in studies by visual inspection as well as with quantitative analysis (see Itil, 1977, for review).

Generally, these later and more precise quantitative studies have used only a single lead, usually at the occiput. This neglects one of the great advantages of electrophysiological techniques—the possibility of assessing local cortical functions in man in a way that neurochemical measures of the blood, cerebrospinal fluid, and urine never can. Animal studies have repeatedly demonstrated neurotransmitter and enzyme differences in different cortical areas, suggesting the possibilities of local differences in drug effect. With advances in computer technology, brain electrical activity maps and simple dot density topograms (Duffy, Burchfiel, and Lombroso, 1979; Dubinsky and Barlow, 1980) are within the range of currently available, relatively inexpensive laboratory computer equipment.

ELECTROENCEPHALOGRAPHIC RECORDINGS

A set of 16 electrodes was placed on the left hemisphere, 12 according to the International 10–20 System (left hemisphere and midline: Fp_1, F_z, C_z, P_z, O_z, F_3, C_3, P_3, O_1, F_1, T_3, T_5), with four additional locations posteriorly (at the centers of squares formed by the regular positions in Fig. 11-1). The EEG was amplified (frequency response 0.3 to 100 cps) and digitized with an on-line computer system (Coppola, 1979). All 16 leads for each epoch were inspected for artifacts and between four and eight 10-sec epochs were obtained. The EEG activity for spectral analysis was digitized at 102.4 Hz (1024 samples/epoch), and low frequency subharmonics were removed by an auto-regressive filter (Coppola, 1979). A window function consisting of 10% cosine taper was obtained by weighing the 50 points at either end of the epoch by a cosine bell. A standard fast Fourier transform was applied, and the power spectrum estimates computed at 0.1-Hz steps. For smoothing, 10 adjacent estimates were summed to yield 1-Hz resolution, with the final estimates expressed as magnitude values in microvolts (μV) (square root of power). Thus, a peak-to-trough 50-μV alpha wave series throughout the 10-sec EEG epoch yielded a value of 25.0. If only 50% of the epoch contained alpha activity, the value would be approximately 12. Additionally, the activity estimates for the following bands were computed by summing adjacent values: delta, 2.1 to 5.0 cps; theta, 5.1 to 8.0; alpha, 8.1 to 13.0; beta, 1 13.1 to 18.0; and beta, 2 18.1 to 30.0.

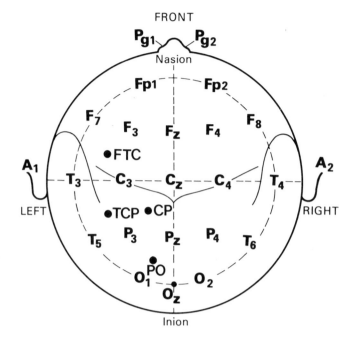

Top of Head

FIGURE 11-1. Electrode Positions on the Scalp, Shown Diagrammatically for the International 10–20 System. Only left-sided electrodes were used, with the addition of four interpolated electrodes, three in the posterior cortex. This array was chosen because it was our impression that contour lines in the topographic maps of Ragot and Remond (1975) and Lehmann (1970) were closer together over this area. Since 16 leads are minimal for topographic definition (Lehmann recommends a minimum of 25) and since antero-posterior differences tend to be greater than right/left, we placed all leads on one hemisphere rather than the standard wide spacing of the 10–20 System over the whole head. Because of a number of lines of evidence that schizophrenia could be related more closely to left hemisphere function (Flor-Henry, 1974, 1976) and because of Ingvar's choice of the left hemisphere in blood flow studies, all leads were placed on the left hemisphere.

BRAIN SURFACE MAPS

First, it is necessary to represent the three-dimensional curved surfaces of cortex on a two-dimensional surface. Since electrodes are not more

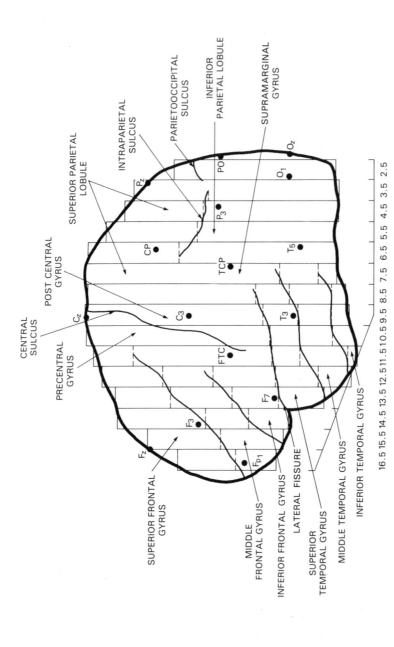

FIGURE 11-2. A Cortical Map Developed by an Anatomical Reconstruction from Whole Head Sections (Buchsbaum et al.; (1982); see text for technique). The numerical scale at the bottom gives the distance in centimeters from the occiput. Although individual variation in head shape and cortex may exist, it should be noted that the proportionality of the 10–20 System is planned to correct for it; residual variation is probably considerably smaller than the 5-cm electrode spacing.

closely spaced than 4 to 5 cm, an accuracy of 1 cm seemed adequate for anatomical features. To provide a lateral view of the brain, we used the series of whole head coronal sections (Thompson and Hasso, 1980), cut at 1-cm intervals. The length of the line segment traced along the scalp and dura on each plan were measured for the left hemisphere for each slice. The base point of each section was formed by the line connecting the nasion with the external auditory meatus and the meatus with the occipital protuberance. The highest point was the longitudinal cerebral figure fissure. The succession of lengths measured at 1-cm intervals formed a surface as shown in Fig. 11-2. The International 10–20 System was applied to the scalp surface and perpendiculars were constructed to the underlying cortex. The major sulcuses and syruses were identified and similarly reconstructed. Thus, an approximately equal area projection was developed.

Evoked Potential Stimuli and Recording

The stimuli were four intensities of light flashes and four intensities of tones, each presented 64 times in a randomized sequence. Each stimulus was 500 msec long, followed by a 500-msec interstimulus interval. The light flashes were viewed on a transluscent screen, illuminated from the rear by fluorescent tubes under computer control (Buchsbaum, Post, and Bunney, 1977). Auditory stimuli were four intensities of 1000-Hz tones, similarly presented, using a computer-controlled oscillator at 50, 60, 70, and 80 dB through two loudspeakers in an acoustically attenuated room (background less than 20 dB at 1000 Hz, with a less than 2 dB variation in the cubic foot surrounding the subject's head). The stimuli were presented in a pseudorandom sequence, so that each intensity of light and tone was preceded by every other tone or light an equal number of times. Evoked potentials were first detrended, using linear regression, and then digitally filtered to remove frequencies below 4 Hz and above 30 Hz, as described (with a different bandpass) elsewhere (Lavine, Buchsbaum, and Schechter, 1980). Eye movements and artifacts were monitored using lead F_{pl}; trials exceeding a threshold of 64 μV were automatically excluded from the average for all leads. Individuals exceeding a 50% trial loss on any condition were excluded (one individual).

For assessment of attentional enhancement, all subjects first received training in the correct identification of the intensity of the visual and auditory stimuli (Schechter and Buchsbaum, 1973). Subjects were then given three different tasks in random order: (1) Light attention (LA), counting the number of visual stimuli that were of the same intensity in a row and ignoring intervening tones; (2) tone attention (TA), counting the number of tones and similarly ignoring lights; and (3) mental arithmetic (MA), subtracting seven serially from 2000. For each condition, the same EP sequence of lights and tones was presented. The schizophrenic patients received only the light attention and tone attention tasks.

The literature on N120 in schizophrenia has tended to reveal smaller N120 than seen in normal controls, even when the attentional task was uncontrolled (see reviews by Shagass, 1976; Buchsbaum, 1979). But, studies have differed in EEG lead derivation, patient medication status, and measurement of N120 relative to a base line or confounded with a P100 or P200 variation. Here we focus on the N120 component, comparing differences observed between off-medication schizophrenics and normal controls. Further results applying topographic techniques to the N120 component will illustrate the problems inherent in interpreting evoked potential data from only one or two EEG leads.

STUDIES OF THE BRAIN PHYSIOLOGY SCHIZOPHRENIA

In an ongoing study, we have so far examined eight young schizophrenic patients (age 18 to 26), all of whom met RDC criteria for schizophrenia (Spitzer et al., 1978) and were off medication two weeks or longer. Sixteen age- and sex-matched normal controls were available for comparison. These were screened for major medical problems and a history of major psychiatric disorders in self or first-degree family members.

Subjects were tested in a quiet, sound-attenuated room. First, EEG recordings were made with eyes open and eyes closed; then, visual stimulation was begun.

ELECTROENCEPHALOGRAPHIC FINDINGS

The low alpha/high beta findings of earlier investigators were confirmed (Fig. 11-3). Beyond merely having low alpha, the schizophrenics

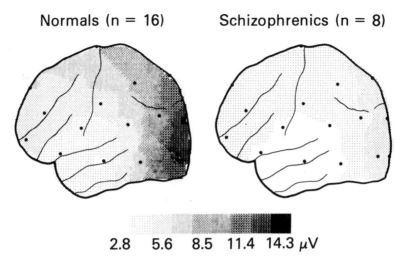

FIGURE 11-3. Mean Distribution of Alpha Activity in Normal Volunteers and Schizophrenics. The normals show a typical off-medication occipital lobe alpha distribution, with an average of 14.3 μV. In contrast, the schizophrenics show much lower alpha levels, with more frontal distribution.

showed different cortical distributions that suggested a qualitative difference in cortical function in the frontal and occipital areas.

EVOKED POTENTIAL FINDINGS

The N120 component showed a parietal/central attentional enhancement that was maximal in the superior parietal cortex. We have not yet analyzed all the data from the schizophrenics, but in the first individual tested, a marked deficit in N120 attentional enhancement appears in the same parietal region (Fig. 11-4). Further studies are underway to assess the generality of this effect.

BLOOD FLOW

Another approach to the determination of local functional processes is to measure blood flow. When the neurons of the brain become more

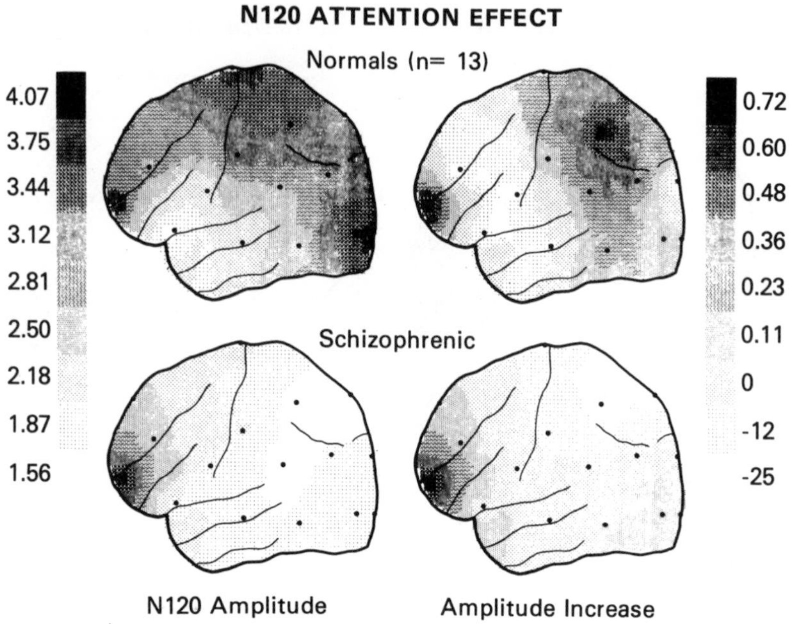

N120 ATTENTION EFFECT

Normals (n= 13)

N120 Amplitude   Amplitude Increase

FIGURE 11-4. The N120 Amplitude (left column) and Amplitude Enhancement (right column) in Normals (above) and Schizophrenic Patients (below). Above right: Mean N120 amplitude in 13 normal volunteers. Scale is on the tone bar to the left, in microvolts. Above left: Mean difference between visual N120 amplitude while attending to lights and visual N120 amplitude while attending to tone stimuli. Scale is on the tone bar to the right, in microvolts of increase with attentional instruction. Topographic map is largely positive, confirming an increase in N120 amplitude with attention (see Hillyard et al., 1978, for review). Attention maximum appears in the superior parietal cortex. Below: A schizophrenic patient shows no parietal attention effect, although the frontal area apparently remains intact.

active, metabolic changes occur, which then dilate the cerebral blood vessels. Thus, the increased metabolic demands can be met by an augmentation of the blood flow in the active region. Conversely, the blood flow is reduced when the neurons become less active (see Sokoloff, 1977). This so-called metabolic regulation (Ingvar and Lassen, 1975) of the regional cerebral blood flow can be utilized to determine indirectly the functional level in a circumscribed part of the brain by recording its regional cerebral blood flow. With multi-regional blood flow measure-

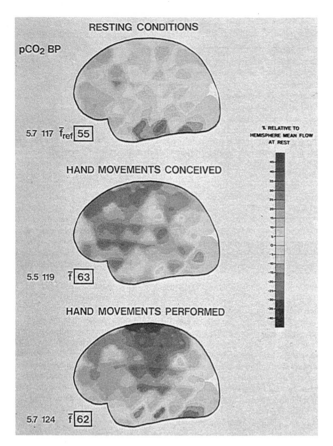

RESTING CONDITIONS

pCO₂ BP

5.7 117 f̄ref 55

HAND MOVEMENTS CONCEIVED

5.5 119 f̄ 63

HAND MOVEMENTS PERFORMED

5.7 124 f̄ 62

% RELATIVE TO
HEMISPHERE MEAN FLOW
AT REST

FIGURE 11-5. Cerebral Blood Flow Patterns (Ingvar and Philipson, 1977). Patterns were obtained from four neurologically normal subjects at rest (A), during motor ideation (B), and during actual movements of the right hand (C). The color scale (right) shows steps corresponding to flow relative to hemispheric mean flow at rest. Note the normal hyperfrontal flow distribution with high flows in the premotor and frontal regions and the very low flows temporally.

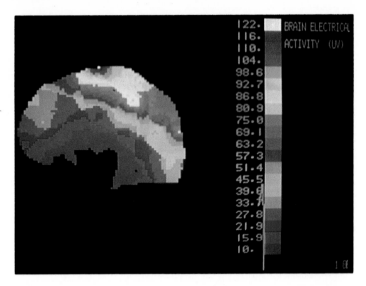

FIGURE 11-6. Somatosensory-Evoked Potential Component P200 Distribution. Note the similarity to the cerebral blood flow pattern in Fig. 11-5, hand movements. The right forearm was stimulated (Buchsbaum, Davis, and Bunney, 1977) and recordings were made from the left hemisphere. A similar blood flow distribution was seen by Foit et al. (1980), with somatosensory stimulation. Our P200 component shows a distribution of both pre- and post-central gyruses. The color scale shows amplitude in microvolts × 10.

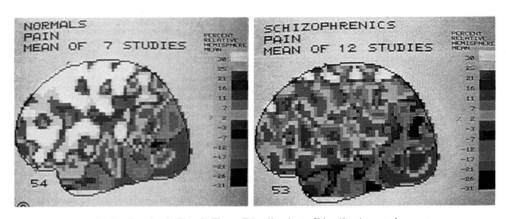

FIGURE 11-7. Cerebral Blood Flow Distribution. Distributions taken, at rest for eight normals (left) and eight highly psychotic chronic schizophrenics (see Franzen and Ingvar, 1975, for clinical details). Note the hyperfrontal resting flow distribution in the normals (seen also in Fig. 11-5). Both groups showed about the same mean hemisphere flow rates, as demonstrated in the early work of Kety et al. (1948), using the nitrous oxide technique.

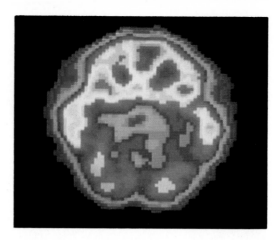

FIGURE 11-9. Glucose Use Imaged by PET in the Brain of a Resting, 25-Year-Old Normal Volunteer, Eyes Closed. Red, orange, and yellow are areas of relatively high glucose use (uptake of 18F-deoxyglucose). This horizontal slice is computed at 41 mm above the canthomeatal (CM) line (joining the outer canthus of eye and the external auditory meatus). The red area in the frontal cortex is the gyrus rectus–cingulate gyrus. In the occiput, the calcarine fissure and the surrounding gray matter are poorly seen, as anticipated because the eyes are closed.

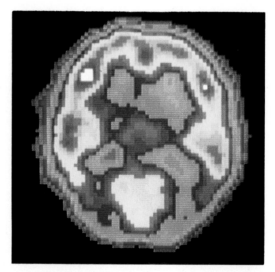

FIGURE 11-10. A Volunteer PET Image at 77 mm, the Low Supraventricular Level. The superior frontal gyrus and the middle frontal gyrus (the white and red spots in the anterior area) show high glucose uptake, whereas the occipital lobe and the inferior parietal and superior parietal lobules show low glucose uptake. The slice at 77 mm is 56% of the distance from the external auditory meatus to the top of head, measured as in Matsui and Hirano (1978).

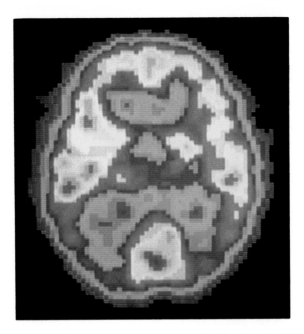

FIGURE 11-11. A PET Scan in a 29-Year-Old Schizophrenic Off Medication, at 49 mm above the CM Line. Note the higher glucose uptake (red area) in the occiput and the lower uptake in the frontal region (cf. Fig. 11-9). The higher activity in the auditory cortex, left, may be related to the presence of "accusatory voices" following deoxyglucose injection.

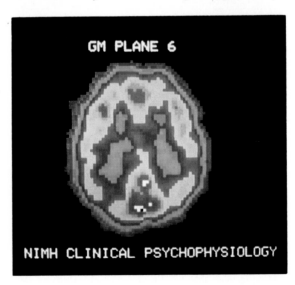

FIGURE 11-12. A PET Scan in the Same Schizophrenic at 71 mm, a Supraventricular Level. The same pattern of greater occipital than frontal activity is seen.

ments, the functional activity in many cerebral regions is measured simultaneously, and thus, the blood flow distribution, i.e., the distribution of cerebral function, is determined. When methods similar to those described for interpolated EEG or evoked potentials (Figs. 11-5 and 11-6; see insert following p. 244) are used, topography computer techniques yield "functional landscapes" of the hemispheric blood flow. Mean landscapes can also be calculated for groups of patients suffering from the same disorder studied under similar conditions.

Measurements of regional cerebral blood (rCBR) were carried out using the intra-arterial xenon-133 clearance technique. A thin polyethylene catheter was placed in the left internal carotid artery for bolus injections of 3 to 5 ml saline, in which 2 to 4 mCi of xenon-133 was physically dissolved. A battery of 32, and later, 256 detectors, placed at the side of the head, recorded the sudden arrival and subsequent slower clearance of the radioisotope from the hemisphere. Surface structures, i.e., the cerebral cortex, are seen better than are deeper structures. The rCBF for each region was calculated in terms of ml/100 g brain/min by a computer coupled to the detector battery. By superimposition of individual flow charts, mean hemisphere flow distributions were calculated and, thus, mean "functional landscapes" in color were produced for the whole group and for subgroups representing different levels of severity of the disease, as well as for controls.

Patients and Controls

Over 30 schizophrenic patients and a series of control and comparison patients have been studied, the majority reported in two detailed communications (Ingvar and Franzen, 1974; Franzen and Ingvar, 1975). Here we review the data on the most psychotic patients and the psychometrically normal, male, chronic alcoholics with the data reprocessed to facilitate comparison with EEG and glucose metabolic rate.

The rCBF Distribution in Controls and in Chronic Schizophrenics

Control patients, when examined at rest, i.e., in a quiet laboratory, with a pad over the eyes, and no disturbance by touch or speech, all showed a typical hyperfrontal resting rCBF pattern, with a high flow in the range of 50 to 80 ml/100 g/min in regions anterior to the Sylvian and the Rolandic fissures and with lower flows in the range of 35 to 50 ml/100 g/min in regions postcentrally in the parietal, occipital, and temporal areas (Ingvar, 1980) (Fig. 11-7; see insert following p. 244). As discussed elsewhere, the normal hyperfrontal activity landscape of the cerebral cortex signals that the resting conscious brain, when awake and undisturbed, is highly active in frontal motor-behavioral cortical regions and much less active in postcentral sensory-gnostic areas.

In the schizophrenic patients, the rCBF distribution at rest was often found to be hypofrontal, i.e., the flow in frontal regions was relatively low and the flow postcentrally relatively high. Since, as mentioned, the total mean hemisphere flow was within normal limits, the hypofrontal pattern shows that chronic schizophrenia is accompanied by an abnormal distribution of cerebral cortical function (Fig. 11-7).

ELECTROENCEPHALOGRAPHY AND BLOOD FLOW RELATIONSHIPS

As early as 1938, Berger suggested that the rhythmic electrical activity of the brain reflected the oxidative metabolic rate of nervous tissue. In attempts to correlate EEG and cerebral oxygen uptake, the xenon-133 clearance technique and single occipital EEG leads have been primarily used (Ingvar, Sjolund, and Ardo, 1976; Tolonen and Sulg, 1981) in patients with various cerebrovascular lesions (Tolonen and Sulg, 1981). Tolonen and Sulg (1981) report power spectral EEG measures and especially note the association between increased slow EEG (delta activity) and low flow in the damaged hemisphere. Comparison of the high frontal delta in schizophrenics with the hypofrontal flow patterns (Figs. 11-7 and 11-8) tends to support this association, even in individuals with no known anatomical cerebral vascular lesion, such as schizophrenics. It should be noted that in Tolonen and Sulg's patients with cerebrovascular lesions, normal hemisphere data showed little blood-flow/EEG correlation. However, Tolonen and Sulg recorded parietal/occipital EEG and frontal regional flow; Ingvar et al. (1976) used similar derivations and mean hemispheric uptake. From the foregoing EEG topography and regional flow maps, the limitations of these non-regional techniques should be clear. Clearly, EEG and cerebral metabolic measures must be obtained regionally and simultaneously to demonstrate their parallel distri-

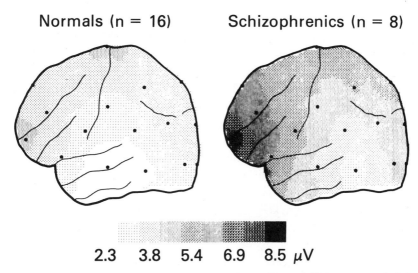

FIGURE 11-8. The EEG Delta Activity in 16 Normal Volunteers and eight Off-Medication Schizophrenics. The normals show relatively low delta levels, with a cap-like distribution; the schizophrenics show a superior and middle frontal distribution. This parallels the reports of delta activity correlating with low cerebral blood flow in patients with cerebrovascular disease; compare the delta topography in schizophrenia here with the blood flow in Fig. 11-7.

bution accurately. Gur and Reivich's (1980) xenon-133 blood flow data during cognitive tasks show regional patterns of change that follow previously reported alpha rhythm results with similar tasks; thus, both task and regional measurement appear critical. Because of the responsivity of EEG (and probably local blood flow) to environmental cues, and the need for normal controls, a non-invasive and non-intrusive method is necessary. Such a method has recently become available—positron emission tomography (PET).

POSITRON EMISSION TOMOGRAPHY

Blood flow in the cerebral cortex and local glucose consumption by the brain appear closely related (Sokoloff, 1977). Sokoloff developed a quantitative autoradiographic method for measuring local glucose consumption in animals using 2 - [^{11}C] deoxyl-glucose (2DG), with a resolution of less than 0.1 mm. Deoxyglucose is taken up by the brain in competition with glucose, but metabolized no further than DG-6-phosphate. Thus, the rate of accumulation of DG-6-phosphate is proportional to glucose use. Labeled with a positron emitter, 18F, its trapped location can be reconstructed with emission computer tomography and the glycolytic rate quantified with the Sokoloff et al. (1977) tracer kinetic model. Although current cortical resolution is of the same order as the xenon-133 blood flow studies, this technique has several advantages: (1) the entire brain, including basal ganglia, thalamus and brainstem, can be studied; (2) glucose uptake is labeled before scanning, so closer psychological control over the subject's state can be maintained; and (3) occipital areas, of special interest in investigation in schizophrenia, are less well visualized in carotid injection xenon-133 studies, since they are primarily supplied by other arteries.

Positron Emission Tomographic Methods

In studies begun, we are simultaneously investigating local glucose metabolism using 18F-2DG with PET and EEG frequency with 16 lead topographic mapping in unmedicated schizophrenics and age- and sex-matched normal controls. Subjects sit in an acoustically treated darkened room with eyes closed for 10 min before, and 30 min following injection of 3 to 5 mCi 18-F-2DG. Following uptake, seven to eight horizontal scans parallel to the canthomeatal line are made. Glucose uptake is expressed in micromoles glucose/100 g tissue/min (Sokoloff et al., 1977). Sixteen lead EEG recordings are made beginning 1 min after injection of the isotope and continuing for 30 min.

Preliminary analysis indicates that most normals show a higher 2DG uptake in the frontal cortex than the occipital cortex (Figs. 11-9 and 11-10; see insert following p. 244). In contrast, this uptake is reversed in schizophrenics with low frontal maximum activity and clear delineation of occipital gray matter (Figs. 11-11 and 11-12; see insert following p. 244). These preliminary results are consistent with the blood flow studies of Ingvar and the PET results of Farkas et al. (1981).

Correlations between specific symptoms and 18F-2DG uptake patterns have been noted. For example, one patient who had auditory hallucinations during the 30-min uptake period showed elevated glucose use in

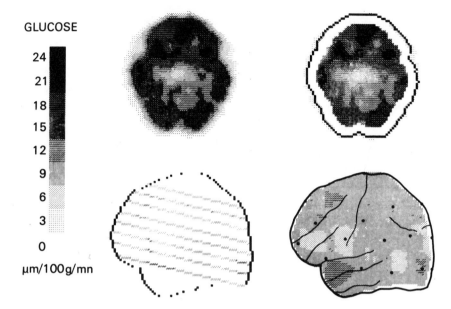

GLUCOSE

24
21
18
15
12
9
6
3
0

μm/100g/mn

FIGURE 11-13. Upper left: PET Slice, as Shown in Color in Fig. 11-9 (insert). The scale, in micromoles of glucose/100 g of brain tissue/minute, is at left. Upper right: the brain is outlined and a 1.5 cm thick cortical slice is peeled from the cortex. The peeled cortex is white. Lower left: Peeled segments from the left hemisphere are scaled to proportions of the lateral scalp view developed earlier (Fig. 11-2) and stacked up and positioned according to the proportion of the CM–vertex distance. Lower right: the stacked peel segments are interpolated to cover the lateral surface, providing a cortical surface view of glucose metabolism. Note the dark areas in the superior frontal gyrus area, similar to the blood flow shown in Fig. 11-7. The blotchy appearance also resembles the texture of the blood flow maps. These lateral view maps can then be compared with EEG and evoked potential maps to examine simultaneously electrophysiological and metabolic processes.

the superior temporal auditory areas in the left, but not the right temporal cortex.

With the use of digital techniques, consecutive PET slices effectively "peel off" the skull and skin layers in an adaptation of a bone-deleting technique (Henrich et al., 1979). Next, a cortical strip is peeled off the slice, conformed to the lateral brain view, and the values between the strips are interpolated. The result is a metabolic lateral view of brain function displayed in gray scale values represented by dot density (Fig. 11-13).

Results of these parallel studies indicate similarities in distribution for certain EEG frequencies. Individual differences in distribution and statistical problems in comparing complex topographic maps are now being studied. These findings are clearly preliminary, and issues of control of mental activity, structure identification, and biological heterogeneity of schizophrenia remain to be explored.

ACKNOWLEDGMENTS

The authors appreciate the contributions of Drs. D. P. van Kammen and R. Waters for clinical information on some patient populations, the PET team (Drs. R. Kessler, J. Goble, R. G. Manning, R. Flynn, and J. Bird), the Clinical Psychophysiology Group (J. Cappelletti, R. Coppola, C. King, J. Johnson, and F. Rigal), and secretarial and editorial assistance (R. Mayeux, B. Carroll, and S. Majors).

REFERENCES

Buchsbaum, M. S. (1979). Neurophysiological aspects of the schizophrenic syndrome. In *Disorders of the Schizophrenic Syndrome* (L. Bellak, ed.). Grune & Stratton, New York, pp. 152–180.

Buchsbaum, M. S., and R. O. Rieder (1979). Biologic heterogeneity and psychiatric research: Platelet MAO as a case study. *Arch. Gen. Psychiat.* 36, 1163–1169.

Buchsbaum, M. S., G. C. Davis, and W. E. Bunney, Jr. (1977). Naloxone alters pain perception and somatosensory evoked potentials in normal subjects. *Nature (London)* 270, 620–622.

Buchsbaum, M. S., R. M. Post, and W. E. Bunney, Jr. (1977). Average evoked responses in a rapidly cycling manic-depressive patient. *Biol. Psychiat.* 12, 83–99.

Buchsbaum, M. S., F. Rigal, J. Cappelletti, C. King, and J. Johnson (1982). A new system for gray-level surface distribution maps of electrical activity. *Electroencephogr. Clin. Neurophysiol.* 53, 237–242.

Coppola, R. (1979). Isolating low frequency activity in EEG spectrum analysis. *Electroencephalogr. Clin. Neurophysiol.* 46, 224–226.

Davison, K. and C. R. Bagley (1969). Schizophrenia-like psychoses associated with organic disorders of the central nervous system: A review of the literature. In *Current Problems in Neuropsychiatry* (R. N. Hemington, ed). Headley, Ashford, Kent, England. pp. 113–184.

Duffy, F. H., J. L. Burchfiel, and C. T. Lombroso (1979). Brain electrical activity mapping (BEAM): A method for extending the clinical utility of EEG and evoked potential data. *Ann. Neurol.* 5, 309–321.

Dubinsky, J., and J. S. Barlow (1980). A simple dot-density topogram for EEG. *Electroencephalogr. Clin. Neurophysiol.* 48, 473–477.

Flor-Henry, P. (1974). Psychosis, neurosis, and epilepsy (1974). *Br. J. Psychiat.* 124, 144–150.

Flor-Henry, P. (1976). Lateralized temporal-limbic dysfunction and psychopathology. *Ann. N.Y. Acad. Sci.* 280, 777–795.

Goldman, H. (1977). Nonunitary disease hypotheses. *Schizophr. Bull.* 3, 2–3.

Gur, R., and M. Reivich (1980). Cognitive task effects on hemispheric blood flow in humans: Evidence for individual differences in hemispheric activation. *Brain and Language* 9, 78–92.

Foit, A., B. Larsen, S. Hattori, E. Skinhoj, and N. A. Lassen (1980). Cortical activation during somatosensory stimulation and voluntary movement in man: A regional cerebral blood flow study. *Electroencephalogr. Clin. Neurophysiol.* 50, 426–436.

Heinrich, G., N. Mai, and H. Backmund (1979). Preprocessing in computed tomography picture analysis: A "bone-deleting" algorithm. *J. Comput. Assis. Tomogr.* 3, 379–384.

Hillyard, S. A., T. W. Picton, and D. Regan (1978). Sensation, perception and attention: Analysis using ERPs. In *Event-Related Brain Potentials in Man* (E. Callaway, P. Tueting, and S. H. Koslow, eds.). Academic Press, New York, pp. 223–321.

Franzen, G., and D. H. Ingvar (1975). Abnormal distribution of cerebral activity in chronic schizophrenia. *J. Psychiat. Res.* 12, 199–214.

Ingvar, D. (1980). Abnormal distribution of cerebral activity in chronic schizophrenia: A neurophysiological interpretation. In *Perspectives in Schizophrenia Research* (C. F. Baxter and T. Melnechuk, eds.). Raven Press, New York, pp. 107–125.

Ingvar, D. H., and G. Franzen (1974). Abnormalities of cerebral blood flow distribution in patients with chronic schizophrenia. *Acta Psychiat. Scand.* 50, 425–462.

Ingvar, D. H., and N. A. Lassen (eds.) (1975). *Brain Work.* Munksgaard, Copenhagen, Denmark.

Ingvar, D. H., and L. Philipson (1977). Distribution of blood flow in the dominant hemisphere during motor ideation and motor performance. *Ann. Neurol.* 2, 230–237.

Ingvar, D. H., B. Sjolund, and A. Ardo (1976). Correlation between dominant EEG frequency, cerebral oxygen uptake and blood flow. *Electroencephalogr. Clin. Neurophysiol.* 41, 268–276.

Itil, T. M. (1977). Qualitative and quantitative EEG findings in schizophrenia. *Schizophr. Bull.* 3, 61–79.

Kety, S. S., R. B. Woodford, M. H. Harmel, F. A. Freyhan, K. E. Appel, and C. F. Schmidt (1948). Cerebral flood flow and metabolism in schizophrenia. *Amer. J. Psychiat.* 104, 765–770.

Lavine, R. A., M. S. Buchsbaum, and G. Schechter (1980). Human somatosensory evoked responses: Effects of attention and distraction on early components. *Physiol. Psychol.* 8, 405–408.

Lehmann, D. (1971). Multichannel topography of human alpha EEG fields. *Electroencephalogr. Clin. Neurophysiol.* 31, 439–449.

Matsui, T., and A. Hirano (1978). *An Atlas of the Human Brain for Computerized Tomography.* Igaku-Shoin, Tokyo.

Meltzer, H. Y. (1976). Biochemical studies in schizophrenia. *Schizophr. Bull.* 2, 10–18.

Ragot, R. A., and A. Remond (1978). EEG field mapping. *Electroencephalogr. Clin. Neurophysiol.* 45, 417–421.

Schechter, G., and M. S. Buchsbaum (1973). The effects of attention, stimulus intensity, and individual differences on the average evoked response. *Psychophysiology* 10, 392–400.

Shagass, C. (1976). An electrophysiological view of schizophrenia. *Biol. Psychiat.* 11, 3–30.

Sokoloff, L. (1977). Relation between physiological function and energy metabolism in the central nervous system. *J. Neurochem.* 29, 13–26.

Sokoloff, L., M. Reivich, C. Kennedy, M. H. Des Rosiers, C. S. Patlak, K. D. Pettigrew, O. Sakurada, and M. Shinohara (1977). The [^{14}C] deoxyglucose method for the measurement of local cerebral glucose utilization: Theory, procedure, and normal values in the conscious and anesthetized albino rat. *J. Neurochem.* 28, 897–916.

Spitzer, R., J. Endicott, and E. Robins (1978). Research diagnostic criteria: Rationale and reliability. *Arch. Gen. Psychiat.* 35, 775–782.

Thompson, J. R., and A. N. Hasso (1980). *Anatomy of the Head and Neck.* C. V. Mosby Company, St. Louis, Missouri.

Tolonen, U., and I. A. Sulg (1981). Comparison of quantitative EEG parameters from four different analysis techniques in evaluation of relationships between EEG and CBF in brain infarction. *Electroencephalogr. Clin. Neurophysiol.* 51, 177–185.

12 | Neurohistological Studies in Schizophrenia

STEVEN MATTHYSSE and
ROGER WILLIAMS

The finding of ventricular enlargement in some schizophrenic patients, as described in Chapters 8 and 10, will undoubtedly generate renewed interest in neurohistological abnormalities in schizophrenia, since ventricular dilation is not a disease, but a sign of unknown pathology. We would like to review the checkered career of neurohistological observation in schizophrenia, to show why this field has been called "the graveyard of neuropathologists" (Plum, 1972); then we will describe some new methods in neurohistology, which we believe will make it possible for future workers to avoid the pitfalls that beset past experimentation in the field.

"THE GRAVEYARD OF NEUROPATHOLOGISTS"

Let us begin with an illustration from the work of the leading European neuropathologists Drs. C. and O. Vogt, in the 1950s (Fig. 12-1). Cell loss in schizophrenia was reported as early as 1897 by Alzheimer. Figure 12-2A shows a normal cell and ten forms of "wasting cells" from a catatonic brain. By "wasting cell," the Vogts meant a cell in which the nucleus loses Nissl substance while vacuoles form in the cytoplasm; the cell body atrophies, and subsequently, the nucleus. Figure 12-2B shows various cells from layer III of the cingulate and prefrontal cortex.

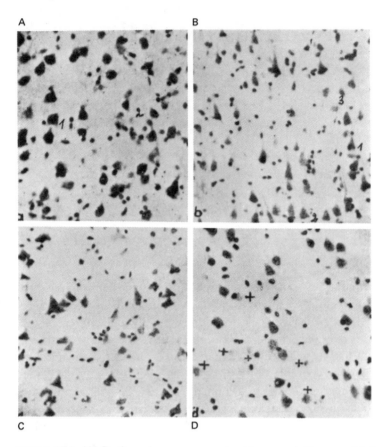

FIGURE 12-1. (A) Prefrontal cortex, normal subject, aged 38 years. (B) Broca's area, catatonic patient, aged 28 years, showing loss of Nissl substance. (C) Same patient as (B), prefrontal cortex, showing cell loss (lacunes) and cellular debris. (D) Cingulate gyrus, acute catatonic patient, aged 18 years, showing more extensive cell loss (+ signs). From Vogt and Vogt (1952).

A student of the Vogts, Buttlar-Brentano (1952), carried out similar investigations on the nucleus of the substantia innominata. This region, the outflow zone of the nucleus accumbens septi, has attracted much recent attention because of the dopamine hypothesis, which may implicate the nucleus accumbens in schizophrenia (Stevens, Ch. 7; Mesulam and Geschwind, 1978; Matthysse, in press). Buttlar-Brentano found the cells of the nucleus of the substantia innominata to be shrunken in catatonic schizophrenia, but not in other schizophrenia subtypes (Fig. 12-3).

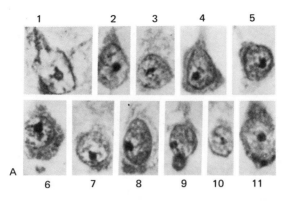

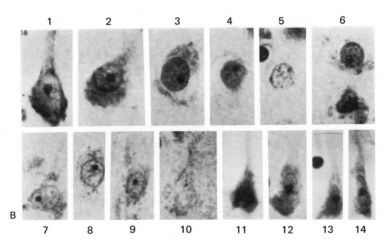

FIGURE 12-2. (A) Normal cell (11) and "wasting cells" (1 to 10) from the brain of a catatonic patient. (B) Cells from layer III of the cingulate and prefrontal cortex: Normal cell (1) and cells from patients with schizophreniform psychoses (2 to 14). According to the Vogts, some cells (2 to 5) show loss of Nissl substance: note fat deposits and cytoplasmic vacuoles. In other cells (7 to 11), the cell body and subsequently the nucleus disintegrate, leaving "ghost cells" containing fat deposits. From Vogt and Vogt (1952).

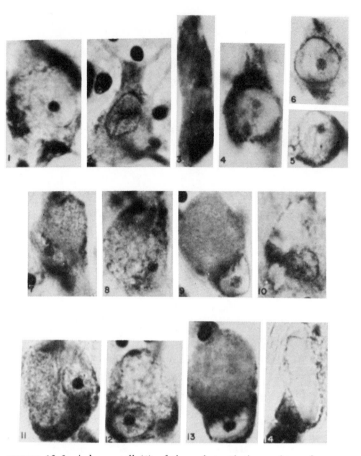

FIGURE 12-3. A large cell (1) of the substantia innominata from a normal subject, aged 24 years. Other cells are from schizophrenic (primarily catatonic) patients (2 to 10) and senile patients (11 to 14). From Buttlar-Brentano (1952).

The cytological changes observed by Buttlar-Brentano include swelling (2), shrinkage (3), disappearing cell body (4, advanced stages, 5, 6), lipofuscin accumulation (7), fatty vacuolization (8), glassy appearance (9), and liquefaction (10). The changes in cells 11 to 14, from the senile cases, are the same as the changes found in cells 7 to 10, respectively, which Buttlar-Brentano interpreted as suggestive of premature aging in catatonic patients.

The problem with these observations is not that they are demonstrably false, but rather that they are so subjective that it is impossible to decide whether they are true or false. To illustrate the lengths to which subjective reporting can go, a quote by the eminent neurologist Papez (1952) from the same volume of the *Journal of Nervous and Mental Disease* in which Buttlar-Brentano reported her observations, proports to describe

> the teeming life of zooid organisms in the brains of patients with mental illness. This zooid infestation becomes evident when one takes the decisive step of examining bits of cortex crushed in normal saline under the dark contrast, phase microscope. These organisms occur in great concentration in the cerebral cortex and thalamic region.

The need for objective methods in the neuropathology of psychoses was recognized clearly as early as 1924 by Dunlap:

> We have considered control brain material, collected from so-called normal persons, without psychoses, to be absolutely necessary in this study. The controls must be of similar age to the dementia praecoxes, must be collected under similar conditions, fixed, embedded and stained by the same methods. It has been harder to find suitable control cases than to find suitable cases of dementia praecox. . . . It is reported that Nissl, who all his life was searching for a normal brain, died without finding one that was wholly satisfactory to him. The supposedly normal brains that I have studied in a series of years, seldom looked alike under the microscope, but varied greatly in appearance, in stainability and in the condition of the nerve cells.

In his best control case, that of a bootlegger shot through the lungs, the nerve cells were "dark, shrunken, with poorly defined, misshapen nuclei; in short, these cells closely resembled what is often described as among the chronic organic changes in dementia praecox." "We have used chiefly cell counting and photography," Dunlap continues, "in order to reduce impression and preconceptions to the minimum." As a test of reliability, he tabulated cell counts by four different observers. Dunlap detected no cell loss in schizophrenia relative to controls.

Wolf and Cowen (1952) extended these critiques (Fig. 12-4). These authors were able to demonstrate cell "shrinkage and sclerosis" in control as well as schizophrenic brains.

It is evident that quantitative methods are necessary for objectivity. There are two quantitative neuropathological studies of schizophrenia in the literature. Colon (1972), using measurement and counting, reported a decrease in the mean thickness of the cortex in several cortical areas in schizophrenia and cell loss up to 70% in layers IV and V and in part of

A   B

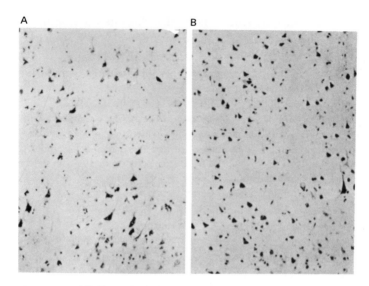

FIGURE 12-4. (A) Frontal cortex, hebephrenic, aged 46 years. Note the "focal nerve cell loss." (B) Frontal cortex, nonpsychotic subject, aged 45 years, with equivalent "focal nerve cell loss." From Wolf and Cowen (1952).

layer VI; a smaller degree of cell loss was found in layers II and III. Unfortunately, the study was based on three patients, aged 60 to 62 years, who were diagnosed schizophrenic, but who showed significant dementia. The author suggests that the cell loss is probably related to dementia rather than to schizophrenia. Dom (1976) measured the numerical cell density broken down by size, in several regions, and reported that the microneuron density was 40% lower in the posterior thalamus from catatonic patients than from controls. The observation was significant at the .018 level, but many comparisons were made in the course of the study. Dom also reported a decrease in the microneuron diameter in the caudate and putamen of the catatonic group.

NEW METHODS IN QUANTITATIVE NEUROPATHOLOGY

We would like to examine the problem of objective measurement in neuropathology from a somewhat more general perspective. Figure 12-5

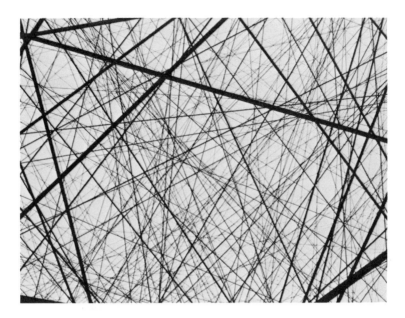

FIGURE 12-5. Randomly Distributed Lines for Which the Angle and the Width Are Not Correlated. From Mandelbrot (1977).

is a collection of lines, which are randomly distributed in angle (isotropic) and in width; there is no correlation between angle and width (Mandelbrot, 1977). If one were to test a hypothesis that, in this general area of the "brain," the "fibers" tend to run from upper left to lower right, it would be easy to convince oneself that the prediction is true. Similarly, one could bias an observer to see a pattern from upper right to lower left. In pattern recognition, the human brain tends to err on the side of false positives rather than false negatives. Perhaps there was more pressure, during evolution, to notice objects in the environment than to be certain that identifications were always correct. Because of the risk of false positives, compensatory conservatism (fear of ending up in the "graveyard") can set in, also unfortunate because it can lead to false negative results.

There is also a more important reason for false negatives. In Fig. 12-6 (Marr, 1977), the lines in the inner portion of the square are restricted to three directions, whereas in the outer portion all angles are equally probable. The eye cannot perceive the difference, although a computer easily can. Subjective pattern perception can miss differences that humans are not programmed to detect.

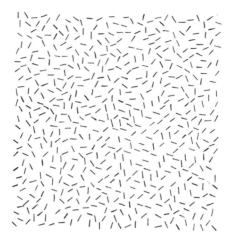

FIGURE 12-6. Square with Two Line Patterns Not Differentiated by the Human Eye. From Marr (1977).

ANALYSIS OF HISTOLOGICAL TEXTURE

We have begun to develop methods of analyzing histological texture, as revealed by the Nissl stain. In order to illustrate this concept, consider area IVa from the *von Economo* atlas of normal human brain (Bucy, 1949; Fig. 12-7). The cells are not arranged at random, but rather in columns, with the long axis of the pyramidal cells oriented parallel to the flow. Parallel order is a feature that has been overlooked in the description of pathological material, perhaps because of the difficulties in quantitating it. Figure 12-8 illustrates why such difficulties increase in certain areas; it shows area IV gamma from the same atlas; and illustrates local rather than global parallelism, since the alignment is parallel in any small region, but the predominant direction changes from place to place.

An interesting recent study by Galaburda and Kemper (1979) reports "unusually coarse appearance and disordered layering" of the left cingulate gyrus in a patient with developmental dyslexia. In this case, the ideal control was present, the patient's own right cingulate gyrus, which was normal. We would like to ask a parallel question: In mental retardation, schizophrenia, and other neuropsychiatric diseases, are there changes in the orderly arrangement of neurons?

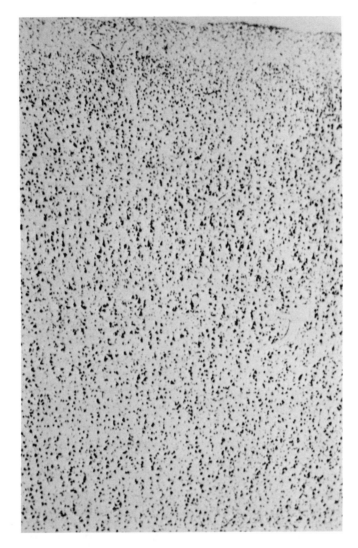

FIGURE 12-7. Normal human brain, area IVa, von Economo atlas, showing global parallelism in arrangement of pyramidal cells. From Bucy (1949).

This question is attractive because it requires only conventional staining methods, but the problem of subjective bias is particularly difficult in determining local and global parallelism. To circumvent this difficulty, we have implemented a computer algorithm based on the Fourier transform. It is analogous, in the spatial domain, to the transform in the time domain that reveals the frequency components of auditory signals.

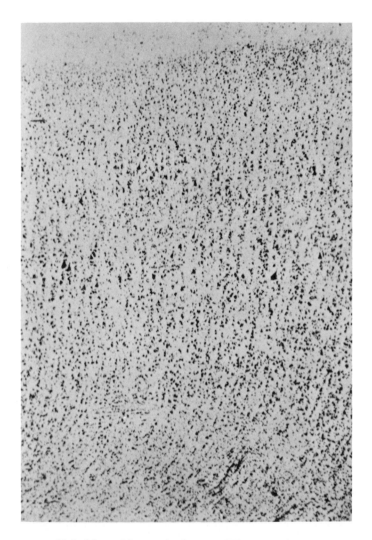

FIGURE 12-8. Normal human brain, area IV γ, von Economo atlas, showing local parallelism in arrangement of pyramidal cells. From Bucy (1949).

Peaks in the spatial Fourier transform occur whenever there is a spatially repetitive pattern. The height of the peak indicates the degree of orderliness of the repetition, and the spacing of the peaks is inversely proportional to the width of the repeating pattern. The technique is illustrated in Fig. 12-9.

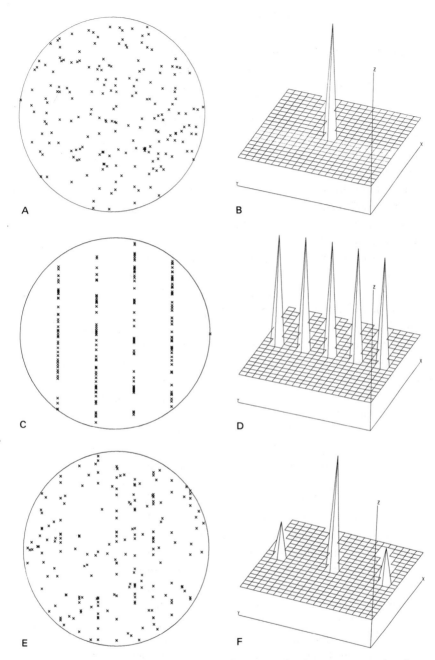

FIGURE 12-9. (A) Randomly arranged pattern of points, computer drawing. (B) Corresponding spatial Fourier transform, with one peak. (C) Columnar arrangement of points, and its Fourier transform (D). (E) Points, one-half random and one-half columnar. (F) Fourier transform of (E).

Figure 12-9A is a computer-drawn pattern of points, randomly arranged in space. The corresponding spatial Fourier transform has one peak, at the origin (Fig. 12-9B). In Fig. 12-9C, a perfectly ordered arrangement of points in columns is shown. The corresponding Fourier transform displays a regular set of peaks (Fig. 12-9D). Figure 12-9E is an arrangement in which one-half the points are random and one-half the points are in regular columns. This is the kind of pattern that the human observer might feel uncertain about classifying. The Fourier transform of this pattern (Fig. 12-9F) gives, in addition to the peak at the origin, which is always present, peaks one-half as high as those in the previous transform, indicating that one-half the points are arranged in an orderly pattern.

It is also possible to Fourier transform the gray levels without first breaking the image up into individual cells. Segmentation of images is a difficult problem for computers, but an orderly arrangement of cells should be observable in the gray levels as well as in the cell center location. Figure 12-10, obtained in collaboration with the Image Analysis Laboratory of Tufts University, is a preliminary example of what can be done without image segmentation. At the upper left is an orderly histological specimen, reconstructed from a digitized photomicrograph. Below it is the gray level Fourier transform. The prominent bright edge, aligned in parallel to the cell columns, indicates the existence of a regular pattern. At the upper right is a similar reconstruction of a specimen in which there is a more random arrangement of cells. In its Fourier transform, below, a faint edge appears, but the intensity pattern is more uniform. These properties of Fourier transforms can be easily quantitated.

The relevance of these techniques to the neuropathology of schizophrenia is highlighted by the recent report by the distinguished anatomist Scheibel of "dendritic disarray" in Ammon's horn of 15 patients diagnosed as schizophrenic (Kovelman and Scheibel, 1979). The normal human hippocampus has a nonrandom, but elusive pattern of cells in Ammon's horn. Kovelman and Scheibel found that the normal orderly palisades of neurons in Ammon's horn were disturbed. "Dendrite domains extended in various directions and were often completely reversed." If confirmed by objective methods, this observation might be an indication of developmental pathology in schizophrenia.

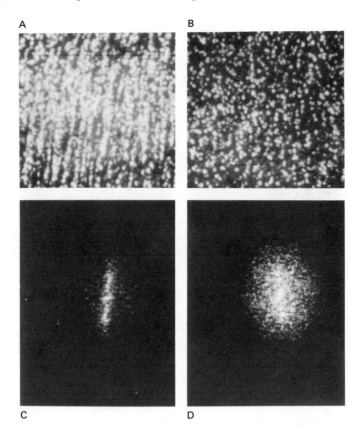

FIGURE 12-10. A histological specimen from a digitized photomicrograph (A), with its gray level Fourier transform (C). A similar specimen in which the cells occur more randomly (B), with its Fourier transform (D). Calculations courtesy of Image Processing Laboratory, Department of Therapeutic Radiology, Tufts University.

DEVELOPMENTAL HISTORY OF THE NEURON USING THE GOLGI TECHNIQUE

We have set ourselves the goal of using the shape of the dendritic arbor, as revealed by the Golgi stain, as an indicator of the developmental history of the neuron and especially as a sign of developmental pa-

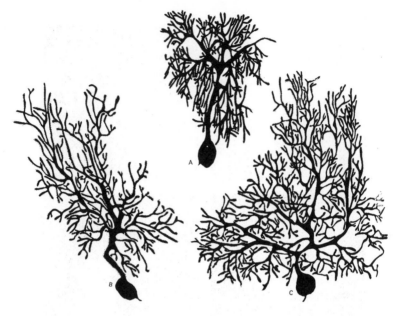

FIGURE 12-11. Cell A is from an irradiated animal and cell B from an animal with a lesion in the cerebellar nuclei. Compare normal Purkinje cell (C).

thology. A classic example of the effect of developmental environment on neuronal morphology is shown in Fig. 12-11 (Bradley and Berry, 1976). A normal Purkinje cell (C) is depicted. The two other cells (A, B) illustrate how the dendritic arbor is altered by changes in the synaptic milieu during development. Cell A is from an irradiated animal; cell B is from an animal with a lesion in the cerebellar nuclei. Even the psychosocial environment can affect the geometry of dendritic trees. In the hippocampal granule cell of the infant rat, the degree of arborization of the proximal portion of the dendritic tree is increased by environmental complexity and decreased by isolation (Fiala et al., 1978). Plasticity can also be detected in adult life, if appropriate measurements are made. Buell and Coleman (1979) have found that elongation of the terminal branches of cortical pyramidal cells in human brain continues for a substantial period after age 55, if senile dementia is not present.

The effect of environment on the shapes of branched structures is better known in the field of botany.

Trees growing in a sunny or windy position are more branched, shorter and less straight, and in general mountain trees have more knots than those that grow in plains, and those that grow in dry spots more knots than those that grow in marshes. (Theophrastus, *Enquiry Into Plants, c.* 350 B.C.)

It is possible for field workers to tell that a tree with bayonet-shaped branches has suffered damage. When the growing tip of a plant (apical meristem) is damaged, a lateral meristem takes over and starts off at right angles and then begins to curve upward in order to reach the light. We postulate that the shape of the dendritic tree will be a record of the life history of the cell, just as it is in the woody tree.

Our work to date has been largely concerned with quantitative analysis of the dendritic geometry of hippocampal granule cells in the mouse. After we have studied the effects of pathological conditions on dendritic morphology in this system, we will be in a better position to apply a similar method to the human brain. The similarity in general morphology of the granule cells will make it possible to use the same descriptive indices for studies of patients.

In a quantitative analysis of dendritic trees, the angle that immediately comes to mind is the angle between the daughter branches at each bifurcation. We call this the *daughter angle*. In previous studies of pyramidal cells from adult rat neocortex, Lindsay and Scheibel (1974) found the daughter angle to be highly variable. Our results on hippocampal granule cells in the mouse are in agreement (Fig. 12-12). Variability detracts from the usefulness of any geometric parameter in characterizing normal or abnormal developmental histories.

We have found that certain other angles are more orderly in the normal hippocampal granule cell. The typical hippocampal granule cell has a "wineglass" shape. In view of the cylindrical symmetry of the cell, we define an "ideal axis" by computing a unit vector in the direction of the vector sum of all branches. This vector represents the general tendency of the outward growth of the cell. We define the *planar angle* as the angle of inclination of the plane of the daughter branches with respect to the main axis of the cell. As shown in Fig. 12-13, on the basis of data on 100 granule cells in the normal mouse hippocampus, it is strongly concentrated around zero. The *bisector angle* indicates whether, within their plane, the daughter branches emerge symmetrically or asymmetrically with respect to the central axis. Figure 12-14 indicates that the bisector angle is also concentrated around zero. These two regular features—the

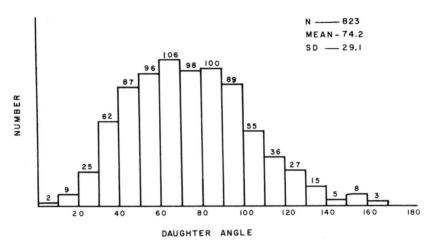

FIGURE 12-12. Graph of Daughter Angles, Mouse Hippocampal Granule Cells.

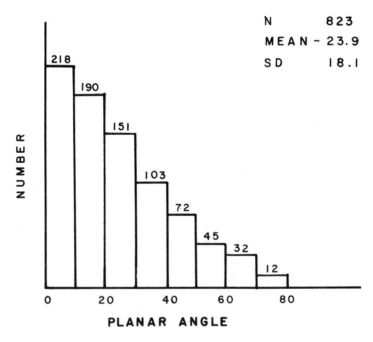

FIGURE 12-13. Graph of Planar Angles, Mouse Hippocampal Granule Cells.

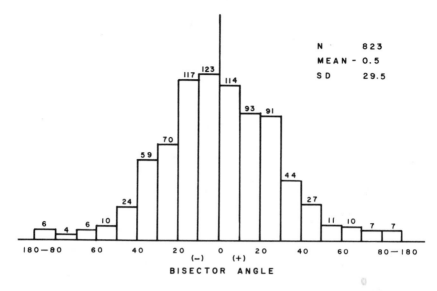

FIGURE 12-14. Graph of Bisector Angles, Mouse Hippocampal Granule Cells.

planar angle and the bisector angle—give rise to the characteristic wine-glass shape of the hippocampal granule cell.

The Golgi method can be used with postmortem material under favorable conditions. Figure 12-15 is from a study by Williams, Ferrante, and Caviness (1978) on the effect of postmortem time on Golgi preparations. The left specimen was fixed at five minutes postmortem, the middle one at six hours, and the one on the right at 24 hours. The 24-hour preparations are not very useful, but at six hours, although fewer cells are stained than at five minutes, the quality of the impregnations of individual cells is good. The availability of brain tissue resource centers at McLean Hospital–Harvard Medical School under Dr. Edward Bird, Wadsworth Veterans Hospital–University of California under Dr. Wallace Tourtellotte, and Addenbrookes Hospital–Cambridge University under Dr. Martin Rossor will greatly facilitate collection of postmortem brain tissue from neuropsychiatric patients.

Quantitative analysis of dendritic geometry in specimens from patients with neuropsychiatric disease should be possible in the near future. Reliable neuropathological changes have not yet been found in schizophrenia, but if there are abnormalities, they may be at a finer structural level than can be examined using traditional methods. Schizophrenic patients

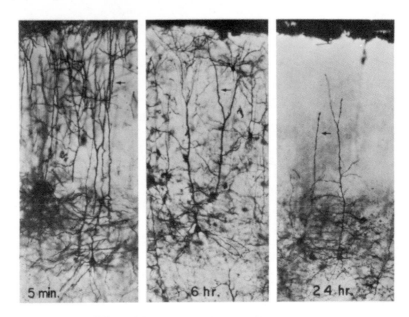

FIGURE 12-15. Effect of Postmortem Fixation Time on Golgi Staining of
Brain Cells. From Williams, Ferrante, and Caviness (1978).

are relatively normal from a neurological perspective, so gross neuron-
atomical abnormalities would not be expected. Many severely mentally
retarded individuals have normal brains when examined by classic techniques, even though some structural defect is almost certainly present
(Williams et al., 1980). We believe that computer-assisted quantitative
methods will help prevent both false positives and false negatives, so that
schizophrenia need be a "graveyard of neuropathologists" no more.

ACKNOWLEDGMENTS

We are grateful to Dr. Richard Sidman for making the computer microscope
in his laboratory available to us, to Drs. Verne Caviness and Alfred Pope for
helpful advice, and to the the Image Analysis Laboratory of Tufts University for
the Fourier transform calculation in Fig. 12-10.
Supported in part by the Schizophrenia Research Foundation of the Scottish
Rite, N.M.J.; U.S.P.H.S. grants R01-NS-12005, R01-MH-34079, 3-P01-MH-
30511, 5-P01-MH-31154; and Research Scientist Development Award 5-K02-
MH-00108.

REFERENCES

Bradley, P., and M. Berry (1976). The effects of reduced climbing and parallel fiber input on Purkinje cell dendritic growth. *Brain Res.* 109, 133–151.

Bucy, P. C. (1949). *The Precentral Motor Cortex.* University of Illinois Press, Urbana, Ill.

Buell, S. J., and Coleman, P. D. (1979). Dendritic growth in the aged human brain and failure of growth in senile dementia. *Science* 206, 854–856.

Buttlar-Brentano, von, K. (1952). Pathohistologische Feststellungen am Basalkern Schizophrener. *J. Nerv. Ment. Dis.* 116, 646–653.

Colon, E. J. (1972). Quantitative cytoarchitectonics of the human cerebral cortex in schizophrenic dementia. *Acta Neuropathol.* 20, 1–10.

Dom, R. (1976). Neostriatal and thalamic interneurons: Their role in the pathophysiology of Huntington's chorea, Parkinson's disease and catatonic schizophrenia. Thesis, Catholic University of Leuven. Leuven, Acco.

Dunlap, C. B. (1924). Dementia praecox: Some preliminary observations on brains from carefully selected cases, and a consideration of certain sources of error. *Amer. J. Psychiat.* 3, 403–421.

Fiala, B. A., Joyce, J. N., and Greenough, W. T. (1978). Environmental complexity modulates growth of granule cell dendrites in developing, but not adult hippocampus of rats. *Exptl. Neurol.* 59, 372–83.

Galaburda, A. M., and T. L. Kemper (1979). Cytoarchitectonic abnormalities in developmental dyslexia: A case study. *Ann. Neurol.* 6, 94–100.

Kovelman, J. A., and Scheibel, A. B. (1979). Dendritic disarray in the hippocampus of paranoid schizophrenics (1979). Abstract, Society of Biological Psychiatry.

Lindsay, R. D., and A. B. Scheibel (1974). Quantitative analysis of the dendritic branching pattern of small pyramidal cells from adult rat somesthetic and visual cortex. *Exptl. Neurol.* 45, 424–34.

Mandelbrot, B. B. (1977). *Fractals: Form, Chance and Dimension.* San Francisco, W. H. Freeman.

Marr, D. (1977). Representing visual information. M.I.T. Artificial Intelligence Monograph *415.*

Matthysse, S. (in press). Nucleus accumbens and schizophrenia, 1981. In *Symposium: Nucleus Accumbens* (J. De France and R. Chronister, eds.) Haer Institute, in press.

Mesulam, M-M., and Geschwind, N. (1978). On the possible role of neocortex and its limbic connections in the process of attention and schizophrenia: Clinical cases of inattention in man and experimental anatomy in monkey. *J. Psychiat. Res.* 14, 249–59.

Papez, J. W. (1952). Form of living organisms in psychotic patients. *J. Nerv. Ment. Dis.* 116, 375–391.

Plum, F. (1972). Neuropathological findings. In *Prospects for Research on Schizophrenia, Neurosci. Res. Prog. Bull.* 10, 384–88.

Vogt, C., and Vogt, O. (1952). Alterations anatomiques de la schizophrenie et d'autres psychoses dites functionelles. In *Proceedings*, First Int. Congr. of Neuropathology, vol. 1, pp. 515–532. Torino, Rosenberg and Sellier.

Williams, R. S., Ferrante, R. J., and V. S. Caviness, Jr. (1978). The Golgi-rapid method in clinical neuropathology: I. Morphologic consequences of suboptimum fixation. *J. Neuropathol. Exptl. Neurol.* 37, 1333.

Williams, R. S. et al. (1980). Neuropathologic studies in four retarded persons with autistic behavior. *Arch. Neurol.* 37, 749–53.

Wolf, A., and Cowen, D. (1952). Histopathology of schizophrenia and other psychoses of unknown origin. In *The Biology of Mental Health and Disease*, New York P. B. Hoeber, Inc., pp. 469–97.

13 | Laterality and Hemispheric Dysfunction in Schizophrenia

HENRY A. NASRALLAH

INTRODUCTION

Laterality refers to the differential activation of the left and right cerebral hemispheres for motor, perceptual, cognitive, conative, or emotive functions. Commonly referred to as cerebral dominance, it implies a specific specialization of each cerebral hemisphere for different neurophysiological tasks. Over the past decade, the role of lateralization of hemispheric functions in psychopathology has become an important area of research.

HISTORICAL OVERVIEW

Only in the past 20 years have the duality, asymmetry, and advanced integration of the human brain been appreciated as a major evolutionary advance that produced the special distinguishing features of humans (Dimond, 1977; Bogen and Bogen, 1969). Up to the 1950s, it was generally believed that the two cerebral hemispheres were duplicate structures, with the left hemisphere being the dominant one. Over the past 100 years, however, there had been several clinical indications that the two hemispheres in humans were different, not duplicate brains, as reflected in clinical lateralization of symptoms. In 1880, Hughlins-Jackson noted that right hemisphere epileptic foci were characterized by "emotional states." Broca (1861) concluded from postmortem studies of aphasic patients that the left temporal lobe was crucial for language. Others (Briquet, 1859; Pitres, 1891; Tourette, 1895) observed that hysterical conversion symptoms occurred more frequently on the left side of the body. Babinski (1914) pointed to the occurrence of hemi-neglect and indifference in patients with left-sided hemiparesis (i.e., right hemispheric lesions). Goldstein (1939) was the first to note the association of catastrophic reactions in left hemisphere lesions, whereas Hécaen, Ajuriaguerra, and Massonit (1951) and Denny-Brown, Meyer, and Horenstein (1952) described the indifference reactions of persons with lesions of the right, or so-called "minor" hemisphere.

INTRACAROTID BARBITURATE INACTIVATION

On the other hand, similar data were obtained from studies of pharmacological inactivation of the cerebral hemispheres by intracarotid barbiturate injections. Terzian and Cecotto (1959) reported a differential response of the two cerebral hemispheres to intracarotid sodium amytal injections, with a "depressive-catastrophic" reaction following the inactivation of the left (dominant) hemisphere and a "euphoric-maniacal" reaction following the inactivation of the right (non-dominant) hemisphere. These findings were generally replicaed by others (Alema, Rosadini, and Rossi, 1961, Perria, Rosadini, and Rossi, 1961, Terzian, 1964, Rossi and Rosadini 1967), but not by Milner (1967), who found no difference after the pharmacological inactivation of the "dominant" and "minor" hemispheres. In another study of unilateral intracarotid amytal injections in patients hospitalized for depression (Hommes and Panhuysen, 1971), it was found that the severity of depression correlated negatively with dominance for speech in the left hemisphere, suggesting that left hemispheric dominance is reduced in depression. Elevation of mood was noted with injections on either side to varying extents, but depressive reactions were probably imbedded in the existing depression of the patients.

UNILATERAL AND BILATERAL ELECTROCONVULSIVE THERAPY

A large literature has appeared during the past 15 years that suggests that electroconvulsive therapy (ECT) applied only to the right hemisphere is as effective as bilateral ECT for the treatment of depression, but that ECT to the left hemisphere, only, is significantly less effective than bilateral or right hemisphere ECT (Halliday et al., 1968; Cronin et al., 1970, Costello et al., 1970). Kronfol, Hamsher, Digre, and Waziri (1978) reported that before treatment with ECT, depressed patients had more abnormalities in testing of right hemisphere functions compared to the left, and that after ECT, whether unilateral right or left, the right, but not the left hemispheric functions improved. Deglin and Nikolaenko (1975) studied the effects of right and left ECT and concluded from their behavioral observations that the dominant hemisphere plays a major role in the regulation of mood. The ECT literature suggests a role of lateralization of hemispheric function in psychopathology.

COMMISSUROTOMY STUDIES

Major advances in the understanding of hemispheric and interhemispheric functions came as a by-product of the commissurotomy studies in patients with intractable epilepsy. The earlier commissurotomy studies (Akelaitis, 1944) failed to show any distinct or consistent behavioral symptoms with agenesis of the corpus callosum or following the complete surgical sectioning of the corpus callosum and anterior commissure, even with extensive neurological and psychological testing. Those negative findings set the prevailing doctrine of the 1940s and 1950s that separating the hemispheres does not cause any change in brain function in humans, and that the dominant left hemisphere continues to function as before. However, animal studies started in the early 1950s, mainly on cats and primates (Myers and Sperry, 1953; Sperry, Stamm, and Minor, 1956; Sperry 1961; Downer, 1962), showed consistently that after surgical separation, each cerebral hemisphere functions independently to a very large extent in most higher activities, including perception, learning, and memory. In addition, the two separated hemispheres could be trained concurrently to perform mutually contradictory tasks (Myers, 1962) and cerebral dominance for a certain task could be experimentally shifted from one hemisphere to the other.

The second series of commissurotomy patients done in the early 1960s were studied more intensively with the use of specialized tachistoscopic techniques by which sensory input to one hemisphere at a time could be achieved. Although clinically and behaviorally the "split-brain" patients were hardly different following the surgical disconnection of the hemispheres, the tachistoscopic testing (Gazzaniga, 1970) demonstrated that the separated hemispheres functioned independently, with the verbal left hemisphere acting as the main executive hemisphere as it did preoperatively. It was also shown that each hemisphere is specialized or dominant for different tasks, with the left hemisphere specialized for verbal, analytical, logical, or propositional tasks and the right hemisphere specialized for spatial, synthetic, intuitive, and appositional functions (Bogen, 1969). Furthermore, and perhaps most significantly, the separated hemispheres appear to contain two independent and different spheres of consciousness in the split-brain patients, which has led to a revolution in the scientific and philsophical conceptualization of self, mind, and the unity of conscious awareness (Sperry, 1968; Puccetti, 1973; LeDoux, Wilson and Gazzaniga, 1977; Sperry, 1977).

GENETIC FACTORS IN LATERALIZATION

Although genetic factors appear to be involved in the determination of laterality, the nature of this involvement is still undetermined. Evidence comes from the presence of anatomical asymmetries in the human fetus related to language function and handedness (Wada, Clarke, and Hamm, 1975). Further evidence comes from the right-ward tonic neck reflex that is present at birth in the majority of neonates, and its correlation with handedness at age 10 years; the correlation of a family history of left-handedness with the degree of perceptual asymmetry in right-handed individuals, and the observation that frequency of right-handedness does not increase after age 4 years (Levy, 1974). Recent adoptive studies have also confirmed that handedness in offspring was a function of biological, but not adoptive parents (Carter-Saltzman, 1980).

It should also be noted that, developmentally, the corpus callosum, which is the major interhemispheric commissure, has been shown to be unmyelinated at birth and that it is the last region in the human brain to be myelinated (up to age 10 years or more) (Yakovlev and LeCours, 1967). Thus, children under the age of three years have, in essence, split brains (Galin, Johnstone, Nakell, and Herron, 1979), which become gradually integrated with maturation, corresponding with stages of cognitive development.

LATERALITY AND BRAIN ANATOMICAL ASYMMETRIES

There are several lines of evidence for asymmetries in the cerebral hemispheres related to motoric laterality. Geschwind and Levitsky (1968) found that in postmortem brains of right-handed subjects, the left hemispheric planum temporale is larger than the right. LeMay and Culebras (1972) and LeMay (1976), using computerized axial tomography, showed that the left occipital pole was longer and wider than the right in many mature right-handers. They also found that left-handers were more likely to show no asymmetry or even an opposite hemispheric asymmetry from right-handers (LeMay and Kido, 1978). Others (Witelson and Pallie, 1973) also reported left–right differences in postmortem brains of newborns.

NEUROCHEMICAL LATERALIZATION IN ANIMALS

Animals do not have an inherent asymmetry of the nervous system. Right and left sides are structurally and functionaly mirror images (Dimond, 1977). However, some asymmetry may develop in response to the environment (Collins, 1977).

Some studies have suggested a neurochemical lateralization in rat brain, which may be significant for the animal model of psychosis. Glick, Jerussi, and Zimmerberg (1977) reported an asymmetry of nigrostriatal dopamine (DA) levels in rat brains, which is related to behavior, in that rats rotated toward the side of the brain with the lower DA content. Amphetamine increases the striatal DA asymmetry and subsequently the frequency of rotations toward the side lower in DA. Stress was also found to have a similar effect on turning behavior. It was also noted that animals with no side preference are the most active and the poorest overall learners. Since DA has been implicated in psychosis and in hyperactive children, these findings may have clinical implications for neurochemical lateralization and psychopathology.

An asymmetry in thalamic norepinephrine in postmortem human brains was reported by Oke, Keller, Mefford, and Adams (1978). Norepinephrine is also an important neurotransmitter for psychiatric illness, and its asymmetry in the human brain suggests a link between laterality and psychiatric symptoms.

The studies of Denenberg, Garbarati, and Sherman (1978) also suggest that early experiences can influence lateralization in rat brain, which may have implications for developmental experiences and lateral psychopathology in humans.

FACTORS INFLUENCING LATERALITY CHANGES IN HUMANS

Laterality changes in humans, usually in the direction of shifting cerebral dominance from the left to the right hemisphere, have been shown to occur under a variety of conditions. These include stress (Tucker, Roth, Arneson, and Buckingham, 1977), sleep (Goldstein, Stoltzfus, and Gardocki, 1972), orgasm (Cohen, Rosen, and Goldstein, 1976), alcohol ingestion (Chandler and Parsons, 1977), hypnosis (Frumkin, Ripley, and Cox, 1978), and ingestion of stimulants and hallucinogens, but not sedatives and minor tranquilizers (Goldstein and Stoltzfus, 1973). Neuroleptics reduce and increase left hemispheric voltage concurrently with symptom amelioration in schizophrenia (Serafitinides, 1972, 1973).

LATERALITY AND PSYCHOPATHOLOGY

There are now several lines of evidence indicating a dysfunction of the left cerebral hemisphere in schizophrenia, which may produce a shift of laterality (Wexler and Heninger, 1979), as well as an impairment of motoric, perceptual, and cognitive lateralization (Gruzelier and Flor-Henry, 1979). A review of this evidence follows.

Handedness

Perhaps the easiest and crudest indicator of motoric laterality and cerebral organization is handedness. Pathological (not familial) left-handedness, or sinisterality, from its root, *sinistre*, has been linked to cerebral impairment (Levy, 1969; Miller, 1971), and both left-handedness and cognitive deficits have been attributed to neonatal brain damage (Satz, 1972). Left-handedness as an indicator of indeterminate cerebral dominance has been linked with temperamental irritability and undue sensitivity to stress (Zangwill, 1960).

The study of handedness in schizophrenia is quite recent. The findings so far have been inconsistent and at times contradictory.

Walker and Birch (1970) reported poorly developed hand and eye preference in a high proportion of schizophrenic children. Oddy and Lohstein (1972) found increased mixed hand-eye dominance, but no excess of left-handedness in schizophrenia compared to the general population. The lack of difference in left-handedness between schizophrenics and controls was confirmed by Wahl (1976). Bolin (1953), Fleminger, Dalton, and Standage (1977), and Taylor, Dalton, and Fleminger (1980) reported on an excess of right-handedness in schizophrenic patients. Lishman and McMeekan (1976) found a significant shift to left-hand preference in young male psychotic patients with delusions, but not in schizophrenics as such. On the other hand, Dvirskii (1976), Gur (1977), and Nasrallah, Schroeder, Keelor, and McCalley-Whitters (1981) reported an excess of right-handedness in male chronic schizophrenic patients. However, when the patients were divided into chronic paranoid and non-paranoid types, Nasrallah, Kuperman, McCalley-Whitters, and Keelor (1981) found the incidence of left-handedness to be significantly higher among the paranoid schizophrenic group compared to the non-paranoid (hebephrenic) group.

It is possible that the contradictory findings of the incidence of left-handedness in schizophrenia may be due to methodological differences in diagnosis as well as differences in sampling, assessment of handedness, age, and sex.

Another approach to the relationship of handedness to schizophrenia comes from the study of twins. Boklage (1977) found that in dizygotic twins, when one has schizophrenia, there was no difference in hand preference between the schizophrenic and the normal twin. However, in monozygotic twins discordant for schizophrenia, there was a discordance for handedness with left-handedness being overrepresented among the schizophrenic twins, whereas in monozygotic twins concordant for schizophrenia, both twins tended to be right-handed and also to have the poor prognosis (nuclear) type of schizophrenia. This suggests that discordance in monozygotic twins may be due to anomalous lateralization in the schizophrenic twin as indicated by left-handedness, or incomplete right-handedness, in the non-schizophrenic twin, which may be due to neonatal brain insult or perhaps to mirror imaging among monozygotic twins (Raney, 1938). Luchins, Weinberger, and Wyatt (1979) have confirmed Boklage's findings and suggested that the schizophrenic illness in discordant monozygotic twins is related to anomalous lateralization and is less severe and has a better prognosis than the type of schizophrenia observed in concordant monozygotic twins, which tends to be a poor prognosis "process" type.

Skin Conductance

In studies in patients with unilateral brain damage (Luria and Homskaya, 1966; Sourek, 1965), an absence of skin conductance responsiveness in the hand ipsilateral to the brain lesion was reported. Gruzelier and Venables (1972, 1973, 1974) and Gruzelier (1973) examined the skin conductance orienting response in the right and left hands of schizophrenic patients and in controls. A significantly lower response was noted in the left hand, suggesting a dysfunction in the left cerebral hemisphere in schizophrenia responsible for the lateralized imbalance in skin conductance. The asymmetry was also found to be related to arousal level (Gruzelier and Venables, 1974). Gruzelier and Hammond (1976) also replicated those findings and described a reversal of the lateralized deficit with chlorpromazine.

Lateral Eye Movements

Another type of research evidence for a left hemispheric dysfunction in schizophrenia comes from the studies of conjugate lateral eye movements (LEM). Eye movements to the left or right have been hypothesized to reflect activation of the cerebral hemisphere contralateral to the direction of the gaze (Bakan, 1971; Gur, 1975). Kinsbourne (1972) used LEM to show that verbal tasks preferentially activate the left cerebral hemisphere and spatial tasks preferentially activate the right cerebral hemisphere. Schwartz, Davidson, and Maer (1975) showed that the right hemisphere was also preferentially activated by emotional material.

Using LEM as an indicator of lateralized hemispheric activation, Schweitzer, Becker, and Welsh (1978) found that the left hemisphere in schizophrenic patients had an overall increase in activity, compared to control subjects, and was inappropriately activated by spatial–emotional tasks. Educational background or medication status had no effect on this finding. They concluded that there was a left hemispheric dysfunction in schizophrenia. There was, however, a sex difference, with women generally, regardless of diagnosis, initiating cognition in the left hemisphere more often than men.

Gur (1978) used LEM in schizophrenic patients to show a left hemispheric dysfunction in the initial processing of visual data and a generalized increase in left hemispheric activation by verbal, emotional, and spatial material. Schweitzer (1979) replicated his original findings of increased left hemisphere activity in schizophrenia, with excessive processing of spatial and to a lesser extent, emotional material in the left hemisphere.

Dichotic Listening

Another mode of assessing laterality is dichotic listening, which was first introduced by Broadbent (1954); it has been demonstrated to be a reasonably reliable method of indicating which hemisphere is dominant for language functions (Kimura, 1967). It involves delivering different words simultaneously to the two ears and noting the number of words correctly identified at each ear. More words are correctly identified at the ear contralateral to the dominant hemisphere.

Polidoro (1970), using a staggered spondaic word test, reported that schizophrenic patients were poor performers overall, but showed no difference from controls on asymmetry. Yozawitz et al. (1979), using two click stimuli as well as staggered spondaic word test, duplicated Polidoro's results and found no evidence for a left hemispheric dysfunction in schizophrenia, but did observe a right hemispheric dysfunction in affective psychosis. He could not find a significant correlation between neuroleptics and magnitude of ear asymmetry.

Lishman et al. (1978) reported that both manic-depressive and schizophrenic patients showed much larger ear differences (favoring the right ear) than controls and concluded that psychosis, per se, rather than the diagnostic category, is the important factor in this asymmetry.

Wexler and Heninger (1979) studied dichotic listening in right-handed schizophrenic as well as schizoaffective depressive and control subjects. They detected laterality changes in all psychotic groups, but not in controls, and found that psychopathology ratings were worst when the laterality was lowest. They concluded that psychotic illness is associated with diminished cerebral dominance.

Electrocencephalography (EEG)

A larger number of studies have consistently found an excess of EEG power in the higher frequencies in psychosis (Lifshitz and Gradijan, 1974). However, only in the last few years have investigators noted the possible lateralization of EEG abnormalities in schizophrenia. Flor-Henry, Koles, Howarth, and Burton (1979) reported an abnormal power distribution in the 20- 35-Hz band in the left temporal region of unmedicated schizophrenic patients. Hays (1977) also found asymmetric EEGs in the theta range among schizophrenic patients without a positive family history, usually lateralized to the left side. Abrams and Taylor (1979) found more temporal abnormalities in schizophrenia and more parietooccipital abnormalities in affective psychosis. Coger, Dymond, and Serafetinides (1979) reported a significant increase of power densities in the frontotemporal regions in schizophrenia, compared to matched controls, as well as a significant increase in power in the right frontotemporal region. Stevens et al. (1979) found desynchronization over the left temporal region during spatial tasks and a reduction of power in the alpha frequency in the left temporal region during periods of auditory hallucinations, together with right temporal slow activities.

Evoked Potentials

Roemer, Shagass, Straumanis, and Amadeo (1978) used a visually evoked response to show lower left hemispheric stability in schizophrenic patients compared to controls or psychotic depressives, suggestive of a left hemispheric dysfunction in schizophrenia.

Buchsbaum et al. (1979) studied hemitachistos copically evoked potential enhancement by selective attention and found a left temporal deficit in schizophrenia similar to patients with left lobectomy. Thus, the evoked potentials data are also suggestive of a lateralized left hemispheric deficit in schizophrenia.

Cerebral Blood Flow and Metabolism

Using computerized clearance of intracarotid xenon-133, Ingvar and Franzen (1974) reported that schizophrenic patients had a normal mean left hemispheric flow, but a decreased blood flow in frontal structures and an increased flow in posterior brain regions. They concluded that since frontal structures control intentional behavior, whereas posterior structures are concerned with perceptual processes, schizophrenia is a hypointentional hypergnostic state. No comparison was made with the right hemisphere.

More recent studies measuring regional cerebral metabolic rate with positron emission transaxial tomography (PETT) (Farkas, 1980; Chapter 11, this volume) have confirmed the hypofrontality suggested by Ingvar, and revealed that schizophrenic patients utilize less glucose than controls in the frontal cortex, lenticular nucleus, thalamus, and cingulate gyrus. In addition, manic patients in the acute psychotic phase had increased glucose metabolism, especially in the frontal cortex, lenticular nucleus, and cingulate gyrus. Buchsbaum et al. (1981) reported an asymmetrical metabolic rate in the posterior part of the temporal lobe cortex, and in the parietal cortex, with a higher uptake in the right hemisphere in schizophrenia not related to age, but associated with past morbid history and family history. The age-related changes were more pronounced in the parietal regions.

Future studies in this new and pioneering area of research promise to reveal in more detail differences in cerebral activity between the normal and the schizophrenic brain, as well as the brain in other psychopathological states. The implications for diagnosis and treatment could be far-reaching.

Neuroanatomical Asymmetries in Schizophrenia

Over the past few years, there have been several reports of computerized axial tomographic (CAT) findings of lateral cerebral ventricular enlargement and structural brain changes in the brains of schizophrenic patients (Johnstone et al., 1976; Weinberger, Torrey, Neophytides, and Wyatt, 1979a,b). Evidence for a subgroup of schizophrenics with reversed cerebral asymmetry on CAT scans was reported by Luchins, Weinberger, and Wyatt (1979). They noted that, in contrast to usual neuroanatomical asymmetries of normal right-handed individuals, whereby the right frontal and left occipital lobes are wider than their counterparts, a subgroup of right-handed schizophrenics without evidence of cerebral atrophy had a higher incidence of reversal of the usual frontal and occipital neuroanatomical asymmetry. They concluded that abnormal lateralization is important for a subgroup of schizophrenic patients who tended to have no atrophic brain changes and to have a milder form of illness with fewer years of hospitalization.

In another study, Luchins et al. (1981) found that for black schizophrenic patients, reversed cerebral asymmetry is associated with an increased frequency of human leukocyte antigen (HLA)-2 A, especially if there was no evidence of cerebral atrophy.

A reversal of cerebral asymmetry has also been observed in children with autism (Hier, LeMay, and Rosenberger, 1978a) and developmental dyslexia (Hier, LeMay, Rosenberger, and Perlo, 1978b), so it does not appear to be restricted to schizophrenia.

The association of embryonic symmetry anomaly with the development of monozygotic twins discordant for schizophrenia has been suggested by Boklage (1977). Others (Kinney and Jacobsen, 1978) also implicate early neonatal brain damage in the development of milder forms of schizophrenia in patients who are not at a genetic risk for schizophrenia.

Finally, Golden et al. (1980) reports that there is a brain density deficit in schizophrenic patients as compared to normal controls. In a more recent study, Golden, Ariel, and Graber (1981) found a decrease in left anterior cerebral blood flow, compared to controls.

To sum up, there is a large amount of evidence, from a variety of research areas, suggesting a lateralized dysfunction in the left cerebral hemisphere in schizophrenia. The areas most likely to be involved in this dysfunction are the left temporal lobe and the temporal–frontal and temporal–limbic connections. More work is needed to clarify the neurochemical nature of this dysfunction, which appears to be a weakening of left hemispheric dominance.

INTERHEMISPHERIC DYSFUNCTION IN SCHIZOPHRENIA

In addition to the data suggesting a left hemispheric dysfunction in schizophrenia, there is a growing body of evidence suggesting an inter-hemispheric integration defect in schizophrenia.

The two cerebral hemispheres are connected by several commissures, the largest of which is the corpus callosum. The finding of significantly wider corpus callosum in chronic "process" schizophrenia, compared to non-schizophrenic psychiatric controls (Rosenthal and Bigelow, 1972), was perhaps the earliest finding suggesting an abnormality of interemi-spheric communication in schizophrenia.

More recently, Nasrallah, Bigelow, Rauscher, and Wyatt (1979) re-ported that the corpus callosum tended to be thicker in early onset, "he-bephrenic" schizophrenia compared to the late onset, "paranoid" type. When the regional thickness of the corpus callosum was examined, the frontal region, but not the occipital region, was significantly thicker in schizophrenia compared to psychiatric controls (Bigelow, Nasrallah, Rauscher, and Wyatt, 1981). The cause(s) of increased thickness of the corpus callosum are still unknown, but the histological study done so far (Nasrallah, McCalley-Whitters, Rauscher, and Bigelow, 1982) suggests that there is increased gliosis in the corpus callosi of late onset schizo-phrenic patients as compared to the early onset schizophrenic group. No difference in the number of fibers per unit cross-sectional area was found.

Beaumont and Dimond (1973) reported a dysfunction in the left hemi-sphere, as well as an impairment of cross-matching between the hemi-spheres, on tachistoscopic testing in schizophrenic patients. They con-cluded that their findings suggest a disconnection of the cerebral hemispheres in the schizophrenic brain, possibly related to a callosal de-fect. Since then, other investigators have found evidence of defective interhemispheric transfer of different perceptual information in schizo-phrenic patients. This includes failure of tactile and intermanual transfer (Green, 1978; Dimond et al., 1979, 1980; Carr, 1980) and auditory trans-fer (Eaton et al., 1980). Etevenon et al. (1979) found EEG evidence of interhemispheric dysfunction in hebephrenic, but not paranoid schizo-phrenia.

A high frequency of schizophrenia-like symptoms in patients with tu-mors of the corpus callosum has been noted for a long time (Elliot, 1969). Recently, Nasrallah and McChesney (1981) found significant depressive and dementia symptoms in patients with corpus callosum tumors, compared to a control group of unilateral tumors. In addition, delusions and hallucinations were associated with tumors located in the anterior part (genu) of the corpus callosum, suggesting that interruption of interhemispheric frontal lobe connections may be associated with schizophrenic symptoms.

The findings of "soft" neurological signs in schizophrenic patients (Cox and Ludwig, 1979; Torrey, 1980), as well as in children at risk for schizophrenia (Fish, 1977), also serve as additional evidence for integrative deficits in the brains of schizophrenic patients.

Dimond (1978) postulated that there are split-brain symptoms in schizophrenia. Nasrallah (submitted), on the other hand, hypothesized that schizophrenic symptoms may be due to weakened inhibitory mechanisms that mediate left hemispheric dominance for consciousness. This may result in the "awareness" by the left hemispheric consciousness of another (right) hemispheric consciousness, which communicates with and "intrudes" on it, leading to Schneiderian-type delusions to explain the "external influence." A test for this hypothesis would be that a total commissurotomy (i.e., complete separation of the hemispheres) should produce an improvement in schizophrenia, since the confusing and inappropriate right hemispheric intrusion into the left hemispheric consciousness would then cease.

CONCLUSION

A large body of evidence supports the notion of a left hemispheric dysfunction and defective interhemispheric integration in schizophrenia. This appears to be associated with a weakening of the normal patterns of lateralization of cerebral dominance. Since schizophrenia is a heterogeneous syndrome (Tsuang, 1975), with many possible etiologies, it may be that laterality shift is a common element of psychosis (Gruzelier and Flor-Henry, 1979) and that in schizophrenia it is related to a specific left hemispheric dysfunction. It is also possible that laterality shifts play a significant role in certain subtypes of schizophrenia only (Gruzelier, 1981).

REFERENCES

Abrams, R., and M. A. Taylor (1979). Differential EEG patterns in affective disorder and schizophrenia. *Arch. Gen. Psychiat.* 36, 1355–1358.

Akelaitis, A. J. (1944). A study of gnosis, praxis and language following section of the corpus callosum and anteria commissure. *J. Neurosurg.* 1, 94–102.

Alema, G., G. Rosadini, and G. F. Rossi (1961). Psychic reactions associated with intracarotid amytol injection and relation to brain damage. *Excerpta Medica* 37, 154–155.

Babinski, M. J. (1914). Contributions à l'etude des troubles mentaux dans l'hemiplegie organique cerebrale (anosognosie). *Rev. Neurol.* 37, 845–848.

Bakan, P. (1971). The eyes have it. *Psychol. Today* 4, 64–67.

Beaumont, J. G., and S. J. Dimond (1973). Brain disconnection and schizophrenia. *Brit. J. Psychiat.* 123, 661–662.

Bigelow, L. G., H. A. Nasrallah, F. P. Rauscher, and R. J. Wyatt (1981). Post-mortem evidence for pathology in the anterior corpus callosum in schizophrenia. Abstracts of the 36th Annual Meeting of the Society of Biological Psychiatry, p. 31.

Bogen, J. E. (1969). The other side of the brain II: An appositional mind. *Bull. Los Angeles Neurool. Soc.* 34, 135–162.

Bogen, J. E., and G. M. Bogen (1969). The other side of the brain III: The corpus callosum and reactivity. *Bull. Los Angeles Neurol. Soc.* 34, 191–220.

Boklage, E. C. (1977). Schizophrenia, brain asymmetry development and twinning: Cellular relationship with etiological and possibly prognostic implications. *Biol. Psychiat.* 12, 17–35.

Bolin, B. J. (1953). Left-handedness and stuttering as signs diagnostic of epileptics. *J. Ment. Sci.* 99, 483–488.

Briquet, P. (1859). *Traite Clinique de Therapeutique de l'hysterie.* Barltiere, Paris.

Broadbent, D. E. (1954). The role of auditory localization in attention and memory span. *J. Expertl. Psychol.* 47, 191–196.

Broca, P. (1861). Remarques sur la siege de la faculte du languge articule. *Bull. Soc. Anat.* 6, 330–357.

Buchsbaum, M. S., W. T. Carpenter, P. Fedio, F. K. Goodwin, D. L. Murphy, and R. M. Post (1979). Hemispheric differences in evoked potential enhancement by selective attention to hemiretinally presented stimuli in schizophrenic, affective and post-temporal lobectomy patients. In *Hemisphere Asymmetrics of Function in Psychopathology* (J. Gruzelier, and P. Flor-Henry, eds.). Elsevier/North-Holland Biomedical Press, New York, pp. 317–328.

Buchsbaum, M. S., R. Kessler, W. E. Bunney, J. Cappelletti, R. Coppola, R. Flynn, J. C. Goble, R. G. Manning, D. P. VanKammen, F. Rigal, R. Waters, L. Sokoloff, and D. Ingvar (1981). Position emission tomography and EEG in schizophrenia. New Research Abstracts. American Psychiatric Association 134th Annual Meeting, p. 50.

Carr, S. A. (1980). Interhemispheric transfer of sterognostic information in chronic schizophrenics. *Brit. J. Psychiat.* 136, 53–58.

Carter-Saltzman, L. (1980). Biological and sociocultural effects on handedness: Comparison between biological and adoptive families. *Science* 209, 1263–1265.

Chandler, B. C., and O. A. Parson (1977). Altered hemispheric functioning under alcohol. *J. Stud. Alcoh.* 38, 381–391.

Coger, R. W., A. M. Dymond, and E. A. Serafetinides (1979). Electroencephalographic similarities between chronic alcoholics and chronic, non-paranoid schizophrenics. *Arch. Gen. Psychiat.* 38, 91–94.

Cohen, H. D., R. C. Rosen, and L. Goldstein (1976). Electroencephalographic laterality changes during human sexual orgasm. *Arch. Sex. Behav.* 5, 189–199.

Colbourn, C. J. (1979). Laterality measurement and theory. In *Hemisphere Asymmetries of Function in Psychopathology* (J. Gruzelier and P. Flor-Henry, eds.). Elsevier/North-Holland Biomedical Press, New York, pp. 65–76.

Collins, R. L. (1977). Origins of the sense of asymmetry: Mendelian and non-Mendelian modes of inheritance. In *Evolution and Lateralization of the Brain* (S. J. Dimond and D. A. Blizald, eds.). New York Academy of Sciences, New York.

Costello, C. G., G. P. Belton, J. E. Abra, and B. E. Dunn (1970). The amnesic and therapeutic effects of bilateral and unilateral ECT. *Brit. J. Psychiat.* 116, 69–78.

Cox, S. M., and A. M. Ludwig (1979). Neurological soft signs and psychopathology: Findings in schizophrenia. *J. Nerv. Ment. Dis.* 167, 161–165.

Cronin, D., P. Bodley, L. Potts, M. D. Matgher, R. K. Gardner, and J. C. Tobin (1970). Unilateral and bilateral ECT: A study of memory disturbance and relief from depression. *J. Neurol. Neurosurg. Psychiat.* 3, 705–713.

Deglin, V. L., and N. N. Nikolaenko (1975). Role of the dominant hemisphere in regulation of emotional states. *Hum. Physiol.* 1, 394–402.

Denenberg, V. H., J. Garbarati, and G. Sherman (1978). Infantile stimulation induces brain lateralization in rats. *Science* 201, 1150–1151.

Denny-Brown, D., J. S. Meyer, and S. Horenstein (1952). The significance of perpetual rivalry resulting from parietal lesions. *Brain* 75, 433–471.

Dimond, S. J. (1977). Evolution and lateralization of the brain: Concluding remarks. *Ann. N.Y. Acad. Sci.* 299, 477–501.

Dimond, S. J. (1978). *Introducing Neuropsychology.* C. C. Thomas, Springfield, Ill.

Dimond, S. J., R. E. Scammell, I. Pryce, D. Huws, and C. Gray (1979). Callosal transfer and left hand anomia in schizophrenia. *Biol. Psychiat.* 14, 735–739.

Dimond, S. J., R. Scammel, I. Pryce, D. Huws, and C. Gray (1980). Some failures of intermanual and cross-lateral transfer in chronic schizophrenia. *J. Abnorm. Psychol.* 89, 505–509.

Downer, J. L. (1962). Interhemispheric integration of the visual system. In *In-*

terhemispheric Relations and Cerebral Dominance (V. B. Mountcastle, ed.). John Hopkins Press, Baltimore.

Dvirskii, A. E. (1976). Functional asymmetry of the cerebral hemispheres in clinical types of schizophrenia. *Neurosci. Behav. Physiol.* 7, 236–239.

Eaton, E. M., J. Busk, M. P. Maloney, R. B. Sloane, K. Whipple and K. White (1980). Hemispheric dysfunction in schizophrenia: Assessment by visual perception tasks. *Psychiat. Res.* 1, 325–332.

Elliot, F. A. (1969). The corpus callosum, cingulate gyrus, septum pellucidum, septal area and fornix. In *Handbook of Clinical Neurology* (P. J. Vinkent and G. W. Bruyn, eds.), Vol. II. Elsevier/North-Holland Biomedical Press, New York, pp. 758–765.

Etevenon, P., B. Pidoux, P. Rioux, P. Peron-Magnan, G. Verdeaux, and P. Deniker (1979). Intra- and interhemispheric EEG differences qualified by spectral analysis. Comparative study of two groups of schizophrenics and a control group. *Acta Psychiat. Scand.* 60, 57–68.

Farkas, T. (1980). Biochemical imaging of the brain. A presentation at the 35th Annual Convention of the Society of Biological Psychiatry, Boston, Mass., September 1980.

Fish, B. (1977). Neurobiological antecedents of schizophrenia in children: Evidence for an inherited congenital neurointegrative defect. *Arch. Gen. Psychiat.* 34, 1297–1313.

Fleminger, J. J., R. Dalton, and K. F. Standage (1977). Handedness in psychiatric patients. *Brit. J. Psychiat.* 131, 448–452.

Flor-Henry, P. (1969). Psychosis and temporal lobe epilepsy: A controlled investigation. *Epilepsia* 10, 363–395.

Flor-Henry, P., Z. J. Koles, B. G. Howarth, and L. Burton (1979). Neurophysiological studies of schizophrenia, mania and depression. In *Hemisphere Asymmetries of Function in Psychopathology* (J. Gruzlier and P. Flor-Henry, eds.). Elsevier/North-Holland Biomedical Press, New York, pp. 189–222.

Frumkin, L. R., H. S. Ripley, and G. B. Cox (1978). Changes in cerebral hemispheric lateralization with hypnosis. *Biol. Psychiat.* 13, 741–750.

Galin, D., J. Johnstone, L. Nakell, and J. Herron (1979). Development of the capacity for tactile transfer between hemispheres in normal children. *Science* 204, 1330–1332.

Gazzaniga, M. S. (1970). *The Bisected Brain.* Appleton-Century-Crofts, New York.

Geschwind, N., and W. Levitsky (1968). Human brain: Left-right asymmetries in temporal speech region. *Science* 161, 168–187.

Glick, S. D., R. P. Jerussi, and B. Zimmerberg (1977). Behavioural and neuropharmacological correlates of nigrostriatal asymmetry in rats. In *Lateralization in the Nervous System* (S. Harnad, R. W. Doty, L. Goldstein, J. Jaynes, and G. Krauthamer, eds.). Academic Press, New York.

Golden, C. J., B. Graber, J. Coffman, R. Berg, S. Block, and D. Brogan (1980). Brain density deficits in chronic schizophrenia. *Psychiat. Res.* 3, 179–184.

Golden, C. J., R. N. Ariel, and B. Graber (1981). Cerebral blood flow in schizophrenics and controls. New Research Abstracts, American Psychiatric Association, 134th Annual Meeting, p. 10.

Goldstein, K. (1939). *The Organism: A Holistic Approach to Biology, Derived from Pathological Data in Man.* American Book, New York.

Goldstein, L., and N. W. Stoltzfus (1973). Psychoactive drug-induced changes of interhemispheric EEG amplitude relationships. *Agents and Actions* 3, 124–132.

Goldstein, L., N. W. Stoltzfus, and J. F. Gardocki (1972). Changes in interhemispheric amplitude relationships in the EEG during sleep. *Physiol. Behav.* 8, 811–815.

Green, P. (1978). Defective interhemispheric transfer in schizophrenia. *J. Abnorm. Psychol.* 87, 472–480.

Green, P., and V. Kotenko (1980). Superior speech comprehension in schizophrenics under monoaural versus biaural listening conditions. *J. Abnorm. Psychol.* 89, 399–408.

Gruzelier, J. H. (1973). Bilateral asymmetry of skin conductance orienting activity and levels in schizophrenia. *Biol. Psychol.* 1, 21–41.

Gruzelier, J. H., and P. Flor-Henry (eds.) (1979). *Hemisphere Asymmetries of Function in Psychopathology.* Elsevier-North Holland Biomedical Press, New York.

Gruzelier, J. H., and N. Hammond (1976). Schizophrenia: A dominant hemisphere temporal-limbic disorder? *Res. Comm. Psychol. Psychiat. Behav.* 1, 33–72.

Gruzelier, J. H., and P. H. Venables (1972). Skin conductance orienting activity in a heterogenous sample of schizophrenics. *J. Nerv. Ment. Dis.* 155, 277–287.

Gruzelier, J. H., and P. H. Venables (1973). Skin conductance response to tones with and without attentional significance in schizophrenic and non-schizophrenic psychiatric patients. *Neuropsychologia* 11, 221–230.

Gruzelier, J. H., and P. H. Venables (1974). Bimodality and lateral asymmetry of skin conductance orienting activity in schizophrenics: Replication and evidence of lateral asymmetry in patients with depression and disorders of personality. *Biol. Psychiat.* 8, 55–73.

Gruzelier, J. H. (1981). Cerebral laterality and psychopathology: Fact and fiction. *Psychol. Med.* 11, 219–227.

Gur, R. E. (1975). Conjugate lateral eye movements as an index of hemispheric activation. *J. Personal. Soc. Psychol.* 31, 751–757.

Gur, R. E. (1977). Motoric laterality imbalance in schizophrenia. *Arch. gen. Psychiat.* 34, 33–37.

Gur, R. E. (1978). Left hemispheric dysfunction and left hemispheric overactivation in schizophrenia. *J. Abnorm. Psychol.* 87, 226–230.

Halliday, A. M., K. Davison, M. W. Brown, and L. C. Kreeger (1968). Comparison of effects on depression and memory of bilateral ECT and unilateral ECT to the dominant and non-dominant hemisphere. *Brit. J. Psychiat.* 114, 997–1012.

Hays, P. (1977). Electroencephalographic variants and genetic predisposition to schizophrenia. *J. Neurol. Neurosurg. Psychiat.* 40, 735–755.

Hecaen, H., J. Ajuriaguerra, and J. Massonit (1951). Les troubles visvo-constructifs par lesion parieto-occipitale droite. *Encephale* 40, 122–179.

Hier, D. B., M. LeMay, and R. P. Rosenberger (1978a). Autism: Association with reversed cerebral asymmetry. *Neurology* 28, 348–349.

Hier, D. B., M. LeMay, R. B. Rosenberger, and V. P. Perlo (1978b). Developmental dyslexia: Evidence for a subgroup with a reversal of cerebral asymmetry. *Arch. Neurol.* 35, 90–92.

Hommes, O. R., and L. H. H. M. Panhuysen (1971). Depression and cerebral dominance. *Psychiat. Neurol. Neurochir.* 74, 259–270.

Hughlins-Jackson, J. (1880). On right- or left-sided spasms at the onset of epileptic proxysms, and on crude sensation warnings and elaborate mental states. *Brain* 3, 192–206.

Ingvar, D. H., and G. Franzen (1974). Distribution of cerebral activity in chronic schizophrenia. *Lancet* 2, 1484–1486.

Johnstone, E. C., T. J. Crowe, C. D. Frith, J. Husband, and L. Kreel (1976). Cerebral ventricular size and cognitive impairment in chronic schizophrenia. *Lancet* 2, 924–926.

Kimura, D. (1967). Functional asymmetry of the brain in dichotic listening. *Cortex* 3, 163–178.

Kinney, D. K., and B. Jacobsen (1978). Environmental factors in schizophrenia: New adoption study evidence and its implications for genetic and environmental research. In *The Nature of Schizophrenia* (L. C. Wynne, R. L. Cromwell, and S. Matthysse, eds.). Wiley, New York, pp. 38–51.

Kinsbourne, M. (1972). Eye and head turning indicates cerebral lateralization. *Science* 176, 539–541.

Kronfol, Z., K. Hamsher, K. Digre, and R. Waziri (1978). Depression and hemispheric functions: Changes associated with unilateral ECT. *Brit. J. Psychiat.* 132, 560–567.

LeDoux, J. E., D. H. Wilson, and M. S. Gazzaniga (1977). A divided mind: Observations on the conscious properties of the separated hemispheres. *Ann. Neurol.* 2, 417–421.

LeMay, M. (1976). Morphological cerebral asymmetries of modern man, fossil man and non-human primate. *Ann. N.Y. Acad. Sci.* 280, 349–366.

LeMay, M., and A. Culebras (1972). Human brain: Morphologic differences in the hemispheres demonstrable by carotid arteriography. *N. Engl. J. Med.* 287, 168–170.

LeMay, M., and D. Kido (1978). Asymmetries of the cerebral hemispheres on computed tomograms. *J. Comp. Assist. Tomography* 2, 471–476.

Levy, J. (1969). Possible basis for the evolution of lateral specialization of the human brain. *Nature* 224, 614–615.

Levy, J. (1974). Psychobiological implications of bilateral asymmetry. In *Hemisphere Function in the Human Brain* (S. J. Dimond, and J. G. Beaumont, eds.). Halsted Press, New York.

Lifshitz, K., and J. Gradijan (1974). Spectral evaluation of the electroencephalogram: Power and variability in chronic schizophrenics and control subjects. *Psychophysiol.* 11, 479–490.

Lishman, W. A., and E. R. L. McMeekan (1976). Hand preference in psychiatric patients. *Brit. J. Psychiat.* 129, 158–166.

Lishman, W. A., B. K. Toone, C. J. Colbourn, E. R. L. McMeekan, and R. M. Mance (1978). Dichotic listening in psychotic patients. *Brit. J. Psychiat.* 132, 333–341.

Luchins, D. J., D. R. Weinberger, and R. W. Wyatt (1979). Anomalous lateralization associated with a milder form of schizophrenia. *Amer. J. Psychiat.* 136, 1598–1599.

Luchins, D. J., D. R. Weinberger, E. F. Torrey, A. Johnson, N. Rogentine, and R. J. Wyatt (1981). HLA-Az antigen in schizophrenic patients with reversed cerebral asymmetry. *Brit. J. Psychiat.* 138, 240–243.

Luria, A. R., and E. G. Homskaya (1966). *The Frontal Lobe and Regulation of Psychological Processes.* Moscow University Press, Moscow.

Miller, E. (1971). Handedness and the pattern of human ability. *Brit. J. Psychol.* 62, 111–112.

Milner, B. (1967). Discussion of the subject: Experimental analysis of cerebral dominance in man. In *Brain Mechanisms Underlying Speech and Language* (C. H. Millikan and F. L. Darley, eds.). Grune and Stratton, New York.

Myers, R. E. (1962). Transmission of visual information within and between the hemispheres. In *Interhemispheric Relations and Cerebral Dominance* (V. B. Mountcastle, ed.). John Hopkins Press, Baltimore.

Myers, R. E., and R. W. Sperry (1953). Interocular transfer of a visual form discrimination habit in casts after section of the optic chiasm and corpus callosum. *Anat. Record* 115, 351–354.

Nasrallah, H. A. Schizophrenia as a disorder in the unity of consciousness. (submitted).

Nasrallah, H. A., and C. M. McChesney (1981). Psychopathology of corpus callosum tumours. *Biol. Psychiat.* 16, 661–667.

Nasrallah, H. A., L. B. Bigelow, F. P. Rauscher, and R. J. Wyatt (1979). Corpus callosum thickness in schizophrenia. New Research Abstracts. American Psychiatric Association 132nd Annual Convention, p. 15.

Nasrallah, H. A., C. Schroeder, K. Keelor, and M. McCalley-Whitters (1981). Motoric lateralization in schizophrenic males. *Amer. J. Psychiat.* 138, 1114–1115, 1981.

Nasrallah, H. A., S. Kuperman, M. McCalley-Whitters, and K. Keelor (1981). Laterality in paranoid and non-paranoid schizophrenia. New Research Abstracts, American Psychiatric Association 134th Annual Meeting, p. 32.

Nasrallah, H. A., M. McCalley-Whitters, F. P. Rauscher, and L. B. Bigelow (1982). Histopathology of the corpus collosum in early and late onset schizophrenia. Proceedings of the Annual Meeting of the American Association for the Advancement of Science, Washington, D.C.

Oddy, H. C., and T. J. Lobstein (1972). Hand and eye dominance in schizophrenia. *Brit. J. Psychiat.* 120, 231–232.

Oke, A., R. Keller, I. Mefford, and R. N. Adams (1978). Lateralization of norepinephrine in human thalamus. *Science* 200, 1411–1433.

Perria, L., G. Rosadini, and G. F. Rossi (1961). Determination of the side of cerebral dominance with amobarbital. *Arch. Neurol.* 4, 173–181.

Pitres, A. (1891). *Lecons Clinique sur L'hysterie et L'hypnotism.* Doin, Paris.

Polidoro, L. (1970). The use of a complex auditory task with acute good morbid paranoid and acute poor premorbid non-paranoid schizophrenics. Doctoral Dissertation, George Peabody College for Teachers.

Puccetti, R. (1973). Brain bisection and personal identity. *Brit. J. Philo. Sci.* 24, 339–355.

Rany, E. T. (1938). Reversed lateral dominance in identical twins. *J. Exptl. Psychol.* 23, 304–312.

Roemer, R. A., C. Shagass, J. J. Straumanis, and M. Amadeo (1978). Pattern evoked potential measurements suggesting lateralized hemisphere dysfunction in chronic schizophrenia. *Biol. Psychiat.* 13, 185–202.

Rosenthal, R., L. B. Bigelow (1972). Quantitative brain measurements in chronic schizophrenia. *Brit. J. Psychiat.* 121, 259–264.

Rossi, G. E., and G. Rosadini (1967). Experimental analysis of cerebral dominance in man. In *Brain Mechanisms Underlying Speech and Language* (C. H. Millikan and F. L. Darley, eds.). Grune and Stratton, New York.

Satz, P. (1972). Pathological left-handedness: An explanation. *Cortex* 8, 121–125.

Schwartz, G. E., R. S. Davidson, and F. Maer (1975). Right hemisphere lateralization for emotion in the human brain: Interactions with cognition. *Science* 190, 286–288.

Schweitzer, L. (1979). Differences of cerebral lateralization among schizophrenic and depressed patients. *Biol. Psychiat.* 14, 721–733.

Schweitzer, L., E. Becker, and H. Welsh (1978). Abnormalities of cerebral lateralization in schizophrenic patients. *Arch. Gen. Psychiat.* 35, 982–985.

Serafetinides, E. A. (1972). Laterality and voltage in the EEG of psychiatric patients. *Dis. Nerv. Sys.* 32, 622–623.

Serafetinides, E. A. (1973). Voltage laterality in the EEG of psychiatric patients. *Dis. Nerv. Sys.* 34, 190–191.

Sourek, K. (1965). *The Nervous Control of Skin Potentials in Man.* Nakladatelstvi Ceskoslovensa Akademic Ved., Prague.

Sperry, R. W. (1961). Cerebral organization and behavior. *Science* 133, 1749–1757.

Sperry, R. W. (1968). Hemisphere deconnection and unity in conscious awareness. *Amer. Psychol.* 23, 723–733.

Sperry, R. W. (1977). Forebrain commissourotomy and conscious awareness. *J. Med. Phil.* 2, 101–126.

Sperry, R. W., J. Stamm, and N. Miner (1956). Relearning tests for interocular transfer following division of optic chiasma and corpus callosum in cats. *J. Comp. Physiol. Psychol.* 49, 529–533.

Stevens, J. R., L. Bigelow, D. Denny, J. Lipkin, A. H. Livermore, F. Rauscher, and R. J. Wyatt (1979). Telemetered EEG–EOG during psychotic behaviours of schizophrenia. *Arch. Gen. Psychiat.* 36, 251–262.

Taylor, P. J., R. Dalton, and J. J. Fleminger (1980). Handedness in schizophrenia. *Brit. J. Psychiat.* 136, 375–383.

Terzian, H. (1964). Behavioural and EEG effects of intracarotid sodium amytal injection. *Acta Neurochir.* 12, 230–239.

Terzian, H., and C. Cecotto (1959). Su un nuovo metodo per la determinazione e lo studio della dominanza emis erica. *Giorn. Psichiat. Neuropat.* 87, 889–924.

Torrey, E. F. (1980). Neurological abnormalities in schizophrenic patients. *Biol. Psychiat.* 15, 381–388.

Tourette, G. (1895). *Plon Nourrit et Cie,* Paris.

Tsuang, M. T. (1975). Heterogeneity of schizophrenia. *Biol. Psychiat.* 10, 465–474.

Tucker, D. M., R. S. Roth, B. A. Arneson, and V. Buckingham (1977). Right hemisphere activation during stress. *Neuropsychologia* 15, 697–700.

Wada, J. A., R. Clarke, and A. Hamm (1975). Cerebral hemisphere asymmetry in humans. *Arch. Neurol.* 32, 239–246.

Wahl, O. F. (1976). Handedness in schizophrenia. *Perceptual Motor Skills* 42, 944–946.

Walker, H. A., and H. G. Birch (1970). Lateral preference and right–left awareness in schizophrenic children. *J. Nerv. Ment. Dis.* 151, 341–351.

Weinberger, D. R., E. F. Torrey, A. N. Neophytides, and R. J. Wyatt (1979a). Lateral cerebral ventricular enlargement in chronic schizophrenia. *Arch. Gen. Psychiat.* 36, 735–739.

Weinberger, D. R., E. F. Torrey, A. N. Neophytides, and R. J. Wyatt (1979b). Structural abnormalities in the cerebral cortex of chronic schizophrenic patients. *Arch. Gen. Psychiat.* 36, 935–939.

Wexler, B. E., and G. R. Heninger (1979). Alterations in cerebral laterality during acute psychotic illness. *Arch. Gen. Psychiat.* 36, 278–284.

Witelson, S., and W. Pallie (1973). Left hemisphere specializations for language in the newborn: Neuroanatomical evidence of asymmetry. *Brain* 96, 641–646.

Yakovlev, P., and A. LeCours (1967). The myelogenetic cycles of regional maturation of the brain. In *Regional Development of the Brain in Early Life* (A. Minkowski, ed.). Blackwell, Oxford.

Yozawitz, A., G. Bruder, S. Sutton, L. Sharpe, B. Gurland, J. Fleiss, and L. Costa (1979). Dichotic perception: Evidence for right hemisphere dysfunction in affective psychosis. *Brit. J. Psychiat.* 135, 224–237.

Zangwill, O. L. (1960). *Cerebral Dominance and Its Relation to Psychological Function.* Oliver and Boyd. London.

Index